AND
DEALERS

Some have observed that the titles of Stephen Brown's management thrillers are suspiciously similar to those of his best-selling namesake, Dan. Some have suggested that Stephen and Dan are twins, albeit separated at birth (one was brought up in the lap of American luxury, the other was raised by feral Irish wolfhounds in the wilds of the Emerald Isle). Some have even suggested that Dan and Stephen are one and the same, since they've never been seen in the same room together. But who knows the true secret of the Brown bloodline? Maybe it's just a quirky conspiracy theory…

AGENTS AND DEALERS

Stephen Brown

First published in 2008 by:

Marshall Cavendish Limited
Fifth Floor
32–38 Saffron Hill
London EC1N 8FH
United Kingdom
T: +44 (0)20 7421 8120
F: +44 (0)20 7421 8121
sales@marshallcavendish.co.uk
www.marshallcavendish.co.uk

A CIP record for this book is available from the British Library

ISBN-13: 978-0-462-09916-3
ISBN-10: 0-462-09916-4

Printed and bound in Great Britain by
CPI Mackays, Chatham ME5 8TD

Timeline

The events described in *Agents and Dealers* take place five weeks before those recounted in *The Marketing Code*.

Fact

Everything in this book is true, with the exception of the first sentence. The second sentence is dubious too, as is the entire introductory paragraph. The rest, though, is the truth, the whole truth and nothing but the truth.

Readers of Dan Brown will be familiar with the Priory of Sion, a shadowy secret society based in Paris. Founded in 1099, the priory not only protects and preserves the holy bloodline of Jesus Christ and Mary Magdalene, but it is the brains behind the mysterious Knights Templar, who are the brains behind the Freemasons, the Rosicrucians and the Hermetic Order of the Golden Dawn.

What is less well known is that the Priory of Sion is the Francophone branch of a clandestine multinational organization. In Spain, it is known as the Priory of Léon. In Greece, it is called the Priory of Priam. In China, it operates as the Priory of Xian. In Singapore, it functions as the Priory of Cyan. In Thailand, it's the Priory of Siam. In Australia, it's Orion. In South Africa, it's Lion. In Israel, it's Dan. In Germany, it's Iron. In Britain, the home of Monty Python, it muddles along as the Priory of Brian. In the United States of Abbreviation, where polysyllabic words are considered downright unconstitutional, it goes by the appropriately plain and simple moniker, P4.

Of all the priory's subsidiaries, by far the most secretive is the branch based in Ireland. So ruthless is the Irish division that even to utter its name risks punishment of the most cruel and unusual kind.

This book lifts the lid on the Priory of...

Read it if you dare.

Prologue

Operation Firefly

Blood looks black by moonlight. Under the lunar lantern, flesh wounds are rapidly spreading inkblots. Head shots are exploding carboys of Quink, with chunks in.

Oberst Friedrich Krueger's battledress was a sodden strip of blotting paper. But the blood that stained the uniform of the Brandenburgers, Nazi Germany's elite commando unit, wasn't his own. Nor was it the blood of his four fearsome companions: the Austrian giant, Otto Skorzeny, all duelling scars and party ideology; Feldwebel Hermann Munstermann, short, squat, savage and as ugly as sin; Oberleutnant Siegfried Grabert, the regiment's boy wonder, hero of the blitzkrieg campaign of 1940 and holder of the Knight's Cross of the Iron Cross; and Jupp Hoven, an acne-scarred archaeologist, with greasy hair and greedy demeanour, who had found the artefact before the war and couldn't wait to get his hands on it again.

Then there was Frank Ryan, the ageing, out-of-shape IRA man, with angina and an attitude problem, who'd been sprung from a stinking Spanish jail especially for the operation. Rumour had it that the head of the German secret service, Admiral Canaris, had interceded with General Franco on Frank Ryan's behalf.

The ink-black blood belonged, rather, to an unsuspecting ARP patrol the Brandenburgers had stumbled upon by chance. Four middle-aged men, playing at soldiers, armed with battered binoculars and a couple of decrepit Webley pistols. School teachers or bank officials doing their bit for the British war effort, probably. They didn't stand a chance. Not against Hermann Munstermann's MP34 machine gun and Otto Skorzeny's silenced Schmeisser, a gift from Hermann Göring himself.

They'd surrendered, of course. They were too shocked to do

a ... ıse. But there was no time for prisoners, let alone the rules ... ngagement laid down in every Wehrmacht paybook. Still stir-crazy, Ryan shouted, "Kill the Northern bastards!" and Munstermann needed no encouragement. Machine guns are messy at close range – spit, sputter, splatter – though the gore is as nothing compared to the noise.

Ordinarily, the raucous bark of an MP34 would've attracted a lot of night-time attention, as would the astonished screams of ARP patrolmen doing the jerky, jumpy, jittery dance of death. This was no ordinary night, however. The spits and screams were drowned out by the throbbing drone of Luftwaffe engines as wave after wave of Heinkels, Junkers JU88s and Dorniers washed over the defenceless city and the crump, crump, crump of bombs, incendiaries and assorted high explosives echoed off the encircling escarpment. It was a TNT thunderstorm, the drumbeats of Bedlam.

Belfast, of course, was well used to thundering drumrolls rattling the casements of its grandiose Victorian thoroughfares. The Orange parades every 12th of July thundered and hammered and reverberated all day. But this was Tuesday 15 April, in the Year of Our Lord 1941, and the noise was like Vulcan's infernal workshop, with Wagner on the Tannoy.

Oberst Krueger was grateful for the cover. The north side of the city was an inferno. From the far side of the Cave Hill, where he and his comrades had parachuted successfully before the main raid commenced, the Belfast conurbation looked like a volcanic crater, active and about to erupt. The moon, the flames, the firebombs, the searchlights added up to a pyrotechnic phantasmagoria. Panic prevailed, with pandemonium in close attendance. Everyone who wasn't getting out of town pronto was preoccupied with fighting the flames.

The air raid was a perfect diversionary tactic, as it was intended to be. The city-wide bonfire was a smokescreen, both literally and metaphorically. Krueger's hand-picked Brandenburgers were charged with the most important task of the evening, the most important task of the war thus far. They were on a mission from God. For God. For Canaris. For Adolf Hitler himself. They were on a mission that would determine the outcome of Operation Barbarossa, the imminent invasion of Stalin's Russia. They were on a mission that, if successful, could give the Führer a birthday surprise he'd never forget. They were on a mission that marked the 25th anniversary of the Easter Rising and, as Ireland was Nazi Germany's stepping stone for the mooted invasion of Great Britain, the occasion was too important to pass unmarked.

Symbolism aside – and ARP interruption notwithstanding – Operation Firefly had gone like clockwork. Five-man team. Lightly equipped. Parachute drop from 1,000 metres. Rendezvous on the outskirts of Templepatrick, eleven kilometres north of Belfast and eight cross-country to their destination. The artefact had to be acquired, its provenance had to be confirmed and, thanks to Frank Ryan's contacts, the exit strategy had to be enacted. Only an Irishman could've come up with a scheme that disguised military operations under a cover of good neighbourliness. A highly placed Irish official had promised that fire engines from Dublin, Drogheda and Dundalk would rush north, bells clanging, to assist the stricken citizens of Belfast. Except that they'd have a few extra passengers on their way back, early next morning. Oddly uniformed passengers, perhaps, and jealously guarding a precious object in their possession. But after an exhausting night of firefighting heroics, who'd be counting or looking too closely? The diplomatic bag of Dublin's German legation would do the rest. Hitler's 52nd would be his happiest birthday yet. Canaris apparently couldn't wait to see Himmler's face with its non-Aryan nose out of joint.

Munstermann bundled the ink-stained bodies into a roadside ditch. "That was unnecessary, sergeant," Grabert snapped in his best brothers-in-arms manner. "The first commandment in your paybook, in case you've forgotten, states that Wehrmachten observe the rules of chivalrous behaviour. This isn't the SS."

"It will be if Himmler has his way," Feldwebel Munstermann replied gruffly, refusing to be cowed by the cocky junior officer. "Canaris is out of his depth. Himmler will move against him. Your precious regiment will be the Reichsführer's plaything this time next year."

"You've jeopardized our mission, sergeant," Grabert retorted officiously. "You'll pay for this insubordination when we return to barracks."

Munstermann glared at the regiment's wunderkind. Knight's Cross or not, he wasn't used to having his bloodlust denounced by a pipsqueak like Grabert.

"Knock it off, the pair of you," Skorzeny interrupted, shouldering his Schmeisser. The Austrian giant's duelling scars were clearly discernible in the enveloping conflagration.

"No more talk," Krueger ordered, in an attempt to impose his authority on the squabbling detachment. "We have a job to do. By my reckoning, our target is just over that ridge, at the bottom of the hill."

The commandos crested Belfast's Cave Hill. They stood on McArt's Fort, an ancient Iron Age settlement, where the United Irishmen famously plighted their anti-British troth in 1795. A fire-filled vista lay beneath them. It was like the entrance to the underworld, or worse. The flames soared heavenward and, reflected in the eerily calm waters of Belfast Lough, sank Letheward as well. The last of the Luftwaffe waves ebbed off into the distance, engine noise drowned out by the crash of collapsing buildings and the mournful sirens' wail.

A bright light lanced up from the wooded hillside below. Three long, three short. The signal. Oberst Krueger looked round at his colleagues, their faces flushed and eyes shining. Jupp Hoven, the youthful archaeologist, was almost beside himself with excitement. "That's it, let's go!"

The platoon scrambled down the steep slope, freewheeling from tree to tree, bush to bush, using the foliage as a brake. Propelled by the combined momentum of gravity and weaponry, it was as close to fun as secret operations ever got. Elated, they were breathing heavily by the time the ground levelled out. Frank Ryan, the out-of-condition local liaison, was down on his knees, hissing and wheezing like a punctured barrage balloon. The light was clearly discernible, as was the dark outline of their destination. It was less than fifty metres distant across a rock-strewn meadow.

"Halt! Who goes there? Stop, or I shoot! Stop!!"

A shot rang out, ricocheting off the rocks and into the copse.

Skorzeny unshouldered his Schmeisser. Tuesday night was inkblot night.

Chapter One

Shoplifters of the World Unite

Shrinkage City, they called it. Shrinkage as in stealing, theft, nicking, knocking, ripping stuff off. It was the Lanzarote of larceny, the Malaga of misappropriation, the Benidorm of blag. It was where lifers went to die, teenage thugs learnt their trade and hardened criminals liked to loosen up. It was where the long arm of the law didn't reach or would get amputated if it tried. It was a rest home for ex-cons, the Champneys of the criminal classes. It made Chicago during Prohibition look like Walt Disney World on Mothering Sunday. If shoplifting were an Olympic sport, it would be the host city in perpetuity.

But that was then, this is now. These days, Belfast is the very model of a modern major metropolis. Five star hotels, Michelin recommended restaurants, shimmering shopping malls, expensive apartment blocks, designer label boutiques, bijou art galleries, cosmetic surgery clinics, magnificent public buildings, picturesque riverside walkways, pretentious arts festivals, dramatic concert halls and pristine pedestrianized streets are all present and correct, though the jury's still out on an all-singing, all-dancing, super-duper sports stadium. The property market is booming. Booming in a good way. Not like before. Before's behind us. Belfast's many and varied paramilitary organizations have been pensioned off – thanks to generous government grants for "decommissioning" – and the ill-gotten gains of the godfathers of yore are being confiscated by the Assets Recovery Agency. The agency costs more to run than it recoups in raids and seizures. But, hey, who's counting?

Jimmy James is counting. So's his sidekick "Moonbeam" McCartney. They're counting down the retail stores in Greater Belfast. Ticking them off, in fact. Five years ago, Jimmy read that Belfast was the shoplifting capital of the world – Shoplifter City they called it in the paper – and Jimmy decided he wanted to be the king of the world, the best shoplifter in the best city for shoplifting in the world. A boy's gotta have ambition, right?

So Jimmy set out to steal something from every single shop in Belfast Urban Area, the continuously built up region from Ballygowan in the east to Ballymurphy way out west, from Whiteabbey in the down-and-out north to Black's Road in the up-and-coming south. Such a task, which surely warrants inclusion in the Guinness Book of Criminal Records on completion, is easier said than done, however. It's not the sheer number of shops that's the problem. Jesus, Jimmy could do twenty on a good day. It's defining what a shop is and what a shop isn't. Are dry cleaners shops? Are banks shops? Are pubs shops? Are estate agents shops? They look a bit like shops. They are found on shopping parades and in shopping malls, nestling among the other shops. But are they "proper" shops? Who decides these things?

Whatever they are, Jimmy discovered, they don't provide particularly rich pickings for the filching fraternity. Money aside, what can you pinch from a bank branch, bar exhausted ballpoint pens on a string? Takings aside, what can you pilfer from a pub, other than beer mats, bar towels or the pint of an inebriated punter? Petty cash aside, what can you snaffle from an estate agent, apart from Photoshopped photographs of unaffordable houses and maybe a desk calendar or two? Till-fill aside, what can you steal from a dry cleaners, beside someone else's ill-fitting outfits and a container or two of narcotic cleaning fluid?

Then there's the problem of chain stores. Does each branch of Boots or Superdrug or W. H. Smith count separately, or does one dipping operation cover them all? And if so, must the operation be mounted on the city centre flagship store or will an outlying outlet do just as well?

Decisions, decisions, decisions. Definitions, definitions, definitions. Where does the urban area stop, for Christ's sake? Is there life after Abbeycentre?

Actually, Jimmy loved wrestling with these undecidable issues. He was a philosopher at heart. A shoplifting sage, sort of. He often waxed lyrical to Moonbeam about the art, the craft, the metaphysics of misappropriation. "It's not the stealing or the swag," he frequently commented, with more than a modicum of self-justification, "it's the battle of wits, it's us against them, it's overcoming the security precautions, the anti-theft technology, the angled mirrors, the CCTV, the alarm tags on the merchandise, the idiotic store detectives, the fat bastards standing guard at the door who can't catch a cold, let alone bird flu. It's the hunter versus the hunted."

"Whatever you say, Jimmy."

"Look at me, Moonbeam," he counselled, "You must always remember that we are in the right. Shoplifting is a noble calling. Don't believe retailers' propaganda about pilferage. They only have themselves to blame. They make their displays as attractive as possible. They lead consumers into temptation. They are serpents in the Garden of Eden. They bombard us with adverts, loyalty cards, money-off deals, three-for-two promotions, buy-one-get-one-free gimmicks. Their aim is to attract us, seduce us, make us buy despite ourselves, despite the fact that we can't afford it, despite the fact that over-consumption is destroying the planet and ecological Armageddon is nigh."

"So it's not just about stuffing DVDs down the front of our jeans, sprinting out of the shop, and pissing ourselves laughing at the bus stop?"

Jimmy James glanced at his scabby companion. A biblical plague of boils adorned his already spotty complexion. Knocking, for Moonbeam, was all about the buzz, the excitement, the orgasmic thrill of the getaway. He thought it was the next best thing to sex. The next best thing to thinking about sex, rather. He'd thought about sex a lot. He'd spent sufficient time on remand to think his way through the Kama Sutra. Or the complete back issues of *Loaded* at least.

Moonbeam wasn't much good at thinking. He wasn't a great shoplifter either. His basic problem was that he had a suspicious face, the kind of singularly sleekit face that security personnel don't like the look of, the kind they keep a watchful eye on and take inordinate exception to. He went through hell on holiday, when airport police, X-ray machine attendants, customs and excise officers etc.

clapped their beady eyes on him. He'd had more hands up his arse than a ventriloquist's dummy. Even Howard Marks, the celebrity drug runner, hadn't had more latex gloves fumbling in his fundament than Moonbeam McCartney.

From Jimmy's standpoint, though, you couldn't beat Moonbeam as a partner in crime. He attracted all the attention while Jimmy did the business. He led the floorwalkers a merry dance, as Jimmy helped himself to whatever tickled his light-fingered fancy. He spent long spells in jail, admittedly, but whenever Moonbeam was out he was invaluable. As a double act, they couldn't be bettered. They were the criminal equivalent of good cop, bad cop. Jimmy, you see, had an innocent face, an innocuous face, a butter-wouldn't-melt face that allowed him to get away with, if not quite murder, then any number of watches, bracelets, books, CDs, T-shirts, trainers, computer games, bottles of vodka, giant Easter eggs, Gillette Fusion razor blades and even a frozen turkey from Tesco. Jimmy's shiny black hair, bright blue eyes, wonderfully winning smile and drop-dead dimples didn't count against him either.

"We don't steal stuff, Moonbeam. We liberate it. We're on the front line of the anti-capitalist movement, guerrilla fighters in the war against marketing. We're the Brand Liberation Front. We are the people. Never forget that."

"Whatever you say, Jimmy."

"Think Zen, Moonbeam."

"Is that like *Nuts*, or *HFM* or *Maxim*?"

"It's not a lad-mag. It's a philosophy, a world-view, a system of thought..." Jimmy despaired for his dopey companion. He wasn't the fastest CPU in PC World. "It's a way to avoid getting caught, Moonbeam."

"Oh. Right. How does it work?"

"It's mental, Moonbeam. All in the mind. The Tao of petty theft. The Prana of peculation. Think yourself invisible. They can't see you. They don't know we're there. We're in and out before they're any the wiser. Shopping's special forces strike again. Another straw on the back of the capitalist camel."

"Can you steal anything if you're a ... a Zen master ... a Zen mastermind, Jimmy?"

"Anything, Moonbeam!"

"*Anything*?"

"Well, within reason."

A sly look crossed Moonbeam's shifty, stoat-like face. "What about power tools? Lawnmowers? Sets of spanners? What about a chain saw, Jimmy? You up for hiding a hedge-trimmer down the front of your kecks?"

If Jimmy James had a fault, it was vanity. In a city where stuff didn't so much fall off the back of a lorry as plummet, Jimmy was the pontiff of plummeting stuff. Or so he believed. "Nothing is beyond a Hatha Yoga practitioner, Moonbeam, not even a sabre-toothed hedge-trimmer."

"Are you sure about that, Jimmy?"

"Look and learn, grasshopper. Look and learn."

Chapter Two

If You Go Down to the DIY Today

"Breathe through your eyes, Moonbeam," the Zen master advised as they stepped off the Carrickfergus-bound Ulsterbus.

"Breathe through your arse?" the adept retorted, refusing to take the tenets of Hatha Yoga too seriously. "I know some people who talk through their arses – mentioning no names, Jimmy – so I suppose breathing makes sense."

"Matter is energy," the nicking ninja intoned. "The meaning of life is theft. Repeat after me, Moonbeam… Ooooommm."

"Om."

"Again, Moonbeam, stressing the O."

"Oooo… my God, Jimmy, would you look at the size of that." He pointed toward a hulking, cladding-covered category killer across an almost empty car park.

Discount DIY had trouble written all over it. An outgrowth of The Troubles, a local euphemism for thirty years of civil unrest, religious bigotry, communal strife and general lawlessness, Discount DIY was a front for a prominent paramilitary organization. The IRA, to be precise. Armed robbery receipts, drug trade takings, protection racket returns, identity theft contributions, life insurance scams and assorted backhanders, blackmailings, bogus compensation claims and prisoners' welfare "contributions" were channelled through Discount DIY's accounts. Its auditors knew which side their bread was buttered on, as did its preferred suppliers, as did the organization's trade-only subsidiary, Discount Supply.

The IRA may not have been the most ruthless terrorist organization in the world – compared to Al-Qaeda or Hamas they were wimps, though they gave it their best shot, so to speak – but their business plan was a work of genius. They'd created a virtuous circle that was the talk of the construction industry. The bars, restaurants, department stores and office blocks they bombed with impunity had to be rebuilt in due course. And rebuilding needs building supplies. It was too good an opportunity to miss and the IRA were nothing if not opportunistic. When business was slack, a well-placed car bomb in a city centre side-street soon had the cash registers ringing merrily. The decorative glass and glazing department was particularly lucrative, since car bombs blew out windows several miles away. It wasn't so much money for old rope, as money for old lags.

Building requisites naturally led to property development, estate agency, insurance brokerage, mortgage provision, quantity surveying, loss adjusting, shopfitting operations, furniture retailing, carpet supplies and office equipment leasing. As the economy picked up, thanks to the IRA's canny investment strategy, they rapidly branched out into restaurants, superpubs, nightclubs, multiplexes, amusement arcades and the many and varied tentacles of the contemporary leisure sector. Surprisingly, they steered clear of taxicab services – because that is where the organization's business activities started and was an unwelcome reminder of the way things were. *Tiocfaidh ár Lá*. Our day will come. Our payday already has.

The beauty of the IRA's diversification strategy was that it opened up all sorts of underhand opportunities. Watered drinks were served in its public houses, ersatz Ecstasy tablets were on offer in its every-night-is-party-night clubs, rigged fruit machines ringed the floors of its amusement arcades, food that had long passed its sell-by date was spiced and served in its carry-out restaurants. Chernobyl chicken, Sellafield steaks, plutonium puddings, grisly rissoles, salmonella seafood specials, e-coli-enriched enchiladas. You name it, they moved it. Gastroenteritis remedies were likewise available from its friendly neighbourhood pharmacy-cum-coffee bars, Pharmalatte.

When the public health authorities got wise to this rancid racket – which took longer than many might think, because Belfast's burghers aren't renowned for their gastronomic sophistication – the IRA's resident marketing gurus simply dipped their date-expired bread into the delicious gravy of themed recreation. People'll eat, drink or do anything if it's wrapped in an interesting theme. Australian pubs, Argentinean steakhouses, Scottish financial institutions, Harry Potter summer schools, *Pirates of the Caribbean* boat trips, Dolce & Gabbana boutique hotels, fast-fashion fast-food restaurants (featuring Kate Moss Coke and Naomi Campbell Happy Meals) attest to the power of a well-thought-out theme.

Sadly, the Hunger Strike chain of Ulster pizza parlours wasn't the most well-thought-out operation, nor was its Dirty Protest decor. So much for success breeding success.

Success, in reality, breeds competition. The IRA-instigated uplift in the Northern Ireland economy had a dark cloud inside its silver lining. After avoiding the province for thirty-odd years – bubonic plague victims were more welcome in Britain than Ulstermen – the big wheels of the post-industrial economy ran their investment vehicles over the place, recognized the money-making opportunities that existed in an overlooked, undershopped, surprisingly affluent UK region, thanks to all those well paid government employees. After burning the place down for a generation, consumers had money to burn, and where there's smoke there's Tesco, Sainsbury, Homebase, B&Q, Ikea, etc.

Discount DIY couldn't compete with the big boys, let alone big boys equipped with Big Brother databases, store location optimization software and a line of credit at the Tony Blair ennoblement exchange. Discount DIY, if truth be told, couldn't compete with anyone, since it was essentially a front, a funnel, a slush fund sluice gate. True, they took things into their own hands from time to time by fire-bombing the cross-channel competition. If you can't beat them fair and square, blow the British bastards up, as it were. But Discount DIY was a cardboard cut-out company that couldn't cut it when it came to the cutthroat crunch. Cutting throats they could cope with, but cutthroat competition was something else again.

The IRA's business model – bomb with one hand, build with the other – was getting green around the gills and stinking to high heaven.

Jimmy James didn't know any of this. How could he, he was an unmarried hick from the sticks and hadn't reached the stage where he darkened DIY stores' doors. Despite his cherubic looks, he'd only ever had one serious girlfriend and she dumped him for demanding conjugal rights before the wedding ring had been received. He'd never given much thought to doing it himself. Six-packs of Guinness he could handle. Flatpacks from Homebase were beyond him. DIY outlets were on his shoplifting list of course, as were all retail store types, but he was working systematically through the city centre before starting on the suburbs.

Still, a challenge is a challenge, a dare is a dare. His Zen of embezzlement had been called into question. Moonbeam must be made to realize that nothing is impossible for a samurai shoplifter with self-belief. Even power tools, which are hard to handle at the best of times and are the sneak thief's equivalent of scaling the Eiger, are not beyond a warrior from the Brand Liberation Front.

Generously, Moonbeam let him make the call on which warehouse to plunder. Would it be bustling B&Q, where the crowds and commotion made it easy to slip in and out unnoticed? Or would it be dingy Discount DIY, as empty as Hunger Strike pizza shops on anchovies-only Fridays, but where employees were so indolent that swiping a complete bathroom suite, plus tiles and grouting, wasn't beyond the bounds of possibility?

They tossed. B&Q lost.

The Carrickfergus branch of Discount DIY was easiest to get to even though it was just outside Jimmy's arbitrarily imposed city boundary. Part of the harbourside shopping park, a half-hearted attempt to brighten up a moribund commuter town, Discount DIY stood sad and forlorn beside a gimcrack cinema, iffy Italian restaurant, rinky-dink marina and cavernous Co-operative superstore. Actually, it was even emptier than usual. Unbeknown to Jimmy and Moonbeam, who rarely read the newspapers or watched anything other than stolen DVDs, Discount DIY had "gone into receivership" the day before. Well, that's what they called it, but when the official receiver-speak had been translated, it seemed that the IRA was shutting up shop, admitting defeat and getting out of the increasingly unprofitable do-it-yourself business. Not only was the DIY superstore's remaining stock deeply discounted, but they were giving it away. Gratis, no strings attached, all you can carry, to anyone that wished to avail themselves of the paramilitaries' munificence.

Never reluctant to partake of a bargain, even a blood-money bespattered bargain courtesy of an officially proscribed organization, the citizens of Carrickfergus descended on the dying discounter like seagulls round a beached sperm whale. So what if it stank to high heaven? Praise the Lord, pass the shopping trolley and grab the garden supplies, gallon drums of Ronseal and giant tins of Crown emulsion while you can.

But Jimmy and Moonbeam didn't know this either. They sauntered through the cleaned-out superstore towards the end of "everything must go" day. The timber department was deforested. The lighting aisle was stripped. The plumbing section had disappeared down the proverbial plughole. The paint display counter had nothing left in stock but ecru, beige, fawn, tan, taupe, magnolia and smidgen of peach. Revolting strips of flock wallpaper rolled across the concrete floor, akin to tumbleweed through Deadwood.

"Are your knocking chakras aligned, Moonbeam?"

"Last time I checked, Jimmy," he replied with a smile. Moonbeam paused at the self-assembly shelving aisle and started fiddling inelegantly at the crotch of his breeks. "What about yours?"

"My chakras are always aligned, Moonbeam. I'm feeling especially lucky today," he said with absolute assurance. "I'll get away with something. The security guards can't stop me, grasshopper."

"Is that because of the Zen?"

"No, it's because I can run faster than you."

The complicit companions laughed. It was just like the good old days before Moonbeam paid his debt to society and Jimmy made a bid for solo glory on *Steal Idol.* Discount DIY had seen better days too. The power tool section was at the very back of the store, adjacent to the customer advice counter, where employees could keep an eye on the outlet's most expensive items. There were no employees in sight, though. There were no power tools for that matter. Not a drill, not a sander, not a paint stripper, neither a circular saw, nor a chain saw, nor indeed a hedge trimmer. Not even the dubious own-brand knock-offs that fry you at the first flick of a switch. Not a sausage, in short.

There was only a sweaty sausage roll, sitting on a display unit at the back of the customer help desk, alongside a big mug of steaming coffee. The DIY "doctor" was either on a house call or he'd slipped outside for a quick cigarette. Bold as anodized brass, Moonbeam leapt over the counter and took a huge bite out of the medic's afternoon snack. He was taking his life in his hands, since the piping comestible was presumably supplied by the IRA's catering corps and consisted of macerated pigs' testicles. Maybe not pigs'. Definitely testicles though, to judge from the look on Moonbeam's scunnered kisser.

"Come on, grasshopper, let's go." Jimmy had had enough. "There's a B&Q up beside Tesco's. We can walk from here."

"Mmmm … nnmm … nnmm … nnmm." Moonbeam's mouth was full of gristle and filler. Polyfilla probably. Tiny bits of flaky pastry spewed out as he tried to speak. So he pointed at something instead. There was a large canvas holdall tucked under the wooden counter, all but invisible from the shopfloor and evidently overlooked by the ravening hordes of local locusts who'd passed through earlier. Munching loudly, Moonbeam motioned toward it as if to say "steal that, mastermind".

Jimmy shook his head and turned to go. Things didn't feel right. His chi was acting up and not in a good way. But Moonbeam was having none of it. Still chewing with his mouth open, he gestured at the purple holdall again, motioning enthusiastically and spluttering something that might have been "I double dare you." It was impossible to tell.

Okay, let's do it, Jimmy thought. Better than nothing. Better than a hedge trimmer down the boxers. Better get out of here before the DIY doctor returns and discovers the attack on his snack. A man can get pretty irate if his Ginsters is interfered with.

Jimmy lifted the hatch, rounded the counter and grabbed the hidden holdall by the handles. Christ, it weighed a ton. He threw it over one shoulder and staggered under the weight. Jesus, it must contain a full set of spanners, plus a judicious selection of hammers, chisels, mallets and monkey wrenches. With Moonbeam in tow, Jimmy made his way toward the front of the store. They'd got as far as plumbing and bathrooms when a disembodied voice spoke up behind them. It echoed throughout the cavernous outlet.

"Sorry guys, you can't take that. It's not an SKU. It's not part of the closing down give-away. Bring it back, please."

Jimmy and Moonbeam ignored him. They were in the Zen zone. They knew no fear. They were invisible. They were a Stock Knocking Unit. They were the Brand Liberation Front.

"Bring it back *right now*, or I'll call security."

The samurai of shoplifting kept walking, steady as she goes. They were nearing the checkouts, all eight abandoned. There was no sign of the security guards. It was as if they too had helped themselves illicitly to some free time or were grabbing what keepsakes they could before joining the ranks of the unemployed. Only the diehard scavengers were still in store, removing the very fixtures and fittings.

"*Who ate my fucking sausage roll*!?" With a roar like a baited bear, the hefty DIY doctor vaulted the counter of his clinic and dashed down the central aisle after the toolkit-stealing miscreants.

The BLF refused to be intimidated by threats or profanities or intemperate accusations of snack snaffling. They continued on, unconcerned. They were on the astral plane of misappropriation. They were experiencing what some commentators call "flow", a heightened sense of preoccupied invulnerability.

Vulnerability was rapidly catching up with them, however.

Accelerating like an ambulance on emergency call, the good doctor's bedside manner left a lot to be desired. "Wait till I get hold of you, you fuckers. I'll fucking kill you!" So much for the Hippocratic oath.

Snack attack retribution had almost reached the nonchalant Zen masters when an overloaded shopping trolley – one of the extra-long, DIY store-style trolleys – suddenly appeared in front of the speeding emergency vehicle. Pushed by a grinning greengrocer, who couldn't believe his luck, it was stacked with a ziggurat of aluminium display racks. It was unavoidable. The deafening crash must have penetrated The Zone, because the shoplifting shoguns glanced over their shoulders, clocked the DIY RTA, promptly sprinted out through the yawning entrance and zipped across the deserted car park, heading in the general direction of Carrickfergus town centre.

Picking himself up painfully, Doctor Death decided that back-up was needed. He pulled out his mobile phone, then hit speed dial. "Billy? Bit of a problem. The holdall's gone."

Chapter Three

Some Like it Hot

Abby Maguire was struggling. Struggling with a vibrator. Struggling with a fistful of vibrators. Giant vibrators with flexi-tips, easi-grips and multi-speed options. Abby was struggling to dress the shop window for its Re-member September promotion, and the Beelzebub vibrators were proving a pain in the backside. No matter how carefully she arranged them, they looked like pornographic porcupines in day-glo plastic.

"They didn't warn me about this at the orientation session," Abby muttered to herself. She was sweating in the heat of the halogen display lighting. The faux-latex Some Like It Hot staff uniform didn't help either. She was flushed, panting, perspiring and, to casual passers-by, looked as though she was enjoying the perks of the job, much like a bartender on the bottle, a pharmacist raiding the drugs cabinet or a Merthyr Tydfil hill farmer dipping his sheep on the sly.

Still, passing trade was minimal at this time of day, so there was no one to witness her wanton window display. Things usually went quiet after 5.00 p.m., only to pick up later on. Friday was Some Like It Hot's late opening night and things could get hairy in the costume hire department – naughty nurse and dirty doctor sets, sinful nun and devilish priest vestments, Nazi stormtrooper get ups, complete with coal-scuttle helmets, stick grenades, swastika armbands and leatherette jackboots. More popular still were the salty sea dog ensembles, comprising souwesters, gumboots, harpoons, naughty nautical gaits and what have you. Only the Harry Potter outfits, consisting of his 'n' her invisibility cloaks, wash 'n' go magic wands and one-size-fits-all fizzing whizbees, came close to the raunchy delights of Moby Dick night.

Well, that's what the customers claimed on returning the

encrusted costumes, though Abby had her doubts. Carrickfergus may have been a hotbed of many things – Christian fundamentalists, Protestant paramilitaries, tattooed Pitbull owners and Tesco loyalty card holders – but sexy swingers with a predilection for stain-resistant, ready-wipe, velcro-fastened pac-a-macs required a pinch of salt, or several.

Hardcore clients aside, the town hadn't warmed up to Some Like It Hot. Opened seven years earlier, the store was situated in West Street, a narrow pedestrianized thoroughfare that ran from the main town square to one of Carrick's two principal tourist attractions, St. Nicholas's twelfth-century church. Along with the nearby Norman castle, St. Nicholas's attracted the vast majority of visitors, and the shops lining West Street benefited from the day-tripper footfall.

Some Like It Hot's arrival hadn't gone unnoticed, needless to say. The good citizens of Carrickfergus, what few there were, took exception to the opening of a saucy lingerie shop within heavy petting distance of St. Nicholas's. Demonstrations, picket lines and brimstone-belching lay preachers attempted to disrupt the intimate apparel operation. However, the promised hellfire simply made Some Like It Hot more appealing to local and national newspapers. Their headline writers had never had it so good and business burgeoned accordingly. When media interest moved on – to the traditional Carrickfergus fare of car parking charges, economic regeneration packages, paramilitary punishment beatings and headless corpses in council estate back alleys – the erotica emporium's marketing-savvy management turned to another hold-the-front-page tactic. A Marilyn Monroe mannequin was installed in Some Like It Hot's shop window. Wearing the iconic white dress from *The Seven Year Itch*, sporting the retail store's raciest underwear, and equipped with a powerful underfoot fan that burst into life at set intervals, the billowing window display attracted all and sundry from near and far. Adolescent boys of all ages were also drawn in rubber-necking, finger-pointing, customer-discouraging numbers. However, a display of monster dildos, labelled Small, Medium and Large, soon dispersed the hairy-handed contingent, though their post-pubescent psyches may have suffered considerable collateral damage.

Still, the fragile psyches of tumescent teenagers weren't high on Abby Maguire's agenda. She had more important things to worry about. The Eco-friendly August posters had to be removed from the shop window ("Calculate Your Carnal Footprint!") and replaced with Re-member September's eye-popping display of pornupines. Then she had to tidy up the shop before the Friday night rush.

Not that the Friday night rush added up to much. Despite the headline-grabbing PR spectaculars and attempts to further inflame Bible-thumpers by setting the white dress uplift interval to seven minutes on Sundays, the sum total of those who liked it hot in Carrickfergus was somewhat disappointing. Business was much better in Belfast, Lisburn, Bangor and above all Cultra, where cross-dressing accoutrements proved particularly popular with local celebrities, high-ranking civil servants, the remaining military personnel at Holywood Barracks and affluent former paramilitaries who owned huge houses on Ulster's so-called "Gold Coast". Gold lamé coast, more like.

Carrickfergus, by contrast, was a blue collar town. Dog collars were pretty popular too, though not the kind of dog collars that Some Like It Hot ordinarily stocked. The oldest settlement on the north shore of Belfast Lough – considerably older than Belfast itself – Carrickfergus had the makings of a major money-spinner. An ancient castle and keep, a Georgian town hall, an impressive Norman church in St. Nicholas's, atmospheric, twisty-turny streets in the Irish and Scots Quarters, and well-preserved remnants of ramparts and walls, brilliantly ticked the right tourist boxes, as did the harbour-side shopping complex on the outer edge of the town centre.

Better yet, the settlement had witnessed more than its fair share of historical incidents, which offered all sorts of tales-for-tourists possibilities. Prince William of Orange, a.k.a. King Billy, landed there with his armies in June 1690 before defeating James I at the Battle of the Boyne a month later. The last witch trial in Ireland took place in the town in 1711, when three hubble-bubblers were sentenced to the toil and trouble of the common pillory. John Paul Jones, the rambunctious American privateer, attacked the settlement with impunity during the War of Independence. Carrickfergus was the centre for gun-running in 1912, when the Ulster Crisis was at its height and northern Protestants were prepared to fight rather than submit to Irish Home Rule. Its former residents included Jonathan Swift of *Gulliver's Travels* fame, Andrew Jackson, seventh president of the United States, Louis MacNeice, the foremost British poet of the "low dishonest decade" that was the 1930s, and "Buttercup", the terrifying ghost of a soldier who was executed in error (possibly on account of his decidedly unmilitary name) and whose troubled spirit stalks Carrick's night-time streets to this very day.

Despite its prodigious commercial potential, the townscape was marred by unattractive pedestrianization schemes, all sorts of cheap and nasty 1960s buildings, an unsightly rash of surrounding housing estates and an intrusive multi-lane dual carriageway that dominated the seafront and effectively separated the town centre from its crown jewels, the castle and the harbour.

The worst blight, many believed, was Some Like It Hot itself. And at times Abby was inclined to agree with them. It wasn't that she was a puritanical blue stocking or anything, but in its increasingly desperate attempts to attract free publicity the store was becoming ever more outrageous, ever more offensive, ever more eroticized. The emporium's traditional stock-in-trade, deliciously feminine de-luxe lingerie, was being supplanted by harder and harder hard-core contents, which were hard to swallow, let alone stomach, much less display. It was turning into the retailing equivalent of aging rock chicks – Britney, Courtney, Madge and more – seemingly determined to shock their way back to the top and only succeeding in making clueless, shameless, knickerless fools of themselves.

The long-term future for Some Like It Hot wasn't Abby Maguire's problem, however. She was simply a university student on work placement as part of her Retail Marketing degree at the University of Hustler. She had no intention of making a career in sexy chemises, peek-a-boo bustiers or see-through bondage gear. The avuncular owners, admittedly, had made her what they thought was an offer she couldn't refuse (a free hand with the edible underwear range, specifically the introduction of lo-cal, high-fibre, omega3-enriched alternatives). They'd painted an attractive career-track picture of managing one of Some Like It Hot's sister stores (Hot to Trot, Pants on Fire, Yes Yes Yes, Once More With Feeling and First Time For Everything). They'd encouraged her to examine the gamut of on-line expansion options (albeit the thought of surfing through XXX-rated websites was enough to make Abby seriously seasick).

All things considered, Ms. Maguire wasn't tempted by a permanent position in Some Like It Hot. She'd seen enough liquorice-flavoured condoms, split-crotch cami-knickers, nearly-nylon naughty nighties, relaxed-fit see-through bodystockings, and boxes of Viagra Max, Viagra SuperMax and Viagra A&E to last a lifetime.

Some lifetimes are shorter than others, though.

Chapter Four

Lie Back and Think

Market research has a lot to answer for, Abby Maguire reckoned as she put the finishing touches to the eye-catching window display. A national survey of 1,200 adult consumers had revealed that September was the sexiest month. September was the month when British women were at their friskiest and men, re-energized after the summer holidays, were ready for a full five minutes of passionate love action. September was the month for romantic weekends in Paris, courtesy of Ryanair and similar low-cost carriers, though there was nothing romantic about Ryanair's cheap and cheerless service. September was also the month that was nine months before June, the official start of the UK's shotgun wedding season. But Abby preferred not to think about that.

She didn't believe the market research, for starters, since she doubted whether people told the truth about their sex lives. Certainly not to interviewers, definitely not to partners, and least of all to themselves. Men exaggerated, women understated and gays were too busy shopping to answer stupid questions.

Still, hers was not to reason why. The owners of Some Like It Hot had read the syndicated research report and decided that September needed an extra-big promotional push, and the Re-member September event was the result. In addition to the usual special offer (buy-one-nipple-clamp-get-one-free), there was a 50 per cent reduction across the entire cock ring range (in price, that is, not circumference). Weekend rental rates on bondage equipment, including handcuffs, chains and shackles of every stripe, were slashed in an attempt to take the strain out of restraint. As if that weren't enough to pull in the grunting punters, loyalty card points were doubled on lubricants, massage oils, delay sprays and ever-popular penile dysfunction elixirs, embrocations, balsams and rubs.

The marketing money shot, however, was the "Win a Weekend of Lurve" competition. Sexy scratch cards were being direct mailed to every dwelling in the Carrickfergus region – all shock horror publicity gratefully received – while entrants were asked to complete the saucy sentence, "Some Like it Hot in Paris Because…" Abby dreaded reading the submissions, though Dick and Betty Biggar, the ebullient owners of the erogenous outlet, were beside themselves with erotic anticipation. Raring to go, they were in Gay Paree for the weekend to finalize the libidinous arrangements, leaving Abby in charge of the shop.

It was a big responsibility. It meant a lot of extra work. If successful, it was sure to lead to extra, extra work. Namely, an October Legover promotion on flavoured body oils; an autoerotic extravaganza in No-partner November; and a super-saucy Christmas Special featuring Rudolph the Red-Nosed Rabbit. Abby frowned at the thought, while hastily rearranging the last of the cotton candy chastity belts.

But at least there's an upside, Abby mused, as she backed out of the hot shop window. The promotion's perfect for her placement project. Her work experience year in Some Like It Hot wasn't all fun and games, let alone slap and tickle. She had to write a 5,000-word essay, a placement-specific report that involved original market research and an assessment of its implications for the sponsoring organization. Dave Kelley, her placement tutor, had arranged a progress meeting for Friday week and she was supposed to have an interim update prepared. The Re-member September promotion was ideal. She had the national sex survey to draw on and a focus group or two with the regulars ought to do the trick.

Hmmmm… a focus group with the regulars, the self-styled Some Like It Hotties? Abby shuddered at the prospect. It wasn't that she was prudish or anything – well, okay, she was a bit, and, looking around, who could blame her? – but she sometimes thought that a modicum of modesty wouldn't go amiss. Morality, too. She should've objected when the placements were assigned. She should have said no. She didn't have a choice. She'd been spurned by several placement student takers, presumably on account of her unacceptable attitude… aptitude… appearance. Some Like It Hot was the only opening available and, even then, it was a family connection that sealed the deal.

Basically, she'd made her vibromatic waterbed and had to lie on it.

Ahead of schedule, Abby had time for a quick break before Friday night got into gear. All sorts of gear. The display racks were fully stocked and groaning with goodies. The teddies, baby dolls and suspender belts were a rainbow in racy red, wedding night white and peek-a-boo pink. The novelty department, with its sex dice, tantric Twister, carnal Cluedo, strip poker cards and happy honeymoon musical underwear (push and it plays *Here Comes the Bride*), was as riveting as always. The costume hire department was ready for action, though there might not be enough French Maid outfits to meet Re-member September's demands. Carrickfergus Rugby Club would be disappointed.

There was just enough time for a free ice cream from the love tub cabinet at the back of the store, next to the carnal costume fitting rooms and ex-stock annex. Abby made her way past the till, where she paused to straighten the safety equipment display, everything from packets of condoms and cans of delay spray to GPS stalker detectors and date-rape drug antidotes. She cast an eye over the Friday Night Specials rack – acrylic tiger-skin thongs, imitation rubber basques in black and blue, padded posing pouches for the embarrassingly under-endowed, etc. – knowing that it'd be empty come 9.00 p.m., closing time.

Abby stared into the ice box of delights, perhaps the most profitable part of the Some Like It Hot operation. What better way to cool down after a night of hotter than hot passion than with a half-gallon carton of Ben & Jerry's Willy Vanilly? Granted, the gloop looked almost as bad as it sounded, but the Willy Vanilly taste sensation beat Chunky Monkey and Cherry Garcia hands down. It was either that or the gay pride perennial, Tutti Frutti, or possibly the bondage brigade best-seller, Double Whipped Dairy Ice Cream. Decisions, decisions.

Tucking lustily into the "bottomless bucket" of Ben and Jerry's, Abby returned to the front of the store and peered outside. The ineptly pedestrianized street was almost empty, apart from a swirl of airborne crisp packets and a lateral moraine of abandoned fish and chip wrappers. Everything stopped for tea in Carrickfergus, bar KFC and Dunkin Donuts at the far end of West Street, where the cheap and nasty pavoirs joined the litter-strewn central square. If only they'd spend a bit of money renovating the place, it could be very, very attractive. She'd heard rumours of a redevelopment project and not before time. Carrick could do with a makeover. She could do with one too. The diet starts tomorrow.

Abby's reverie was disturbed by a commotion outside the shop. Someone was in stitches, laughing uproariously. Two blokes were standing in the middle of the street, dressed in the usual Ulster uniform of blue jeans and black bomber jackets. One had his head thrown back in hysterics. The other was doubled over, with his hands on his knees. He had a huge purple holdall slung over his shoulder and was gasping for air. Then, glancing up at his snorting companion, he too started laughing uncontrollably, holding his side with the pain.

"Damn druggies," Abby swore beneath her breath. They were obviously on glue of some kind, with crack cocaine chasers by the look of it. Abby knew what was coming next. They'd spot the Some Like It Hot window display and, as intoxicated passers-by were wont to do, they'd start nudging each other. This'd be followed by obscene comments and accompanied by attempts to enter the premises. She was calling the police.

The smaller of the two chuckle brothers, the one with a decidedly suspicious face, did a double take on the store. The model of the Parthenon had attracted his attention. Well, the Pornenon was a bit of an eyeful, if she said so herself. With its Doric columns made from fluted vibrators, pediments constructed from carefully layered love eggs and portico of artfully assembled penile propellers (don't ask), it far surpassed her previous sex toy recreations of Sydney Opera House, Buckingham Palace, Carrickfergus Castle, RMS *Titanic* and the Taj Mahal.

Backpacker adjusted his load and started walking towards the main square. His still giggling companion, captivated by the arresting window display, was clearly one of the some who like it hot. He was transfixed by the day-glo pornupines and frankly amazed by the melt-in-the-mouth arrangement of milk chocolate butt plugs. Despite the dampening effect of the heavy-duty, graffiti-resistant, reinforced plate glass, Abby could hear him call out "Hey, Jimmy, take a jook at this."

Wiping his eyes, the guffawing bagman turned round. Holy shinola! It was Jimmy James, Abby's former boyfriend. She hadn't seen him for several years and, would you credit it, he was looking better than ever. He scanned the store front and, although Abby shrank back quickly, it was too late. A look of confusion crossed his face, then the light of recognition dawned. He shook his head, smiled in that devilishly cute way she knew so well, ran a hand through his shaggy, jet-black hair and headed straight for the door.

"Hi Abby. Long time no see. You're looking..., you're looking..." He glanced at the half-empty carton of Ben & Jerry's. "... as though you're enjoying yourself at uni."

"Well, you know how it is first semester. The twenty-pound weight gain and all that."

"And twenty each semester thereafter. How many years have you been at Hustler now? Three, isn't it? Four?"

"Still shoplifting, Jimmy? I'd recognize that post-theft euphoria anywhere. Still giggling because you got away with it? Still planning to join the recreational shoplifter hall of fame, alongside Winona Ryder, Farrah Fawcett, Jennifer Capriati, Courtney Love, Eric Clapton and Britney Spears? I've got news for you, Jimmy. They were celebrities *before* they dabbled in dubious discounts. They didn't become celebrities *because* of their knack for knocking. Grow up. Get a job. Get a life."

Jimmy James cracked a wry smile and raised an eyebrow inquisitively. "Post-theft euphoria?" he echoed sarcastically. "Recreational shoplifter? Knack for knocking? Dabbled in dubious discounts? Who taught you to talk like that?"

"That's education for you," Abby snapped. "You should try it sometime."

"And end up working in a sex shop?"

"I'm on placement," she replied. "I didn't have a choice. My tutor insisted. And it's not a sex shop, actually. It's an intimate apparel emporium."

"I'll say," he laughed. "Tell me, Abby, do you get a staff discount?"

"No, but we have a special offer on delay sprays that might interest you."

He wasn't laughing any more. "That's rich. You never used to be interested in sex. Times have changed, eh?"

"Wrong again, Jimmy. It wasn't sex I wasn't interested in. It was sex with *you* I wasn't interested in!"

Jimmy glared at her, eyes blazing. Abby glared right back. She wasn't going to be embarrassed by a recreational shoplifter. The adult entertainment industry was a noble calling. Well, okay, perhaps not. However, she wasn't going to crumble in front of him, no matter how gorgeous he looked.

The tension was broken by the shop door opening with a bang. "Jimmy. Come quickly. They're after us. It's King Billy..."

"King Billy?" Jimmy seemed dumbfounded. But only for a second or two. "Jesus Christ," he gasped in panic, while adjusting the shoulder strap of his weighty holdall. "Better leave this here. Abby, mind this for me. I'll be back for it later. We'll talk then. I promise."

Taken unawares, Abby didn't have time to refuse, much less say "No way, Jimmy!" There wasn't time to do anything, as the terrified twosome tore out of the shop and sprinted up the pedestrianized street, slipping and slithering in their haste.

Some people never change! Abby thought, booting the bag of swag in frustration. It felt like it was filled with breeze blocks. Muttering murderously, she manoeuvred the bulky purple holdall behind the counter. Prosecuted for handling stolen goods. While on placement. In a sex shop. I'll be a laughing stock. I'll be sent down from uni, whatever that means. Damn you, Jimmy James. I'll give you what for later.

Having secreted the holdall in the costume fitting room, she hurried to the front of the store. The half-empty carton of Willy Vanilly was sitting in the shop window, where she'd set it down under her ex-boyfriend's disdainful gaze. He's no bloody oil painting. Well he is, actually.

Suddenly, the oil painting pelted past the store, running down the hill at full tilt with his spotty sidekick in hot pursuit. He skidded to a stop and looked round anxiously. There was terror in his eyes. The pair dashed up a dark alleyway directly opposite. Abby couldn't make out what was happening. A bulky but muscular man, brandishing a baseball bat, ran after them.

Abby hared back to the counter and picked up the phone. Nine, nine, nine. Don't let it be busy. Or a call centre. Or off-shored. Or menu-driven. Hurry up. Hurry up! For God's sake hurry up!! "I'll kill you, Jimmy James," she blurted out. "I swear, I'll kill you for this."

Click. "Not if we kill him first, fatty." Click.

A huge, stainless steel knife was pressed on the phone, breaking the connection.

Click. "Would ye like to join him, love?" Click.

Chapter Five

Hey Joe, Where You Goin' With That Knife in Your Hand?

The intruder had a horrible speech impediment. He was clicking and clacking like a demented dolphin. Some Like It Hot saw its fair share of crazies, usually on Sundays when Pentecostal protesters dropped by with their placards, psalms and prayers for the sinners within. However, cleft palate was wielding a very big knife – a big, ex-abattoir knife with a seriously serrated blade. Abby knew better than to argue with a belligerent senior citizen on a Jim Bowie bender. She put the phone back on its cradle and turned to face her cackling assailant. Bald as a coot on chemotherapy, with a face like an elephant's scrotum during a cold snap, he was Igor's uglier twin brother. Only with dentures.

Abby'd been frightened by many grisly sights in her life, not least a Daniel O'Donnell gig at Belfast's Waterfront Hall, but this wasn't one of them. Psycho senior citizens held no fear for sex shop workers, though randy senior citizens wearing plastic macs and playing with themselves were another matter entirely. Tempted to make a crack about big clicks/small dicks, she almost laughed in the face of the wizened dwarf. He cut her off, however.

Click. "Ye know him, fatty?" Click.

"Who?"

Click. "Yer thievin' boyfriend, Jimmy no-fingers James." Click.

"No fingers?"

Click. "No hands, knees, ears, tongue or bollocks, when Billy's finished with him." Click. He laughed malevolently. There's no joke like your own joke.

Abby glared down at the cleated crumbly. "No, I don't know

No-fingers," she said forcefully. "I *do* know that if you don't get out of here right now, the police'll hear all about it."

Never underestimate an OAP, especially an OAP with a Davy Crockett complex. Psychos have the strength of ten men, or so they say, and even Saga psychos in sex shops punch well above their weight. And their height. The blow, when it came, arrived like a left-field sledgehammer. Sent flying, Abby sprawled across the countertop, scattering packets of condoms, upsetting arrangements of date rape antidotes and sending vials of lubricant sliding along the glass-topped counter like shots of whisky in a wild-west saloon. Cans of It's A Miracle delay spray cascaded to the marbled floor, a metallic thunderstorm, where they were joined by broken bottles of One Night Stand anti-impotence elixir, which crashed and shattered on impact.

Winded, Abby tried to catch her breath and, while the OAP was savouring the moment, she seized her chance, shoved him aside and made a dash for the door. But she wasn't as fast as she used to be. Igor stuck out a foot, tripping the rubber-suited sprinter. Abby crashed face-first into a giant, dildo-shaped display case containing giant dildos. The store's prize collection of super-vibrators was strewn all over the shop.

As she struggled to disentangle herself from the wreckage, Abby's jaw ached indescribably. But not as much as her neck. Igor was on top of the placement student, one hand on her throat, thumb and forefinger jammed either side of her windpipe.

Click. "Don't fuckin' lie to me!" Click. "Breathe a word to the police and ye'll be joinin yer boyfriend in the bone yard, ye fat bitch." Click.

Well, Abby may have been packing a few extra pounds, courtesy of the obligatory undergraduate diet of beer 'n' pizza, plus an occasional tub of Ben & Jerry juice. But to be called a fat bitch by a vertically challenged dickhead with a speech defect was decidedly out of order. Grasping and flailing, she managed to latch on to a giant vibrator. Hard plastic ... pointed tip ... fluted shaft ... The Saturn 5. She rammed the supersized dildo into his left eye, while flicking the on-switch. It slithered across the cornea like an electric screwdriver seeking purchase on the denuded slot of a star-head.

The effect was instantaneous. Igor screeched and peeled away, his left hand clamped against the injured orb.

The Bowie knife was still in the gargoyle's other hand, though. Abby didn't hesitate. She grabbed a 500 ml can of It's A Miracle delay spray from the scattered counter-top display, whipped off the sure-lok, press-n-twist, kiddie-protection cap, jammed the well-shaken canister into his prune-in-vinegar face and, with nary a thought for CFCs or her burgeoning carbon footprint, gave him a blast that must have turned the entire ozone layer into a pair of fishnet tights. Then she blasted him again. And again. He had more aerosol propellant in his lungs than Scud missiles have rocket fuel.

The shriek was genuinely terrifying. Like his Frankensteinian namesake, ancient Igor lurched across the shop floor, staggering, stumbling, smashing into display racks and shelving units. Baby dolls, bustiers and bra-and-panty sets were flung this way and that as the floundering OAP tore at his streaming eyes. It was a live-action version of *The Scream*, at 120 decibels or so.

Abby ran to the telephone, picked it off the floor and punched 999, her fingers trembling with adrenaline. Turning her back on the raging pygmy was a serious error of judgement. A bellow from the bowels of the earth rent the air. Abby wheeled round, only to catch the baleful sight of the Devil himself, complete with horns, forked tail and gleaming hunting knife, bearing down on her. Igor had got tangled up in the costume department's Old Nick outfit. Had he stumbled into the autoerotic department instead and attacked in the guise of a blow-up doll, Abby's momentary hesitation might have proved fatal.

As it was, she was saved by the spillage. Slippery at the best of times, the marbled shop floor was smeared with spilled lubricant, littered with buzzing vibrators and liberally sprinkled with glass from the broken bottles of penile dysfunction embrocation. Charging toward her at full tilt, while screaming like a banshee on a triple loop roller coaster, Mephistopheles stood on a Beelzebub vibrator, slipped sideways and landed face down in the glutinous mess. He got to his feet, the side of his head covered in genital gel, and made another mad dash for Abby. He lost his footing on the greasy floor once more and, wildly rotating his arms for counter-balance – he looked like a geriatric on the dance-floor, desperately doing the hoochie-coochie – skidded into the designer label lingerie section. Diaphanous delicates by Dior, silken slivers *à la* La Perla and little wisps of Egyptian cotton courtesy of kittenish Kylie were torn asunder by the furiously slashing blade of psycho shopper.

Aghast yet unaccountably amused, Abby turned back to the phone. Damn and blast, it *was* menu-driven! Press one for police, two for ambulance, three for fire tenders, four for air-sea rescue, five for floods and mudslides, six for hazardous chemical spillages, seven for avian flu, foot-and-mouth or analogous infectious diseases, eight for all other emergency services including dangerous dogs, cats stuck up trees, escaped farm animals and big hairy spiders in the bathroom. Desperate, Abby didn't have time to decide. A cross-dressing devil, draped in ribbons of slinky silk and see-through, super-sensual satin, was emerging from the wreckage, screaming like a demon who'd eaten a cheeseburger too quickly and was afflicted with terminal trapped wind. He wrenched the luxury undergarments from his tear-stained face, rubbed his hideously bloodshot eyes, slowly removed his drool-dripping dentures and started running toward Abby in a rugby tackle crouch. The evil imp grabbed her round the midriff and such was his momentum that the entire glass-topped counter, complete with heavy cash register, toppled around the tangled twosome. Abby battered the brute about the head with the hefty handset of the telephone, a retro-chic classic in brass and bakelite, but he held on like a miniature giant squid with superglue-supplemented suckers. Frantic, she blasted him full-face with yet more of the foul-smelling delay spray. At such close range, the impact on the incubus almost defied belief. Truly, the torments of hell are as nothing compared to the anguished howl that rang round the walls of the intimate apparel emporium.

Squealing like a stuck piglet watching *Babe Three: The Slaughterhouse*, the wounded dwarf still wouldn't relent. Summoning up a well of hideous strength, he propelled Abby rapidly backwards and slammed her against the rear wall, close to the ice cream cabinet. Pinning her by the throat, he pulled a spare switchblade from somewhere and clicked its blade open in front of Abby's fearful face. The toothless gargoyle spluttered something, though his saliva marinated words were indistinct, almost incoherent. "I used to be a family butcher," he slobbered. "I've dismembered bigger heifers than you, fatty." A grotesque smile distorted his already distorted features. "Slicing up Fenians is my speciality," the gummy bigot dribbled (or did he say Friesians?).

"You're right," Abby replied, refusing to be cowed by the mutant lovechild of Mini Me and Mad Bastard. "I am a left-footer. And here's proof, you Protestant arsehole." Drawing upon her rapidly dwindling strength, she kneed the fiend in his unprotected crotch. Even the Devil's wedding tackle can't take a direct hit like that. His bloodshot eyes started suddenly, rolled upwards and turned inwards like a Harold Lloyd impersonation. Poleaxed, he collapsed to the floor in a heap, clutching his stomach and moaning something about mummy, daddy, mummy, daddy. Using all of her remaining strength, Abby gave him one more mighty kick in the knackers. Just for luck.

Inexplicably euphoric despite her terrifying ordeal, Abby turned and made a beeline for the door. I'm outta here…

A monster was blocking her path.

Well over 185 cm., with rippling muscles that were rapidly turning to fat – extremely intimidating fat – the monster sported a tiny black goatee, boasted an enormous gleaming pate, had more tattoos on his arms than a heavy metal-loving Maori chieftain and possessed an alarmingly wry smile on his incongruously pretty face.

"What the fuck's going on here?" he barked.

"Thank God," Abby blurted out. "This… this madman attacked me… I tried to fight him off… Please call the police."

A rumbling laugh rolled around the shattered store. "Did the fat girl get the better of you, Joe? Wait till I tell the boys in the Butchers Benevolent Society." The newcomer chuckled to himself then casually revealed a baseball bat that was hidden behind his bison-like back. It was covered in blood and what appeared to be bits of brain matter. He looked down at the bloody bat and then looked up at Abby. He didn't have to say anything. Nor did he.

Chapter Six

In Emergency Break Glass

Within what seemed like milliseconds, the beefy newcomer picked Abby up with his left hand, lifted her completely off the ground and started shaking the shop assistant like a rag doll with rickets. "Listen up…," he said softly, taking in her name tag, "… Abby. I like a girl with a bit of fight. This country was built on fighting spirit…"

"Yes," Abby gasped, struggling to touch the ground with her toes, "that's why it's such a shithole."

He shook her again. "Don't interrupt me when I'm talking, Abby. And don't even think of kicking me in the clinks. Because I'll tear your fuckin' head off." The monster set her down with a smile. Defiant, she scowled back at the muscle-bound brute. But didn't make a move. He turned back to his fallen companion, "Are you okay there, Joe?"

The old man struggled to his feet. He pushed the heels of his palms into his still streaming eyes, rubbed vigorously, and took a couple of deep shuddering breaths. He looked like death warmed up in a microwave. Joe may have had the heart of a lion and the strength of Popeye after the all-you-can-eat spinach smorgasbord, but his wizened testicles were firmly lodged somewhere near the base of his spine. It might take several weeks before they crawled back into his drawers, which was a revolting thought in itself. Joe's speech impediment was unimpaired, though it seemed to be operating an octave or two above its normal register.

Click. "Aye, I'm okay." Click. "Step aside, Billy, I'm goin' to kill the fat fucker." Click. Shoving the bent and buckled display racks aside, he picked his way through the shop floor carnage and stooped to retrieve his hunting knife and switchblade, which lay where they'd fallen among the shards of glass, pools of lubricant, puddles of erectile elixir and madly buzzing vibrators, many with purple tips waving. The look of disgust that crossed his prudish, prune-like face was priceless.

"I think you've had enough excitement for one day, Joe." Billy wiped the top of his bloody baseball bat with the cup of a 38D Wonderbra. "We both have. Abby here is going to tell us where our stolen property is. Then we're going to leave and let her tidy up."

Click. "I'll be back, frilly knickers." Click.

"Anytime, Arnold," she replied in a mock *Terminator* accent.

Mr. Muscle chuckled in admiration at Abby's naïve nervelessness, then passed a hand over his glistening pate in pretend exasperation. "That's enough, the both of you." Smiling, he started stroking his goatee idly. "Where's the holdall, Abby?"

She looked at him resolutely, refusing to be browbeaten or bullied. "What did you do to Jimmy James, you thug?"

"I asked you first," he laughed, though his periwinkle eyes were glinting rather than twinkling.

"You won't get away with this."

"I will, love," he said quietly. "I've been getting away with it for years." His voice descended to a menacing whisper. "Now, where did you put my property?"

Terrified though she was, Abby wasn't going to let the intimidating bastard get away with it. The silence in the store was deafening. Even the Beelzebub vibrators had stopped buzzing, though some sexy-flexis writhed on the floor like an infestation of flesh-coloured slugs. The room reeked of It's A Miracle delay spray, its musty, choking aroma enveloping everything and everyone. So much for retail store atmospherics.

The goateed giant grimaced. "Do you know who I am, Abby?"

"Yes," she answered calmly. "I'm sure I've seen your face on TV. *Crimestoppers*, wasn't it? Maybe it was an Ulster's Most Wanted poster."

The ice-blue eyes stabbed right through her. "I don't think so, love. I own this place…" He raised his tat-matted arms aloft. "This town… this country. The police are in my pocket. Don't even think of contacting them. If you do, you're dead," he added matter-offactly. "As I said, Abby, I like people with spunk, no matter what foot they kick with. Now, do yourself a favour and tell me where the holdall is. I won't ask you again."

Obstinate first, last and always, Abby subscribed to the traditional Irish credo, whatever you say, say nothing. Resolute, she remained mulishly mute, even though she'd nothing personal at stake, other than the welfare of (and loyalty to) a feckless ex-boyfriend.

It was the speed of the creature's reaction that surprised her. Three parts thug to one part thoroughbred, Billy was very quick on his feet, even when the going was heavy. Or sticky, as in this particular instance. He grabbed Abby by the hair and shoved her face to within a millimetre of a large shard of glass, standing proud among the wreckage of the counter. Taken aback, she glanced involuntarily at the costume fitting room, where Jimmy's ill-starred goods were secreted. Billy spotted the tell-tale sign and, holding her by the scruff of the neck – akin to a feral cat with its kitten – he physically hurled her towards the rear of the shop. Slipping and sliding on the treacherous floor, she crashed into the heavy swing door, knocking it open with a crash and landed face-down on the polished vinyl floor. She turned to see Billy looming behind her, rapidly scanning the room, which was filled with stock boxes, costumes for hire and a couple of curtained changing cubicles.

"Let this be a lesson to you, Abby. Don't try to punch above your weight." Smirking in a sickeningly self-satisfied manner, he caught sight of the purple holdall in the corner behind some boxes, swaggered over to his objective, pulled back the zip fastener and looked inside, carefully checking its contents.

There was something about his smug strut, the way he thought he owned the place, that got Abby's goat. She looked around for a weapon. The costumes-for-hire prop box was just within reach. Policeman's truncheon. Cowgirl spurs. Dominatrix flail. Harry Potter broomstick. Doctor 'n' nurse endoscope. Captain Ahab's barbed harpoon...

Abby wrenched the harpoon out of its holder and hurled it at Billy with all her might. Interrupted by the racket, the bald brute whirled round and was half on his feet, almost facing his female assailant, when the harpoon caught him amidships. A look of shock and surprise crossed his face, as he stumbled backwards into cardboard boxes of Victoria's Secret scanties. Abby could see he was seeing his life flash in front of him and that it wasn't a pretty sight. He clutched the spear to the folds of his fleshy belly, stood upright, staggered slightly and stared down at the still quivering lance. Groaning, he gradually pulled it away. Grinning, he threw it to the floor at Abby's feet. The tip had buckled on impact, as it was designed to do. It was a theatrical harpoon, akin to toy knives with spring-loaded blades.

"Health and Safety'll be the death of you, love," he chortled.

"Go on, do your worst," Abby shouted. "You'll get your comeuppance some day."

"No, love. You're gonna get your comeuppance, right now." The brute started unbuckling his jeans. "Violence is an aphrodisiac, better than Viagra by far. Has no one ever told you that?" He grinned lustily, licking his lips in carnal anticipation. "It's your lucky day, lady."

Abby thought she was going to be sick. She made a grab for the fireman's axe. But the monster was too quick off the mark, his belt-buckle jangling with the exertion. He grabbed her by the throat and threw her across the polished vinyl floor, where she sprawled flat on her back, the rubberoid uniform riding up invitingly.

Towering above her, unbuttoning his fly furiously, the rampant animal announced, "I've had a thousand women."

Unimpressed, Abby retorted, "Had, as in had a look at their photos in dirty magazines?"

"They loved every minute of it."

"Is that what they told you? Do you really think any of them would dare criticize your performance? I bet there's a tribute website, though. Billy's Really Tiny Willy dotcom. Average rating, no stars."

"You'll be seeing stars in a minute, love," he leered, thrusting his pelvis forward in a revolting manner he probably considered sexy. "Get your knickers off."

Abby bit back the bile that was burning the back of her mouth. "You're wasting your time, buster," she spat, trying to discourage the creature. "I'm wearing Marks and Spencer's magic knickers. They're made of vulcanized rubber with super-adhesive, carbon-fibre panels and NASA-approved stealth fighter technology. You need a crowbar to get them off."

"I'll show you a crowbar, love." He dropped his jeans and exposed a pitiful sight, Red Hand of Ulster Y-fronts.

Abby laughed out loud. "A crowbar? More like a miniature nail file."

"We'll see about that," he roared, tearing off his underwear and exposing his penile pride and joy.

Backing away crab-like across the oilcloth floor, praying that the stream of insults would dissuade the animal rather than incite him to further violence, Abby hastily countered. "You're in the wrong shop. This isn't Acorn Antiques."

The burly beast threw himself on top of her, knocking the breath out of the writhing, struggling, thrashing shop assistant. "Aye, and you make Jo Brand look like Slimmer of the Year." He started pulling down her clamped-on, limpet-like control pants. It sounded like a plunger being extracted from a blocked sink. She grabbed and scratched and clawed at his face. That only enraged him. She gripped her elasticated chastity belt for grim death. He pulled and yanked and yanked and pulled. He was having no joy. Thank God for St. Michael. He wasn't giving up, however.

Despite her panic-parched mouth, Abby managed to summon up sufficient saliva to spit in his face, which was a fatal mistake in the circumstances. She spat again. And again. She spat and spat until she had no spit left.

Chapter Seven

Where There's a Willy

Monsters like Billy are sensitive brutes. The tiniest thing can bring out their inner psychopath, though there's usually a moment or two of deceptive calm before the bloodthirsty beast is unleashed. Belittling their sexual prowess is bad enough. But spitting on them is usually a one-way ticket to a shallow grave. Only untoward remarks about Oedipal matters, or the tribulation of male pattern baldness, are more likely to receive automatic death sentences. The latter, indeed, usually invites mutilation before murder mercifully intervenes.

Billy No-dick sank back on his hunkers. He painstakingly wiped the gobbets of spittle from his fleshy face and smoothed the soiled goatee with a well-practised move involving finger and thumb, starting with the moustache, finishing under the chin. "I'm going to kill you, you fat bitch, when I've finished fucking you."

"Go ahead, you bald bastard," Abby countered in as calm a voice as she could manage in the circumstances. "What's twenty seconds here or there?"

"Twenty seconds is a long time in my business," he replied, wiping his sputum-streaked hands on a huge haunch. "I can cause a lot of pain in twenty seconds."

Abby had nothing to lose. "Yeah, so they say on Baldy Billy's Bendy Willy dotcom."

The animal's otherwise impassive face twitched ever so slightly. Stroking his goatee again, he announced nonchalantly, "Actually, I think I'll kill you first and fuck you afterwards."

"Not for the first time, I bet. I bet your mother's proud of you."

"She is," he said. "She was," he corrected.

"Oh, that's not what Billy's Hairy Scary Mummy says on My Waste of Space dotcom."

The creature's features started twitching uncontrollably. His huge, shank of beef-sized shoulders were heaving. His massive paws did a perfect Parkinson's impersonation. "I'm going to kill you slowly, you evil bitch. I'm going to rip your rubber knickers off and ram them down your throat."

Knowing that the end was near, Abby threw caution to the wind. "Thought you liked feisty women, Billy. Thought you liked the fighting spirit that made Ulster what it is. The problem with people like you is that you can't handle real women. Mummy's boys like you come into shops like this full of mistaken masturbatory fantasies about what women want. You don't understand women at all. You're suffering from a mental disorder. You say you've fucked a thousand women. You haven't. You've fucked your mother a thousand times. And she didn't think much of your performance either. You're pathetic, Billy. You're Oedipussy whipped. Get professional help."

Given the nature of the beast, Abby expected to hear a bellow like a constipated water buffalo with irritable bowel syndrome. Instead, to her absolute amazement, Billy No-dick suddenly burst into tears. Great racking, rolling sobs rippled from his pneumatic shoulders to his bloated belly. Great hairy hands covered his improbably pretty face as he wept uncontrollably. If anything, Billy's lachrymose demonstration was even more frightening than before, though at least he didn't start sucking his thumb or pull out a comfort blanket.

Abby backed away from the wounded animal as fast as her sturdy legs could carry her. Clearly, she'd touched some kind of primal maternal nerve. Her hightail retreat was halted by the paltry panel door of the ex-stock annex, a part of the building she'd never been in before, for fear of the X-stock it might contain. Seizing her chance, she tugged frantically on the flimsy door handle, but it was jammed solid.

Turning to face her psychotic pursuer, Abby was determined to look into his eyes at the last. He hadn't moved. His head was bowed, though the heaving sobs seemed to have subsided to an occasional passing shudder. He slowly lifted his great glistening head and glared at her. The light in his psycho-killer eyes gradually grew in intensity, like an old oil lamp when the wick's turned up. Desperate, Abby pulled and kicked and pounded on the painted panel door. It shifted slightly but remained stuck fast.

Suddenly, a siren started up. Somewhere outside the shop. Rising and falling, rising and falling, coming ever closer. Billy No-dick stopped dead and listened attentively to the Doppler wail, judging its direction and ETA with obvious expertise, as though he were a Native American tracker with an ear on the railroad.

Igor burst into the costume room. The genital gel had taken anaesthetic effect. His wrinkled face was frozen into a rictus mask, startled eyes staring maniacally. He looked less like a stroke victim than the paralysed recipient of extreme plastic surgery from a back street beautician. "It's the peelers, Billy," he clucked, drool cascading from one side of his cavernous gob. Click. "Someone's spotted the stiffs up the alley." Click. "They'll be here in a couple of minutes." Click. "Kill the bitch and let's go." Click.

Billy nodded curtly, lumbered up to Abby, pulled her away from the recalcitrant doorjamb and forearm smashed her into a pyramid of stock boxes. He rattled the handle and studied the snib. Then with a huge heave, he wrenched the annex door open. It was still juddering as he popped his head inside to check that there was no way out. "I promised you a slow and painful death, love. I'm a man of my word. Inside. Now. I'll be back later."

Abby weighed her options. She didn't have any. Igor was blocking the only way out, glistening hunting knife in hand. Calmly, she picked herself up and walked proudly toward the condemned cell. She paused in front of her half-naked nemesis, puckered up provocatively, stuck her thumb in her mouth and, in the most infantile voice she could manage, cried, "I want my mummy."

With a roar, Ulster's Oedipus shoved her into the ante-room, then slammed and snibbed the door behind her. She struggled to her feet and hobbled back to the doorway. Despite the humming of the flickering fluorescent light, she could hear the security shutters on the shop front coming down, as her attackers made their escape. Presumably, the police would assume that the shop was closed, like most of the others on Friday evenings in Carrickfergus town centre. She had to attract their attention. Someone's attention. Anyone's attention. She had to escape before the brute got back. Shouting was pointless because the seventeenth-century walls were substantial stone blocks, a metre thick at least.

But that didn't stop Abby trying. She yelled and bawled and beat a tattoo on the door. To no avail. She was exhausted, drained, desperately tired. Her head was buzzing. It felt muzzy, heavy, like it was swaddled in cotton wool. Her cries were dampened, furthermore, by the detritus in the annex, which was some kind of dumping ground for discarded display units, out-of-date shop fittings and unfashionable retail store paraphernalia. She'd never seen anything like it. It was an Aladdin's cave of commercial cast-offs, packed with retail artefacts from the innumerable establishments that had occupied the premises down the years. There were male and female mannequins and mannequin body parts. There were bolts of dress material and curtain material in cotton, poplin, rayon, muslin, chiffon, crinoline and crêpe de Chine. There were stuffed owls and foxes and badgers and humming birds in Victorian glass cases. There were cigar boxes and tobacco tins and clay pipes of all shapes and sizes. There were tea chests and biscuit barrels and massive screw-top jars that once held gobstoppers and mint humbugs. There were pewter Toby jugs and china cruet sets and tottering piles of willow-pattern crockery. There were radiograms and record players and metamorphosed stacks of shellac discs in brown paper sleeves. There were hawsers and windlasses and box compasses and giant wooden pulleys. There were rucksacks and groundsheets and tents and torches. There were saucepans and bedpans and ceramic hot water bottles. There were impressively mounted ibex horns. There was a giant stuffed bear. There was a complete suit of armour. There was an enormous anchor that must have weighed a ton. There was a great, brass, sit-up-and-beg cash register with keys like a Remington typewriter and prices displayed in pounds, shillings and pence. There was even a gigantic haberdasher's wall unit, dotted with glass panels and deep drawers and countless little hidey-holes for ribbons, buttons, brocades and broderie anglaise. Dark and looming and hewn from the finest mahogany, the adipose armoire should have occupied pride of place in a shopkeeping museum. In certain respects it did.

Abby was in the retailing equivalent of Tutankhamen's tomb. However, she wasn't planning to become a mummy anytime soon. She shouted and screamed, again and again. As before, the noise was absorbed in archaeological layers of bric-a-brac. She was alone, abandoned, just like the dumped stuff that surrounded her.

As the adrenaline ebbed away, Abby started shaking uncontrollably. It was all too much. Billy-like, she burst into tears, tears that she cursed herself for as they cascaded to the unvarnished pine floor. Almost killed, nearly raped, bruised and battered, and all-but hoarse from her vocal exertions, Abby could be forgiven for a shedding tear or two. Yet bizarrely, the thing that bothered her most, the thing that hurt more than anything, was being called fatty. They'd all called her fat. Even Igor, the ugly old git. She *was* fat. She'd let herself go. She was ashamed of her beer 'n' pizza university lifestyle. She only had herself to blame. If she ever got out of this mess, she'd diet and diet and diet and diet. And get her former figure back if it killed her.

If Billy didn't kill her first.

Abby sank to the floor in despair. Something stirred behind the huge haberdasher's cabinet. Possibly mice, probably rats, though the way things were going feral timber wolves couldn't be ruled out completely, nor could mutant man-eating alligators from the old-town sewers. "Get a grip, Abby," she said to herself. The sweat cooled on her clammy brow. She could feel a slight breeze from somewhere, a draught from underneath the monstrous display unit. There must be another way out. She vaguely remembered Betty Biggar calling it the rear entry room. She'd assumed it was a crude joke. But on reflection...

Re-energized by the prospect of escape, Abby leapt up, cleared a path through the retail marketing midden, grabbed an edge of the giant, acanthus-incised cabinet and pulled with all her might. She wiggled her fingers behind the mahogany monstrosity and tried again. No joy. She ripped dozens of drawers out of their beautifully bevelled sockets, scattering buttons and bows and bobbins to the four winds. Still no movement. Only a slight wobble from the top-heavy tallboy. Encouraged, she planted her back against the uneven stone wall and shoved the empty unit as hard as she could. It shifted. She squeezed in behind, pressed her foot flat against the fixture's unpolished backboard and pushed, pushed, pushed, giving everything she had. It was the leg press from hell. But it worked. The heavy mahogany behemoth toppled over with a sound like a felled giant sequoia landing on a Murano glass factory. Shellac discs disintegrated, taxidermist domes exploded, willow-pattern crockery shattered on impact, the suit of armour collapsed in a clattering heap. Only Metallica in concert comes close to the cacophony.

When the dust of ancient days had dispersed sufficiently, Abby examined the wall where the display unit had stood. It was no different from the rest – rough, thick, solid as the rock it was. So much for the rear entry escape route. She stamped her foot in understandable frustration. Miraculously, the floor rang hollow. Dropping to her knees, Abby rapidly brushed away the dust and soon discovered the source of the slight draught under the colossal cabinet. It was a carefully concealed trap door with a wooden ring-pull lying flush against the floorboards. Only the most acute, or desperate, observer could've spotted it. Abby was desperate. She yanked on the handle, determined to overcome three hundred years of grime-gummed resistance. But she almost fell over backwards, such was the ease with which it opened.

A cool breeze wafted from the inky blackness below. She thought she could hear a faint rushing noise, like waves beating on the seashore. Perhaps the cellar was acting like a giant conch shell. More likely her blood pressure had rocketed. A set of rickety wooden steps descended into the void. There was no sign of a light switch, though there was definitely something scurrying, flapping, writhing below. Tentatively, she placed her foot on the first step. It was solid, as were the second and third. The fourth, however, gave way with a resounding crack. Abby plunged into the Stygian abyss beneath her feet.

Chapter Eight

The Nuremberg Rally

"Give us this day our daily whisky. And just a wee droppie mair fer luck, laddie."

The barman looked lost, but quickly got the gist of it. Trendy hotel bars tend to attract off-beat, off-kilter, off-their-face people, especially on Friday nights when conventioneers hit town. However, the apparition that was swilling the wee droppie whisky in Boynann's Bar at the Carlton Hotel – a minimalist monument to modernism, all pale ash, black leather, stainless steel and recessed strip lighting – was something else again.

Heinrich Hühnerkacke, the bartender, had seen and served quite a few characters in his time. Albeit nothing like the apparition who sat opposite. Rosy of nose, florid of face, bushy of eyebrow, stubbled of chin, craggy of cheekbone, military of bearing and wearing an extravagant tam-o'-shanter with bright red bobble, the wee droppie customer had professional Scotsman written all over him. The tartan trews were a give-away too. Unless, of course, he was a professional golfer, sinking a short putt on the nineteenth green.

Heinrich knew better than to pass comment on the customer's attire. It was more than his job was worth. He needed the tips and, hampered by a perpetually mournful expression, Heinrich compensated with super-slick service. Secretly pulling guests' names from the hotel computer also helped, because there's nothing quite like the personal touch to generate generous gratuities. When they signed for their drinks with a room number, Heinrich put two and two together and came up with five-star customer care. It wasn't standard hotel policy, but as the bar manager often said, take care of your customers and they'll take care of you.

"Certainly, Professor Brodie," Heinrich replied obsequiously, pouring a sizeable shot of Johnnie Walker Black Label. "Is there anything else I can do for you?"

"Aye, there is," Brodie said, knowing full well what the bartender was up to with his real-time relationship marketing. "I need to borrow a conference room for 45 minutes or so. I'm in town for tomorrow's Citroën shindig and I need to rehearse my speech." The sixty-something professor knocked back his whisky in one and winked at the barman. "Lubricating the vocal cords, laddie."

"The Citroën convention is not popular here," Heinrich ventured, a little bit too vehemently for his own good.

"Oh aye? Why's that?" the grizzled guest inquired. "Big conference. Big money. Big business for hotels." He raised his finger for another libation. "Big tips for attentive barstaff."

Heinrich hesitated. He rubbed his nose nervously, reluctant to speak and even more reluctant to risk ruining the potentially remunerative relationship he'd been cultivating so assiduously. "You will see for yourself tomorrow morning, Professor Brodie." Dutifully, he poured another stiff Johnnie Walker and turned on his heel. "I'll contact the manager right away, sir."

"Afore ye go," the Scotsman smiled, rattling his glass, "add a couple of jiggers of Jägermeister to that. And maybe a wee dash of Underberg."

Heinrich started at the strange request, then complied deferentially, though it took a few minutes to assemble the unorthodox ingredients. "Is this a Scottish cocktail?" he asked. "I've never combined Johnnie Walker, Jägermeister and Underberg before." He lifted the fizzing mixture from the bar and held it up to the light, assessing colour and consistency against the halogen spots. It looked like toxic sludge. Smelled like it too. He set the stinking snifter in front of his customer, trying not to gag.

"No laddie," Brodie answered. "It's one of my own." He reached for the treacled tipple and raised his glass in salutation. "You've heard of criminologists and campanologists? Well, I'm a cocktailologist. I like to experiment." He sipped and shuddered.

Affecting unflappability, Heinrich entered into spirit of things. "What is it called, this experimental cocktail?"

The impassive hunk of Grampian granite thought for a moment, swallowed his stiffener in a single bite, gritted his ochre teeth, coughed once or twice, then wheezed, "The Nuremberg Rally."

Startled, Heinrich scuttled off at high speed. Pale faced, black clad, pony-tailed and unaccountably flustered, he was reminiscent of a raven in a bird bath.

Ten minutes later, Professor Pitcairn Brodie was practising his speech in the Bibliothek conference room. He didn't really need to rehearse, because he'd delivered countless iterations of his catch-all presentation, "The Alchemy of the Blank Brand". Only the Blank changed. Blank became BMW, Nike, Ikea, Armani, Virgin, Ryanair, Siemens, Perrier, Absolut, Puma, Sony, Zara, Vioxx, Corus and countless others. He made the same four points about alchemy, then segued into a specially tailored section on Blank. He sometimes wondered if there was an actual brand out there called Blank. He had of course heard of Arthur Blank, the founder of Home Depot, and then there were those Blank CDs and DVDs that his bit-torrent-obsessed research assistant kept going on about. But by and large he'd drawn a blank on Blank and basically lacked the IT skills to enlighten himself.

As a consummate conference performer, Professor Brodie was conscious of the perils of complacency. He always did a dry run the night before a big speech, even though wetting his whistle was becoming an increasingly necessary part of the process. Audiences, he'd found, were funny creatures. Much as they appreciated a polished presentation, especially one delivered without notes or prompts or autocues or – hawk, spit! – PowerPoint slides, they could readily detect rehashed, reheated or under-rehearsed performances. Short-changed audiences, he believed, were akin to tiger sharks. Perfunctory or pre-packaged speeches were like blood in the water and they reacted accordingly, particularly when big-name, high-fee, all-mouth-no-outcome management gurus were involved. He'd seen many a cocksure speaker on the conference circuit ripped limb from limb. He refused to let it happen to him. Even at his age. Even after innumerable iterations. Even if it meant forgoing the fräulein-filled fleshpots of Nuremberg on a funky Friday night during Altstadtfest.

The theology professor's keynote speech may have been

canned, but it was far from corny. In a world where glib gladhanders garnered huge consultancy fees from quick-fix "solutions" or one-word, acronym-encrusted "interventions", Pitcairn Brodie's rollicking reminder that marketing management is an essentially alchemical exercise – similar to seeking the philosopher's stone or the elixir of life – unfailingly went down a storm. It drew upon a 3,000-year-old tradition, not yesterday's headlines or the next big thing, much less the buzzword du jour. It challenged the B-school-inculcated idea that marketing was a hard science, contending it was actually closer to magic. It resonated with front-line managers because alchemy placed great store by tiny details, infinite care, prodigious patience, getting things absolutely right, the kind of things that day-to-day management invariably involved. Above all, alchemy was preoccupied with the process of transformation, turning base metal into gold. Even the dullest executive could see the connection between their own leaden organizations and the glittering gilded future where profits were illimitable, employees were content and customers were delighted in perpetuity.

Even the dullest manager, moreover, could detect the stench of a keynote speaker going through the motions. So Brodie rehearsed his routine in the Bibliothek conference room like his life depended on it. He projected his rich, rubicund voice. He paused for laughter as appropriate, imagining the tide of hilarity rolling toward him. He checked his hand-gestures in the full-length mirror that the hotel manager had thoughtfully provided (though his thoughts had to be channelled with a conjuration of euros). He worked his way through the four alchemical points without so much as a whisky-warped stammer or cocktail-lubricated mumble. Brodie then turned to the bespoke component of his speech, the all-important element that makes or breaks every performance.

"Today, *mes amis,* we sit at the very centre of the medieval Alchemical Triangle, bounded by Frankfurt, Prague and Munich. We are communing in perhaps the most magical place on the planet, a site of incredible primordial power. We are celebrating the one hundredth anniversary of André Citroën's incomparable insight, the insight that's commemorated by your world-famous logo."

Brodie knew from past experience that his audience wouldn't

know the full history of the company they worked for. Businesspeople in general and sales reps in particular were so preoccupied with the future – with next quarter's targets – that making them feel part of the tradition they belonged to was a sure-fire way of securing their support. However, the company history had to segue seamlessly into the pre-prepared part of the talk. Otherwise it was blood in the water time.

"I'm talking helical gears, brothers and sisters, the helical gears that André stumbled upon not very far from here and instantly realized a great company could be built thereon. To this very day, André Citroën is lauded as an engineer of genius. And so he was. He was also the man that supplied the steering mechanism on the *Titanic*. But we won't hold that against him."

Pause for laughter.

"He also gambled away a fortune on the gaming tables of Deauville and Monte Carlo and lost control of his company as a consequence. But business life is a crap shoot at the best of times and André firmly believed that a big win was right around the corner, as indeed do most salesreps and road warriors."

Pause for rueful laughter.

"André Citroën's greatest gifts, however, lay in the alchemical art of brand building. It's not something he's normally given credit for, but the evidence speaks for itself. In striking contrast to his competitors, for example, Citroën's very first car came fully loaded. Buyers of André's Type A got a complete package: bodywork, bonnet, wheels, tyres, lights, horn, toolkit, driver's manual and even an electric self-starter, which was unusual to say the least in 1919. And still unusual in Daewoos today."

Pause for smug laughter.

"Alongside the company's all-in products, Citroën was blessed with prodigious promotional acumen. He advertised incessantly and with gusto. Numerous full-page newspaper ads, countless thousands of posters, billboards beyond number and 150,000 road signs embellished with his company's double-chevron logo were just the start of it. Paris was brought to a standstill in 1924 when the opening of the annual Motor Show was greeted with an aerobatic display above the Eiffel Tower and a smoke trail that spelled out

'Citroën' in kilometre-high letters. Between 1924 and 1934, the Eiffel Tower itself was illuminated from tip to toe at André's expense. The Citroën sign was visible for 100 kilometres and helped Lindbergh navigate his way to the City of Light at the climax of his landmark trans-Atlantic f-f-f-f-flight."

Brodie stuttered, stammered, lost his place. Infuriated, he cursed, shouted and metaphorically kicked himself. He ripped off his tam-o'-shanter and hurled it to the floor, only to pause and carefully rearrange his cantilevered combover. He could sense his imaginary audience turn against him as the cracks in his performance started to appear. He stopped the phoney show, groaned aloud in frustration, took a couple of deep breaths and tried to psyche himself up for the climax. Hesitation is death, he reminded himself. Perfection is possible. Failure is not an option. You're a Scotsman, remember. Waterloo. Balaclava. Rorke's Drift. Passchendaele. El-Alamein. The Beehive Bar on Saturday nights.

"Of course, you already know this. You've all seen the photographs of the Citroën-lit Eiffel Tower. What you may not know about your company's founder is that he was a Freemason, one of the most eminent Freemasons in France. André Citroën was a leading light of the Illuminati, arguably the world's most famous secret society, a secret society that was founded less than fifty kilometres from where we're sitting today. André Citroën was a practising alchemist. Not an alchemist who tinkered in the laboratory with alembics and retorts. But an alchemist who understood that the *prima materia* of alchemical legend is the unsurpassable power of the human imagination. Imagination is the secret of alchemy. Imagination is the secret of business success. Imagination is the secret of Citroën, as a long line of incredibly imaginative cars from the Traction Avant to the 2CV attests. Imagination is the key to your company, your brand, your future, your alchemical essence."

Professor Brodie grimaced, growled and grumped his way out of the empty conference room. He was not very happy with his imperfect rehearsal. He checked his watch, an irritating reminder of an earlier performance, a peerless performance, The Alchemy of the Breitling Brand. Just time for another Nuremberg Rally, or several, before hitting the sack. *Sieg Heil.*

Chapter Nine

Tales From the Crypt

Terrified, Abby looked around in panic. She had tumbled into a web wide world. The cellar was completely filled with huge, shaggy cobwebs which looped and criss-crossed like creepers in a jungle clearing. If not quite the lair of Aragog, or the nest of Shelob, it was where Carrick's arachnids came to party on Friday and Saturday nights.

The scurrying of the rats was kind of scary too, but not as scary as the dripping pincers of the giant Ecstasy-fuelled tarantula that was coming, coming, coming to get her. Eekk.

"Get a grip!" she shouted at herself. "There isn't time for this." Abby didn't know how long she'd been lying there, because the fall from the crumbling staircase had knocked her out. However long it was, it was far too long because Billy the Killer could be back any minute. The yawning trapdoor above her head was well out of reach. The ruins of the staircase lay at her feet. She grabbed the most promising lump of broken banister rail and started thrashing away at the cobwebs, cutting a path through the subterranean jungle. Every so often she stopped with a start, as sticky fronds tickled the back of her neck and sent a shiver down her spine. Increasingly frantic, she whacked as hard as she could, determined to confront the Son of Shelob, the Daughter of Queen-Alien, the septic spawn of Jabba the Hutt or whatever urban myth made flesh lurked in the corners.

Wooosh. Wooosh. Wooosh. Abby wielded her wooden light-sabre with aplomb and within a couple of minutes had hacked a path through the underground undergrowth. The cellar was approximately seven metres by seven. Made of enormous untrimmed stones, its uneven walls reminded her of Carrickfergus Castle. Seemingly hewn from the living basalt, they looked just as solid and secure as the Norman fortress itself, though the darkness made it difficult to tell. The pool of fluorescent light from the trapdoor didn't quite reach into the nooks and crannies, where the super-sized funnel web spiders with great venomous fangs secreted themselves, waiting to pounce. She could hear them scuttling. Or was it the monstrous, disease-ridden, flesh-eating rats…

"Enough. Enough. Calm down. Deep breaths, Abby. This isn't getting us anywhere. There's bound to be another way out of here. There must be." The breeze she'd felt upstairs was coming from somewhere. Somewhere round here. She could still sense it. She wasn't giving up hope and, if the worst came to the worst, she'd make Billy and his malevolent monkey come down to get her. Maybe the murderous mummy's boy was even more afraid of spiders than she was. She doubted if the poisoned dwarf was, though.

"Hello? Hello? Hello? Anyone there?"

Abby was dreaming … hallucinating … away with the fairies. She was starting to hear voices. She thought for a moment that someone was calling out to her. She shook her head violently to stop the buzzing, the incipient madness.

"Hello. Hello. Is everything all right?" The voice was getting closer, becoming ever-more sing-song. "Hellooo…ooo."

Someone was coming. Someone concerned for her welfare. Someone who didn't have murder in mind, someone whose voice she vaguely recognized. She could hear the panel door of the ex-stock annex being unsnibbed and a person picking their way through the retailing debris. "Hello," she shouted, striding into the pool of light beneath the trapdoor. Looking up, Abby was convinced that she'd hit her head in the fall. Either that or she was in some kind of coma. There was no other explanation for it. "Dr. Kelley, is that you?"

"Yes, Abby, of course it is! I'm here for our meeting. We're supposed to be discussing your assignment. We have an appointment. Are you hiding from me?" Kelley asked incredulously.

"But the meeting's next Friday," she complained, forgetting about her situation for a second and reverting to the usual student-supervisor relationship.

"No Abby. It's *this* week," he insisted. "Friday, the first of September, at 5.30 p.m. I'm sure of that. Well, I'm pretty sure of that," Kelley corrected. "And you won't get out of it by hiding in a cellar!" Standing at the edge of the trapdoor, hands on hips, he looked around with exaggerated exasperation and more than a tincture of camp asperity. "Nice store you're running here, darling. Is it a postmodern merchandising plan or the old treasure hunt routine beloved by crafty antique shops? Comme des Garçons do something similar, don't they? Guerrilla retail stores. Dishevelled displays. Deconstructed layout. Here today, gone tomorrow. There's method in your marketing madness, right? Half-closing the security shutters is a fantastic ruse, darling. Encourages customers to rush in before the shop shuts and the best bargains are gone. Correct? Shopkeepers' creativity never ceases to amaze me."

Abby almost burst into tears with relief. It was all of five seconds before she remembered that the Billy boys could be back any minute. "Dr. Kelley, you've got to get out of here. Right away!"

"Well, Ms. Maguire," he said with pretend professorial pomposity, "we can of course reschedule our meeting if it's inconvenient. But I think that you should at least come out of hiding, if only to arrange the appointment." Laughing, he continued in a mock-officious vein, "It might adversely affect your marks if you don't."

This was no time for jokes, especially Dave "the Rave" Kelley jokes. Abby quickly filled him in on the details of what'd happened. Expurgated details. There'd been a break in at the store. She'd finished up in the basement.

"Okay, Abby, I'm calling the police," he said forcefully. "Actually, I'm going to get them. I noticed a police car on my way here, close to the entrance of the churchyard. I'll be back in a minute. Hold tight, we'll soon have you out of there."

"No, no," Abby yelled up at him. "Whatever you do, don't call the police. I'm dead if you do. *You're* dead if you do." Struggling to keep her voice calm, she briefly explained who was behind the break-in and what would happen if the police got involved.

Even in the harsh strip lighting of the stock annex above, Abby could see the colour drain from her lecturer's youthful face. His little-boy-lost look had taken on a haunted aspect.

Dr. Kelley swallowed and cleared his throat. "Come on out of there," he croaked. "Let's go. I know someone we can talk to. Quickly, Abby. Quickly."

"I would if I could," she answered. "But the steps are broken and I can't get out."

Swiftly appraising the situation, Dr. Kelley took the kind of decisive action that academics are renowned for. He lay flat on the knotted pine floor and, spreading his legs for extra purchase, reached down for the student. "Grab my hand. We'll have you out in a jiffy."

"You'll never hold my weight," Abby replied, mortified. "And anyway, I can't stretch that far."

"Give me a minute, Abby, I've got an idea." Kelly stood up again and, akin to an ancient Egyptian grave robber, rummaged through the retail detritus above. He retrieved a coil of heavy nautical hawser, tied one end to the anchor and dropped the rope into the cellar. "Okay, grab a hold and I'll pull you up." He struck a pose like an abseiling instructor but evidently lacked the basic muscle power to lift his hefty student.

Optimistically, Abby attempted an Indian rope trick instead. Shinning up shaggy ropes was a lot easier in PE classes at school. Marks's magic knickers made climbing a lot tougher than she remembered.

"Jeez, I'm a wimp," Kelley cursed, wiping his brow. "We need a plan B."

"God, I'm a fat cow," Abby wailed, easing off her constrictive control pants – she had to roll them down like a piece of plasticine – and trying again. Rope burns on the nether regions were the least of her worries. But she still couldn't hoist herself up the hairy hawser.

Kelley sifted anxiously through the archaeological deposits once more, extracting a powerful torch from the marketing midden. He spread himself on the floor again, leant into the cavernous cellar and clicked the rubber button. Nothing. Nada. It was as dead as the stuffed bears, badgers and humming birds in the annex overhead.

"There's a lamp in the changing room, Dr. Kelley. The costumes. The Welsh coal miner ensemble. The Loins of My Father outfit. There's a miner's lamp... Hurry!"

After a few minutes' banging and thumping, Kelley returned, illuminated lamp in hand but decidedly green around the gills. "Do… do… do people really dress up in Eskimo and Polar Bear outfits?"

Despite her dire situation, Abby couldn't help smiling at Dave's endearing naivety. "Of course," she replied. "Nanookie of the North is Ireland's favourite pastime. You haven't lived until you've searched for the north-west passage."

"Do they really play at Cardinals and Swiss Guards round here?"

"God, yes!" Abby shouted, amazed he'd imagine otherwise. "It's become very popular on the back of Dan Brown's books. There's an Opus Dei costume in the S&M department as well. We throw in a penile cilice for free."

"But the Tellytubbies' group sex costumes are just a joke, right?"

"God, no!" Abby couldn't believe what she was hearing. "They're one of our most popular lines! Tinky Winky's tantric turn-on."

Even in the unflattering fluorescent light of the ex-stock annex, Dr. Kelley looked shocked to the core. "There are some very sick people in Carrickfergus, that's all I can say."

"Yes, and two of them are after me! Could you get a move on? Please? I'm sure there's another way out of here. I felt a slight breeze at one stage."

The lantern descended into the dark. Kelley was holding it at full stretch. "Do you really feel a breeze?" he asked, while taking in the geography of the basement. He seemed transfixed by the sight. "Remarkable," he mused. "Remarkable. Quite remarkable."

"Christ," Abby whispered under her breath, thinking that you can't take an academic anywhere. He obviously imagines he's in the senior common room at Caius College, Cambridge. "Dr. Kelley. Dr. Kelley. Earth to Dr. Kelley."

"I know what this is," he announced triumphantly. "The legend is true. I know where we are. I know what to look for. Stand back, I'm coming down." Kelley slithered down the hawser like a mamba doing the Mambo. He held the light aloft as he descended.

Shadows angled and bounced off the uneven stone walls, making it even scarier than before. There was no obvious sign of another way out. Standing beside his student with lantern-arm extended, Kelley drank in the space, entranced. "Try not to laugh, Abby, but I used to be a goth. I spent a lot of time in graveyards. I've studied the history of Carrickfergus and there's a legend that an ancient tunnel runs from St. Nicholas's church to the Castle. They also say that some of the buildings in the old town connect to the tunnel…"

"But this isn't a tunnel, Dr. Kelley. It seems like a pretty solid cellar to me."

"Seems that way, but it's not. This is a medieval panic room, an Elizabethan souterrain, complete with secret escape route. The ancient Celts called them fogous. There should be a camouflaged gap, a niche, in one of the corners. The walls look as though they're real but they aren't. It's an architectural optical illusion."

Frrrrrrrrrr. Frrrrrrrrrrr. Frrrrrrrrr.

"What's that noise?" Abby gasped fearfully, knowing only too well what it was.

"Someone's closing the security grille," Kelley confirmed. "I raised it myself when I arrived for our meeting." He smiled encouragingly. "There must be people in the shop. Maybe it's the police."

"Why would the police close the shutters behind them? There's no reason to. Unless someone doesn't want to be disturbed. It's Igor and Billy No-dick."

Kelley stared at her.

"Sorry, did I say No-dick? I don't know why I said that."

The lecturer shook his head, placed a finger against his lips and made a hand signal that said "Check the corners, quick."

Frrrrrrrrr. Frrrrrrrrr. Frrrrrrrr. Clang.

Chapter Ten

There's Riches in Niches

They struck gold in the third corner they tried. Not that a 49-er would have recognized it, much less an alchemist. A narrow gap, twenty centimetres at most, had been left between two of the basement's rough stone walls. Cobweb covered and deftly disguised, the niche was virtually invisible to the naked eye. It looked more like a subsidence problem, or the work of cowboy builders, than a potential passport to freedom.

I'll never get through that crevice, Abby thought, not in a million years. Not without six months on the Atkins, several sessions of Dyson-powered liposuction and someone to shove vigorously from behind, like those guards on the Tokyo underground.

The rattle of metal filtered down from the main shop floor, as scattered display racks were kicked and heaved aside. The indistinct mumble of masculine voices announced the return of the goateed organ grinder and his midget monkey. Either that or the local trannies had turned up in pursuit of the special offer on party dresses, plus disposable posing pouch.

"Come on," Kelley insisted. Catching Abby's sceptical expression, he continued, "It doglegs left and opens out almost immediately. Think of it as squeezing through a narrow turnstile." He could see she remained unconvinced. "We've no choice," he said with finality. "I'll lead the way." He extinguished the lantern and, grasping Abby's hand firmly, squeezed himself sideways into the tiny cobwebby fissure. A skinny so-and-so, he disappeared instantly.

An almighty roar rent the air upstairs. The unlocked door of the ex-stock annex had obviously been discovered. "Where is she?" someone bellowed. "The fuckin' cow's not here. The fat bitch has escaped."

Click. "Maybe she's hiding, Billy." Click.

Abby jammed herself into the crack. The walls were biting into her, tearing at her bust, belly and bottom. Although the rubberoid staff uniform provided some protection – thank God for S&M – she felt like a lump of sweaty cheddar in a cheese grater. Centimetre by bodice-ripping centimetre she advanced. The gap was getting narrower and narrower, tighter and tighter. Then she hit a solid wall. She was stuck. She was entombed. She was buried alive. She was the woman behind the wall in that Edgar Allan Poe story. Panicking, she could hear a row raging in the annex above. Bellowing Billy was bullying his clicking sidekick for failing to secure the panel door properly, failing to close the security shutter fully, failing to… "What the fuck?" They'd discovered the open trapdoor and the rope dangling down… "What in the name of fuck?" They'd spotted the broken remains of the staircase, scattered on the cellar floor. Abby could sense their confusion. It must have seemed like a locked room mystery. In reverse. Agatha Christie and Dorothy Sayers were never like this. Where's Hercule Poirot or Lord Peter Wimsey when you need him?

At least Abby'd be entombed with a smile on her face. She tried to turn her head. There was a hairy Highland Terrier on her shoulder. A Highland Terrier with an extra set of legs, three additional pairs of eyes and mandibles the size of bananas. It was the biggest spider she had ever seen. She was going to scream. The terrier scuttled across her shoulder and stopped at the base of her neck. She bit her lip. The terrier climbed up the side of her head and into her hair. She bit her lip harder. The terrier paused to catch its breath then walked over her cheek and sat on the bridge of her nose. She was about to scream the cellar down. The terrier waded through the cold sweat on her forehead, stepped tentatively on to the wall and skittered off into the darkness. She could taste blood in her mouth.

In the struggle to evade Aragog, Abby had managed to shift her shoulders slightly and rearrange her feet. She was being pulled hard from behind, as Kelley contributed his two-pennyworth. All of a sudden, with a rip and a semi-stumble, she slipped free of the L-shaped vice. The ante-chamber – or tunnel, she couldn't tell – was pitch black, but at least there was room to breathe. Kelley wrapped himself around her with relief. She could smell his after-shave. Calvin Klein's Escape for Men, with a top note of musty cobweb. He pressed his mouth against her ear and hissed, "Don't move. I'll be back in a sec." Fumbling, he slipped the lantern into her hand and disappeared off into the darkness.

Alone in the black velvet void, still shaking from the Highland Terrier encounter, Abby could sense the old, pre-teen tremors rising in her chest. Terrified by ghost stories from her raconteur father, she'd slept with a night-light until she was twelve and, even as a 24-year-old adult, she sometimes lay in night-time terror listening to creaks on the wooden staircase and gurgles from the defective radiators of her student flat…

A disembodied hand touched her shoulder. She jumped several score centimetres into the air. Had she jumped like that in the cellar, she'd have been out of the annex and away.

"This is it!" Kelley whispered excitedly. "The secret tunnel to the castle." Despite their situation, his ordinarily cod-camp voice was brimming with boyish enthusiasm. "Come on. Keep your head down." He held her tightly by the arm as they inched their way – one eagerly, one gingerly – into the oppressive indigo. The flagstone floor was surprisingly smooth underfoot, the rough stone walls less than an arm's length away. The tunnel sloped gently downwards and, after a short straight passage, curved steadily to the right. After approximately forty metres, Kelley stopped for a moment, then switched on the miner's lamp.

Protecting her eyes against the painful blaze of light, Abby spotted a posse of pink-eyed rats stampeding down the passage-way. They seemed unreal in the incandescence, a herd of mini-buffaloes viewed from above. At least the corbelled, low-roofed cavern was cobweb free, which is more than could be said for Kelley. One side of his face, his head, his body was sporting this season's Black Widow collection. "Takes you back to your goth days, eh, Dave?"

Brushing himself off with difficulty, he made the most of a bad sartorial situation. "Spider webs? Wonderful for the complexion, darling. Beats Crème de la Mer hands down. Hard to get hold of, of course. But that's the beauty of exclusivity."

"You think Cobweb de Carrickfergus has brand-building potential, Dr. Kelley?"

"Well, Ms. Maguire, if you can sell Tellytubbie romper suits – rumpy pumpy romper suits – you can sell just about anything. Tulle d'Arachnid might be more acceptable as a brand name, though."

"Yes, and squeezing through that razor maze might make a great lipo alternative or cellulite removal device. Maximum cellulite attack."

"Well, darling, women *do* like to suffer for their appearance. The more suffering a product inflicts, the more good they think it does them. We could be on to a winner."

"Why stop at scent and cellulite, Dr. Kelley? We could set up a gothic spa. Undertaker makeovers. Cobweb therapies. Gravestone exfoliants. Frog spawn face-packs. Embalming fluid enemas. Coffin-shaped immersion tanks. Dr. Frankenstein's cosmetic surgery clinic. Count Dracula's garlic-free diet. Burke and Hare's body parts replacement service."

"Costs an arm and a leg, Abby."

"Buy one eyeball, get one free."

"Branches in Whitby, Salem, Elm Street, Rue Morgue, Boot Hill, Sleepy Hollow, Transylvania, the Dead Sea..."

"And Indian graveyards everywhere!"

Gallows humour, they call it, humankind's inexplicable tendency to laugh in life-threatening situations. Especially common among medics, morticians, military types and Mafia hitpersons, gallows humour is irrepressible, inescapable, instinctive, innate. According to Sigmund Freud, the man who put the id into kidding and was famous for his funny walk, The Freudian Slip, it is a vitally necessary defence mechanism.

Scary movie goers nevertheless know that gallows humour is a harbinger of further horror.

Abby and Dave's lucky escape was no exception.

The gently curving stone tunnel terminated in an ancient wooden door. Constructed of massive oaken planks and huge iron hinges, it looked as solid as the volcanic plug that supported Carrickfergus Castle. Its ancient latch had rusted solid. No amount of pushing, pulling and shoulder-charging made the slightest dent in the immovable obstacle. There was no alternative but to turn back in the hope that the top end of the tunnel still opened into St. Nicholas's churchyard and that their pursuers hadn't found the entrance crevice.

"Oh for a tube of lubricant," Abby sighed, jiggling the jammed latch up and down to no avail.

Dr. Kelley looked sheepish, embarrassed almost. "Would, erm, some delay spray help at all?" he inquired, reddening slightly. "I, erm, picked up a can in the store. It was just lying there on the floor. It's for a friend who, erm, has a slight problem with, um, with premature... ahem... I'll pay for it, of course."

Smiling, Abby didn't need lamplight to detect Dave the Rave's embarrassment. The heat in the tunnel was palpable. "Well," she said, stifling a giggle, "delay spray's supposed to relax the muscles. No harm in trying. Give it here." Abby shook the canister vigorously, shoved it into the solidified latch and gave the sucker a sustained burst of the musky, smelly, choking aerosol. Pausing momentarily, she rattled the rusted mechanism once more. No joy. Kelley attempted a jerk or two, with the same outcome.

"WD40 usually takes a couple of minutes," Abby rationalized. "Maybe It's a Miracle is the same. I'll give it another go. Stand back, Dr. Kelley. This stuff can really make your eyes water."

"Hurry, Abby."

"Patience, patience."

"Better make it snappy, Abby. I think something's coming down the tunnel. I thought I saw a light flickering on the wall."

"There's no way Thugzilla will get through that gap. No way on earth..."

"Ssssshhhh. I can hear a noise. Something's clicking, I think."

"... Igor might, though."

Chapter Eleven

Bombs, Bullets and Beyond

"Sssssshhhhh." Kelley switched off the lantern. Billowy blackness engulfed the two of them again. Apart from the faint rumble of road traffic – they must have been under, or close to, the Marine Highway – nothing stirred in the low-ceilinged passageway. "Sorry, my mistake," Kelley murmured. "I must be imagining things. The delay spray fumes are affecting my thought processes."

"Yes," Abby replied with asperity, "most men think with the brain between their legs, so that certainly makes sense." Irritated, she pressed down hard on the lubricated latch. With a sharp click it released. "Yes!" She pushed the creaking, groaning door open. It howled on ossified hinges and juddered across the flagstones within.

Abby paused at the portal and listened attentively, just in case Igor had heard the echoing commotion and was lurching down the tunnel in hot pursuit. Kelley slipped past his partner in grime then switched on the lantern, while Abby secured the old door behind her.

"Wow," he exhaled. A dry-stone vault rose above them, its corbelled ceiling rising at least five metres overhead, the thrum of nearby traffic clearly audible in the resonant space. Despite the dancing shadows, they could see that three additional doors dotted the circumference of the circular chamber, identical to the one they'd come through. A line of narrow stone benches encircled the outer dry-stone wall and an old well occupied a stepped basalt plinth in the centre, beneath the apex of the barrel-vaulted rotunda. "Wow!" he repeated.

"Does this take you back too, Dave? Is this where Carrick's goths sacrificed goats and virgins at midnight?"

"No. God no," Kelley replied distractedly, while gravitating toward the plinth. He looked around in awestruck amazement, then launched into a garbled historical rationale for what they'd stumbled upon. This involved secret tunnels to a Cistercian Abbey on the edge of the old town, the miraculous healing well of King Fergus – subsequently blessed by St. Patrick himself – stories of a pagan druidic temple where St. Nicholas's church now stands, and a digression on dry-stone vaults which suggested prehistoric rather than medieval origins. The thing that confused Kelley most was the fact that the chamber hadn't been found before, especially as teams of rabid archaeologists descend on Carrickfergus at the slightest sniff of a significant discovery and a medieval stone passageway plus prehistoric corbelled vault would be huge news. Huge. He surmised that building contractors must have covered it up during the construction of the Marine Highway back in the future-first 1960s, because a big archaeological dig would have held things up for donkey's years, possibly decades. The march of progress was all, back then, the past conveniently ignored.

What Kelley's rambling historical hypothesis boiled down to was that one of the wooden doors probably led under the town square towards Tesco, the second almost certainly wound up in the castle's keep and the third headed for the old gas works and saltpetre warehouses that lined the harbourside before the development of the marina-cum-retailing complex.

Foolishly, Abby asked him what saltpetre was.

"Saltpetre's a local speciality," Kelley replied with a smile, obviously warming up for another mini-lecture. "There are salt mines just up the road, close to where my family lives. Saltpetre was a food preservative that used to be used in the making of gunpowder. Way back when, they put it in soldiers' rations and prison diets in order to... erm... inhibit their natural urges. It was an anti-aphrodisiac, I suppose."

"A bit like delay spray?" she interrupted.

"Well, no way spray, perhaps."

"I like the sound of that," Abby said. "So, how do we get out of here so that I can place an order?"

"Well, the castle route's inadvisable. It'll be closed for the night and we'll be stuck in the keep till morning. The harbour route most likely ends up among underground gas gubbins or saltpetre storage whatsits. Better not go there. The Tesco door's our best bet."

"Every lintel helps?"

Kelley groaned at the pitiful pun, though his equally pitiful rejoinder was drowned by a hideous howling noise that roared down the passageway from Some Like It Hot and pealed like a colossal bell in the conical chamber. Abby clamped her hands to her ears trying to shut out the fearful racket, while suspecting that the source was Billy No-dick's infuriated discovery of her abandoned control pants.

With a new sense of urgency, plus a squirt or two of trusty delay spray, they managed to heave open the heavy oaken door to Tesco. And immediately wished they hadn't. It smelt like Humpty Dumpty's droppings the day after the dinosaur egg eating contest. Putrid to start, the pong got stronger and stronger and stronger as they made their way along the narrow corridor. "We must be under the town square somewhere," Kelley said, his hand covering his mouth and nose for protection. "The drains are two hundred years old if they're a day. And blocked for most of that time by the smell of it. Come back, Dynorod, all is forgiven."

"I think I'm going to be sick."

Such was the stench that, if they'd had a canary in a cage to accompany the miner's lamp, the critter would be dangling upside down from its perch, asphyxiated. Coughing and gasping and retching, they returned to the clinkered vault, where Abby immediately made for King Fergus's miraculous well, splashing her face and neck with its refreshing baptismal waters.

"Okay, Abby, let's try the harbour exit."

A quick spritz of It's a Miracle eased open the encrusted door. A salty tang greeted them, gently clearing their heads. The passageway curved rapidly down and away to the right. As they hurried along the cool tunnel, they were forced to scramble over enormous piles of rubble and deep drifts of hard core, casually dumped by the couldn't-care-less road-builders of the 1960s. Bit by bit, the rough stone and low ceiling gradually gave way to old-fashioned, nineteenth-century brickwork, with more than adequate headroom. A red light glowed in the far distance. Bizarrely, it was an emergency exit door, a much larger version of those in cinemas or cold stores. The letters "U.S.E." were painted in gold gothic lettering above the lintel.

"U.S.E.?" Abby asked.

Kelley shrugged. "Ulster Saltpetre Exports, I expect."

Abby placed her hand on the metal bar across the middle of the door. "What do you think? Burglar alarm?"

"Only one way to find out. It's either that or a tour of the sewers to Tesco's. Or a kip in the castle keep." He placed his hand on top of Abby's and pressed the aluminium bar. The door opened with a solid metallic clunk. The throb of a power plant hummed in the darkness. Air conditioners hissed. Distant red lights marked additional emergency exits from the vast space. Kelley hit a bank of switches and, with a flash and flicker, serried ranks of strip lights kicked into action. It was a warehouse. A colossal warehouse. A warehouse unlike any other. Rack after rack of automatic weapons filled the cavernous storage facility to the brim. Aisles of Armalites, shelves of Kalashnikovs, cut cases of M14 carbines, palettes of rocket-propelled grenades, open displays of assorted assault rifles, dump bins of SVD Dragunovs, beloved by snipers, sharpshooters and assassins for hire. Boxes of ammunition were stacked in one corner. Carefully wrapped packages of high explosives stocked chill cabinets along an outer wall. Glass cabinets of luxury, pearl-handled handguns occupied an easi-browse boutique in the centre of the store. An Uzi concession sat off to one side, with the complete range on incredible offer, everything from micro-sized pistols to major-league machine guns. Huge swags of camouflage netting drooped down from the ceiling, akin to acoustics-enhancing panels in a concert hall. An elaborate lattice of Miniman anti-tank guns was pyramided like a monster display of beans in a supermarket special promotion. Racks of backpacks, battledresses, boots, belts, leggings, jerkins, tunics, ammo pouches, water bottles, forage caps and so forth filled a fashion aisle to overflowing. A retro kit corner contained Thompson, Lewis and Bren machine guns, Colt pistols, Winchester rifles, webbing belts, gabardine slicks and steel helmets of every description, including a spiked monstrosity from the First World War.

It was nothing less than a terrorist's Tesco. It was an armament

Ikea. It was Guns-R-Us. It was Kit-U-Like. It was McMunitions ("I'm Loadin' It"). It was Bomber King ("The Home of the Whacker"). All it needed to complete the crazy picture was a couple of ten-items-or-less express checkouts, with tempting impulse displays of knives, garrottes, grenades, silencers, telescopic sights and knuckledusters.

Abby and Kelley wandered around, utterly gobsmacked, trying and failing to make sense of the lunacy. Oblivious to the dangers of their situation, they slowly circumnavigated the aisles of destruction, like recreational shoppers on a Saturday afternoon. They were mesmerized, stupefied, aghast at the evidence of careful marketing planning and advanced in-store systems – barcodes, planograms, DPP space maximization displays, computerized inventory control programmes. It was state of the retail art.

A special caged section was chock-a-block with stencilled crates bearing the trefoil radiation symbol. "Plutonium pick 'n' mix," Kelley muttered, curling his fingers round the protective wire mesh, which he shook with indignant disdain. "This is madness. This is lunacy. This is the dark side of retail management."

Abby was tempted to make a glib remark about Dave the Rave's rattled cage, but thought better of it. "I guess this is where Saddam off-shored his WMDs," she suggested instead. "No wonder the inspectors couldn't find anything in Iraq. Should've gone to U.S.E."

Kelley grimaced and walked away, towards the distant bank of checkouts. Just beyond the final aisle, a thick white line was painted across the concrete floor, with the letters U.S.E. beneath. "So much for Ulster Saltpetre Exports," he said curtly.

"More like Ulster Slaughter Expo."

Massive brushed steel doors, leading in all likelihood to a loading bay, occupied the end wall of Death Mart, beside which lay a carpeted back-office area, all glass partitions, baffle-sided cubicles, cheap office furniture, pine veneer desks, flat screen displays and generic telemarketing kit. Kelley sat down at the nearest workstation and with a "why not?" shrug at Abby, fired up the desktop. "Got to keep up with the latest retail marketing technology, right?"

"So my lecturer keeps telling me," Abby replied over her shoulder, as she wandered off into the call centre silo, wondering what further horrors were in store.

When the PC burst into life, Microsoft's start-up theme tune was gratifyingly absent. The replacement was unforgettable, however. A jaunty jingle, based on an old TV advert for Martini, tinkled from the tinny speakers:

Anytime, anyplace, anywhere,
There a wonderful war we can share.
If the fight comes, try the right ones,
That's U.S.E.

The company logo then coagulated on screen.

Appalled, Kelley hammered on the keyboard, trying to glean more information about the grisly facility.

"Got anything?" Abby asked, having returned from her exploratory peregrinations.

"No, dammit. Password protected. I know what U.S.E. stands for, though. You'll never guess."

Abby shook her head, waiting to be enlightened.

"Untraceable Shooters and Explosives."

"That figures. There's a boardroom over in the corner. It's got a big polished table and luxury leather chairs. The lot."

"How the other half lives, eh, Abby?"

"There are portraits of ex-executives on the walls. Or maybe they're wanted posters in oils."

"Are our pursuers among them? Recognize anyone?"

"Nah. They're all retired."

"Retired as in deep-sixed, I presume."

"I imagine so. Come and have a look. Mug shots like you wouldn't believe."

The twosome's idle banter was interrupted by a whooshing, whirring sound, similar to a slowly descending lift or defective hydraulic equipment. A panel adjacent to the brushed steel doors started blinking rapidly. "Time to take our leave of Saddam's storage facility, darling."

"Gotta get something first."
"Quick, Abby, quick. They're definitely coming this time."
"Last out, switch off the lights."

Chapter Twelve

Little Boy Blue

"What on earth were you thinking of?" Dr. Kelley shouted, his youthful face contorted with all-too adult and decidedly unacademic rage.

"Only doing what you taught me!" Abby shot back, giving as good as she got. "Well, not you," she added, in as cutting a voice as she could manage. "I never bothered turning up to *your* classes. Just doing what my lecturer in Buying taught me."

"Don't pin this on Professor Winstanley," Kelley snapped, ignoring his student's insubordinate jibes. "You're an extremely foolish young woman. You're going to get yourself into very serious trouble, if not killed." Fizzing with anger, Dave the Rave stormed off across the castle car park. Several passing pedestrians, out enjoying an evening stroll by the harbour, relishing the unseasonably mild on-shore breeze, listening to the happy clink of halyards against yacht masts in the marina, understandably assumed some kind of cataclysmic lovers' tiff was unfolding. But it was much more serious than that. Pausing by his car, an unmistakable, bright pink Morris Minor, Kelley announced in a peremptory manner, "I'm going straight to the police station. You can come with me if you like. It's entirely up to you, Abby." He opened the ancient car door, glared at her over the gleaming roof, and started folding himself into the front seat.

"If you do," Abby answered curtly, "they'll kill you too. They don't know you're involved. I'm the one they're after. If you run squealing to the police, word'll get back to them and they'll kill us both. If they can secrete an enormous arms dump within spitting distance of a national monument, in a place crawling with tourists and traders, under the noses of council workers and teams of eager archaeologists, do you really think they haven't got ears in the walls of the local police station?"

Kelley backed out of the garish car, almost stumbling as he unwrapped himself. With one leg planted awkwardly in the foot well, he looked like an ungainly teenager. "That's probably true. Fair dos. But did you really have to take *that*?" he yelled, almost apoplectic with anger. "When you said you wanted a souvenir, I thought you meant a mouse mat or a key ring or sheet or two of U.S.E. stationery. Not a frigging holdall filled with high explosives or somesuch. Do you imagine they won't notice that it's missing, especially as it was sitting on the boardroom table?"

"Yes, and do you really think they won't notice the computer you left on, or discover the miner's lantern beside an emergency exit, a miner's lantern with 'Property of Some Like It Hot' stamped on the underside?"

"That's different."

She jabbed her finger toward him, infuriated. "No it's not, Doctor high-and-mighty Kelley. All roads lead to Abby Maguire and I'm dead meat unless I have some insurance." She heaved the heavy holdall on to her shoulder and after an involuntary wobble, such was its unexpected weight, she set off toward the Belfast bus stop. "This," she said, lifting the shoulder strap of the imperial purple monstrosity an indicative fraction, "is obviously very important to them. They stole it from me in the first place. That's why they broke into the shop and trashed it. That's why I have it now for negotiation purposes. Professor Winstanley told us that the secret of successful negotiation is to make sure you have something the other party wants, something that's worth more than what you want from them."

Kelley looked momentarily nonplussed. "So you *didn't* steal it? You're stealing it *back*? That's different. That changes things completely. What's in the bloody thing that's so important? A complete set of Tellytubbie sex toys? An elephant's dildo? Moby's Dick?"

"Sorry, Dave, it's a bit more complicated than that. I'm stealing back what they stole from me and what was stolen from them in the first place. I don't know what's in it. But I do know that its contents are sufficiently important to kill people when a clip round the ear would've sufficed."

"They've killed people already?" he gasped, then remembered what he'd witnessed earlier. "Of course, the police cars and scene-of-crime tape at the churchyard." He put a hand across his eyebrows in anguish. "What in the name of God have you got us into, Abby?"

"I don't know, Dave. But it doesn't involve you. I'll take it from here. Thanks for your help. I couldn't have got out of the cellar without you." Turning on her heel, Abby made her way to the nearby bus stop, where she glared at a pair of astonished adolescent boys, whose eyes were popping out at the Amazon's raunchy rubber ensemble, a post-pubescent fantasy made flesh. Realising she'd no money for the bus fare, Abby stomped on for fifty metres or so then stuck out a thumb, certain that the costume would soon work its erogenous magic.

A car pulled up. It was Kelley's Morris Minor. She looked away, ignoring him, shaking her head resolutely, struggling to fight back the tears. He clambered out of the car, with an abject expression on his little boy lost face.

"Look, Abby, I'm very sorry for what I said. Please come with me. There's no point in heading home. They'll be waiting for you, wherever you are, wherever you go. My family lives a couple of miles from here. In Kilroot. You can stay for the night. There's someone in Coleraine who might be able to help. Someone with connections. We can contact him in the morning."

"Thanks Dave. But no thanks. This isn't your mess. I'll sort it out myself."

"It *is* my mess," he decreed. "I'm your supervisor, your tutor. I arranged the work placement. I'm ultimately responsible for what happens in Some Like It Hot."

"Ooh-err, missus."

Kelley laughed out loud, a snorting, braying, hiccoughing laugh that was too embarrassing to be affected. "Please, Abby? I'll even show you my knick-knacks."

"Let me guess, your etchings are being framed?"

"Correct."

"On one condition, then."

"What's that?" Kelley grinned.

"You give me an A for my placement assessment."

"An A? An A? I'll have to think about that, darling." He rubbed his chin thoughtfully, eyes irrepressibly twinkling. "An A double-plus at least, Ms. Maguire."

"You have yourself a guest, Dr. Kelley. I even packed an overnight bag on the off chance."

"Hmmm. On reflection, Ms. Maguire, I feel I should deduct one of your pluses for your failure to spot the escape route from the cellar and perhaps another for your reaction to the rats in the tunnel. Then there was that unfortunate gagging incident in the town square branch line to Tesco. Actually, now that I think about it, a C minus might be more appropriate. I'm sure the external examiner will concur."

Abby punched him playfully as she settled into the pink velour passenger seat, kitbag safely stowed in the boot. "Hit it, David. Kilroot here we come."

As they slowly circled the central roundabout and trundled away from the main Belfast carriageway, Kelley provided a potted summary of the history of Kilroot. Its principal claim to fame is that it was once the home of Jonathan Swift. Lord of the Lilliputians, spokesperson for the Yahoo party and modest proposer of cannibalism as a cure for Ireland's eighteenth-century food shortages, Swift's first job was as a clergyman in the manse-, glebe- and church-less prebend of Kilroot. Settled by cantankerous Scotch-Irish dissenters, the Carrickfergus region had insufficient Anglican parishioners to make Swift's calling rewarding, let alone remunerative. But he put up with life in the sticks for five years, often making the long, slow coach journey to Dublin, passing Belfast's Cave Hill en route. Silhouetted against the evening sky, Cave Hill was shaped like a great recumbent giant, and local legend had it that Conor McArt, the once and future king of ancient Ulster, lay there in a somnambulant state waiting for the call from his quarrelsome people. Suffice it to say, the story of the sleeping giant gave Dean Swift the idea for Gulliver, his greatest literary hit. Although he hated the place with a vengeance, Kilroot was the making of Ireland's pre-eminent satirist.

Lord knows what he'd make of it today. Even Swift's rapier wit would be hard pressed to do justice to Kilroot's current state. A massive smokestack, so tall it boasts navigation beacons for passing aircraft, surmounts a power station of breathtaking Brutalism. It makes the worst excesses of architectural modernism look rococo by comparison. It makes Teesside look like San Tropez. Worse still, it is neither hidden behind stands of mature trees nor tucked away in a face-saving hollow. The power station, rather, occupies the most prominent site imaginable, near the entrance to Belfast Lough, an exquisite natural harbour. Cloned from the unspeakable Sellafield gene pool, it is a painful cold sore at the pouting mouth of the estuary.

"The good news," Kelley said, idly chatting to his rubber-clad passenger as they chugged along the Marine Highway, past the bonny banks of Bonnybefore, birthplace of US president Andrew Jackson, and on through the inappropriately named village of Eden, "is that Kilroot power station is a lot less unsightly than it used to be. An ICI chemical plant once occupied an adjoining site, though it's long shut down and since replaced by an industrial estate. Happy days."

Abby was bewildered, to put it mildly, by Kelley's chit-chat. "You seem to be taking it very personally, Dave. Does the power station block the view from your parents' house, or something?"

The bright pink, almost painfully pink, Morris took a left at Eden service station, then started climbing through the undulating hills, past the subterranean salt mines and deep into the country-side. "Oh, it's a lot worse than that, Abby."

"Really?"

"We sold them the land!" Kelley's eye-popping vehicle stopped before an enormous pair of wrought iron gates. They were topped by an impressive heraldic shield riddled with unicorns, crosses and chevrons. He leaned over to an intercom-CCTV arrangement, pressed a crested button and adopted an affected public school accent. "What ho, bro. Just passing. Can you put us up for the night, old bean?" The intercom crackled in the affirmative. The gates slid open automatically and closed silently behind them. Kelley's veteran car crunched along the curving driveway, past billowing pillows of blooming rhododendron and stately groves of sessile oak. A deer park, duck pond, rose garden, mini-maze and several singularly striking marble follies flowed past as the drive meandered and oxbowed its way through yews, sycamores, horse chestnuts and primordial monkey puzzles. Abby couldn't believe her eyes. It was like an establishing shot from a television adaptation of Jane Austen, Anthony Trollope, Evelyn Waugh or John Galsworthy.

"Welcome to Castle D'Anger, darling. We normally dress for dinner. But S&M chic is perfectly acceptable." The welcoming wings of an impeccable Palladian mansion reached out to greet them. Its three storeys, four chimneys, seven bays, hipped roof and semi-circular, greensward-carpeted courtyard were pretty impressive, especially for someone from a small, hard-scrabble hill farm high in the Sperrin Mountains. But it was particularly impressive on this occasion. A party of beautiful people – dinner-jacketed, ballroom-gowned, cummerbunded, silk-scarved, bow-tied, pearl-necklaced – was dripping down an ornamental double staircase, which swept up to a monumental front door behind a splendid statue-dotted balustrade and veranda. A white stretch limousine sat at the bottom of the sandstone staircase, its uniformed chauffeur holding open a door for the revellers.

"Tra-la, tra-la, ta-ta, ta-ta," trilled the leader of the photogenic pack. "Just off to the Opera House. Must rush. Must rush. Overtures wait for no man. See you later, big brother. Maybe tomorrow."

"Toodle-pip," Dave the Rave called out. "What is it this time, Robert?"

"*Lucia di Lammermoor*," the opera-lover replied in a light baritone, then burst briefly into song, "*Fra poco a me ricovero, darà negletto avella.*"

Abby could hear champagne corks popping as the limo sped off in a cloud of laughter. "Your brother has a beautiful voice. Is he a professional singer?"

"Trained for it," Kelley said curtly, his scowl-scarred face aflame. "Gave up. Lacked application. Always has. Always will."

"Sorry I asked," Abby muttered, rapidly retreating from the family feud. "I didn't mean to," she continued, flicking a glance at her frowning, purse-lipped companion. "Is... is... everything okay?"

"I'm going to kill that so-and-so one of these days."

Chapter Thirteen

Piano Nobile

"Sorry about last night, Abby." Dave Kelley's boyish face was, if not quite full of shame, certainly less puckish than usual. A blush flushed his attractive, snub-nosed features. The effervescent brown eyes and dark curly hair lacked their usual lustre. "You didn't need to see that exhibition of, um, sibling discord. I'd be very grateful if you kept quiet about it. Careless talk and all that."

"Not a problem, Dave. It's our little secret."

"Thanks, darling," he said, without the usual kitsch cadence.

Abby nibbled a corner of lightly-buttered, diet-day-one toast, took an awkward sip of Earl Grey from the D'Anger Castle crested teacup – she wasn't used to high maintenance crockery – and set her heavy silver cutlery at a polite angle on the bone china plate, before continuing. "I don't know what you're so worried about. All families fight. My parents fought like mad dogs and crazy cats and they were easy-going compared to my little sister and me. And as for my kid brother..." She paused and swallowed slowly while waiting for linguistic inspiration to strike. It didn't. "My point is that families are families are families."

"That's true, Abby, but the D'Angers aren't like other families. Our history is a tad tempestuous, shall we say."

"Tell me about it."

"I shall. I shall. Once you've finished your breakfast. I'll give you a guided tour of the old place as well." Kelley stood up, placed his crumpled linen napkin on the table and made his way to the door of the stately, high-ceilinged dining room. A monument to Edwardiana, it boasted an elaborate crystal chandelier with matching wall sconces, an enormous gilt mirror above the Carrara marble fireplace, a colossal, damask-covered, candelabra-dotted dining table that seated twenty or so, and a magnificent ebony sideboard groaning with silver-salvered comestibles – crispy Irish bacon, fresh Irish eggs, succulent Irish sausage, soft Irish soda bread. It broke Abby's heart to resist. She stared outside instead, attempting to keep temptation behind her. The dining room enjoyed spectacular views across the lawns, through the copses, over Belfast Lough, towards the County Down coast. The dark smudges of the Mourne Mountains loomed beyond. If it weren't for the psychopaths on her trail, Abby could have dallied there for days, eating herself into oblivion.

As they sauntered through the "big house", a colloquial term for Anglo-Irish Ascendancy mansions, Abby couldn't help feeling that Kelley's patter was too pat for comfort. It had all the authenticity of a guided tour – practised, polished, undeniably fascinating, yet ultimately soul-less. His heart wasn't in it. Built between 1750 and 1754, on the site of two earlier castles, the ruins of which form part of folly-filled gardens, Castle D'Anger is one of the finest Palladian buildings in Ireland. Parts of the frontage were refurbished in vermiculated rustication during the 1850s on the recommendation of Charles Lanyon, the celebrity architect of the time who built Belfast's Custom House, its Jailhouse and Queen's University, though inmates of the latter two are hard to tell apart.

"Yes, Dave, but do you have Sky-Plus?"

Dr. Kelley ignored her facetious comment and continued his tour guide monologue, Castle D'Anger for Dummies. "The courtyard quadrants, lit by pairs of oval lunettes, are particularly fine features, as is the peerless *piano nobile*, as is the iconic columned pediment at the rear entrance, though that's a later addition."

"So, where do you keep the wheelie bins?"

"Incidentally," Kelley ploughed on regardless, "the interior's main staircase is outstanding, if in need of a little TLC, and the original plasterwork, marquetry, and mouldings are in fair-to-middling condition. But the electrical wiring," he glanced at his guest and smiled slyly, "is so antiquated I suspect it was installed by Thomas Edison himself. Michael Faraday, possibly. Our carbon footprint is the size of Finn McCool's."

"Is that with or without his seven league boots?"

"Listen up," Kelley chided. "You might learn something."

Abby put a hand to her mouth in mock astonishment. "Do you expect me to take notes or ask questions afterwards, Dr. Kelley? Or submit an essay by the end of the week, sir?"

"The old library, I'll have you know, is one of the finest this side of Trinity College, with first editions of Wilde, Yeats, Tennyson, Scott, Darwin, and even a prize copy of Isaac Newton's *Principia*. Swift himself made use of it when he lived down the road. No one uses it now, least of all Robert," he added glumly.

Yippee, Abby thought. An old library. What is it with academics and old libraries? "Oh, I'd like to see that," she lied.

"We'll save the highlight of the tour for the end, shall we? Let me show you the grounds first." He looked her up and down, with approval. "My sister's dress suits you, by the way. Was her room all right? Did you sleep well?"

"Like a log. It was wonderful, thank you. Do you think she'll mind the borrowings?"

It was a sultry September morning, dew on the grass, birds in the branches, hazy sunshine dappling the walkways. "Yes, I'm pretty sure she'll mind the borrowings. But she's staying with friends in Dublin. I think you're safe for a few days." The twosome strolled slowly round the grounds, pausing to admire the rose bushes, the ivy-covered ruins that predated the castle and the pellucid ornamental pond with a travertine fountain of Triton blowing waterspouts from his wreathèd horn. Kelley skimmed stones while telling tales of his illustrious ancestors, who'd been around since the Norman conquest. Soldiers, sailors, churchmen, scientists, politicians, judges, air aces, governors of American colonies, lord mayors of Carrickfergus during the Williamite wars of the seventeenth century. The D'Anger sense of duty, commitment to community service and all-round noblesse oblige was oppressively palpable, as was the decline and fall of the Ascendancy. The cost of running the estate, the piecemeal disposal of parcels of land and, of late, the younger brother's reckless expenditure on his jet-set lifestyle.

Most people find it hard to sympathize with the landed gentry, especially the much-loathed scions of the Anglo-Irish Protestant Ascendancy. But as Kelley recounted his familial tribulations, and realizing the weight of family history that sat on the current generation's shoulders, Abby began to get a sense of what Corporate Social Responsibility really means. Obligation. Dedication. Altruism. Trust. Easy to say, difficult to do.

They wandered through a narrow, shadowy glade in the deer park, towards one of the many mossy follies posing picturesquely on the periphery of the estate. Kelley looked the part in his olive Barbour jacket and obligatory green wellies. Abby shivered involuntarily in her borrowed Givenchy dress. "There's something I don't get. Where do the Kelleys fit into the picture? All you've talked about is D'Anger this, D'Anger that, D'Anger the other. Admiral D'Anger, Archbishop D'Anger, Governor D'Anger and no doubt Dirty Uncle D'Anger who you'd prefer not to mention. How do the Kelleys fit in? Please tell me that Ned Kelly's one of your ancestors and that you come from the black sheep side of the family. Gene Kelly, maybe. Machine Gun Kelly, too. Grace Kelly, even. But not Gerry Kelly. Please."

With a gentlemanly flourish, he wrapped the Barbour round her trembling shoulders. "I think you'll find that Ned, Gene, Machine Gun, Grace and Gerry are Kellys with one 'e'. Two es are much, much more exclusive, Abby."

"So I see," she said, taking in his exquisitely tailored Hackett jacket, classic country check shirt by Turnbull & Asser and tweedy flat cap courtesy of, inevitably, Holland & Holland.

Abashed by his blatant blue-blood brand array, Kelley started colouring up again. A reticent smile flickered at the corner of his mouth. "Remember I told you that I used to be a goth?" Abby nodded and smiled her encouragement. "Well, Kelley's my stage name. My real name is David D'Anger, hence the DD nickname that… um… sometimes circulates among students… along with Dave the Rave… Danger Mouse… and others too dreadful to mention. But Kelley's my stage name and as lecturing is a form of performance, I kept it when I joined the University of Hustler."

"A stage name?" Abby retorted, in an imitation of Lady Bracknell, as performed by countless amateur dramsocs and Oscar Wilde appreciation societies. "*A stage name*?"

Skewered by his guest's expectant grin, Kelley coughed into his tightly-bunched fist and murmured, "I used to be in a band."

"Brass band? Flute band? Bagpipe band? Orange Order, Masonic handshake, kick-the-Pope, blood-and-thunder band?"

"Rock band."

Stifling a sudden shriek of laughter, albeit with difficulty, Abby pressed home her conversational advantage. "Goth rock? Hmmmm, let me see. Let me guess. No, no, don't tell me. Jesus and Mary Chain? Sisters of Mercy? Evanescence?"

"Next question."

"The Damned?"

"Next question."

"The Mission?"

"Moving swiftly along."

Abby had to cover her mouth to prevent an unladylike snort escaping. "Did you have many hits? Something I might know? Any chance of a chorus or two, just to remind me? Are you, ah, still gigging?"

"Pass."

"Fair enough," Abby said sympathetically. "However, while I'm waiting to see your CD liner photographs, can I ask you something else?"

David D'Anger, a.k.a. Dave the Rave, a.k.a. DD Kelley rockstar, settled himself on an old lichen-covered log at the edge of a beautiful leaf-strewn copper-beech glade and adopted an authoritative pose, as if running a seminar for remedial retail marketing students. "Fire away."

A ferocious burst of cawing erupted from the rookery overhead, forcing Abby to repeat the question. "You referred to your kid brother's extravagance. But if you're his big brother, how come you're not Lord of the Manor? I always thought the eldest son inherited the noble pile. Is that not the case in your family?" However, she could tell from the cumulo-nimbus clouds scudding across his boyish face that he'd heard her perfectly well the first time.

After waiting for the raucous chorus to quieten down, Kelley looked her straight in the eye. "I was disinherited."

"Mary, Mother of Marilyn Manson! I know Smashing Pumpkins

tribute bands are bad, but disinheritance is a bit extreme."

He sighed and said nothing.

Abby knew what was coming. "Next question, eh Dave?"

Kelley shook his head as he stood up wearily, his knees cracking in tune. "No. I'll tell you all about it if you wish. Though perhaps we should save it for the journey to Coleraine. It's a three hankie job. Let me just show you the library before we hit the trail." Setting off at a quick clip down the leaf-limned path, which rustled deliciously underfoot, he turned to his tardy companion, as she zipped up the voluminous Barbour and struggled with the studs. "I think it's my turn now. Let me ask *you* a question."

Abby caught up, though she so wanted to start kicking leaves in the air and forget about her troubles. "How can I possibly refuse? Though I should tell you in advance, Dave, that tenant farming, hedge schools and potato famine-fuelled trips in coffin ships are the height of our ancestral achievements."

Arms akimbo, Kelley gazed directly into her eyes. "What's in the holdall?" he inquired politely. "I take it you've opened the thing by now. And I presume it wasn't a dead body or assorted body parts."

The rookettes started up again in the beech trees behind them. An importunate fire alarm sounded in the far distance. It was oddly ominous on a peaceful Saturday morning. "Yes, I opened it before breakfast. No body parts, I'm afraid. Much worse than that."

Kelley helped pop a couple of the Barbour studs and pulled up her corduroy collar, with a nod of sartorial approval. "Copies of my band's debut album? Ah, the horror, the horror."

"Money," she replied. "It's full of money. Twenties, tenners and fivers mainly. At least a million, maybe more. I haven't counted it yet."

Stunned, Kelley looked askance at his regally-dressed house guest. "Money? Millions? Illegal arms trade millions? We're going to die gruesome deaths, Abby."

She smiled by way of reply. "There's nothing like dying young in the music business, Dave. It's a great career move. Especially for goths. Try to look on the bright side."

The crows' chorus came back for an encore.

Chapter Fourteen

Phishers of Men

The taxi arrived at 11.00 a.m. Although he wasn't speaking until early afternoon, Professor Pitcairn Brodie liked to get to the conference venue well ahead of time. AV equipment had a mind of its own and, as tantrums were an ever-present possibility, it was necessary to enter into negotiations prior to every presentation. For years, Brodie had refused to employ audio-visual aids, relying on his natural charisma, spellbinding oratory and outlandish outfit – a complete Scottish kilt with all the trimmings – to hold the audience. In a world of grey-suited businessmen, packing PowerPoint and not much else, Brodie's antithetical approach stood out from the me-too, ho-hum, yada-yada crowd. The widely circulated rumour that he had nothing under his kilt, a rumour he had done much to propagate, unfailingly ensured a full house of inquisitive rubberneckers who hung on his every word while hoping for a grisly glimpse of the Trossachs.

Brodie didn't disappoint.

The kilt wasn't the key to his success, however. Nor indeed were the alchemical ideas he artfully articulated. Audiences took in very little, by and large, especially hung-over or partied-out audiences, as was often the case with corporate junkets. His secret was mnemotechnics. The art of memory. As a classically educated theologian, Brodie was familiar with the techniques that the ancients used to improve their memories. When printed books were rare and oral storytelling traditions held sway, clerics were required to learn masses and masses of biblical information by heart, as did the druids, oracles, shamans and priest-kings before them. They did so by mental imaging methods. So stupendous were the resultant feats of memory that great orators were simultaneously revered and feared. Mnemotechnics was the work of the devil, some said in the Middle Ages, and with good reason, because the procedure was perfected by infamous medieval occultists – Agrippa, Lull, Fludd, Bruno, the deadly Dr. Dee. But as alchemy was an integral part of the western occult tradition, Brodie had no compunction about using magic mnemonic techniques when discoursing on brand alchemy.

It was apt, after all.

Although the showman-scholar didn't need audio-visual aids to hold an audience – his two-hour, one-man, no-safety-net shows, delivered without notes or prompts or scripts or stutters, were more than sufficient – Brodie appreciated that today's visually literate audiences need something to look at while the message is communicated orally. So he made creative use of a throat microphone and Microsoft's media player. As he talked, synchronized images of rising flames, spreading ripples, pulsating sound waves and suchlike, syncopated on the big screen behind him. It was bravura stuff, especially as most other speakers on the circuit worked on the mistaken assumption that the best way to impress a torpid audience was to up the PowerPoint ante by increasing the number of slides or by flicking through them at an ever faster rate.

It didn't work that way.

In the past, the ebullient theologian had led audiences in riotous chants of "Out, PowerPoint, Out." But not today. Today's showstopper was Brodie's legendary lie-detector "test". Ostensibly attached to an alleged lie-detector machine, he promised the audience that every word he was about to speak was the truth, the whole truth and nothing but the truth. And he had the equipment to prove it. Thus, when he assured the audience that he held the key to marketing success, effective brand building, long-term competitive advantage or whatever it happened to be, the leaping lines behind him indicated otherwise. The more sincere he got, the more his pseudo-hypocrisy was exposed. Hilarity ensued. He was impossible to follow. He often thought of introducing klaxons, which would go off when he told a particularly extravagant whopper – such as when he said how much he loved the audience – but the technology was temperamental and the noise adversely affected his mnemotechnique.

Such were the perils of the consultancy circuit.

What the Nuremberg auditorium lacked in advanced AV equipment and crystalline acoustics, it more than compensated in aesthetics. The Emperor's Hall of Kaiserburg Castle, which sat resolute on a hilly outcrop overlooking the old town, was a baroque masterpiece of gilded panels, priceless tapestries, intricate parquet and imperialist oil paintings of armoured emperors on rearing chargers. The look was somewhat spoiled by Citroën's looming logo, massive reproductions of which were slotted and shoe-horned into every available space. Bright red, chevron-slashed banners bearing the legend "One hundred years of helical gears" were wallpapered around the auditorium and hung in loops from the ornate ceiling, undulating slightly as the turbid air slowly circulated. Huge, sepia-hued photographs of André Citroën himself, looking vaguely sagacious in his owlish glasses, alternated with the double-chevron standards.

An apathetic audience was listening listlessly to a grinning guru from Las Vegas, who pontificated plaintively on his cutting-edge company's off-the-shelf "solution" to Citroën's manifold ills and who just happened to have the key to the organization's future profitability. It seemed to involve some kind of corporate cosmetic surgery. Brand Botox, Distribution Abrasion, Retail Rhinoplasty, Competition Filler, Logistics Laser Surgery, Value Chain Depilation, Logosuction and the like. You couldn't make it up. What management metaphors will these people come up with next? And they have the nerve to charge six-figure sums for this stuff? Appalled, Brodie listened attentively for ten minutes, taking in the atmosphere. Every audience has its quirks and the Kaiserburg's was quirkier than most. He scanned the logo-lashed, chevron-spattered conference programme for a suitable break in the proceedings, one that'd give him time to set up his Mediaplayer-dependent alchemical extravaganza. There was a fifteen-minute coffee interlude immediately after the amiable airhead from Stupidity Associates, or whatever his awful company was called.

Even at his worst, Brodie was much better than that.

The next but one session, he noticed in the glossy brochure – which contained seriously airbrushed colour photographs of the unprepossessing speakers – was his own. The first speaker was Dr. Hugh Dolt, a self-important academic from Manchester, who was expounding on tyre-kickers, nose-pickers, arse-lickers, price-dickers and other customer types. The bleary-eyed delegates will be looking forward to that one, Brodie surmised, since they mainly consist of Citroën showroom personnel and fleet sales managers, flown in at great expense to celebrate the multinational's illustrious past and move mountains of metal for the foreseeable future. Luckily, the execrable content of academics' presentations rarely lived up to their arresting titles. Ironically, the attention-grabbing titles merely served to raise audience expectations, only to dash them with oratory of butt-numbing monotony.

No threat there, then.

The second speaker, from yet another solution-selling consultancy – a subsidiary of an internationally renowned accountancy firm, no less – purported to be a brand whisperer. A *what*? Brodie read the brochure again with disbelief. Like the Montana farmer of Robert Evans's bestselling book, as played by Robert Redford in the hugely successful Hollywood movie, Chuck Conestoga claimed to be able to turn any brand, no matter how frisky, no matter how lame, no matter how temperamental, into a thoroughbred, a champion, a world-beater, a winner of the Melbourne Cup of brand share, the Kentucky Derby of customer satisfaction, the Grand National of competitive advantage, the Belmont Stakes of brand equity, the Prix de l'Arc de Triomphe of long-term profitability.

Horseshit, Brodie reckoned.

Smiling affably at the somnolent conference delegates on either side, Professor Brodie got up to leave the dozing auditorium. Unimpressed by the obviously second rate speakers in his session – he was going to slay this audience – the Scottish theologian started humming a favourite childhood hymn:

I will make you phishers of men, phishers of men, phishers of men
I will make you phishers of men, if you follow me.
If you follow me
If you follow me
I will make you phishers of men, if you only follow me.

Chapter Fifteen

Dear Abby

According to glossy tourist brochures, febrile in-flight magazines and sundry Sunday newspaper supplements, the North Antrim coast is one of the wonders of the natural world. Alongside Urulu, Victoria Falls and Yosemite Valley, it is a place that begs to be visited before the Grim Reaper swings his scythe. In-flight magazines admittedly aren't the most reliable tourist information providers, but even best-selling, no-nonsense guidebooks, be they rough or lonely, acknowledge that the Antrim Coast Road is worth the trip. Built during the 1840s, as an Irish Famine relief project, the A2 coast road runs from Larne to Ballycastle, a distance of 66 kilometres. Narrow and twisty, the undulating, occasionally precarious carriageway clings to the base of steep chalk cliffs, thrusting basalt headlands and mist-shrouded, bracken-banded mountainsides. Nine fairy-filled glens punctuate this forbidding sea wall, their sheltered serenity a balmy contrast to the sweeping, spume-filled, crescent-shaped bays that chamfer the edge of Ulster's Amalfi.

A tourist thrombosis at the height of the season, when sclerotic strings of tour buses and people carriers clog the service economy's pulmonary artery, the Antrim Coast Road returns to rude health during June and September. The road is empty. The views are uninterrupted. The weather, thanks to the miracle that's global warming, is often unnaturally excellent. For a couple of hours at least. Indeed, one of the primary attractions of the Antrim coast is that its micro-climate frequently provides the four-seasons-in-one-day scenario that Crowded House once sang about. The clear skies and bright sunshine that bring the west coast of Scotland within apparent touching distance soon cloud over as passing showers sweep in, their dark promise of precipitation discernible from many kilometres away. Visibility drops to zero, the sparkling seas turn slate grey and the cold winds of winter bend the stunted bushes at ever more acute angles.

The infinite variety of the North Antrim littoral – glistening glades, tumbling streams, rolling hillsides, bustling harbours, peaceful churchyards, crumbling castles, vaunting viaducts, vanishing lakes, one-horse hamlets – is complemented by the stories that clothe the glens and uplands, their prose as purple as the heather, their content as black as the peat bogs. There are stories of Robert the Bruce and his never-say-die spider; stories of Finn McCool, the temperamental titan who tore up the Giant's Causeway; stories of the Spanish Armada, which came to grief on galleon-unfriendly reefs and shoals; stories of the disastrous 1639 soiree at Dunluce Castle, when a sudden landslip tipped the revellers into their salt water graves.

The story Abby Maguire was listening to wasn't as tumultuous as those that sheathe the glorious Glens of Antrim. But it was tragic in its own way. Dave Kelley explained, with much hesitation and not a little regret, how he'd lost his inheritance. Abandoning his adolescent gothic fantasies and dreams of rock 'n' roll stardom, he studied management at uni, took a master's in marketing at Trinity, prepared a business plan to turn Castle D'Anger into a sustainable tourist attraction, and secured the necessary funding thanks to Northern Ireland's rapid transition to peace, prosperity and ever-increasing popularity among once-wary holidaymakers. Then fate took a hand. In keeping with family tradition, Dave decided to give something back to society. He offered his services as a tutor for the Open University, taught at Maghaberry women's prison, fell in love with a beautiful serial killer who was serving sequential life sentences for conspiring to murder several British soldiers, and married her in a moment of passion-propelled madness. Appalled, his father disinherited Dave in favour of Robert, the sybaritic second son. Dave's wife, having secured an early release on the strength of the D'Anger family connections, promptly left him when there was no prospect of inheritance. Distraught and disillusioned, with only a couple of ramshackle commercial properties to his name, Dave turned to higher education, took a lecturing post at the University of Hustler and enrolled for a doctorate under Professor Emer Aherne.

"Jeepers, I thought Britney Spears had marital problems," Abby interjected in the irreverent Ulster manner, trying to remain sympathetic without resorting to soap-opera-style syrup. "But a convicted serial killer takes the biscuit. You must have a masochistic streak, Dave. We all thought you were gay."

Kelley laughed. "No, darling, I'm not gay. I camp it up a bit for the students. Lecturing is a branch of show business. I discovered that on my very first day, as a petrified junior lecturer facing an audience of two hundred expectant undergraduates, most of whom either didn't want to be there or were hungover from the night before or had wandered into the class by accident. You've got to grab the punters' attention, darling. You've got to entertain them and, while they're laughing and having fun, you try to ensure that they take a couple of key points away with them. Too many university lecturers are sad, middle-aged men who look like badgers..."

"Smell like them too," Abby added.

Steering erratically with one hand, Kelley held his nose with the other and faux-frowned across at his travelling companion, boyish enthusiasm bubbling once more. "So, I camp it up a bit in class. No harm in that, though my esteemed colleagues don't see it that way. However, the graduates remember me long after they've forgotten the..."

"Badger breaths."

"Well, I was going to say the monochrome set, but hey." Laughing, he turned the carnation-coloured retromobile into a particularly tight bend, where the road surface had buckled due to subsoil slippages and the local council hadn't repaired Mother Nature's roller coaster. It wasn't exactly Alton Towers, but it was exciting all the same, especially with a driver who believed that as he'd paid his road fund licence, he was entitled to make full use of both sides of the carriageway. At all times. Regardless of oncoming traffic. In a car that may have lacked airbags and ABS, but was fully loaded with metal fatigue.

Thankfully, they stopped in Carnlough for a local, low-cal ice cream and sat on the picture-postcard harbour wall watching the fishing boats bob up and down with the swell. The smell of seaweed was overpowering. A font of local historical knowledge, Kelley told tales of Glenariff fairy glen, tales of economic hardship and bloody conquest, tales of Oisin, the great Gaelic poet buried on a hilltop above Cushendun, tales of his family's participation in the once-important iron ore trade between North Antrim and Central Scotland, tales of his brother's attempts to dispose of the irreplaceable D'Anger Castle library, which he'd fought tooth and nail. He offered to swap his town centre properties, but Robert didn't want to know.

Revelations are reciprocal. You tell me your back story, I'll tell you mine. Although Abby's life experience was less extensive than Kelley's and much less littered with lords, ladies, demesnes, diminishing fortunes and troublesome inheritance issues, it was no less noteworthy for all that. Talking about it also enabled her to defer discussion of the one million pound gorilla in the boot. As they drove on, skirting the resplendent Torr Head, she told him about her father's suicide. On her sixteenth birthday, of all days. She told him about her mother's mental disintegration. And the struggle to keep the family farm going. She told him about her younger brother and sister, who she had to bring up single-handed. Naturally, she didn't mention her predatory uncle or the priest who took sexual advantage of her situation, or the eating disorders that plagued her late adolescence or the extended family who refused to assist the embarrassing "Mad Maguires". She did, however, talk about her time on the killing line of the local slaughterhouse, where she supplemented the family income and earned just enough to see her brother and sister through to adulthood. It was there that she acquired the nickname that tormented her at the time, but now felt natural, somehow.

"Nickname? What nickname, Abby?"

"Abby."

"Huh?" Alarmingly, Kelley took his eye off a steep hairpin bend to look at her intently. "I thought your forename was Abigail."

Abby shrugged her shoulders regretfully. "No, no, it's not. Abby's short for abattoir. Abattoir Maguire they used to call me… round the village… on the way to chapel…" Her voice trailed off.

"Jesus."

"Well, Dave, the way I look at it, Abby's a lot better than my real name. Lesser of two evils and all that."

"I don't want to ask, darling. But tell all, tell all."

"Husky. My real name's Husky Maguire. My father was a bit of a nature buff, a wildlife enthusiast. My brother's called Marsupial, for goodness' sake. My sister's Dingo. Actually, I didn't mind Husky when I was young and slim. However, I've put on a few pounds since then and, given the choice between Husky and Abby, it's a no-brainer, as they say."

"But you're not fat," Kelley said gallantly. "You're no size at all, darling."

Adopting her best *Sound of Music* voice, Abby sang, "I am sixteen going on eighteen... And size twenty you'll see, after a bucket of KFC."

Kelley laughed. Or he would have done if his stomach hadn't fallen away, when cresting a rise at Ballintoy. Undoubtedly the most spectacular sight on the North Antrim coast, the road squeezes between steep cliffs then suddenly plunges precipitously. The Atlantic Ocean is spread out as far as the eye can see. Curly waves and crimped breakers hurl themselves at the cliff bottoms below. The only sign of human intervention is a terrifying, thread-like rope bridge connecting the mainland to a tiny off-shore island.

Despite her life-long fear of heights, Abby agreed to interrupt their journey and cross the heart-stopping chasm. It's a rite of passage, Kelley explained. It guarantees good luck and long life, he insisted. It's something every Ulster man and woman has to do at some stage, he said with a straight face. It is akin to kissing the Blarney Stone down south, he swore blind. Whereas Munster men and women get the gift of the gab in return for a stony snog, Ulster men and women are turned into fearless warriors on crossing the Carrick-a-Rede rope bridge.

Put like that, Abby could hardly say no, especially as good luck was sorely needed, long life looked unlikely and she'd require a show of fearless warriorosity when Igor and Billy No-dick showed up, looking for their loot. Resolute, Abby marched across the trembling rope bridge, wisely refusing to look at the jagged rocks thirty-five metres beneath. Kelley bounded across, occasionally grabbing the frayed handrails while swaying alarmingly from side to side.

"I'll get you for this," she cried, holding on for grim death. "I'll kill you, Kelley."

"Glad to hear it," he shouted. "It's my specialist subject."

"Sorry?"

"I did my doctorate on it, Abby. I'm an expert."

"You did your PhD on Carrick-a-Rede rope bridge? Wasn't that dangerous? Uncomfortable? Risky?"

Kelley wrapped an arm round her shoulders as they walked back toward the cerise Morris, along the winding cliff-top path to the shale-surfaced car park. "No, Abby, My thesis wasn't on extreme sports. It's on revenge."

"Revenge?"

"Revenge!"

"Figures."

Chapter Sixteen

Revenge Is a Ready Meal Best Microwaved

"What motivates business men and women, Abby? What *really* motivates them? Is it making money or getting rich or social responsibility or providing employment or spotting gaps in the market or, as economists would have us believe, profit maximization?" Kelley was warming to his subject, and his increasingly erratic driving bore witness to the fact. Still, there wasn't far to go. They'd stopped off at the Giant's Causeway and, in Dr. Johnson fashion, were duly underwhelmed. They drove past Royal Portrush's splendid golf course – and the less splendid caravan parks opposite – parked beside the Harbour Bar and had a brief bite of lunch in the adjacent Ramore Restaurant.

"All of these things are important," Kelley acknowledged, his eyes shining with enthusiasm, the self-assurance of the zealot. "But there's another fundamental factor, a primal human emotion that academic types tend to overlook. Revenge. The desire to get even, to settle the score, to right perceived wrongs, insults or slights, to give someone a taste of their own medicine. *That's* what drives many business people on. Some of the greatest businessmen of our time were failures at school or dismissed as hopeless cases – Richard Branson, Philip Green, Alan Sugar, Duncan Bannatyne, Felix Dennis, Donald Trump, Henry Ford, Steve Jobs – so they were very strongly motivated to prove themselves, to show that the system got it wrong. Others, like Martha Stewart or Madonna or Maurice Saatchi or, once again, Steve Jobs, were very publicly humiliated at the pinnacle of their success. However, they refused to slink away and accept the defeat. They came back even stronger than before, determined to rehabilitate themselves in the eyes of the world, to give their knockers, mockers and detractors what for."

"So this research of yours has nothing to do with your personal circumstances, Dave?"

"Of course not," he replied, shocked at the very suggestion. "I'm an academic, aren't I? I'm a marketing scientist, committed to the disinterested pursuit of objective truth and value-free knowledge. Purely for its own sake."

Abby found it difficult to keep her face straight. But she did her best as Dave ranted on, waving his arms about, much as he would when lecturing to a class of 200 undergrads. The harried waiters didn't have a clue what the demented diner was signalling for. So they ignored him. Abby didn't have that luxury, not that she really minded. Dave was a nice guy. A nutter, but nice.

"Consumers also retaliate when they feel like it, and they often do. They wreak retribution on the retail stores that treat them badly or slight them in any way. They bad-mouth the brand to friends, they post negative on-line comments, they swap horror stories at dinner parties, they mess the perpetrator about with late payments, rubber cheques and cavalier returns, they set out to waste the time of snooty shop assistants or enjoy informing them that they've lost a sale and missed their commission."

"Like Julia Roberts in *Pretty Woman*?"

"Yes, *exactly* like *Pretty Woman*," he said vociferously. "My respondents often mentioned that movie spontaneously." He jabbed his fork for emphasis, scattering lettuce on the tabletop like bread upon the waters. "That scene resonated with an awful lot of women."

"Well, Dave, it's good to know that you're not getting back at your late father or your spendthrift brother or your evil ex-wife or anything like that. It's gratifying to hear that your interest in revenge is purely academic."

The irony was lost on him. Dr. Kelley was on a roll, recounting his revengeful research findings with post-prandial pleasure. Post-coital almost. "Taking new clothes back to the shop, after wearing them for an evening out, is another favourite retribution tactic among female consumers..."

Much as Abby was enjoying the meal, she wasn't sure she

could take much more of this. Dave was working his way through his entire doctoral thesis. By the look of him, he still had several sizeable chapters to go. "Oh, I'm sorry to hear that," she interjected. "Some Like It Hot's customers must really hate me. They return stuff all the time."

"No, darling," Dave replied, with a flamboyant gesture. "They return intimate apparel because their men have no idea of their size, or their sexuality, or even what turns them on."

"And you do, Dave?"

He ignored the question by looking round for the bill. He waved at a waiter, though in light of Dave's earlier hand signals, he was understandably ignored as the restaurant exacted its revenge. "Mind you, women have no idea about men either. Haven't a clue, darling."

Vaguely insulted, because she prided herself on knowing exactly what men wanted – and preventing them from getting it – Abby answered tartly. "Oh, I reckon we have a pretty good idea, Dave. I know I do."

Dr. Kelley turned to her with the aloof, immensely irritating, I-know-better expression that's often etched on men's faces, usually when driving or ordering in restaurants. "No, Abby, I'm afraid you don't," he said with finality, then changed the subject to his magnum opus once more, something about the four stages of the Revenge Life Cycle: Rejection, Retribution, Rivalry, Regret.

Abby was at the regret stage. She wished she'd never broached the subject, especially when he cranked up the car and started on the revenge motif in popular culture – *Carrie, The Godfather, Die Hard, Thelma & Louise, Paradise Lost, Hamlet, Moby Dick, Dallas, Don Giovanni,* Dan Brown's books. Thankfully, the tower block that dominates Hustler University soon loomed into view and informed her that Dave wouldn't have sufficient time to recount his appendices or itemize his entire list of references.

Much loathed by the locals, Hustler's Coleraine campus is not a thing of beauty. The sixties incarnate – Ronan Point meets Park Hill – it's not so much dreaming spires as leaking roofs. Its principal claim to fame is that the architect originally entered his reinforced concrete design for the competition to build Stirling University and came second to a scheme based on an especially sadistic Swedish prison. So he transplanted his rejected runner-up to the bonny banks of the River Bann. Cruel and unusual punishment doesn't begin to describe it.

If Hustler's Coleraine campus is reminiscent of a Chechen public housing project, Dave Kelley's office was situated in one of Grozny's less salubrious suburbs. Even Uncle Joe Stalin at his most psychotic never banished dissidents to a gulag more inhuman. At the end of a long, uncarpeted corridor, the grimy plate glass of which provided an uninterrupted view of a scruffy delivery bay and electricity sub-station, his office nestled uncomfortably between bathroom and store cupboard. Many an undergraduate had set out to find Dave the Rave's secret hidey-hole and returned, traumatized, by the design walk of death.

The office itself was airy and attractive, though anything semi-stylish would have looked good, given the setting. An arrangement of plump, cushion-covered sofas occupied one corner of the room. A large Louis Vuitton trunk, complete with leather corner-covers, lozine edge-trim and luscious LV logo, served as a surrogate coffee table. The walls were lined with framed reproductions of modern artworks, only one of which she recognized, an entirely apt print of Warhol's dollar bills. The sturdy built-in bookcases were replete with bulky volumes on retail management, marketing research, brand building and Idiot's Guides to doing doctorates. Only idiots did them, surely.

As Abby took in the occasional tables cluttered with delicate Japanese netsuke, colourful Lalique glassware and bits-and-bobs of bespoke Belleek pottery, she recalled Kelley's lectures about the primordial power of objects, artefacts, possessions, things. Whether it be the Turin Shroud, the Holy Grail, the Black Stone, the Sacred Lotus, the Ferrari F430, the Hermès Kelly, the iPod Nano or the contents of museums worldwide, humankind was inordinately susceptible to the intoxicating power of physical objects, especially physical objects that had been owned or touched by famous people – Mozart's piano, Shakespeare's quill, Churchill's cigar, Madonna's conical bra, Paris Hilton's prison uniform. He illustrated his lecture with a clip from *Raiders of the Lost Ark*, the scene where the reliquary is finally opened and its stupendous superhuman power is unleashed. That, he said, captures the primal appeal of tangible things, everything from Manolo Blahnik stilettos and Montblanc Meisterstucks to BlackBerry Curves. Looking around her lecturer's office, Abby could see that Kelley was a boy who loved his baubles.

Wearily, she dumped her bright purple holdall onto the sofa, where it bounced once or twice before settling. "So, who's this person that's going to save our bacon? Does he normally come into uni on Saturday mornings?"

With an anxious sigh, Kelley explained the situation in an uncharacteristically staccato gabble. "He's a bit odd. Only works at night and weekends. Peregrine Faulkner, he's called. English. Regimental tie type. They gave him an emeritus professorship six months or so ago. Nobody knows why. Unspecified services to Hustler. Plays his cards close to his chest. However, I have it on good authority that he was a spook in the past."

"As in ghosts, ghoulies, things that go bump in the night? As in goths, Dave?" Abby added with an irreverent smirk.

"As in Bond, James Bond," Kelley replied, in a terrible Sean Connery accent.

"MI5? MI6? Don't tell me there's an MI7."

"No, no. Not as far as I know. Perry's part of the Irish equivalent. G2, I think it's called."

"He's a kind of O'07?" She had to indicate the apostrophe with her fingers, since the quip was otherwise incomprehensible. Still, her Pierce Brosnan was better than Kelley's Connery.

Kelley smiled pensively, his body language insinuating "Keep that crack to yourself when we meet him." He sat down beside the bulky holdall and patted it warily. "May I take a look?"

"Of course," she said casually. "A million pounds may not mean much to you, Viscount D'Anger, but it's a fortune for hill farmers like me." Abby pulled back the stiff zip of the imperial purple carrier bag, with Nike swoosh couchant. It jerked, caught, stuck, stuttered and, after the teeth were firmly pressed together, finally opened with a resounding rip. The bag was brimming with ready-counted, pre-wrapped fivers, tenners, twenties, fifties and hundreds, the last of which she'd never encountered before, let alone handled. The scene was just like a Hollywood heist movie, only for real.

Kelley picked up a packet of fivers, riffled the ends with his thumb and, with a rueful shake of the head, stuffed it back in the bag. "Let's see if Perry's at home."

"Aren't you going to ring him?"

"He never uses the phone. As I said, he's a bit odd. He's a couple of doors down. I only got to know him because we're near neighbours, both banished to the cancerous bowels of the building."

"Can you trust him?"

Kelley's anxious smile and uncertain look returned. "Who else can we turn to, darling?" His "darling" was devoid of the usual efflorescent intonation.

With a regretful smile, Abby reciprocated. "Here's another fine mess I've got you into, Dave."

"Chin up. We're in this together."

"Chins up, you mean."

"Try to keep things in perspective, Abby. Just wait till you see Perry."

Chapter Seventeen

There's No Spook Like an Old Spook

Peregrine Faulkner's office was right round the corner from Dave Kelley's, albeit down two flights of stainless steel stairs that reverberated underfoot. Situated between a colossal boiler room, all lagged pipes and large glass dials, and a disused computer laboratory, long since bypassed by university-wide wi-fi, Faulkner's lair was even more inaccessible than Kelley's, if such a thing were possible. The Minotaur's labyrinth was a stroll in the park by comparison.

There was no nameplate on the professor's office door, nor any sign of life. Only a push-button keypad, plus retinal scanner, indicated the presence of something unusual.

Unusual doesn't begin to describe it. After several increasingly urgent knocks and echoing calls of "Perry, it's me," the security-chained doorway opened a crack. A sliver of face evaluated the visitors, before deadbolts were thrown and they were ushered inside. Even though it was a beautiful Saturday morning in early September, the Venetian blinds were firmly battened down. Faulkner's office was in semi-darkness. A puddle of electric light under the desk lamp struggled to pierce the pervasive gloom. It was as hot as a sauna in Hell, only sweatier. A faint miasma of body odour filled the strangely spartan space. The strictly functional desk, plastic stacking chairs, metal filing cabinets, industrial style bookshelves and narrow camp bed in the corner bespoke several serious personality disorders, though it's hard to tell with emeritus professors. Or any professors, for that matter.

He didn't look like Sean Connery, much less Pierce Brosnan, let alone Roger Moore. He looked more like a taller version of Peter Lorre. If he had to be described in a single word, that word would probably be slippery, possibly shifty, definitely slimy. Several strands of greasy black hair were plastered across his shiny scalp, his sallow, pock-marked face had a waxy, unhealthy pallor, his fleshy nose had the consistency of a knobbly seed potato, loose folds of skin flapped under his once receding, now withdrawn chin, and the glassy grey eyes weren't so much protuberant as suggestive of an untreated thyroid condition.

It was the voice, however, that Abby found especially disconcerting. She expected a sibilant lisp, a bit like Gollum or Hannibal Lecter, but instead received a cannonade of impeccable pronunciation, the kind of accent that's nowadays confined to the BBC archives and gung-ho wartime newsreels. Last heard during the Queen's Christmas broadcast for 1959, the vowels weren't so much strangulated as throttled at birth. The effect was not only closer to escutcheon than estuary, but Faulkner sounded as though he was crunching escutcheons as he spoke. "Welcome, my dear boy, welcome," he said, rubbing his hands unctuously. "What can I do for you and your fair maiden this fine morning?"

Kelley rapidly explained the events of the previous evening, while Faulkner took notes, periodically glancing up with a vaguely concerned expression, occasionally shaking his head ever so slightly and, at one particular point, barely suppressing a chuckle. When Dave had finished, the ex-intelligence officer set down his old-fashioned fountain pen, sank back slowly into his chair, clasped his hands behind his head, which exposed the unspeakable underarm tarnish of his once-white shirt, and stared silently at the seedy suspended ceiling. He must be seventy if he's a day, Abby reckoned, probably older.

"Well, my dear boy, what can I say? You are in extremely serious trouble, though you already know that. The issue is how we can formulate an exit strategy that keeps casualties to a minimum." He turned his watery eyes on Abby. "You are a very foolhardy young woman. Brave, but foolhardy. Still, at least you have something with which to negotiate. I fear they will kill you anyway."

"Not if I kill them first," Abby retorted angrily.

The well-spoken spook rolled his baleful eyes. It was as if he were dealing with a delinquent child, which in a way he was. "Quite. Quite. The only positive aspect, young lady, is that both sides are involved. Discount DIY is a front for the republican movement, one of the IRA's many money laundering vehicles. The operatives you encountered are prominent Protestant assassins, leading members of the UVF. You are stuck in the middle. You cannot kill them all, my dear, although mainstream Irish society would doubtless be delighted if you did." A supercilious smile creased his smarmy features, as he ran a hair-smoothing hand across his sweaty, sebaceous scalp. "You are safe though, David. Provided you pay them off or arrange appropriate reparation. I am sure they will settle amicably with someone of your stature, breeding and impeccable family background."

"Sorry, old chap," Kelley replied in an adopted Anglo-Irish accent, the clipped tones Abby'd last heard when he was conversing with his errant younger brother. "I am obliged to stand by my student, Perry. Pastoral duty and all that."

Although she was touched by her lecturer's unnecessary loyalty, to say nothing of his stiff-upper-lip Blitz spirit, Abby was unhappy with his choice of father confessor. The oily bastard reeked of expediency and appeasement, which was not what she expected from a supposed Irish superspy, even an obviously Ascendancy superspy. "What did you find so funny?" she snapped. "I saw you smirking during Dave's account of our situation. You think this is a joke? The ignorant Irish amuse you, do they? We don't need your help, Mister Super Intelligence Officer. Let's go, Dave, we're wasting our time here." She stood up and stalked across to the door, only to find that it was firmly locked. She whirled round, about to unleash a torrent of good-old Fermanagh invective, when Faulkner's constricted, cut-glass cadences carved through Abby's rapidly descending red mist.

"Ah, the Irish fighting spirit. There is nothing quite like it. Politically correct stereotyping be damned," he enunciated jubilantly. "We are the finest, fiercest people on the planet. You are simply wonderful, my dear. If anyone can extricate themselves from the unfortunate situation in which you find yourselves, I suspect it might just be your good self." He attempted an avuncular smile, unsuccessfully, before continuing. "Now, come over here and hear me out." It was a voice that didn't brook any opposition. As there was no way out, Abby did as she was instructed. "For your information, young lady, I *am* Irish, born and bred in Wexford, albeit educated at Eton and Oxford. As you rightly observed, I did indeed smile during David's summary of your misguided mission. I smiled at U.S.E., my dear. During the decommissioning debates, the IRA leadership talked about putting their weapons beyond use. The British and Irish governments assumed that this meant getting rid of them completely. Not a very likely scenario. Putting them beyond U.S.E., the white line painted across the Carrickfergus warehouse, is a sublime example of Irish republican double-speak. Hence my smile. It was a smile of admiration, young woman. But not one of approval."

Chastened, yet wary, Abby retook her seat, hard and uncomfortable though it was. Kelley reached across and squeezed her shoulder affectionately. "It'll be okay," he mouthed silently, with a little smile of encouragement.

The espionage expert pushed himself away from the desk, stood up with a groan – gammy leg, presumably – and started pacing around the murky room, thinking aloud all the while. "Here is what I suggest. Make a written record of everything that has happened to you. Make several copies. Address them to the police, the police ombudsman, the Inland Revenue, leading newspaper columnists, the arms decommissioning body, the Assets Recovery Agency, a cross-party selection of politicians, and perhaps a high court judge or two. Ensure that they will be posted in the event of your untimely death, even if it looks like an accident. Most of the letters will be ignored or intercepted by the enemy, but one or two are likely get through. The UVF cannot afford that, nor can the IRA, especially if you make it clear that they are in commercial cahoots. That would not go down well with the rank and file. Thus, I think you will find they are keen to negotiate."

Kelley cleared his throat. "That's a very scattergun strategy, Perry. Whatever happened to surgical strikes? It also means negotiating face-to-face with the miscreants and telling them what'll happen if they renege. We're not dealing with reasonable people, here."

"On the contrary, dear boy, I think you will find that they are *very* reasonable people. They are not ideologues, if indeed they ever were. They are businessmen. Commercial arrangements are paramount. If something threatens to destabilize the brand, or disrupt channels of distribution, or adversely affect consumer confidence, they will do everything they have to do to normalize business relationships. They dislike unpredictability. They are vulnerable to scattergun strategies, which are inherently uncontrollable. Hence, they should see sense. Wise heads may well prevail. You won't know until you sit down with them. Watch your backs, though."

"What do you think, Abby?" Kelley asked solicitously, the staccato delivery betraying his uncertainty. "Sounds like a workable plan to me. But it's your call. You've faced them before. Can you do so again?"

It was all Abby could do to resist snorting with derision. "Oh, I can face them all right. I'm not sure if I can stop myself wringing their necks."

"The plan's worth a try, I reckon," Kelley said firmly. He eased out of his chair and made ready to leave. "Many thanks for your help, Perry. I owe you one, old man."

"Delighted to be of assistance, dear boy."

"What do you think our chances are?"

"Slim," Faulkner replied flatly. "But with Abby by your side," he added, before leering Lorre-like, "I'd say non-existent..."

Furious, Abby reached into her handbag and felt around for the delay spray. There was still a squirt or two in the can. If it was good enough for Igor, it'll be perfect for Perry, by Jove.

"...until such time as she learns to keep her emotions in check," the ex-intelligence officer went on. "Bravery is one thing, bravado is something else again. I've seen many brave men swagger into early graves. Valour and vigilance go hand in hand. Caution is as important as courage when it comes to counter-terrorist work. And that, make no mistake, is what you are engaged in."

"You just said they were businesspeople, brand-minded managers and the like!" Abby spat, still flustered by Faulkner's deliberate provocation, which proved his point perfectly. She'd responded exactly as anticipated and he knew it. And he knew that she knew that he knew it.

"They are, my dear. Of course they are. However, businesspeople are terrorists too. You have to be completely ruthless to manage a brand properly. There is no room for sentiment in business or espionage. Surely they teach you that in class."

Kelley slipped an arm round Abby's waist and steered her toward the office door. Still infuriated, she shrugged him off. Faulkner stood by the doorjamb, preparing to open it for his Saturday morning visitors. He reminded her of a succubus, one of Satan's sulphurous sidekicks. A musty aroma enveloped him, like a mushroom cloud of musk. As before in Carrick's subterranean sewers, Abby thought she was going to be sick.

"There's one other thing, dear boy."

"Fire away, Perry old chap."

"The money, may I see it?"

Abby elbowed her companion surreptitiously, while willing him to show some common sense. But reciprocity demanded an "Absolutely."

Five minutes later, Faulkner was rummaging though Abby's holdall, which sat on the sofa where she'd left it. Unaccountably, she felt personally violated by his hand-rubbing lasciviousness. All-action, the supposed superspy held a randomly selected fiver up to the light in Kelley's office, rubbed it repeatedly between finger and thumb, and flicked it roughly, listening attentively to the snap of the paper. He pulled a second packet out of the bag, fifties this time, and went through the same process. A third sample of hundreds was interrogated in a similar fashion. He wafted the notes under his nose, sniffing deeply, akin to a specie sommelier or fetishist.

"I have a magnifying glass somewhere, should you consider it necessary, old chap." The mockery in Dr. Kelley's voice was unmistakable.

"That won't be required," Faulkner retorted abruptly. "The notes are counterfeit. No doubt about it, dear boy."

Chapter Eighteen

The Plaid Piper

Brodie slipped out of the Emperor's Hall of the Kaiserburg, just as the glib goon from Stupidity Associates was waxing lyrical about Advertising Campaign Angioplasty, Display Unit Detox, Product Range Peels, Executive Suite Exfoliation, Competitor Collagen Filler, et cetera. He was clearly working himself up to a clichéd climactic line of "Because You're Worth It" banality. Is he worth the consultancy fees he's commanding, Brodie wondered.

He wandered outside, head up, shoulders back, kilt stirring in the breeze by the battlements. The inner courtyard of the Kaiserburg was ablaze with scarlet Citroën pennants. It was akin to a post-industrial medieval tournament with its jousting knights, attentive squires, strolling players, dulcet minstrels and fabulous fair maidens. A cobbled outer courtyard, the original bailey, was also comprehensively bedecked in the company's red and white chevron logo, with the conference slogan overwritten in black copperplate script. The "one hundred years of helical gears" theme was further reinforced by an impressive display of the motor car maker's complete range of models from 1919 to the present. The Type A, Type B, Type C, DS, Dyane, Bijou, Saxo, AX, BX, ZX, 2CV, 7CV, 10CV, H Van, Traction Avant, Mehari and many more, all stood to shimmering simonized attention in a corporate *concours d'élégance* which swept past Sinwell Tower, through Heaven's Gate, down the steep-sided Hasenburg, to the top of the old town.

The first and most obvious alchemical parallel, Brodie mentally rehearsed as he swaggered along Albrecht Dürer Strasse, kilt sashaying with every carefully rehearsed roll of the hips, is the philosopher's stone, that special magical ingredient that turns base metal into gold. Every management consultant worth his or her salt claims to possess the philosopher's stone of management, the supernatural solution that'll turn organizational lead into stakeholder gold. None of them work, as the alchemists eventually found out. But that didn't stop them trying, nor did it dissuade princes, pontiffs and people with more thalers than sense from funding alchemists' quixotic quests. Alchemy was essentially about transmutation, turning one thing into another, and transforming dysfunctional organizations or products or brands or indeed people is what today's alchemists aspire to.

There was something wrong! As he sauntered along the impeccably kept shopping street, Brodie tingled with a strange sense of apprehension. For some unaccountable reason, he felt he was being followed. The irrational fear that many feel while walking alone in a forest started preying on his mind. He was losing concentration, which was fatal for an exponent of mnemotechnics. Focus, focus, focus…

The second alchemical element is equally familiar. *Prima materia*, the elixir of life. I think it was Father Ted Levitt who said that the purpose of business is to stay in business. In the main, managers are not motivated by making profits as such – profits are a consequence not a cause of exemplary business activity – but by remaining in the game for as long as possible. Failure, remember, is the norm in business life and anything that promises to put off the fateful day is seized upon by grateful managers. Unfortunately, there are many, many charlatans who promise eternal life but their panaceas are useless snake oil, usually harmless, occasionally poisonous. Genuine alchemists called such people "puffers", a term that's still used about marketing types today. Not that I'm suggesting any of our distinguished convention presenters is a postmodern puffer. Perish the thought.

Something's definitely amiss! Professor Brodie was used to being followed. Whenever he swaggered down Princes Street in full highland regalia, he was often followed by little boys and astonished onlookers who couldn't believe their eyes at the one-man tourist attraction perambulating by. The perennial piper at the gates of Princes Street Gardens often struck up with Brodie's magnificently rousing signature tune, "Hail to the Prof." But this was different. This wasn't right.

The third alchemical analogue is inscribed in an aphorism that encapsulates The Great Work, "like begets like". The clustering of shoe retailers in shopping streets; the instant manufacture of me-too imitation products by cut-throat competitors; the regional clusters of complementary organizations in Silicon Valley, Hollywood, Detroit, northern Italy, et al; marketers' insatiable appetite for brand extensions and extensions of brand extensions and extensions of extensions of brand extensions; car makers' fondness for many and varied model ranges, each of which offer innumerable options and specials – and all of which are driving consumers crazy trying to choose from the insane cornucopia of motoring possibilities – are just some among many examples of "like begets like" in business. Even the textbooks that claim to tell students the secrets of marketing success are identikit imitations of Kate Phillips's original. They too are examples of "like begets like". Alchemy is everywhere!

Turning into Agnesgasse, Brodie glanced over his shoulder apprehensively. Nothing. Only the usual crowd of onlookers pointing and laughing at his extravagant outfit. Even in the heart of lederhosen country, the Brodie tartan stopped them in the street. It was the same everywhere he went, though the atmosphere was edgier this time. What is the problem here? Where's the warmth he normally felt? Was it his conference delegate's badge? Citroën standards dangled from every other streetlamp. The intervening poles were hung with supersized portraits of André, as before. Deal with it later. Focus on the forthcoming presentation! Otherwise calamity beckons.

The sixtysomething Scottish symbologist stopped and stared. He was staggered by the sight before him. He rubbed his eyes with disbelief and stared again. It wasn't very often Pitcairn Brodie lost the power of speech, let alone locomotion. Except on the rare occasions when he imbibed too many self-concocted cocktails in The Dome or analogous dens of Edinburgh iniquity. However, the apparition that greeted him in Nuremberg's Rathausplatz not only gave Brodie food for thought, but it proved a veritable heaped plate of sauerkraut, schnitzel and weisswurst, with double helpings of dampfknudeln in custard. A five-metre replica of Transformer, the massive robot used in Citroën's Europe-wide television advertisements for the C4, pranced and cavorted and moon-walked in the restaurant-ringed square, immediately in front of a flag-draped St. Sebaldskirche. The robot was wearing an XXXXXXL André Citroën T-shirt, with the conference theme stencilled on the back. It did handstands and headstands. It juggled with an oversized set of helical gears. It pirouetted daintily with logo-striated streamers in time to rap 'n' rave music. It gyrated around a giant tableau of Citroën Picassos, artfully arranged and overpainted to look like Pablo's *Les Demoiselles d'Avignon*. The professor's face was a picture too.

Brodie was finding it very difficult to concentrate. The fourth contemporary parallel is found in the distinction medieval alchemists made between the practical and the philosophical sides of their art. Alchemy wasn't simply a practical proto-laboratory process involving steaming retorts, noisome alembics and bubbling bains marie. It was a complete philosophical system of psychological self-transformation through a fixed sequence, symbolized by the colours *negrido* (black), *albedo* (white) and *rubado* (red), with personal enlightenment being the ultimate goal. The same is true of Freemasonry, furthermore, where brethren distinguish between operative and speculative sides of the craft. This practitioner/theorist split is equally evident in 21st century marketing, where those who can do and those who can't sit on their obese asses in business schools, thinking great theoretical thoughts that bear no relation whatsoever to everyday marketing reality.

Circling back to the Kaiserburg, as zero hour approached, Brodie took a detour through Hauptmarkt. The entire front of Frauenkirche, the oldest Gothic church in Bavaria and the site of the city's first synagogue, was concealed behind a gigantic, 30-metre Citroën flag, its red, black and white motif discernible from every corner of the city's busiest shopping plaza. The red and white awnings of the crowded market stalls seemed to kneel in supplication before Citroën's superhuman standard.

The theology professor was livid, furious, incandescent. There'd be hell to pay. He'd see to it.

Chapter Nineteen

Rabbit Rage

If it weren't for the smell of freshly-brewed coffee permeating Kelley's office, the gloom would have been intolerable. Stunned and unbelieving, Abby slumped on the capacious settee, clutching a plush cushion to her chest. Kelley wrestled an Ascaso Arc coffee maker, brewing and frothing and hissing to his heart's content, anything to divert attention from the dead animal in the room. The unzipped money bag lay supine on the Louis Vuitton coffee table, its high denomination innards exposed like intestines. Faulkner felt around in the gaping incision, a sterling surgeon searching for disease-free tissue. Every so often, he'd pull out a packet, examine a note at random, and go through his rubbing, flicking, sniffing routine. At one stage, he disappeared off for a few minutes and returned from his office with a jeweller's loupe. He stood beside the picture window, scrutinizing the whorls and watermarks, shaking his head sorrowfully.

"They are all forged, I'm afraid." Faulkner took a seat on the sofa as his host distributed eco-friendly Fair Trade coffee and carbon-neutral chocolate biscuits.

"That's hardly our fault," Kelley protested, suspecting that the parties to the exchange wouldn't see it that way.

The retired operative didn't see it that way either. His best guess was that the UVF would hold the pair of them personally responsible for the counterfeits. Kelley and Abby had inserted themselves into the distribution channel and taken title to the merchandise. They were accidental middlemen. The value chain was around their necks and they were dealing with people who'd think nothing of tightening it.

Naturally, Dr. Kelley saw things differently, arguing that if the UVF were proper businesspeople, as Faulkner claimed, then a polite, carefully-worded telephone call should clear up the confusion.

The spymaster demurred. Why, he asked, would either para-military party want to clear up the confusion? The IRA isn't going to confess to counterfeiting, let alone cheating the UVF, not when it has a couple of patsies to pin it on. Nor is it in the UVF's interest to believe the patsies, because they now owe them £1 million. Even if the UVF knows the money was forged by the IRA, that's not their problem any more. It's the patsies' problem. As far as the UVF's concerned, the patsies are yet another revenue stream, a welcome little windfall.

Confused by the spook's euphemisms and circumlocutions, Kelley cut to the chase. "What are you really saying, Perry? What's the bottom line here?"

"The bottom line, dear boy, is that unless you can come up with one million pounds between you, the UVF will make you pay in another way. And even if you manage to scrape together enough money, they will probably kill you in any event, regardless of the insurance letters you have written and posted to influential figures. I can see the media spin already. 'Lecturer and Student Lover in Counterfeit Cash Conspiracy'. Disinformation is the easiest thing in the world to disseminate, especially if there are media organs you can squeeze. Squeezing organs is a UVF speciality."

Abby bristled at the student lover remark, though not as much as she should have done. Mindful of Faulkner's earlier advice on emotional equipoise, she drily replied, "Lucky the Lottery draw's tonight. I'll be a multi-millionaire by 9.00 p.m. Get me to a lottery ticket machine, Dave, and we're home and dry."

"You have more chance of finding gold at the end of the rainbow, my dear," Faulkner replied with crushing condescension. "Even if you manage to sell the family farm, which is unlikely given the state of the agricultural property market, you will never gather up the money in time. Unless of course your distant relatives in Some Like It Hot help out, and there is not much chance of that, since they refused to assist in the past, at a time when you really needed it. And, as for you dear boy, your family troubles are no secret. Aristocrats do desperate things when they are in dire straights, even to the extent of consorting with counterfeiters and criminals."

Equipoise be damned. Abby couldn't restrain herself. "How do you know about the farm… my family… the shop? What business is it of yours? How did you discover I'm distantly related to the Biggars? I didn't know myself till six weeks ago!"

Professor Faulkner picked up a chocolate biscuit, bit deeply, chewed the crumbly cud and replied in clipped, cynical tones, while masticating noisily. "Do you not listen to the radio, young lady? Or watch breakfast television? You are all over the news. A wrecked sex shop in Carrickfergus. A placement student left in charge while the owners were away. An extreme case of PMT, they say, or possibly her family circumstances. Or possibly Rabbit rage. So many sex toys, so little time. The owners are worried about your wellbeing. They have circulated a photograph, my dear, though it… it… hardly does you justice."

"What else did they say?" Kelley demanded.

"No mention of you, dear boy, if that's what you mean. You are in the clear from what I can gather."

"I've told you before," Kelley insisted angrily, "Abby and I are in this together. I can get hold of a million, if need be. I can sell my property portfolio, though that might take a while. If the worst comes to the worst, I'll do a deal with my brother."

"And your brother will be happy to go along with that, will he?" Faulkner said superciliously. "Has a peace treaty been signed at Castle D'Anger? If so, it must rank right up there with the accord between Ian Paisley and Martin McGuinness."

Kelley took his seat on the sofa and leant right forward, staring intently into the watery eyes of the old man opposite. "Yes, Peregrine, he'll be happy to deal if I waive my interest in D'Anger Castle library. The library was left to me, but because the codicil wasn't clear whether the word library refers to the books alone or includes the room in which they're stored, he's been unable to redevelop D'Anger without my say-so. So I'm sure we can thrash out some kind of mutually satisfactory arrangement."

"You… you… you… don't have to do this, Dave," Abby spluttered, her syntax disintegrating with appreciation. She knew how much the library, the castle, the estate meant to him.

"I do, Abby, I do have to do this. You're my Sexy Student Lover in the Counterfeit Cash Conspiracy, aren't you?"

"In your dreams, darling," Abby replied with a smile.

Emeritus Professor Peregrine Faulkner stood up and brushed some crumbs from his malodorous off-white shirt. "I shall leave you two to it, dear boy. Good luck. If you need anything else, don't hesitate to call."

"But you never use the phone, old chap, much less answer it."

"Quite, quite." Faulkner oozed his way to the door, only to coagulate and squirm back, rubbing his hands unctuously. "One last thing, dear boy. Was there anything else in the kitbag besides cash? No note or token of any kind? Terrorist organizations have strict codes of conduct, in my experience. Exchanges between criminal fraternities usually include token gifts, the same as they do in many other businesses. Sweeteners, kickbacks, bottles of Scotch, soccer tickets to sports events, severed heads, little fingers, an eyeball or two. Nothing like that? It might help if there were."

Kelley shook his head slowly. "Sorry, old..."

"Actually," Abby interrupted, "there *was* something else." Ignoring her lecturer's admonitory look, she reached into her borrowed Hermès handbag and, after scuffling around for ages, pulled out a battered leather case. "It's a dagger. A bayonet. German. Nazi. Second World War. It's similar to one we have in the shop, only real."

Faulkner looked bemused. "In the shop, my dear? Only real?"

"The costume department. Adolf and Eva, Goebbels and Gilda, Hermann and Hitler Youth if you're that way inclined. We do a Nazi theme night every 9th of November. It's very popular with golf club committee members."

"May I?"

Abby handed him the scuffed slip case. Faulkner removed the weapon carefully, scrutinizing the insignia with an expert eye, easing the blade out of the scabbard and sliding it back with a metallic hiss. "Nothing special, my dear. The S84/98 bayonet was standard Wehrmacht issue. It's in reasonable condition but there are thousands of them in circulation." He turned the worthless object over a couple of times. "SS ceremonial daggers, the *Dienstdolch*, are much more valuable, especially the 1933 Holbein-style pattern with silver sig runes, decorated scabbard mount, regulation portepee knot and swastika-surmounted eagle on the grip. They were presented at a special ceremony, often by Himmler himself." Faulkner handed the bayonet back to her with an oily smile. "You might want to hold on to it though. For personal protection."

"Right," Abby replied caustically. "Thanks for that."

"Unless."

"Sorry?"

"Let me look at it again. Standard army equipment is often personalized, as you might expect. Not only with name tags, but individualized markings." Faulkner inserted his loupe with a flourish and held the bayonet close to his face. He examined the scabbard carefully, then the blade, then the boss. He whistled. "Good Lord. This is incredible, my dear. Amazing."

"What? What?"

"This is Otto Skorzeny's rune. I'd recognize it anywhere. Old Scarface himself. My word. My goodness."

Abby was at a loss. "Scarface? Skorzeny? The French politician?"

"Colonel Otto Skorzeny," Faulkner said with a look of disdain, appalled by the confusion with Sarkozy and taken aback by the ignorance of the younger generation, "was the greatest German hero of the Second World War. The commando's commando, he was Adolf Hitler's bodyguard. He rescued Benito Mussolini from captivity. He took Budapest almost single-handed. He led the charge at the Battle of the Bulge. He was awarded the Knight's Cross with Oak Leaves, Germany's highest military honour. He received a Totenkopfring from Himmler, imbued with the blackest of black magic, some say. He organized the SS Wolfpack division at the end of the war and is believed to have been the brains behind *Die Spinne*, the Spider, the organization that helped former SS officers escape to South America."

Caught up in the boy's own escapades, Machine Gun Kelley added his two-pennyworth. "A bit like *The Odessa File*, old man?"

"Very similar. Very similar, dear boy. Colonel Skorzeny was a great self-publicist, so some of the stories were exaggerated in the retelling. But he did make a post-war fortune in the import-export trade, in various real estate dealings and in other business interests."

"A marketing man?" Kelley exclaimed. "I should've guessed it!"

"Scarface was quite a character," Faulkner continued. "Huge man. Incredible warrior. Commanded total loyalty. That could be a very valuable bayonet indeed, young lady. You might just have another bargaining chip."

Abby slipped the protective case back into her commodious handbag. "There's something about the story that I don't understand, Professor Faulkner. You say the bayonet is standard Wehrmacht issue. Yet you also told us that Skorzeny was an SS officer. Surely he'd carry the SS dagger you mentioned, the Dienstdolch or whatever it was."

"Yes, exactly. Well spotted, my dear. That's the really fascinating thing. Why on earth would an SS officer – the quintessential SS officer – inscribe a common or garden Wehrmacht bayonet? Perhaps it is a fake too, just like the counterfeit money. If you get a chance, young lady, take it to a military memorabilia dealer. It could be worth an awful lot of money."

"A million pounds, say?"

"Possibly. Possibly. Depends on the state of the collectables market. Let me see it again for a sec."

Chapter Twenty

Cool Hand Dev

Abby studied Faulkner as he studied the Skorzeny bayonet, turning it round and round, sheathing and unsheathing the gleaming weapon, listening to the blade slide in and out with a delicious hiss, and rubbing his thumb over the iconic commando's spider-shaped rune on the time-worn boss. She'd seen that look before. On many occasions. Her abusive uncle had it. Her predatory priest had it. Her first boyfriend had it. The grubby middle-aged men in plastic macs who mooched around Some Like It Hot on Wednesday afternoons, claiming that they were "just looking" or buying surprise gifts for their partners, even though their wives left them long ago and their girlfriends were either imaginary or inflatable, had it too. It was a look of untrammelled desire, carnality, lust. Desperation almost. "For an Irish intelligence officer," she said, "you seem very well informed about Skorzeny and the Nazis and the like. My grandfather told me that Ireland was strictly neutral during the Second World War, just like Switzerland and Sweden. President de Valera wanted nothing to do with the warmongers and he kept the country out of it."

"Hardly," Dave Kelley snorted in derision. "My family fought in the Second World War and the Great War and the Boer War and the Crimean War and with Wellington at Waterloo and with Marlborough at Blenheim and with William at the Boyne and against Harold at Hastings. Take it from me, Abby, southern Ireland was *not* strictly neutral between 1939 and 1945. Far from being even-handed, de Valera and his cronies did everything in their power to help Hitler. The lights of Dublin, Drogheda and Dundalk were kept on to guide the Luftwaffe's night bombers. U-boats were refuelled and provisioned off the west coast. De Valera denied Britain access to its former deep water naval bases in Cork and Donegal, which meant that countless Allied lives, including several belonging to the D'Anger family, were needlessly lost on the North Atlantic convoys because of his so-called policy of neutrality. The Irish army even wore German coal-scuttle helmets, for God's sake!"

This was obviously a sensitive subject, steeped in family history. Abby thought he was going to stand to attention when he mentioned the Duke of Wellington, or snap a salute at least. Family history must mean an awful lot to him. Disinheritance must have been devastating. "The whole of the Irish Republic was a nest of Nazi spies," he ranted, "many of whom slipped across the border to report on the north's munitions factories, materiel production, defence emplacements, troop movements and the convoys that assembled in Belfast Lough before heading out into the North Atlantic. Not only were the Irish not neutral, Abby, but de Valera actually visited the German Embassy in April 1945 to offer the Irish government's official condolences on the death of Adolf Hitler. This was *after* the world became aware of the extermination camps, the Holocaust. De Valera claimed the reports of the death camps were exaggerated Allied propaganda..."

"Calm down, Dave," Abby said, when she finally managed to slip a word in edgeways. "Okay, so my grandfather got it wrong about de Valera. What does it matter? It's ancient history."

The oleaginous operative coughed, coughed in a way that spoke volumes, in a way that said, "Actually, dear boy, you are mistaken." Abby never realized a cough could be so expressive, though she'd never met an intelligence officer before, much less read John Le Carré.

"It is not ancient history, my dear young lady. It is wrong-headed history." Sportingly, he patted Kelley on the knee, affecting affection. "I know you come from a long line of Ulster servicemen, David. But do not let family loyalty or outmoded ideals of noble sacrifice or Protestant Ascendancy myth-making blind you to what really went on during the Second World War. I was there, young man. I did my bit. And I can tell you for a fact that the Republic of Ireland was *not* in cahoots with Hitler. De Valera was in an impossible position. His nascent nation state had only been independent for a couple of decades. Many citizens still considered themselves British or remained sympathetic to the Empire. Many of his former IRA henchmen thought he had betrayed the cause of Irish nationalism by accepting partition. Winston Churchill was demanding access to Irish naval bases to help secure the North Atlantic trade routes. And the Nazis had plans to invade Ireland if de Valera acceded to Churchill's demands. You must appreciate that Ireland was very, very important strategically, especially after the fall of France and the capture of Norway. If the Germans had occupied Ireland, which was virtually undefended, they would have encircled Britain, effectively closing the door on the North Atlantic convoy routes which Britain depended on and could not have survived without, regardless of the bravery of the Fighting Few in their Spitfires or the Dad's Army legionnaires who intended to fight the stormtroopers on the beaches."

Faulkner paused for a reaction, but got none from his spellbound listeners. "Ironically," he continued, "the act that gave Germany a legitimate excuse to invade southern Ireland was an act of charity toward the people of the North. When Belfast was blitzed in April 1941, de Valera permitted Irish firemen to travel north in order to assist their over-stretched Ulster brethren. Dublin was bombed by the Luftwaffe a few days later, as a rap over the knuckles for breaking neutrality and helping the enemy. To his credit, de Valera ignored the threat. However, if it hadn't been for Hitler's invasion of Russia in June 1941, when he took his eye off the western front, the invasion of Ireland would almost certainly have gone ahead. Operation Green it was called."

Shell-shocked, Kelley drained his Fair Trade coffee and set the mug down with a sigh. "It was never put to me like that." He made a face of resignation, possibly regret. "My family...," he said, then stopped, the disjunction between D'Anger myth and de Valera reality too much for him.

"It was far, far worse than you can ever imagine, young man. In 1940 and 1941, when Britain stood alone before America entered the war, no one gave your country a hope in hell. The losses in the North Atlantic were horrendous. Britain's armed forces were ill-prepared and poorly equipped, no match whatsoever for the might of the Wehrmacht."

"Plucky Brit, Tim Henman, two sets down to Roger Federer at Wimbledon, going into a tie-break in the third," Kelley quipped bitterly. "What ho."

"Correction, facing match point at 5–0 in the third, with Federer to serve," the sometime spook added. "It was as bad as that. People did desperate things."

"Such as allowing German spies free run of the land of not so saintly scholars."

Faulkner returned the Skorzeny bayonet to Abby, then went on. "David, you must realize that the situation looked very different in the early days of the war. Adolf Hitler was not regarded as the demented lunatic he is deemed to be today. On the contrary, he was a very canny operator and he surrounded himself with very canny operators. In November 1940, he offered de Valera a huge cache of weapons, weapons the British army abandoned at Dunkirk. This offer, which came from the Führer himself, must have been very, very tempting. The Irish armed forces were desperately short of equipment and de Valera feared an imminent British invasion – yes, a *British* invasion, based on detailed plans drawn up by General Bernard Montgomery."

"But de Valera said no?" Abby asked, fascinated despite herself by the hidden history lesson.

"Dev knew a poisoned chalice when he saw one. He knew that there was no such thing as a free gift. He knew that it would be impossible to ship secret consignments of arms into Ireland without the British finding out. Churchill would have had the perfect excuse for full-scale invasion, an excuse he was looking for because he desperately needed the naval bases. Except… except… except."

"Except what?"

The old operative smiled slyly at her. "Except that a British invasion of Ireland would have outraged Irish-American opinion, and Churchill's attempts to persuade the United States to join the fight against Hitler would have been dead in the water, which was exactly what the Nazis wanted."

"Hmmmm. You've got to hand it to him," Kelley acknowledged with a note of grudging admiration. "De Valera was a very astute tactician."

"He was," the spymaster agreed. "He was a mathematician. He knew how to calculate the odds, how to play his hand at diplomatic poker. The stakes could not have been higher, dear boy, and given the extremely poor hand Dev was dealt, his poker-faced performance was impeccable. Not a single wrong move or slip-up. If he had gone into business, he would have made a fortune and been right up there with Ireland's greatest entrepreneurs."

Intrigued by his reasoning, which was unlike anything she covered in class, Abby asked the all-important, bottom-line question: "Where did you fit into all this, Professor Faulkner? What does Skorzeny's bayonet have to do with it?"

"Ah," he smiled unctuously. "During the war, I was a low-level operative, keeping tabs on the Nazi spies that young David here imagines were running amok in our green and pleasant land. Most of them were amateurs, who were picked up within hours of arrival. Only one evaded capture for a long time, Hermann Goertz, and he turned out to be an embarrassment to the German delegation. He let the secret plans to invade Ulster, a Nazi alternative to Operation Green called Operation Kathleen, fall into our hands in 1940. We passed them on to MI5, in an attempt to keep Churchill off our backs. Actually, the Germans only had one competent Irish spymaster, a man called Adolf Mahr. He was an eminent archaeologist and the director of Ireland's National Museum before the war. He was an expert in Celtic art and ancient monuments, and a personal friend of Dev's. His archaeological background enabled him to travel all over the country without arousing suspicion and he helped gather the information that found its way into Operation Green and Operation Kathleen. But, as chance would have it, he was reporting back to his bosses in Nuremberg when the war broke out in September 1939 and he couldn't return to Ireland. So you see, children, the so-called Nazi spies were amateurs by and large."

"Skorzeny wasn't an amateur, though," Kelley chipped in. "Not according to what you said about his wartime record."

Faulkner excreted a diarrhoeic chuckle. "Skorzeny was a superhero, dear boy. Many believed he was a powerful black magician. He retired to Ireland, you know."

"What?" Abby and Kelley gasped simultaneously.

"Oh yes. He lived here after the war. Owned an ex-Ascendancy mansion in County Kildare. Ran his import-export operation from there."

Stunned, Kelley found it difficult to speak. "Import-export, as in helping Nazi war criminals escape?"

"My dear boy," Faulkner said smarmily, "I have already told you too many state secrets this morning. I cannot possibly tell you any more. It is more than my life is... well, suffice it to say that a lot of former Nazis settled in Ireland after the war – Menten, Mengele, Mahr and many more."

"So, my family haven't got their facts completely wrong. Despite the post-war apologists, Dev must have been basically pro-Hitler, otherwise he wouldn't have harboured Nazi war criminals."

The former spook stood up, straightened himself, and prepared to depart. "As your beautiful companion pointed out earlier, it was all a very long time ago."

A few moments later, back in his dimly lit office by the boiler room, Professor Peregrine Faulkner picked up the phone. "Hello... Miss Day... May I speak with Dr. Kane? Not there... Meeting a client... Ah, I see. Well, could you ask him to contact the Business School's... how can I put this... principal benefactor? I have come across something of enormous interest."

Chapter Twenty-One

The Bitch is Back

The departure of Peregrine Faulkner should have cleared the air in Kelley's office. Instead, it brought on a bout of bickering. The good doctor passed comment on his student's failure to mention the bayonet. The feisty student replied that it was none of his business. She hadn't asked for his help in the first place. She could take care of herself. She didn't need his collateral. She couldn't allow him to risk his birthright or family name or professional reputation. He owed her nothing. He didn't have to stick by her.

The good doctor, momentarily abandoning the cavalcade of postmodern personas that he adopted and adapted at will – gay icon, landed gentry, goofy good guy, goth but not forgotten – persuasively explained that he had to see things through. If only for himself. He'd failed in his pastoral duties once before, a couple of years previously. A placement student was being bullied. He hadn't spotted the problem. He was preoccupied with his divorce/disinheritance debacle at the time. The placement student had a serious psychotic episode that he'd prefer not to talk about. He should have recognized the warning signs. The university inquiry exonerated him. But he still felt responsible. This was his chance to make amends.

An opportunity to put things right.

If this was another persona, it was Kelley's best performance yet. Because Abby, who'd learnt the hard way that men making true confessions were either searching for a mother surrogate or angling for a shag, believed him. A mawkish scene was avoided, however, when the good doctor's boyish optimism returned and he threatened to deduct further marks from her assignment. When that failed to raise a smile, he threatened to play one of his former band's CDs. Not the good one, the rock opera one. Abby said that she'd be forced to stab him with the Skorzeny bayonet. She'd plead self defence. No court in the land would convict, especially if the CDs were entered as evidence and played in the well of the court.

He laughed out loud, snorting and guffawing as was his wont. His cheeky smile lit up the room. Dave wasn't the best lecturer in the world, Abby recalled. He was too easily distracted by questions from the floor, questions he responded to like a hound chasing a hare, blissfully unaware that his students were taking the mickey. But his enthusiasm more than made up for the shambolic delivery. His camp act had everyone in stitches and, largely because of his foibles rather than despite them, Dave the Rave Kelley, a.k.a. DeeDee Kelley, a.k.a. Daffy Dave, a.k.a. numerous other terms of undergraduate endearment, was much loved by the student body. Even the jocks, and the macho men, and the coffee bar anti-capitalists, and the too-smart-to-study poseurs made a point of attending his classes and seminars. Unlike many other academics, moreover, he always had time for everyone, whether he was their adviser of studies or not. Nobody was made to feel like a number or an imposition or a mere contribution to the university's coffers, a top-up fee in jeans and T-shirt.

"The thing is, Abby, you just don't understand men in general and what rock music means to guys like me in particular."

Abby wasn't sure if he said guys or gays. "Yeah, you promised to explain the mysteries of the male psyche to me. I can't wait to be enlightened. If it has something to do with Mars versus Venus or subliminal messages on Led Zeppelin albums, I'll stick this dagger up your derriere, David."

"Promises, promises," he replied, adopting the iconic teapot pose of camp comedy, one arm bent on the hip like a handle, the other imitating a limp-wristed spout. "I'll tell all about manliness later, darling. You've got a letter to write and I've got to ring my esteemed brother." Noting her you-really-don't-have-to look, Kelley continued breezily, "He's well connected in the memorabilia business, since he's been selling off what isn't tied down at Castle D'Anger. If anyone can put us in touch with a Nazi art expert, it's Robert."

Playfully, Abby threw a packet of counterfeit fivers at him. He was reaching for the phone at the time. It started ringing just as he touched the handset. The wad of fivers hit him full in the face and landed on his antique satinwood desk with a splat, though Kelley hardly seemed to notice. "Who on earth could that be?" he asked anxiously, withdrawing his hand from the suspect device. "Unless Perry's breaking the habit of a lifetime..."

Abby urged caution. "Maybe you shouldn't answer it, Dave. Seriously. Let's find a safer spot somewhere. They might have tracked us down."

Undeterred, he picked up. His face fell. Then fell further. Then further still. "You *can not* be serious." An infuriated look crossed his ordinarily sunny features. "If this is a joke, it's not very funny." Dark thunderclouds gathered around his forehead. "No, I didn't check my email this morning. It's Saturday." The jawline set hard, brows beetled ominously. "You might have told me about this. Is a heads-up out of the question?" He slammed the phone down. "Bitch." He punched his desktop computer into life. "Fucking bitch." Clicking his mouse venomously, the miffed academic squinted over the flat-screen at his phlegmatic companion. "Pardon my French."

"Your ex-?" Abby asked.

"Worse."

"Worse than a serial killer who married you, left you and cost you your inheritance?"

"Yes, that's true," he grunted. "But at least my ex- was a babe. Emer's just a bitch."

"Emer?"

With an uncharacteristic frown that teetered on the brink of a scowl, Abby's tutor sat back and adopted his most professional manner, arms firmly folded, lips tightly pursed. "Professor Emer Aherne, the Irish marketing superstar, who's written numerous books, hob-nobs with gurus like Kate Phillips and jets around the world at the University of Hustler's expense..."

"What's a superstar doing ringing you, Dave?" She meant it as a joke, but the jibe shot straight over his attractively tousled head.

"... wants me to present her paper this afternoon," he said. "She's too busy to fly back from the States. Too busy to attend the conference that she bloody well organized. She expects *me* to present *her* paper. At two hours' notice! She emailed it to me yesterday afternoon, apparently, forgetting that Ireland is six hours ahead of Chicago." Infuriated, Kelley kicked his raffia waste paper basket in frustration, scattering memos, post-it notes and circulars from textbook publishers across the pale grey carpet. The spillage only made him angrier.

"Why didn't you tell her to piss off?"

Judging by the cut of his jib, Abby's irreverent remark had struck home. He must have considered those very words on countless occasions. Eventually, he composed himself and smiled sadly. "Ah, the innocence of youth. Professor Aherne supervised my PhD. I graduated last year."

Bewildered by the mores of academe, Abby wouldn't let go. "Well, if you've got the qualification, Dr. Kelley, surely you're out of her clutches."

"Ah, the innocence of youth," he reiterated. "I'm even more obliged to her than before, because she controls my professional destiny. If I apply for promotion, she will be asked her opinion of me. If I try for a lectureship elsewhere, her job reference will determine my fate. If I write academic articles that'll help me get promotion or a post someplace else, her name will be attached to them and she'll take much of the credit, even though I've done all the work."

"Sounds like you're an indentured servant, Dave, a scholarly serf or somesuch."

"That's pretty much it, Abby."

Despite her seminars in touchy-feely customer care, Abby couldn't resist a told-you-so remark. "Well, now you know how the peasants on the D'Anger demesne felt, and how Irish tenant farmers were forced to live, and how women were subordinated…"

"My ex- wouldn't disagree, Abby. But at least I've seen the back of her. Professor Aherne's got me in an academic arm lock and I can't refuse her request. Her order. She's the Director of Hustler Business School, for heaven's sake."

"I'm coming with you."

"Sorry?"

"To the conference. I'll be your glamorous assistant."

"It's not that kind of event."

"It's mainly men, though?"

"Mainly."

"I'll distract them."

"I've no doubt you would, Abby. But…"

"But what?"

"It's being held in a monastery, a retreat, a Redemptorist retreat house in the hills above Belfast. It's very spiritual. It's pretty remote. It's almost otherworldly. It's not the place for glamorous assistants. Aherne holds a conference there every couple of years, it's the antithesis of the usual five star venues with hot and cold running room service and pay-per-view porn channels. Not that I… um… would ever… erm… watch… um. It's an anti-conference, I suppose, a form of scholarly flagellation, basically."

"Jeepers, Dave, if you'd told me, I've have brought an S&M selection from the shop. We're running a buy-two-cilices-get-a-flail-free promotion."

"Damn, I missed that," he laughed. "Do you take plastic?"

"Plastic. Leather. Steel. Rubber. Acrylic. Ebony. Feathers. You name it, we take it, we make it, we make out with it."

"I'm okay for feathers, thanks all the same." He nodded towards a free-standing elk-antler coat rack, which was draped with the signature feather boa he wore during lectures and seminars. "I have my own plumage, as you can see. But tell me, madam, is the leather real or fake?"

"Fake, of course."

"So, you'll take counterfeit cash for it?"

"That'll do nicely, Master D'Anger."

"St. Stephen's, here we come."

Kelley's student pulled up sharp, barely controlling a gasp. "Did you say St. Stephen's? St. Stephen's Retreat House?"

"Yep, it's up in the hills above Belfast. Off the Antrim Road. Between the Zoo and the Castle. Do you know it?"

"Sort of," Abby replied, as painful memories flooded back, unbidden.

"Let's go, darling," he said, with a decisive clap of the hands. "We should be safe enough there."

Chapter Twenty-Two

Nothing Succeeds Like Excess

Dave's optimism didn't last. The task that had been dumped on him would have daunted most people, but being dumped on at a time of considerable duress was beyond daunting, somewhere between bullying and blackmail. Despite his natural tendency to think well of people – as his students intuitively recognized – Dave spent much of the journey to Belfast mumbling maledictions against his high-profile mentor, Professor Emer Aherne. Abby had never heard of her, though the semi-autonomous character of Hustler University campuses meant that she knew little of life at the other three sites.

Aherne, apparently, was one of the world's foremost marketing gurus, in her own mind at least. She swanned around international conferences, flew first class here, there and everywhere, conducted an occasional seminar – sorry, masterclass – on Hustler's high-fee executive programme, published unreadable article after unreadable article in unintelligible academic journals, served on copious back-scratching committees of the great and good, and surrounded herself with doctoral students, who did the intellectual heavy lifting while she took most of the credit.

Aherne, Dave explained, had made her name arguing that marketing was an art rather than a science. Previous generations of academics claimed that marketing was either a hard science or capable of becoming a science in the tradition of economics, psychology, physics and chemistry. They went to extraordinary lengths to develop complex theories, equations, formulae and axioms that explained and predicted marketplace behaviour.

Emer Aherne, by contrast, said marketers could learn much more from successful self-promoting, marketing-savvy artists like Salvador Dali, Charles Dickens, Damien Hirst and 50 Cent than by conducting daft laboratory experiments on reluctant undergraduate students, let alone developing grandiose theories of everything. Marketing was not a science, she insisted, and never would be. Marketers should look to the arts and humanities for inspiration rather than the hard sciences.

"And they took her word for it?" Abby asked innocently. She came from an argumentative family and found it hard to believe that an academic discipline could be so accommodating to contrarian views. Aherne was basically arguing the opposite, just for the sake of it. Her petulant kid sister did that all the time. Ignoring her usually solved the problem.

Dave's gloom lifted momentarily. "God no! Quite the reverse. She became notorious. The great she-devil. It was fantastic publicity for her, made her a superstar."

Abby understood immediately. "Ah, so it was the Madonna thing that you talked about in class. Stir up controversy, get people talking, sell the concert tickets."

"That's exactly what it was, though I think Aherne stumbled on the method by accident. Most academics don't market themselves the way artists or rock stars do. It's not the done thing. Academics make their name through published research on the tiny area of marketing science they specialize in. Madonna-style self promotion is completely contrary to the prevailing scholarly spirit."

"But if you don't subscribe to the prevailing scholarly spirit … the scientific spirit?" Abby interjected.

"Exactly. Aherne could justify her behaviour because she rejected the existing scientific ethos. And she exploited her situation to the full, becoming more and more notorious along the way. She maintains that she's an artiste – with a capital A – and that her work should be judged by artistic criteria. Everyone hates her, but you have to give the queen bitch credit. She blew the science, science and more science model out of the water. She marketed herself brilliantly."

Smirking, Abby couldn't help but see the funny side. "So, what you're saying, Dave, is that most egg-headed, big-brained, super-intelligent marketing academics don't know how to market themselves."

He reached across the gearstick and touched her forearm for emphasis. "Yes, it's amazing, darling. None of them has a clue. Academic conferences are so bland you wouldn't believe it. No élan at all, darling. You'll be bored to tears this afternoon."

Boredom didn't sound so bad after what Abby had been through during the past eighteen hours. Tedium she could live with. Or live longer with, all being well.

"Anyway," Kelley continued, warming to his hated theme. "Aherne wrote her big book, the book that sealed her reputation, the book you'll remember from my class because it was on the reading list."

"Oh yes, of course," Abby bluffed. "I remember it well. The title escapes me just now, unfortunately."

Kelley threw her a sceptical look, though his eyes were twinkling. "*Nothing Succeeds Like Excess*, it was called. Basically, she showed how the giants of Irish literature were OTT marketers at heart."

"The giants of Irish literature? You mean like Cecelia Ahern?"

"Hardly," he laughed.

"Marian Keyes?"

"Purlease…"

"Not Maeve Binchy, surely?"

"Hmmmmm," he hesitated. The Dave the Rave that she knew and admired was emerging from the Emer Aherne-instigated gloom. "Let me think… eeerrrr… nope!"

Abby played along. "Ah, I get it. It's a man thing, right? Patriarchy prevails. The *male* giants of Irish literature. It's gotta be Colin Bateman."

"Jesus."

"Jack Higgins?"

"I said literature, not tosh."

"Not Dan Brown, then?"

Kelley screwed up his face with confusion and distaste comingled. "Dan Brown? The *Da Vinci Code* guy? He's not Irish, he's American."

"Oh, I thought he was Irish. Only an Irishman could hate the Catholic Church that much."

Kelley mused. "He might be Irish-American, come to think of it. *Angels and Demons* was so misogynistic that there must be some Guinness swilling around in his gene pool."

Wrestling with the thought of Danny Boy Brown setting about the Roman Catholic hierarchy with a knobbly shillelagh, Abby heard her tummy rumble ominously. It wasn't used to salads for lunch or indeed anything with less than several hundred calories of nutritious sucrose, alimental aspartame and good bacteria cheeseburgers. "Got it!" she cried. "Roddy Doyle... *The Van*. Fish 'n' chips... That's marketing, isn't it?"

"After a fashion, darling."

"He wrote *The Commitments* as well, didn't he?"

"Yeeeesssss," Dave replied apprehensively. His social interaction alarm bells were ringing. Oh oh. Oh oh. Don't go there, they chimed. He knew where his passenger was heading with this. The next question would be about his rock star experiences, something he'd really rather not discuss.

But he was too late. "Tell me about your time as a rock star, Dr. Kelley."

Hoist by his own leotard, Dave decided that he was running out of petrol and promptly pulled in at one of the many service stations on the main road between Coleraine and Belfast. He topped up the Morris Minor with a token amount, bought some sweeties from the confectionery counter and, assuring Abby that her blood sugar level was probably quite low on account of the recent stress and strain, managed to keep the conversation away from his long-abandoned rock star lifestyle. "As the title of *Nothing Succeeds Like Excess* suggests, the Irish literary giants Aherne outed as marketers were Oscar Wilde, George Bernard Shaw, Samuel Beckett, James Joyce and W. B. Yeats."

Abby struggled to resist the Fry's Chocolate Cream. It was calling out to her, whispering sweet sugar-rush nothings, as her tummy rumbled its assent. "But surely," she said, ignoring the beloved bar's beguiling blandishments, "Yeats was the most anti-marketing, anti-commerce, art-for-art's-sake aesthete that Ireland's ever produced."

Kelley looked over at her, wanting to speak but prevented by a mouthful of Mars bar. "He was," he said, after a bout of he-man munching. "He was indeed. How do you know that? So you *did* skim the books on my reading list, after all. Miracles will never cease."

Abby shrugged. "Erm. Not quite, Dave. My dad was a bit of a poet. He preferred writing poetry to tending the farm. He had a thing about Yeats. 'Sailing to Byzantium', 'Under Ben Bulben', 'The Wild Swans at Coole', 'Easter 1916'. I got the distinct impression that Yeats hated the trading classes. Didn't he call them greasy till fumblers and suchlike?"

Kelly nodded. "Yes, he did. But Aherne showed that he was actually a very canny marketer who understood that anti-marketing sells well, especially among artistic types. You know the anti-capitalist entrepreneurs we have these days, those who pretend that they're cool, that they're hippies at heart, that they believe in peace, love and understanding, the ones who sell an anti-commercial message?"

"What, like Richard Branson, Anita Roddick, Ben and Jerry, those guys from Innocent Drinks?"

"Exactly. Well, W. B. Yeats was the Victorian equivalent of Richard Branson or Anita Roddick, except it was poetry and artworks he was selling. He was brilliant at it too, a self-marketing genius. To this day, most people think of him as an elitist who ignored marketing considerations. Whereas the complete opposite's true." Kelley sighed loudly. "Well, that's what I'll be arguing in two hours' time. I'll be slaughtered. Ripped limb from limb."

Baffled, Abby asked, "But why? If it's true, what do you have to worry about?"

Kelley's shoulders sagged noticeably, despite the surging sugar rush. "Because many people at the conference will be proper Yeatsian scholars, scholars from the humanities, non-business school types. They're intrigued by the poem."

"Poem? What poem?"

Teeth gritted, Kelley machine-gunned out the sentences. "During her researches for *Nothing Succeeds Like Excess*, Aherne discovered an unpublished poem by W. B. Yeats. She uncovered it at St. Stephen's Retreat several years back. Apparently St. Stephen's sits on the old route to the top of Cave Hill, overlooking Belfast. In 1899, W. B. Yeats and Maud Gonne, the light of his life and the inspiration for his peerless love poems, made a pilgrimage to Belfast, with a view to celebrating the rising of the United Irishmen one hundred years earlier. The uprising commenced at the top of Cave Hill. Yeats and Gonne climbed up the hill and spent some time together at St. Stephen's. Yeats wrote a poem there and gave it to the Redemptorist priest as a parting gift. At one of her conferences, Aherne presented a paper on Yeats. The current priest gave her the unpublished poem. Or she wangled it from him in some way. She can be quite a charmer when she wants to be. The poem itself was nothing special, though any unpublished poem by such an important artist is noteworthy. It was the subject matter of his confessional ballad that really caused a storm. The poem was about marketing. Yeats basically admitted that he was a marketer first, last and always. This caused ructions in the artworld, as you can imagine. Many thought the poem was a fake. Controversy has been raging about it ever since, much to Aherne's delight."

"Ah, I see."

"Hence today's conference," Kelley added morosely. "Hence the Yeatsians who'll be there, sharpening their knives. Hence the presentation I'm being forced to make, because that conceited cow is too cowardly to face them."

Abby didn't know what to say or how best to comfort him. Even if she did, she didn't get a chance to deliver her assistance. As the wheezing saloon topped a blind hill, their progress was rudely interrupted. A long queue of cars snaked between two striking lines of roadside Scots Pines, known locally as The Frosses.

"Road block. Up ahead. It's the bloody police. Damn and blast!"

Chapter Twenty-Three

Anarchy in the Kaiserburg

It had all been going so well. Brodie had fired his usual fusillade of warm-up jokes. Not see-you-Jimmy jokes, since there were limits to his exploitation of the hackneyed Scottish stereotype. Jokes that only sales and marketing managers appreciate. Jokes about the 4Ps and the four alchemical elements of earth, air, fire and water (most new products are landfill in waiting, advertising equals hot air, price cutting spreads like wildfire, distributors dilute profits, etc.). Jokes about the four humours and top management types (with uproarious reference to executives in the audience). Jokes about alchemists' interest in numerology and their reputation as charlatans. Just like accountants. Jokes about the great ninth century Arabian alchemist, Jabir, whose name is still recalled today in the word "gibberish". Not that Citroën's CEO talks any of that...

He then explained, with a carefully rehearsed look of sorrow and fist pressed regretfully against the forehead, that alchemy is often portrayed as a half-baked precursor to "proper" chemistry. Alchemists made many genuine discoveries – phosphorus, porcelain, antimony, oxygen, the circulation of the blood – and developed laboratory techniques that were improved during the Scientific Revolution of the eighteenth century and perfected thereafter. "This view is completely wrong!" Brodie roared, thereby electrifying the audience and amusing them at the same time, because the lie-detector apparatus made its first great leap at this point. No one twigged that it was operated by a hand-held pressure pad, which Brodie pumped for punctuation at crucial points in his presentation. Or whenever he felt like it. What the hell.

"Alchemy was *not* an early form of proto-science," Professor Brodie pontificated, "though some great scientists practised it assiduously, Newton, Boyle and Leibniz among them." By this stage, you could hear a proverbial pin drip, because the lie detector "proved" he was telling the truth. The audience was totally engrossed, exactly where the redoubtable rhetorician wanted them. "Alchemy was an art form," the Scottish sexagenarian enthused. "Alchemy *is* an art form! Alchemy is closer to music, painting, poetry or sculpture than it is to science. Exactly akin to marketing, branding, advertising, PR or sales pitches" – he ostentatiously paused at this point, subliminally encouraging every salesperson in the audience to make the connection between spellbinding oratory and spellbinding selling – "alchemy is a form of dance."

With a sudden yelp that echoed around the auditorium, Professor Brodie assumed the first position of the famous Scottish sword dance. He jigged and whirled and whooped and swirled so high that his kilt rose alarmingly, prompting the more demure onlookers to cover their eyes while peeping pruriently through their fingers. As for the rest, the vast majority shouted and stomped and clapped in time. They had never seen the like of it, not even from Tom Peters. A few brave souls actually joined in, jiving enthusiastically and jitterbugging inexpertly in the Emperor's Hall aisles.

The great symbologist had the audience in the calloused palm of his mighty Highland hand. The presentation was pretty much on cruise control from here on in, provided he didn't stumble over the bespoke element he'd rehearsed so conscientiously the night before. He could see the sinking faces of the speakers in the next session – a diamante-draped dominatrix hawking "burlesque" brands, a ponytail from a creative hotshop pushing "experiential" approaches and a fatigues-wearing buzzcut who loved the smell of fresh spam in the morning – as the realization dawned that there was absolutely no way they could follow the master. They were admitting defeat prior to taking their place on the podium and powering up their pathetic PowerPoint presentations. They might as well quit while they were ahead and hail a taxi to the airport. Brodie felt sorry for them (he did, he truly did), but he also knew that the conference circuit was Darwinian, where only the fittest speakers survive.

As the alpha orator stared out at the serried mass of Citroën salespersons, all rapt, all leaning forward, all with that curious transfixed expression he'd seen so many times before, the Scottish theologian was disgusted. Disgusted at the sight of them; disgusted by their flag-waving and back-slapping and all-round exultation; disgusted by the smug, self-satisfied, self-congratulatory occasion, which a lackey was video-recording for corporate posterity and keepsake DVDs.

But most of all, he was disgusted with himself. He detested the way he was manipulating the crowd so cynically. He loathed the lie detector because everything he did was a lie, even the lie-detector. He abhorred his willing acceptance of the Citroën shilling, its thirty pieces of corporate silver. He hated the fact that this was only the first of several corporate gigs where he'd cynically perform his alchemical roadshow for more blood money, for more bags of shekels. He was a pimp for capitalism. He was party to the bread and circuses of business life. He had sold his soul to the Devil. He was selling his soul in Faust's home town.

Infuriated, Brodie tore off his throat mike and threw it to one side. Raging, he removed the lie-detector armband with a mighty rrriiippp of Velcro. Irate, he raised the conference laptop above his head and, with cables dangling like a giant stinging jellyfish, smashed it at his feet. Apoplectic, he kicked the heavy podium and, when it refused to budge, put his shoulder to the thing and sent it flying, scattering papers and glasses and half-filled carafes of water.

The audience roared. They thought it was part of the act. Rock 'n' roll, some shouted. All right, others cried, drawing out the syllables. Scotland the Brave, yelled one delirious dealer from Dumbarton. Citroën's sales force drones were witnessing a cathartic enactment of all their rebellious, stick-it-to-the-man fantasies, an angry articulation of their personal frustrations, impeded career paths and prevailing feelings that despite all the company's platitudes about caring, partnership, togetherness and our-people-come-first, they were little more than cannon-fodder, foot-soldiers, corporate grunts who'd get slaughtered if they failed to hit their targets. Citroën's infantry went wild. If they weren't quite rioting in the aisles, or ripping the auditorium's seats up, they were definitely thinking of removing their name-tags and throwing the conference packs away.

It was only when he started tearing down the Citroën banners situated at the edge of the stage that some realized something was amiss, that perhaps Professor Brodie's belligerent behaviour wasn't part of the act. Far from being a corporate equivalent of The Who, smashing guitars and kicking drum kits over, this was an anarchic, post-punk professor on a mission to destroy. Either that or he'd over-indulged in another important alchemical discovery, the distillation of alcohol.

Three burly security guards, dressed in scarlet, logo-liveried blazers, rushed on stage to prevent further damage to Citroën's sacred brand image. The organization's internal marketing activities were being unacceptably undermined in real time. As a statuesque Scot of military build and bearing, Brodie was more than a match for the minders. He nutted the first, who fell down like a Premiership footballer in the penalty area and started rolling around dramatically, the big jessie. He grabbed the second by the chevron-covered lapels – the Citroën suit looked like a McPrison uniform – and hurled him backwards off the platform with a crash, bang, wallop. The third backed away hurriedly, but Brodie was having none of it. He yanked up his kilt by the hem and while the heavy was distracted by the sight of the Scotsman's claymore – it was more of a dirk, actually – he felled the numptie with a humungous Highland haymaker.

Another primal roar went up from the riotous crowd. Seats were being kicked over, cushions were flying willy-nilly, Citroën's expensive giclées were ripped from their moorings in a mutinous frenzy of wanton destruction. There was no stopping them. It was post-industrial pandemonium. It was… it was… it was *wonderful.*

Chapter Twenty-Four

Machine Gun Kelley

Long queues of traffic are not unusual on the A26, the main road between Coleraine and Belfast. As the north coast is Ulster's playground, mottled with golf courses, holiday resorts, sandy beaches and visitor attractions, most notably the Giant's Causeway and Bushmills Distillery, it plays host to innumerable unsightly caravan parks. Inevitably, the Belfast road is chock-a-block with Airstreams, Buccaneers, Crusaders, Odysseys, Romahomes and Sprites. The traffic, though, is seasonal. Caravans of caravans head north in June and return south in September, the precise dates dependent on the weather, personal holiday entitlements, the amount of sick leave that can be screwed out of public sector employers and, above all, the need for mutual protection. Caravans travel in convoys. They have to, on account of the irritation Airstreams *et al.* trigger among commuters, sales reps and the road rage susceptible, who find themselves stuck behind barely mobile mobile homes. It's a postmodern re-enactment of the North Atlantic convoys that used to pass very close to the Causeway Coast during wartime. Except today's snarling wolfpacks of BMWs and Lexuses aren't equipped with torpedoes or limpet mines or deck-mounted artillery, more's the pity.

Caravans' seasonal migration wouldn't be a problem if the A26 were a multi-lane highway or a dual carriageway of some description. For much of the time, however, it is a single-lane artery, clogged with thrombotic traffic and coronary-inducing hold-ups. Especially in September. September is the cruellest month. That's when Belfast-bound caravans are supplemented by tractors, hay wagons, combine harvesters and similar items of slow-moving agricultural equipment. Bringing in the sheaves, they call it. Driving drivers insane, everyone else calls it.

Motorized meltdown occurs when the police chuck a road block into the mix. Police checkpoints used to be an everyday occurrence on Northern Ireland's roads. Acting on a security tip-off or, more likely, a simple sadistic desire to frustrate the travelling public en masse, they'd close the carriageway without warning and check every car as it crawled past the barricade, on the off chance of finding bomb-making equipment in the boot, or a balaclava-wearing terrorist at the wheel.

Road blocks, happily, are a rarity in the New Northern Ireland, where peace and reconciliation prevail, where the economy's booming, where ex-assassins are pillars of the community and where even the most indigent can afford a top-of-the-range caravan, dammit.

Kelley's sacrilegious outburst was understandable. Something very serious, he correctly concluded, must have occurred if the main road was closed and every car, caravan and tractor was being stopped. The fact that they had a sack full of counterfeit money in the back seat, looking for all the world like a Semtex-stuffed car bomb, also gave the saloon's occupants cause for concern. As the line of traffic inched forward, they could see that it was something to do with road safety. Unarmed police officers were doling out flyers to each driver and exchanging a few reduce-speed pleasantries before waving them on. Speeding? In September? During the annual caravan trek? Chance'd be a fine thing!

"Afternoon, sir." The policeman, like all policemen, looked as though he might start shaving some day soon, though his regulation babygrow wasn't the most authoritative of uniforms. Pocketing his pacifier, he handed Kelley a leaflet. It offered a £10,000 reward for information about the disappearance of Ms. Abby Maguire. An old photograph of the missing woman, possibly taken from a passport or driving licence, was reproduced on the front. "Have you seen this woman on your travels this morning?"

Kelley studied the colour reproduction intently. "Never seen her before, officer. What's the problem?"

"Oh, she disappeared from a shop in Carrickfergus last night. Wrecked the place. The owners are very concerned. She's a student at Hustler, apparently."

"I'm a lecturer there, officer. But I don't recognise…" He glanced at the leaflet again. "… Ms. Maguire. Sorry."

The policeman bent down and, talking across the driver, addressed the front seat passenger. "What about you, miss?"

Abby took the flyer from Kelley and scanned it nonchalantly. The photograph dated from her bad old bulimic, anorexic, self-harm-dominated days. The perm wasn't her most flattering look, either. She glanced up, only to catch the policeman staring at her suspiciously. He looked down at the flyer and back at Abby.

"What's your name, miss?"

"Juliet D'Anger, officer."

It was all Kelley could do to stop spluttering. You don't acquire a new sister every day.

"Do you have any identification?"

Kelley held his breath.

" 'Fraid not, officer. Nothing except an Xtravision membership card. Will that do?" She handed him a dog-eared video library card, a card that screamed movie junkie, couch potato, Doritos chips and Dominos pizza. A slob, in short.

The policeman looked suitably unimpressed. "What's in the kitbag?"

"Dirty washing, officer," Abby answered calmly.

Kelley was keeking kittens, staring straight ahead.

The constable's lapel-mounted radio suddenly crackled into life. He ignored the incoming message. "Will you open it for me, miss?"

"No, I won't."

Kelley dropped a second litter.

Pustular though he was and prepubescent though he appeared, the constable wasn't used to being defied. "Excuse me?"

Abby turned on him, dealing with the impudent boy as she would any uppity adolescent. "It's full of my little brother's smelly rugby kit, not to mention his unwashed underpants. I travel to Coleraine every other week to collect it, otherwise his mummy gets terribly upset and starts worrying about his welfare. So big sister has to pick up and pack all his cast-offs and take them home for washing and ironing, while he spends Saturday afternoon in the

Harbour Bar. His kit's stinking out the car as it is and it's wrapped up in plastic bags. If you want to open the holdall, constable, feel free. But please open it well away from the car. And wrap it up again when you've finished."

Cowed by the unexpected outburst, the youthful policeman did as he was bid. He walked round the shocking pink museum piece, while chatting into his two-way. He opened the near-side rear door and popped his head in, only to back away rapidly when a nauseating, overpowering, eye-watering smell hit him. He slammed the door without further ado, gasping. "Why don't you put it in the boot?"

"That's where I've stashed the dead body," Kelley replied offhandedly. "A caravanner. Killed him on the Ballymoney bypass. I'm saving some room for the farmer I'm planning to shoot between here and Ballymena. So the kitbag stays in the back, officer."

"Good thinking," he laughed and waved them on. "Drive safely."

The odd couple managed to keep their faces straight for a couple of hundred metres or so, but when the car rounded a bend, hysteria reigned. Abby kissed her trusty, life-saving can of It's a Miracle, while Kelley took credit for talking them out of it. He was even more delighted by the discovery that his snooty, opera-loving sister was a secret Xtravision member.

"It was in the handbag I borrowed," Abby explained. "I hope its disappearance doesn't cramp her style or ruin her Saturday night viewing."

"She's in Dublin for a fortnight. She'll never notice it's missing. Like all women, she has dozens of handbags, one for every conceivable occasion. Anything else in there?"

"Only her passport and driving licence," Abby replied. "And a Kong Dong vibrator. But that's mine."

Kelley roared with laughter. "Nothing suitably scandalous that I can use against Juliet?"

" 'Fraid not," Abby answered, rummaging around to make sure. "It's good to know that you get on so well with your brother and sister, Dave."

Wisely, Kelley refused to be drawn. Family squabbles, or property sell-offs, or library de-accessions, or the fate of the demesne were unpleasant private matters best not talked about, except in emergencies. Instead, he took shameless credit for talking them out of a tight corner. "That policeman fancied me, darling. Did you notice?"

"Talk sense, Dave."

"If it hadn't been for me, darling, he'd have body-searched us both and spread me over the bonnet with my arms and legs outstretched."

"Dr. Kelley, if you thought a strip search was in the offing, you'd have jumped at the chance and spread-eagled yourself without further ado."

"True, darling, true."

"But you're not gay, Dave!"

Resoundingly trumped, Kelley tried to talk his way out by claiming that he put the camp into campervan and, although he wasn't actually gay, he was sufficiently gay to detect a frisson of gayness in others. The uniformed services, he further opined, consisted of three types of people: openly gay, closeted gay and gays in extreme denial, hence the psychopathology of police forces. Their obsession with uniforms, parades, neatness and obeying orders was poof positive.

"Interesting theory, Dr. Kelley. And you can tell all that from a two-minute conversation?"

"A single glance suffices, darling. I've seen it countless times before."

"When was that, Dave?"

"Oh, you know, when I was on the road with the band." Damn! Too late. He'd fallen right into her true confessions trap, baited earlier.

Abby couldn't believe her luck. This was manna from music biz heaven. "Tell me about your time on the road," she teased. "Goth rock, wasn't it?"

"Heavy metal," he muttered, as a blush began to appear on his boyish cheek. "I gave up goth when I was sixteen. Sorry I ever mentioned it."

They'd reached the M2 motorway. The lumbering vestige of Britain's once-glorious car industry accelerated sluggishly, attendant tyre noise almost drowning out the conversation. Almost, but not quite. "What was the name of your band again?"

"Love Pump."

Abby stared out as the fields and hedgerows flashed past, her fist in her mouth. She knew that if she looked at his bashful face, she'd simply explode. "Love Pump, eh?" The electricity pylons were especially interesting in this part of the world.

"It's a joke," the driver grumped. "It's from *Spinal Tap*. You know, the spoof heavy metal documentary? The keyboard player picks out a beautiful, heart-rending tune on the piano and when asked what it's called, he replies 'Lick My Love Pump'."

Five minutes or so later, hands over her face, still peeping through her fingers at the passing pastoral scene, Abby just about managed to continue. "Lick Your Love Pump, is it?"

Cornered, Dave the Rave had no alternative but to recount his riotous rock 'n' roll accomplishments. How he'd left his bed unmade in numerous anonymous motel rooms; how he used to throw wet towels on the floor then let housekeeping pick them up; how he'd steal shower caps, cakes of soap and, on one unforgettable occasion, a monogrammed bath robe; how he ate all the free biscuits with the complimentary tea and coffee facilities, even the shortbread ones; how he always left the TV on standby and replaced expensive mini-bar items with cheaper store-bought snacks; and how he folded the toilet rolls into a devil's horns point, thereby spooking the rest of the band.

Abby couldn't help herself. What's a girl to do? It wasn't so much Dave's stories of rock god debauchery as the expression on his face while he told them. If he'd been caught stealing apples from an orchard, he couldn't have looked more guilty, more innocent, more loveable. She really shouldn't have started giggling when he itemized the tracks on the band's first album – "Enter Love Pump", "Love Pump Rising", "Addicted to Love Pump", plus covers of "Pump it Up", "Pump Up the Volume" and "Porn in the USA" – but there's only so much testosterone a girl can take without tittering.

"Nearly there," Kelley scowled, in a vain attempt to maintain his dignity. He then laughed at the absurdity of his past life.

The future absurdity was about to begin.

Chapter Twenty-Five

The St. Stephen's Shambles

Taking care to remain within the speed limit, Abby and Kelley cruised along Belfast's Antrim Road, high above the city, where they caught tantalizing glimpses of the recumbent conurbation between slatted curtains of horse chestnuts. The pink Morris snaked past the Zoological Gardens, slithered through several sets of traffic lights and coiled itself in the centre of the road, turning right into St. Stephen's Redemptorist retreat.

A Roman Catholic missionary order, dedicated to working among the poor, the needy and the dispossessed, the Redemptorist movement was founded in 1732. From humble beginnings in Amalfi, where St. Alphonsus Ligouri dedicated his life to the destitute peasant communities around Naples, Cogregentio Sanctismipimi Redemptorti expanded rapidly in the mid-nineteenth century. It reached the British Isles in 1843 and, thanks to the energetic evangelism of the magnificently named Reverend Bob Coffin, the Redemptorists made rapid headway in that resolutely anti-Catholic country. A separate Irish subsidiary was established in 1898, with four main centres of operation in Limerick, Dundalk, Esker and Belfast. So successful were the Belfast Redemptorists that a spanking new facility was built in the 1960s, though several premises on the picturesque site – most notably, an impressive Victorian priest's residence – long predated the retreat house.

An oasis from the hurly-burly of the modern world in general and Belfast's in-built bigotry in particular, St. Stephen's runs a variety of counselling services for people in trouble, be it personal, familial, marital or substance abuse-related. With 85 spartan bedrooms on two gender-sequestered wings at opposite ends of the main building, as well as kitchens, refectories, quiet rooms and a beautiful octagonal chapel, St. Stephen's is a mini Catholic Mecca for those in need of peace, quiet, solitude and spiritual succour. It also provides conference facilities for hire.

As they mounted the curling access road, which wound its way up the precipitous, hazel-hung sides of Cave Hill, Abby was struck by the serenity of the scene. Even though the Antrim Road, a congested arterial route into the city centre, was only a couple of hundred metres away, the grounds of St. Stephen's were a pietistic world apart. The tranquil silence, punctuated by beatific bird song, was working its relaxing magic even before they'd parked the car, let alone strolled around the magnificent grounds, imbibing the divine nectar of the scattered statues, grottoes and Stations of the Cross.

Saintliness, sadly, was in short supply at the conference venue. There are few things more malevolent than academics with their noses out of joint, except possibly scholars whose names have been misspelled in the programme. Not only was the St. Stephen's conference programme a typographical game of Scrabble, but no one seemed to be in charge. The self-obsessed organizer, Professor Emer Aherne, had chosen not to fly back to the event she'd arranged, which was bad enough. But placing two clueless students on the registration desk was a recipe for disaster. Bedrooms had been wrongly allocated, the strict gender segregation policy had been breached and the retreat's head honcho, Father Conn Mannion, had to step in to repair the administrative damage. But not before a nerdish junior lecturer, having performed his ablutions in the communal washrooms, returned to what he thought was his cell, promptly dropped his swaddling towel and found himself staring at two alluring female postgrads, who struggled manfully not to laugh at his unimpressive CV.

Stepping into the rosewood-panelled lobby, Abby and Kelley found St. Stephen's public areas replete with puce-faced professors, snarling senior lecturers and ranting, raging readers from many and varied academic institutions. American, Asian and Australasian intellectuals were milling around, pouring imprecations on the absent Irish organizer. The conference had started badly that morning, when the hi-tech AV equipment malfunctioned at an inopportune moment during Professor Aherne's welcome address via satellite link. Things got worse when desperately needed beverages failed to materialize during the coffee break, and if it hadn't been for the intercession of Dr. Ian Kane, an unflappably affable colleague of Aherne's at Hustler Business School, who turned up unbidden when he'd heard what was happening, the whole event would have degenerated into farce before lunchtime. However, double-helpings of home-made Irish stew washed down with lashings of Bushmills whiskey – Ulster's preferred holy water – somehow saved what was left of an otherwise disastrous start.

Partaking of the devil's buttermilk is dangerous at the best of times. But when it's free, and available in unlimited quantities, and being poured down the necks of intemperate, foul-tempered, less than gruntled academics – at lunchtime – there are only two possible implications for the afternoon conference sessions. Either the entire audience falls fast asleep, their dreams of scholarly glory punctuated by snores, snorts, involuntary flailings and frantic dashes to the loo for the prostate trouble tormented, or they're turned into a baying mass of kill 'em, hang 'em, flog 'em intellectual illiberals, who pounce unmercifully on anything involving sloppy thinking, half-baked theorizing or improper research procedure. Given the mood of the conference prior to the lunchtime libations, the latter scenario was the only realistic post-prandial outcome.

And so it proved.

As Dave was on first, they only had time to register at the front desk and stow their stuff in a couple of hastily allocated bedrooms before Kelley was called into action. Although the conference room was quite small – it seated sixty at most – it was not only packed with mutinous malcontents but extremely warm in the afternoon sunshine, which poured unremittingly through large, plate-glass windows. In classic sixties style, the windows couldn't be opened to let in balmy breezes fresh from the mountaintop. The delegates, accordingly, were sweating raw alcohol, the heady aroma of which further inflamed their gladiatorial passions.

Dr. Kelley would have been given a rough ride even if he'd presented his own doctoral research. However, he was in an utterly impossible situation. He was delivering someone else's paper. That someone else was Professor Aherne, who was responsible for the shambolic organization and unforgivable typos on the conference programme. The audience contained many academics who weren't based in business schools and detested those who were. Many of the delegates were dyed-in-the-wool Yeatsians, who shared the master's alleged aversion to horrid marketing types. Aherne's paper was essentially a reprise of her controversial theory that W. B. Yeats was a marketing man in disguise. And, worst of all from Kelley's perspective, he'd been told to read the paper aloud, in keeping with humanities conference traditions, rather than extemporizing in his usual flamboyant, energetic, Dave-the-Rave manner, the oratorical technique that electrified hung-over undergraduates on Monday mornings at Hustler.

The room was buzzing as Kelley took his place behind the imposing lectern. With his dispirited, hangdog expression, Dave looked like a distempered cocker spaniel that had been caught in a rainstorm after an appointment at The Dog's Bollocks neutering salon. His vital spark was absent. He was defeated before he started. Abby was convinced she could hear a collective growl from the crowd as Dave cleared his throat nervously. She sank down in her seat, cringing in anticipation of the carnage to come.

Kelley hadn't a hope. Stumbling and stuttering, obviously unused to reading aloud, he barely managed to recount that Yeats came from a mercantile family before angry mutters rose from the multitude. He only got as far as summarizing Yeats's self-marketing aptitude, by means of ostentatious outfits and attention-grabbing behaviours, when the first "nonsense" rent the learned air. He'd hardly touched on Yeats's astute management of the Abbey Theatre, where he stirred up Madonna-esque controversy because it was damn good box office, before cat calls screeched from all corners of the sweltering room. The first walk-out occurred when he alluded to Yeats's commercial inspiration for "The Lake Isle of Innisfree", a striking shop window display on the Tottenham Court Road.

Worst of all, Kelley made the mistake of mentioning Professor Aherne's infamous "lost poem", which had propelled her to the forefront of Yeatsian scholarship, even though she was a rank amateur, business school based and a marketing charlatan to boot.

The word uproar hardly does justice to the blood-curdling howl that went up when the absent organizer's name was dropped into the cerebral imbroglio.

Dave looked devastated, distraught, desolate. If not quite on the point of passing out, he appeared pale and sickly and, above all, lost. Abby's heart went out to him. Watching the poor guy wilt under the attack was painful enough. But she knew that it wasn't his fault, that he'd been put in an impossible position, that he was a brilliant public speaker under normal circumstances. She found herself getting more and more annoyed. She wasn't going to stand for it. An undergraduate student she might be, a final-year retail marketing undergraduate on placement, but by God she refused to kow-tow to a bunch of boorish academics – arts and humanities academics especially.

Abby rose to her feet. The torrent of invective halted momentarily, as the audience wondered what was going on and attempted to size up the statuesque woman with the glittering eyes, aggressive mien and determined look on her face. She seized the silence. "W. B. Yeats was a Nazi! Yes, a Nazi. You sit there, convinced that he wasn't a marketer, when he was much, much worse. He was an arrogant elitist. He believed in maintaining the Ascendancy bloodline. He urged eugenic action against the common Catholic herd, people like me. He was a member of O'Duffy's Blueshirts, the Irish equivalent of Hitler's Brownshirts. He wrote marching songs for General O'Duffy's thugs and selected the colour scheme for their flag. He quit the Blueshirts not because they were fascist but because they weren't fascist enough. He was repeatedly compared to Adolf Hitler by his contemporaries. His closest friend was Ezra Pound, a notorious anti-Semite. The one true love of his life, Maud Gonne, wrote articles praising Hitler in the late thirties, made numerous anti-Semitic remarks and denied the existence of the death camps. The basic difference between W. B. Yeats and Adolf Hitler was that Yeats was all talk and no action. The man was Hitler Lite. He was a Nazi through and through. Being a marketer was the least of his failings."

She sat down, shaking uncontrollably as the adrenaline surged through her system, dispersing into the air like a rhetorical force field. The room was completely silent. Not a mutter. Not a snort. Not a harrumph. Not a scratch of felt-tip pen or rustle of the typo-ridden programme. She could hear the birds twittering outside. She had spoken the truth. She had forced her intellectual elders and betters to face facts, the uncomfortable facts they spent their careers massaging, ignoring, excusing or brushing under the carpet of "genius".

Out of the mouths of babes and retail marketing undergraduates.

Chapter Twenty-Six

Beat the Retreat

The September sunshine trickled through the hazel groves on the hillside behind St. Stephen's. From time immemorial, climbing Cave Hill had been a popular pursuit among local residents and visitors alike. Breathtaking views from the summit across resplendent Belfast Lough, a hill-girt natural harbour, made the exhausting yet exhilarating trek worthwhile.

Cave Hill, of course, offers more than sunny vistas across a city that calls itself the Rio of the North (primarily on account of the crime, squalor and party-loving parallels). Like so many places in Ireland, it is a repository of time-worn tales and yarns of yesteryear: stories of God-fearing Victorian families who loved to roll their Easter eggs down the escarpment's cascading slopes; legends of the Iron Age fort that still stands on the summit, where Ireland's coronation stone sat for thousands of years before disappearing mysteriously in 1898; rumours of treasure hidden in the five man-made caves that dot the precipitous cliff face and once provided a hide-out for Ness O'Haughan, the notorious Ulster highwayman; narratives of the sleeping giant who inspired Jonathan Swift and whose face is clearly discernible in silhouette, thanks to a rocky ridge known locally as Napoleon's Nose; and ineradicable memories of the United Irishmen who fomented revolution from the top of the hill in 1795 and whose desire for national self-determination – Protestants and Catholics in happy harmony – resonates now as never before.

Stories were in short supply as Abby and Kelley wandered around the warren of wooded paths behind St. Stephen's retreat house. Kelley was in an understandable funk about his performance, a humiliation he'd never live down. Dave wasn't to blame, Abby argued. He'd had no time to prepare. He was facing an extremely hostile audience with a predisposition toward crucifixion. He'd been forced to deliver the paper in a wholly unfamiliar manner. Yet her heartfelt attempts to help him see the bright side – noting that the audience was roaring drunk and unlikely to remember too much about it – did little to lift Dave's gloom. Even resorting to egregious flattery, by reminding him what a fantastic lecturer he was (not that she wanted to swell his head or anything), failed to do the trick.

Abby had never met anyone so mutable, so subject to mood swings, so prone to the psychic see-saw of euphoria and abjection. She was forced to accept the truism that artistic types in general and flamboyant showpersons in particular are unusually prone to the blues. They live through their work, and when work is going badly, life isn't worth living.

The only surefire way to get them out of the glooms is to outgloom them. Get things into proper perspective, Abby said, the UVF was going to kill them. Sourpuss scholars were the least of their problems, she stressed, because they had to find £1 million a.s.a.p. Things have been worse, she added; think back to the gigs you played as Love Pump. Now that's what I call embarrassing…

The reverse psychology tack raised a momentary smile, though it wasn't till she broached the subject of her father's suicide, and the reasons behind it, that Dave the Rave finally started to come round.

"He killed himself because of Seamus Heaney?" Kelley stared at her, appalled, wondering whether she was winding him up. "I don't believe you!"

"It's true," Abby sighed. "You know, if my dad had killed himself in a noble cause, or because he mismanaged the farm, or on account of letting his family down, I suppose I could live with it. But he killed himself because of jealousy, rivalry, spite. He went to school with Seamus Heaney. He was a much better poet than Seamus, everyone said so. His poems were included in the school magazine, whereas Heaney's weren't. Then Heaney went on to university. My father stayed to work the farm. Heaney became famous. My dad didn't. It rankled, festered, ate away at him. He lived for poetry, Dave. In the evenings, he used to recite 'The Tower' in its entirety. An impromptu rendition of 'The Fiddler of Dooney' or 'The White Birds' or 'He Wishes for the Cloths of Heaven' was his idea of after-dinner entertainment. We just wanted to watch *Top of the Pops*..."

"Ah, so that's how you know so much about Yeats."

"And Love Pump," she added. "My father firmly believed he was the greatest Irish poet since Yeats, and when Famous Seamus received that accolade, you can imagine the effect it had on him. Then, when Heaney won the Nobel Prize in 1995, it was just too much. So he topped himself, without a thought for the rest of us. He was fifty-five at the time. That's the annoying thing. At that age, you'd think he'd have a bit of sense. But no, not my bastard father."

Shaken that someone actually remembered Love Pump's one and only appearance on *Top of the Pops* – surely she was bluffing – Dave politely enquired about Abby's family circumstances. Her father's first wife died young, without issue. Her mother married the middle-aged widower when she was seventeen. He was a catch, they told her. Think of the land, the farm, the legacy...

"What's that?" Abby suddenly shouted, startled. "A shadow in the trees. See? There!" She pointed towards a dense copse of hazel, her arm tracking a dark object of some kind.

Kelley stared intently, following her finger, but couldn't make anything out. "It's just a trick of the light, Abby."

"Sssssshhhh." They stood silently, listening to the forest. Strangely, there was no birdsong. Even the wind in the treetops had ceased. A mosaic of light and shade, grass and leaves, bushes and branches, lay like a green gingham tablecloth across the glade. The arboreal calm, if not quite eerie, was oddly oppressive. There was a slight rustling in the undergrowth up ahead. Abby gripped Kelley's upper arm tightly and scanned the narrow path in front of them. She looked around, trying to get her bearings. They were lost. The labyrinth of forest trails behind St. Stephen's had claimed its latest victims.

It wasn't St. Stephen's fault, of course. It was Belfast City Council's. In its infinite wisdom, the Council had established a country park between its two adjacent properties, the Zoological Gardens and Belfast Castle, a baronial pile widely used for wedding receptions. St. Stephen's nestled between the castle and the zoo. But because the boundaries between the properties were porous, many retreat residents got lost in the woods behind the priest's house and either finished up as spectral figures in someone's wedding photographs or found themselves staring into the African elephant enclosure, an experience that proved unnerving to those just saying no to drugs or alcohol and suffering attendant withdrawal symptoms.

Such occurrences would have prompted many city councils to secure the boundaries between the respective properties. Belfast City Council, though, was nothing if not marketing minded, and it quickly realized that stories of "haunted wedding photographs" were a wonderful added attraction, though not as wonderful as the escaped animal scam. There's nothing like an escaped animal to generate free publicity and attract legions of local sensation-seekers to the Zoological Gardens. Hence, when visitor numbers were slipping or looked unlikely to hit the ambitious targets set by the city fathers, a rhesus monkey or ring-tail lemur or giant sloth inexplicably made a bid for freedom. Indeed, certain cynics among the citizenry concluded that the extent of the visitor shortfall could be calculated from the perceived ferocity of the escaped creature. A bird of paradise meant that managers were pretty much on target, a posse of penguins suggested that year-on-year numbers had slipped slightly, and when one of the smaller big cats went on the lam – a lynx or ocelot, say – it was a sure sign of panic in the management suite. One year, at the very height of The Troubles, when the tourist trade had all but evaporated, a fully grown lion was unleashed. For several days it ran amok among North Belfast's leafy suburbs. At least one senior citizen had the fright of her life while washing the dishes. Larry the Lion materialized at her kitchen window, mane akimbo, searching for scraps or maybe a chew or two of crunchy crumbly.

Far from attracting additional visitors, unfortunately, the council's prodigious PR stunt precipitated widespread panic, led to the closure of numerous local schools and, as fearful citizens cowered in their homes, duly caused a few heads to roll among the zoo's senior management team. Heads, incidentally, that could have been used to recapture the creature rather than a cruel, cowardly and much less commercially mindful tranquillizer dart.

Public relations is not an exact science, sadly.

"There's definitely something there, Dave."

"Maybe it's a fox or a stoat or a pine marten," he whispered, wondering why he was whispering. "There's nothing to worry about."

"No, it was bigger than that." Ordinarily, animals didn't bother Abby. She grew up on a farm, after all, and had killed them for a living. But there was something about the forest atmosphere that unsettled her. Animal emotions were easy enough to intuit. She'd pretty much encountered them all – fear, rage, curiosity, protectiveness, territoriality. This was something different, however.

As different as a ravenous panther.

A sleek black shape filled the path in front of them, tail flicking excitedly from side to side. The beast looked fully grown, if fearfully undernourished. It turned to face them and snarled, though the sound that emerged from its bright-red, fang-filled jaws was more like a hiss than a roar. "Don't move," Kelley murmured. "I was in Kenya once and the keepers at the game reserve told us to stand still if confronted."

"Everyone knows that," Abby snapped. "I've faced down angry animals before. The key is to hold its stare. Whatever you do, don't look away or break eye contact or turn your head towards me," she continued from the side of her mouth. The panther crouched, its red eyes blazing, rear haunches slowly sliding from side to side as it appraised its prey.

"If it comes at us," Kelley urged, "run straight towards it, shouting as loud as you can. That should scare it off, unless it's absolutely starving or protecting its young."

The panther sank lower, preparing to pounce. The fur on its neck bristled, ears pinned flat against its head. The claws curled in and out of its paws menacingly. The scarlet tongue swept around its dripping dewlaps in delicious anticipation. The rear haunches moved more and more rapidly…

Suddenly, a ferocious bout of barking burst the bubble of

silence. Something was snarling furiously behind them. Kelley turned to look, but Abby shook him forward. The big black cat hissed venomously, as if on hydraulic springs, then leapt off into the undergrowth, which rustled and shook for a moment before falling silent.

They turned to greet their rescuer, only to see a youthful, black-clad trainee priest, struggling with the leashes of two straining Rottweilers, which snapped and yapped uncontrollably. He was wobbling with the effort. The choke chains were taut yet apparently incapable of restraining the heaving, ravening hounds.

"Heel!" Abby roared at the top of her voice, pointing directly at the roiling attack dogs. The young priest's rabid charges instantly complied, sitting silently at heel, licking their spume-flecked chops repeatedly while staring up imploringly at Mistress Maguire.

"Thank you," the chubby acolyte gasped. "Thank you." Evidently out of condition, he was panting more than the dogs. "Father Mannion is looking for you, Dr. Kelley. You too, Miss D'Anger. He wants a quick word."

Abby knelt down with a smile, chucked the throats of the bipolar Rottweilers and crooned a couple of canine sweet nothings. They licked her face enthusiastically, then raised a front paw apiece in subservient salutation. "What are they called?" she asked, raising her face to the flushed novitiate.

"Genesis and Revelation."

Kelley snorted. "Hellfire and Damnation, surely."

Chapter Twenty-Seven

Rage Against the Machine

Squat and stolid and steadfast, the Kaiserburg fortress had seen off its share of barbarian hordes and suffered the militaristic ministrations of, among others, King Karl IV, Napoleon Bonaparte, Bomber Harris and General George S. Patton. However, the Great Citroën Riot ranks among its most memorable moments. For five full minutes organizational anarchy reigned, though it felt at least ten times that. Chairs were thrown, water coolers were upended, conference programmes whizzed across the auditorium like lethal frisbees, fisticuffs erupted between agents and dealers of different nationalities and among different divisions of the corporate hierarchy. Human resources didn't stand a chance, not when R&D set about them.

"Stop!" Brodie shouted, his arms aloft, spreadeagled. "Listen to me!" he declaimed. His face was flushed, his breathing heavy. The insubordinate corporate groundlings immediately fell silent. Only the tearing sound of collapsing giclées, brought down by their own weight, interrupted the post-storm calm. "Citroën should be ashamed of itself," the Scottish symbologist said in a controlled tone that carried to every corner of the richly-decorated room, without the aid of a microphone. "You are celebrating one hundred years of helical gears. Yet your company has no sense of history. Don't you know where you are? Don't you realize what you're doing? Don't you appreciate the terrible memories you're disturbing? This is Nuremberg! This was the symbolic centre of National Socialism. This was the beating heart of the Nazi party. This is where the anti-Jewish Nuremberg Laws were passed. This is where the hate magazine, *Der Stürmer*, was published. Your red, white and black banners are a grotesque echo of the Nazi party's livery, not to mention its swastika, the most loathed logo in history.

You've bedecked the town in flags and streamers that recall the revolting rallies that took place here, *every September*, before the Second World War. You are celebrating your marketing prowess in a city that experienced the Nazi party marketing machine at full throttle!"

The pumped-up audience, wannabe insurgents one and all, settled back into their seats as the theologian delivered his sermon, though they didn't particularly like the homily they were hearing.

"You may not be aware of this, because you're all too young to remember. But the Nazis were masters of experiential marketing decades before your next speaker but one was born. They were masters of marketing full stop! Hermann Göring was a salesman by profession, who married into the Beamish brewing dynasty from Cork. Rudolf Hess was a soda pop dealer who came from a family of middle-eastern merchants and had a business school education. Joachim von Ribbentrop worked in advertising, Adolf Eichmann was an agent for Daimler-Benz, Franz Six owned a Porsche dealership. Joseph Goebbels was a PR genius who hustled on the trading floor of the Cologne stock exchange and lectured part-time at the local trade school, and his first job with the Nazi party was as its business manager."

The still-seditious delegates flicked furtive glances at each other. They were slightly confused, somewhat bemused, wondering where this dressing down was going, exactly.

"The SS!" Brodie bellowed. "Yes, the SS. The *Schutzstaffel* was founded to sell advertising space in the Nazi party newspaper. Their uniforms were made by Hugo Boss. They positioned themselves as an exclusive brand to attract the most elite recruits. The *Ahnenerbe*, the SS division behind the death camp experiments, was sponsored by Mercedes and BMW, among others. The slush funds that kept the National Socialists going was donated by big business, even though the Nazis denounced capitalism and desired to destroy it. IBM supplied the tabulating machines that kept impeccable track of the Holocaust, to its eternal shame. The less said about Swiss banks, the better."

Harangues are hard to take at the best of times. But a holy-roller harangue by a money-grubbing consultancy type, in the midst of the sponsoring company's celebration of its richly deserved success, was unacceptable, unbelievable, unforgivable, in fact.

"And then," Brodie went on regretfully, "there was Adolf Hitler. An Austrian, an outsider, an uneducated no-hoper, a testicularly-challenged nonentity with a laughably mincing gait, he persuaded an exceptionally cultured, extraordinarily gifted, extremely class-conscious society to buy his bill of shoddy, shameful goods. Hitler was the biggest huckster in history. He was a marketing master, the marketing master of the master race. The solution he sold was the Final Solution. The brand he endorsed was the Aryan brand beast. His principal source of personal income came from the sale of his image rights. That's right, his Führer brand image rights. That says it all, I feel, as does the photograph that Hitler kept on his desk at all times, a photograph of Henry Ford. Yes, Henry Ford, the man Ted Levitt described as the greatest marketer of the twentieth century." He paused for two full beats. "The second greatest, I fear."

Astonished by Brodie's on-going outburst and relentless condemnation, the deflated, detumescent delegates stared at each other in shocked silence. "Marketing is a form of magic," the imperious theologian explained. "And just as there is black magic and white magic, so too there is black marketing and white marketing. Black marketing involves the sale of unnecessary or unsafe or exploitative or wasteful products or the invention of non-existent ailments or anxieties or concerns that marketers then relieve for a price. Restless Leg Syndrome. Female Sexual Dysfunction. Social Anxiety Disorder. Sports Utility Vehicles. Voice-activated Central Car Locking."

Brodie paced the podium in full flow, eyes blazing, comb-over bouncing. "White marketing, on the other hand, is when our powers of persuasion are used for good causes or socially responsible actions or in order to better inform consumer choice. Anti-smoking, global warming, fair trade, food labelling and so forth. Sadly, I saw precious little white marketing during my stroll through Nuremberg this morning. Citroën has gone over to the dark side! I'm told that Bill Hicks, the American comedian, long dead, urged marketers and advertisers to kill themselves on account of the atrocities they're responsible for. After today, I'm inclined to agree with him."

As the endorphins finally dissipated, and drained down the plughole of token rebellion, the Citroënistas turned against the teller of unwelcome home truths. The fact that the on-screen lie detector line remained flat reinforced the uncomfortable feeling that they were getting it straight, unadulterated and, if not quite from the horse's mouth, certainly from a forthright Shetland pony. The court jester was only playing his time-honoured function – telling it like it is – though the delegates were in no mood for wise fools.

An ugly situation might have been avoided, even at this late stage. But Brodie still had the coup de grace to deliver. "André Citroën was Jewish," he said. "Citroën was one among many Jewish commercial geniuses." Brodie paused for effect, four beats this time. "What were you people thinking of? What persuaded you to commemorate his legacy in such a grotesque way? You're a disgrace to his illustrious name!"

An angry shout of "Get off!" erupted from the back of the hall. Catcalls rained down on the tartan-clad, sporran-sporting professor. But Brodie hadn't quite finished. "André Citroën was a Freemason, one of the foremost in France. The Citroën logo is not a representation of helical gears, it's a depiction of the masons' compass and square. You all work under the sign of the masons, and while Freemasonry may not mean much to you, the Nazi party set out to destroy what they called the worldwide Masonic–Jewish conspiracy. It wasn't just Jews they gassed. It was gypsies, Slavs, artists, Freemasons and many more. Freemasons were especially despised; Jewish Freemasons like André Citroën were at the top of the Nazi party extermination list. There was an anti-Freemason museum in this very town during the dark days of National Socialism. There's a Citroën banner on the building today. Maybe that's a good thing, a symbolic thing. But I don't think so!"

A salvo of complimentary pens landed on the stage close to the infuriated Scottish academic, bouncing and pinging off the fallen podium. A fusillade of breath mints followed suit, their rattles and ricochets like a leisure industry Lewis gun. Brodie soldiered on through the crossfire of Biros and Mintos, as a hefty glass paperweight in the shape of Andre's helical gears crashed into the videoscreen behind him, narrowly missing his head.

"Many people believe that the Citroën logo actually depicts the Spear of Destiny, the Holy Lance, the deeply occult artefact that bestows enormous power on its possessor. Adolf Hitler appropriated it from the Hofburg in Vienna, after the *Anschluss* in 1938, and returned it to its original home here in Nuremberg, first in St. Katharine's church, then in the Kaiserburg. The very building we're in at present. The very building Citroën has commandeered for its orgy of corporate necrophilia. You people are dallying with the blackest of black magic. The Spear of Destiny was supposedly returned to Vienna in 1946, but I know for a fact that that's not true. The spear is out there. Citroën beware!"

A mocking laugh arose from the rear of the auditorium. "Get off, you nutta," called one estuary-accented Little Englander, proud owner of a dealership in Sevenoaks. The rest of the rabble joined in. Head held high, Professor Pitcairn Brodie navigated through a sea of angry faces, steering a course down the centre aisle, despite the continuing squall of Bics, the typhoon of Tic-tacs and the tempest of organizational invective. He sailed serenely outside, into the Castle's inner courtyard. He circumnavigated Empress Kunigunde's singing-ringing lime tree, drifted past the hellish Heathens' Tower, tacked by the low-slung Heavenly Stables and set sail for the nearest Altstadt tavern. The theologian heaved a sigh of the righteous. His career as a consultancy circuit captain was shipwrecked.

Or so it seemed.

Chapter Twenty-Eight

Devil May Care

"A black panther, you say?" The priest looked sceptical, then wrily amused. His bright eyes danced with delight in a ruddy face that belied the advancing years, if not its fondness for the company of Arthur Guinness, Jack Daniels, Johnnie Walker and sundry Bells, Jamesons and Whyte and Mackays. "There must be a desperate visitor shortfall this year." He briefly explained the zoo's promotional strategy to his disbelieving guests, though his jocular attitude suggested he was having them on. "There's only one problem," he continued, pouring large tumblerfuls of brother Bushmills for the shaken twosome. And an even larger one for himself.

Kelley cradled the healing libation, while Abby sipped hers with distaste. "What's that, Father Mannion?"

"Call me Conn," he replied, finishing his drink and pouring another. A silver cigarette case was produced from an inside pocket of a comfortably rumpled clerical jacket and passed around. The fact that there were no takers didn't persuade the host to refrain.

"What's the problem, Conn?"

"The zoo doesn't own a black panther. Never has. It's got a couple of mangy lions, a pair of flea-bitten pumas, a big, bone-idle Bengal tiger and a grimy polar bear that doesn't like the cold." He dragged deeply on his cigarette. "No panthers, though."

"So what was it?" Kelley countered. "A lucky black cat that crossed our path?"

Laconically, the octogenarian priest flicked the end of his fag, depositing ash in a deconsecrated patera. He must have been extremely handsome when he was younger, a spiritual dynamo of faith, hope, charity and outreach, as well as the catalyst for impure thoughts among his flock, male and female alike. "Quite the opposite," he said, blowing a smoke ring in the shape of a sacred heart.

"Sightings of big black cats usually portend death."

Abby and Kelley glanced at each other knowingly. Abby had another sip of Irish. It wasn't quite so bad this time.

"If you believe the local legend, that is."

Kelley wasn't convinced. "So, if the panther doesn't rip you limb from limb, Conn, it puts the mockers on you instead?"

"So they say," Father Mannion said. He refreshed the glasses, mainly his own, and, swigging and smoking alternately, regaled them with tales of local worthies who'd sold their souls to the devil. Most people who make a bargain with Old Nick, he explained, are carried off to the infernal regions when their time is up. But not the Irish. Because the Irish have a bit of devilment in them already, Satan turns them into his representatives on earth, feral creatures that spread mischief, malfeasance and misbegotten malediction.

"We encountered a wild animal of some kind," Kelley insisted, "not the Goat of Mendes in an acrylic cat suit."

The priest exhaled slowly, appraising his visitors through the foul-smelling fug. "There are many variations on the Faust Legend. Mephistopheles moves in mysterious ways. He appears in diverse guises – cats, dogs, panthers, politicians, dictators, *poets*. Or so the story goes..."

Ah, so that's what this yarn is about, Abby twigged as the penny plummeted. Her intemperate outburst on Yeats the fascist. Not the kind of thing that should be raised on hallowed ground, in the house of the Lord, the place where Yeats's lost poem was found, yada, yada, yada. Excommunication here we come. Or a hatful of Hail Marys at least. Whoop de doo. She refused to raise the subject, however, forcing Father Mannion to articulate his censure explicitly. Instead, she looked around the reception room, while pretending to sip her remedial whiskey. It was chintzy yet comfortable. Old sagging sofas, seriously scuffed occasional tables, threadbare-pattern Axminster carpets, deeply dusty velvet curtains, a contorted chandelier with many of its bulbs missing, a very well stocked drinks cabinet, and a crackling log fire, which filled the room with good cheer, irrespective of the season. The walls, surprisingly, were not covered with votive prints, or pietistic portraits or even serried shelves of good books, let alone Good Books. There were dozens of photographs of Father Mannion standing alongside celebrity visitors to his hilltop operation. Bobby Kennedy, Teddy Kennedy, Brian Kennedy, Richard Harris, Charles Haughey, Bertie Ahern, Conan O'Brien, Tom Clancy, Shane MacGowan, Bono, Cherie Blair, the sainted Seamus Heaney, J. K. Rowling, Jeffrey Archer, Brad Pitt, Paris Hilton and many more.

"They've all been here at some stage," he said, following her gaze. "Belfast's the last place the press or paparazzi would think to look for them and the people around town tend to keep themselves to themselves, understandably enough. So, when the pressure gets too much for the Sinéad O'Connors and Madonnas and Dan Browns of this world, or the luxury lifestyle starts turning their heads, St. Stephen's helps ground them again. It's a spiritual spa, I suppose."

"But I thought Madonna and Dan Brown and Sinéad O'Connor had been condemned by the Catholic Church."

"Surely Sinéad took holy orders at one stage," Kelley corrected, proving that his subscriptions to *Heat*, *Hello* and the gay glossies hadn't gone to waste.

"Sinners and backsliders are welcome here," Father Mannion replied. "If it weren't for the temporarily mentally disturbed, we'd be out of business." He raised the half-empty bottle of Bushmills and made to top up everyone's glass, but as his was the only one empty, he had to make do with a show of auto-hospitality. "Even W. B. Yeats was welcome here, and sinners don't come much bigger than him."

Abby was fed up beating around the bush, never mind the bottle of Bushmills. "Look, Conn, I'm sorry about my Yeats outburst. I didn't mean to defile your premises." Can I go now, sir? she felt like adding. Am I forgiven? What's the penance?

The rubicund priest burst out laughing, his weatherbeaten face crinkling like a crushed paper bag. He scratched the side of his head in bemused amusement, his formerly ginger hair now a sagacious shade of grey. "The purpose of this chat isn't to chastise you. Willy Yeats was an old rogue, an out-and-out occultist and an Anglican to boot. He was also a fascist, as you forcefully pointed out. But I'm afraid you've got the wrong end of the stick. Yeats wasn't a Hitlerite, though Maud Gonne was. Nor an anti-Semite, though Maud Gonne was. Hitler was a Yeatsian. Yeats had more influence on Hitler than Hitler had on Yeats."

"No way!" "That's news to me!" Kelley and Abby shouted simultaneously, taken aback by Father Mannion's counterintuitive notion.

"Way," the priest replied, gesturing affably at Kelley. "Of course it's news to you, Juliet," he added, raising his glass in salutation, "because no one wants to damage the myth of Irish poetic genius or adversely affect the tourist trade in Sligo." He caught them glancing at each other, exchanging "he's pissed" expressions. "And no, I'm not the worse for wear or spinning you another shaggy dog story about big black cats." He downed his Bushmills for emphasis and wiped his mouth with the back of a liver-spotted hand. "The facts are as follows. Yeats was awarded a medal by the Nazis in 1934. Correct?"

"Yes, I'd heard that," Abby answered, the bell of half-forgotten memory tolling in the distance.

"The medal was awarded for *The Countess Kathleen*, Yeats's version of the Faust legend."

Kelley nodded as Abby shrugged, the outer limits of their Yeatsian knowledge surpassed.

The priest paused, like all master raconteurs, then delivered his killer soliloquy. "Many have wondered why Adolf Hitler was so knowledgeable about Ireland. Most assume it reflected his belief that Germany and Ireland shared a similar Celtic heritage, which of course they did. The real reason was much simpler. Hitler was here. Adolf Hitler spent the famous 'missing year' of 1912 in Liverpool, where he stayed with his step-brother, Alois, who taught him the rudiments of salesmanship. Alois was an agent for safety razors and he tried to interest Adolf in a dealership. Alois's wife was called Bridget. She came from Dublin. She was an artistic type. She met Alois in the National Museum and, late in life, trod the boards to make ends meet. As her husband was often on the road, Bridget returned to Dublin regularly, in order to see her family. She took Hitler on a couple of occasions. One time, they attended a performance of *The Countess Kathleen* at the Abbey Theatre. W. B.

Yeats was theatre manager at the time. Hitler met him afterwards. With mutual interests in the occult, they had a lot to talk about. Hitler's English was poor, but Yeats was a bit of a motor-mouth and needed no encouragement. He talked about his plans for a Celtic Mystical Order, based on a crannog in Lough Key, County Sligo. He talked about the Hermetic Order of the Golden Dawn, which was descended from the Rosicrucians by way of a magical lodge based in Nuremberg. He talked about Cave Hill in Belfast, with its subterranean slumbering giant, the Irish equivalent of Hitler's hero and personal role model, Frederick Barbarossa. Barbarossa, as I'm sure you know, means red beard. Barbarossa was believed to be of Irish extraction, the Red Branch warriors of Ireland were based in Ulster, as was Cu Chulainn, Ireland's Iron Age killing machine…"

"Barbarossa was the code name of Hitler's assault on Russia," Kelley interjected. "Wasn't it?"

"Correct, Dr. Kelley," the priest assented. "And Kathleen was the code name of Hitler's intended invasion of Ulster, named after the Yeats play, naturally." He pulled another cigarette out of the slim silver case and tapped it gently on the top, settling the tobacco. There was something etched on the cigarette case surface, something that looked like an eagle with wings outstretched, perched upon a swastika. But the case was back in an inside pocket before Kelley could be certain. "However, Hitler invaded Russia instead, two months after the air raid on Belfast."

"I don't see how the two are connected," Kelley said, confused by the direction Conn Mannion's narration was taking. "What's a small-scale Luftwaffe raid on Belfast got to do with Hitler's full-scale invasion of Russia?"

"Oh, it has everything to do with everything," the priest answered with another of his crinkly bag smiles, though the eyes weren't twinkling this time. "And not simply because small events can have very big consequences, according to chaos theory." Casually, he brushed a pellet of cigarette ash off his creased black jacket. "Yeats told Hitler about the spear, you see."

"Spear? What spear?" Abby interrupted, getting caught up despite herself.

"The spear that was found in Belfast. The spear kept in St. Stephen's."

"St. Stephen's Spear? Never heard of it," Kelley snorted.

"No, you wouldn't have," the priest replied drily, lighting his cigarette, inhaling deeply and exhaling through his roseate nose. "Does the Spear of Destiny mean anything to you?"

Kelley turned to look at Abby, his jaw slack with astonishment. His companion remained unmoved, evidently unfamiliar with the legend of the Holy Lance. "The spear that pierced the side of Christ? On the cross?"

"Correct," Father Mannion answered with a conspiratorial smile. "Would you like to see it?"

Chapter Twenty-Nine

The Music of the Spears

Father Mannion rummaged through an old roll-top desk in the corner of the room, its role as a writing instrument long since abandoned. It worked better as an emergency drinks cabinet. An orchestra of empty and half-full whiskey bottles clanked discordantly. Kelley turned to his companion and mouthed "Spear of Destiny?" in a deliberately exaggerated fashion. He pointed at his right temple and rotated his index finger slowly, while rolling his eyes together. Abby responded by raising an imaginary glass to her lips and waggling it repeatedly. The priest is paralytic.

Indeed, for one of the holiest relics in Christendom, the spear that Longinus the Centurion used to put Jesus out of his misery on the cross, the spear that was second only to the Holy Grail in the pantheon of religious artefacts, the spear that featured alongside the peerless chalice in countless medieval Grail legends, the spear that inspired innumerable works of religious art, not least Richard Wagner's final opera, *Parsifal*, the spear that was reputed to be in the Kunsthistorisches Museum, Vienna, along with the rest of the Reichkleinlodien regalia, the spear that gave its possessor unlimited power, superhuman power, possibly apocalyptic power, the spear that must have been six-foot long if it was an inch, was strangely reluctant to reveal itself. Misplacing car keys is one thing, losing the TV zapper down the back of the sofa is another. But there's really no excuse for forgetting the whereabouts of Christianity's pre-eminent keepsake.

The priest must have pulled open every drawer in the multi-drawer desk, including the little miniature ones situated above the writing surface, before he found what he was looking for. He returned to the cosy fireside area with a half-full bottle in one hand and an exquisite rosewood reliquary in the other. "Holy water," he said, raising the dusty bottle of Tullamore Dew in salutation. "There's a tradition that viewing religious objects must be accompanied by food and drink." It was an ancient Irish tradition that he'd invented all of two minutes before. A bowl of nibbles duly appeared in the centre of the scuffed coffee table, between the bevelled bottle and the burnished box. They looked a bit like dog biscuits. Abby demurred.

Father Mannion poured sizeable ceremonial drinks, said a few words of bibulous grace then settled down to explain the spear's provenance. "Are either of you familiar with the stories about Adolf Hitler and the Spear of Destiny?" A shake of the head from Abby and an equivocal wiggle of Kelley's outstretched hand encouraged the aged priest to continue his extempore address. He told them the much-recycled tale of Hitler's epiphany in the Hofburg, where the impoverished artist was transfixed by the mesmeric power of the Holy Lance and, after researching its historical background, vowed to acquire the sacred spear for himself someday. In 1938, his very first post-*Anschluss* act was to remove the artefact from its cabinet in Vienna and transport it to Nuremberg on a special, heavily guarded train. Nuremberg was not only the rightful home of the spear, but also the spiritual locus of National Socialism. Occultists to this day contend that Hitler's stupendous successes on the battlefield owed much to his ownership of the Spear of Destiny.

"But surely he still had it when the war turned against him after Stalingrad," Kelley interjected. "Did the spear lose its power, or something?"

"Ah," the religious raconteur smiled cryptically, "you're running ahead of yourself. You're missing the most obvious point, the crucial question that nobody seems to ask, no matter how many times Hitler's epiphanic story is told." He settled back in his shabby armchair, blowing smoke rings toward the moulting crystal chandelier, forlornly askew in its Victorian ceiling rose. He was waiting for a response that he knew would never come. Like all good storytellers, Mannion understood the importance of building anticipation by means of the pregnant pause.

But he hadn't reckoned with Abby. "Well," she said deliberately, choosing her words with care, "what I can't understand is why a black magician like Hitler would want a Christian relic. If he wasn't a believer in God, if he was a Satanist, a practising magician of some kind like W. B. Yeats, surely he wouldn't venerate the spear or accept that it possessed enormous primal power. Surely the spear wouldn't work for a non-believer. Belief's all-important, isn't it?"

"Belief's the key to all ideologies," the octogenarian priest confirmed, "consumerism included." He looked pointedly at Abby's Chanel skirt, Chloé blouse and Jimmy Choo slingbacks, blissfully unaware that they were borrowed from a full-on fashionista. "But bluff not belief is the real key here. The legend of Hitler's encounter with the Holy Lance dates from 1972, when it was recounted in a best-selling book of alternative history by Trevor Ravenscroft. *The Spear of Destiny* sold millions of copies worldwide. It was a huge hit at the time."

"A bit like *Holy Blood, Holy Grail,*" Kelley chipped in, "the book that Dan Brown used for *The Da Vinci Code*?"

Father Mannion raised his glass in respectful acknowledgement. "Exactly like *Holy Blood, Holy Grail.* And just like *Holy Blood, Holy Grail,* Ravenscroft's book was based on a Sunday newspaper article that appeared more than a decade earlier, an article Ravenscroft didn't refer to. That article was written by a journalist from Belfast, a man called Max Caulfield. Caulfield wrote lots of other things, including a book on the Easter Rising and a novel set in Belfast featuring a reluctant IRA hitman, but the yarn about Hitler's desire for the Spear of Destiny was his greatest work of fiction."

"And the truth, I suppose, is stranger than fiction," Abby said sceptically. "Are you seriously going to tell us that Christianity's greatest relic after the Holy Grail was stashed here in Belfast, not in Vienna or Nuremberg?" She took a slug of the emboldening whiskey, then gestured toward the rosewood container. "And if the spear was here all along – in *that* box – why would a Satanist like Yeats tell another Satanist, like Adolf Hitler, all about it? Wouldn't they have more Satanic things to talk about? How to summon up the devil, perhaps? Or a big black panther?" Abby finished her drink in triumphant refutation and thumped the empty tumbler down on the table. She didn't say a word. She didn't have to. Her meaning was perfectly clear. Get out of that one, Father Bullshit.

The cleated cleric reached for a handful of nibbles, chewed, coughed, swallowed and screwed up his face with distaste. "The truth is much stranger than that, Juliet. As I told you earlier, way back in 1898 when this house was newly built, we were plagued with irreligious people tramping across our property en route to the summit of Cave Hill, where they worshipped at the pagan coronation stone. So we took steps to rid ourselves of the troublesome throne. Underneath the coronation stone was a spearhead, an ancient Iron Age spearhead, a spearhead clearly of enormous symbolic significance. Given the history of this place, we were pretty certain that the spear was Cu Chulainn's fearsome Gáe Bolga, itself a refashioning of Wandering Aengus's Terrible Spear, itself a reincarnation of Lugh's Magic Spear, Lúin, itself a descendent of Odin's infallible lance, Gungnir. Celtic and Germanic traditions begin to merge the further back you go. They are part of the same tradition. It is no accident that both Odin and Cu Chulainn repeatedly exhibited the 'battle frenzy' that accompanied their terrible trademark weapons."

"So, the St. Stephen's Spear was actually a powerful pagan weapon, one certain to appeal to Satanists such as Yeats and Hitler?" Kelley inquired, taking a handful of nibbles. After retching on one, he politely slipped the remainder into a trouser pocket for later disposal.

"Correct," the aged priest replied. "Yeats was particularly keen to get hold of it. The spear was one of the four central symbols of his Celtic Order of Mysteries, along with the cauldron, the stone and the sword. He was obsessed with the Order when he visited Belfast in 1899, when he sat in this very sitting room, when he wrote the poem that your colleague Emer Aherne exploited for her own self-aggrandizing purposes. Yeats tried to acquire the St. Stephen's Spear on numerous occasions. He had a thing about Cu Chulainn, the Hound of Ulster. In an attempt to curry favour, he gave us the rosewood receptacle in front of you. Such was his arrogance that he actually sent us an unpublished manuscript at one stage. A crime novel, it was. A thriller, as I recall. An Agatha Christie-style whodunnit. He said it was certain to be a huge bestseller and that St. Stephen's could retain the copyright, plus all the subsequent royalties, in return for our occult lance."

Abby and Kelley found this hard to believe, since there is no known record of Yeats writing a thriller. An abandoned novel, yes, but nothing so déclassé as a page-turner. "How did St. Stephen's react to the offer?" Abby asked out of courtesy.

"It was before my time," Father Mannion replied, reaching for another canine nibble, before thinking better of it. "My understanding is that we seriously considered doing the deal during the dog days of the Great Depression, because we badly needed the money. Yeats sent the manuscript, we read through it and tried to assess its marketability. And then we came to an arrangement. But he died in January 1939, before he could collect Cu Chulainn's spear. Pity about that."

"What happened to the manuscript?" Abby inquired.

"Oh, we still have it. We considered putting it out in the mid-1950s, but Willy's younger brother, Jack Yeats, objected strenuously, threatened legal action and all sorts. He was a bit of a novelist himself and didn't want to be overshadowed yet again by his renowned big brother. In the end, we let sleeping Yeats lie. The book wasn't very good, anyway. The manuscript's still around here somewhere. Would you like to see it?" The sprightly man of God leapt from his seat, accompanied by a plume of holy dust, and beetled back to the roll-top desk-cum-drinks cabinet, where he rummaged and tugged and clattered once more. "Actually," he declared, looking back briefly over his shoulder, "I reckon he'd have sold our spear on to Hitler. A hard-nosed businessman was W. B. Yeats."

"But surely," Kelley cut in, after taking a slug of Bushmills to remove the revolting aftertaste of the sulphurous dog biscuit, "Hitler would have been interested in the St. Stephen's Spear himself. Surely he was in a position to offer much more than an impoverished Irish poet could."

Bent over double, rootling around in a bottom drawer, Mannion stopped searching for a second and stood up. One hand on the roll-top, ruddy face frighteningly flushed and grey hair dementedly dishevelled, he panted, "That's quite correct. He did. We arranged a swap, our spear for their spear. It made a lot of sense. We're Christians, they're Satanists. A religious relic for an occult totem. A spear for a spear. Fair exchange is no robbery."

"If that's the case," Abby interrupted, "how come the Holy Lance is in Vienna's Kunsthistorisches Museum today?"

"That's a fake," Father Mannion said curtly. "Made by Heinrich Himmler. It occupied pride of place in Wewelsburg Castle, the spiritual headquarters of the SS. After we made the exchange, it was put on display in Nuremberg instead of the original. Nobody knew any better. Himmler's fake was returned to Vienna in 1946."

"When, exactly, did you make the exchange?" Kelley asked.

"April 1941. I was a novitiate here at the time. I remember it well. I'll never forget it, in fact."

"Why did you wait until 1941?" the marketing academic continued, determined to pick holes in Mannion's far-fetched yarn. "Could you not have made the swap before then, especially as Hitler acquired the sacred lance in 1938?"

"Ah, here it is!" Mannion exulted, pulling a bulky manuscript out of the bottom drawer. He fanned it out while strolling over to Abby. It crackled attractively, like a log fire at Michaelmas. He handed the typescript to her, with a shrug. "See what you think." Refocusing his attention on Kelley, he removed the cigarette case from his inside pocket and, pausing to extract another stick of nicotine, set it down on the coffee table, facing his guest, swastika side up. He dragged deeply and exhaled slowly, recalling fond memories of his Hitlerite youth. "These things take time. Adolf Mahr, Ireland's leading Nazi and a famous archaeologist, formally verified the artefact and reported back favourably to his paymasters. But the outbreak of war interrupted the exchange. We thought of transporting it south to the German legation in Dublin, but the embassy was under constant surveillance by G2 and MI5. The Abwehr, Nazi Germany's military intelligence, sent several spies over early on in the war. They were amateurs, though. In the end, an elite group of commandos parachuted in during a bombing raid on Belfast and we made the spear swap. Ten years after the war, when the media started to wonder about Hitler's extraordinary hold on the German people, thereby exposing the occult roots of Nazism, we encouraged a local journo to plant the diversionary Spear of Destiny story, which was subsequently popularized by Ravenscroft's bestseller. His misappropriation of Caulfield's newspaper article was a very lucky break, believe it or not, because the yarn is repeated in every book about Hitler's occult inclinations, even though it doesn't make theological sense."

Kelley reached across the table and touched the beautiful rosewood reliquary, which was about twenty-four centimetres by eight. He could sense its primal power. Despite his easy familiarity with antiques and Castle D'Anger's objets d'art, it was the most incredible object he'd ever encountered. "And the Spear of Destiny is inside, is it?"

Silence descended as the storytelling priest considered his answer. "No, I'm afraid not, Dr. Kelley. The spear was stolen several years ago. We've been trying to get it back, without much success. Normally, you'd report that kind of thing to the police. But in the circumstances..." His answer tailed off. "The reliquary is empty. For the time being." He stubbed out his cigarette decisively and stood up. "Oh yes, there's something else you should see before you go."

Outside, in the woods, a dark shape slipped silently through the trees.

Chapter Thirty

Come Into My Parlour

The priest's residence occupied a commanding site, approximately fifty metres behind the main retreat house, its stout Victorian stonework a sharp contrast to the slipshod sixties construction of the central conference complex, chapel excepted. Faint sounds of boisterous laughter drifted up from the retreat's rear patio, where an impromptu barbeque marked the end of a hard day's academic discussion.

Small groups of scholars shimmied across the lawns, talking animatedly with much gesturing and arm-waving. Musters of peacocks strutted behind, ignoring the ill-bred blow-ins, as late-afternoon shadows crept towards a striking alabaster statue of the crucifixion. A flock of starlings erupted from the wooded hillside above St. Stephen's, its tranquil atmosphere temporarily interrupted by their tumultuous cries. Genesis and Revelation, Father Mannion's ever-eager guard dogs, joined in the bellicose chorus, with much yapping and snarling and bristling of back.

With a shuddering shove, the florid-featured priest opened the stubborn French windows of his sitting room, and stepped outside. His whiskey-thickened voice, commanding the Rottweilers to calm themselves, carried back from the rear of the house.

"What do you think?" Kelley asked his dumbstruck companion, who was beginning to doubt her doubts about Conn Mannion's dubious account.

She shook her head with incredulity. "It's so unbelievable I'm beginning to believe it, especially after yesterday's... adventures."

"Me too," Kelley concurred.

"Ireland's a bizarre place at the best of times, but when one half of the island's fighting for the Allies and the other half's neutral yet stuffed with Nazi spies, some pretty strange stuff must have been going on."

"Most of my family was in the armed forces at the time, fighting for King and country. However, they thought nothing of taking the train down to Dublin for the weekend, in pursuit of 48-hour R&R, even though they knew the city was sympathetic to the enemy. The black market, apparently, almost beggared belief. Tea was in particularly short supply down south and all sorts of tealeaf smuggling scams went on. The currencies were interchangeable at the time, don't forget. Irish notes and coins were legal tender up here and British pounds likewise down there."

"Yes, I remember my father showing me the old Irish coinage," Abby said wistfully. "Beautiful it was. There was a big chicken on the penny, a wee wren on the thruppence, a funny looking pig on the shilling and an enormous carthorse on the two and six."

"Yeats designed them, you know. I intended to mention it during my speech this afternoon. Aherne's speech, rather," he corrected gloomily. "As proof positive that the man was basically money-minded."

Diplomatically, Abby shifted the subject away from Dave the Rave's earlier trauma. The dogs had stopped barking and the starlings had settled back into their bower behind the retreat, murmuring amongst themselves. In the patio below, the pig-out was becoming ever-more boisterous, as half-cut academics got the party into gear, learned thoughts momentarily forgotten. A fiddle struck up a merry jig. It was accompanied by the pitter-patter of the bodhrán, the keening wails of tin whistles and the antiphonal whoops and yells of professorial party animals. "What I can't quite understand," Abby said, flicking through the Yeats novel in a desultory fashion, "is why he's telling us this stuff."

"The reason's very simple," Father Mannion said as he stepped inside, closing the warped French windows behind him. "Let's repair to my study. I have a surprise for you." The priest opened an interconnecting door to the room beyond and led the way.

The study was spartan and spare, a sharp contrast to the shabby comfort of the sitting room. Its uncarpeted floor echoed underfoot as they stepped inside. Perhaps it was the glass of neat whiskey she'd swallowed with a flourish, but Abby was convinced that the central circular table was stacked with money – money that looked painfully familiar.

"You really should have transferred it to a different coloured holdall," the man of God said good-naturedly. "I recognized it on your arrival." He waved them into seats around the table as he reached into a mahogany chest of drawers – no rummaging this time – and pulled out a pistol. It was an old-fashioned handgun, black and angular. A Luger by the look of it. "Stowing the bag under your bed wasn't the smartest of moves either," he continued, smiling. "Try to be more careful in future. If there is a future."

"At least we've come to the right place for our last rites," Abby retorted, refusing to be intimidated by an old man with an older weapon. She'd seen worse during the previous 24 hours, though she sensibly sat where the gunman of God indicated.

"Speak for yourself, darling," her co-captive cut in camply, before taking the seat directly opposite. "I may be a lapsed Presbyterian, but everyone knows that Ulster Protestants go straight to heaven. As for you, Father, you'll never get out of Purgatory. Give my regards to Adolf and the rest of your hellish pals."

"Enough," the crinkly cleric snapped. "The good news is that the money's all present and correct. So I won't have to kill you slowly. Genesis and Revelation will be disappointed, though..."

Having faced down a feral panther, Abby remained unfazed by the crumbly churchman's terror tactics. "All the *counterfeit* money, you mean."

"Correct. All our *counterfeit* money."

"Ours being the IRA's, I take it?" Kelley cut in. "What's the IRA doing passing counterfeit cash to the UVF, in any event? Cretinous as they are, did you really think your sworn enemies wouldn't notice?"

The Luger-toting churchman chuckled drily. "Of course they'll notice. They're expecting it. We have a mutually beneficial arrangement. IRA Inc, the organization I'm honoured to serve, has many admirable qualities. However, logistics and distribution aren't among them. UVF and Sons, on the other hand, has got a wonderful arrangement with one of the clearing banks, where they supply the ATM machines at all our major airports. As passengers always stock up on sterling when they're travelling to Britain, the counterfeits are quickly disseminated throughout the system thanks to unthinking taxi drivers, theatre box-office employees, coffee- and sandwich-bar counter-staff and so forth. Because it's spread so thinly and widely, no one really notices. And because it's mainly fivers, which are fairly rare nowadays, no one quite remembers what they look like."

"Nice to know creativity is alive and well in the North," Abby said sarcastically.

A smirk of self-congratulation crossed the devout counterfeiter's countenance. "We deliver, they distribute. Everyone's a winner. The UVF may be our worst enemies and main competitors, but we cooperate when it's in both our best interest. Hands across the ethnic divide and all that. We aren't barbarians, you know."

Kelley was sorely tempted to remind the not-so-holy roller that his organization was much worse than barbarian, unless killing, maiming, bombing, kidnapping, kneecapping, racketeering, drug running, brothel keeping and associated ancillary activities like punishment beating, armed robbery and protection money extortion were considered civilized in Conn Mannion's neck of the woods. But he decided on discretion rather than valour. "Well, if you've got your money back, your holiness, and it's all present and correct and accounted for, what's to stop you letting us go? We'll call it quits."

"Sadly, that's not possible." The priest sighed with fake regret. "You know too much, I'm afraid. You've seen the inner workings of our organization. You are aware that we work hand-in-glove with our sworn enemies, the UVF. If that were to get out, our reputation would be ruined."

"Your reputation for terrorism, gangsterism, assassination, bomb making?" Abby spat. "Far be it from us to damage your precious reputation, Father!"

"Quite." The black-clad priest cocked his black-clad pistol. It made a well-oiled click.

Sounds in good condition, Kelley surmised. He was only too familiar with the preoccupations of the hunting-shooting-fishing set, though he'd no time for field sports himself. He caught Abby's eye. He knew what she was thinking; what are our chances if we rush him? He's old, he smokes, he's had a bellyful of whiskey, his reactions are bound to be sluggish. Tip the table together and go for it. Kelley shook his head imperceptibly. Abby looked back at him querulously, then blinked in assent. He turned back to stare at the pontificating priest, while searching for something to distract him.

"You also, unfortunately, stumbled upon a particularly important handover," Mannion went on, "an extra-ordinary operation, if I can put it like that. As I told you in the other room, our most precious artefact was misappropriated several years back. Since then, as you've probably noticed, the Catholic Church has lost much of its magic. These days, people believe in brands and shopping and conspicuous consumption rather than the teachings of God. People believe irreligious nonsense about the alleged descendants of Jesus Christ and Mary Magdalene, thanks to badly written novels by blasphemers. People have lost faith in the Papacy, the church and the priesthood, on account of sensationalist stories about purported paedophile priests. It is impossible to recruit novitiates these days, much less persuade young people to take holy orders. The glory days of the post-war church, when recruitment rocketed in the third world in particular, are fading rapidly. And the loss of the spear is the root cause of our current difficulties."

"The reputation of your other employer has also deteriorated of late," Abby added acidly. "Brand IRA is not what it was. That killing-kidnapping-kneecapping positioning strategy doesn't have the pizzazz it used to. The product life cycle rides again, eh, Father?"

Conn Mannion pointed his Luger directly at Abby, his expression cold and heartless, ruddy amiability abandoned. "Products aren't the only things with life cycles," he said, then stopped suddenly as if listening to a noise outside. "Sssshhhh," he hissed, spreading his arms out wide, like a swimmer doing the breaststroke. Now was the time to upend the table and take a chance. But Kelley was otherwise occupied, staring intently at the wall. Silence reigned. There was no sound, save the creaking of the old house as the heat of the day diminished, and the clattering of a distant céilídh band further down the slippery slope. "Anyway," the ungodly IRA godfather continued, "we've heard a rumour that the spear's reappeared. A military memorabilia dealer in Scotland has information on its whereabouts. UVF and Sons have warehouses full of weapons, our cast-offs included. They know every arms dealer in Europe and beyond. The arms industry is based on bribes and backhanders, as BAE bears witness. Hence our sweetener. Hence our free gift for the memorabilia dealer. What did you do with the bayonet?" He levelled his pistol at Abby's head, with one hand under the other for support. He'd either done this before or watched every episode of *24*, *CSI* and *Law and Order*. "You have five seconds, Kelley. Five..."

The retail marketing lecturer replied casually. "That photo over there, Father Mannion."

"What of it?" the priest replied, refusing to take his eyes off Abby, who returned his gaze venomously. "Four..."

"It's Dan Brown, isn't it?"

"Ten out of ten for observation, Kelley. I already told you that Brown stayed here. He turned up when his first three books failed to sell and his career was going nowhere. Many come here when they suffer a personal crisis. That's the purpose of this facility. Three..."

"But why have you added a toothbrush moustache in felt-tip pen? He looks the spitting image of Adolf Hitler. Did he upset you with his dictatorial demands or his irreverent treatment of the Catholic Church? Or is there some deeper connection between the two?"

"I'm losing patience. The bayonet, where is it? Two..."

"Ah yes. Now I get it! The Brownshirts... the Brown House... Eva Braun. Dan Brown is a descendent of Eva Braun and Adolf Hitler. He's part of Hitler's hidden bloodline!"

"Nonsense. Time's up. One..."

Chapter Thirty-One

The Hit Man Cometh

"Hold it right there, old man," a cut-glass voice commanded from the doorway. "Put the gun down. Slowly. No sudden moves or I'll shoot." Peregrine Faulkner was standing beside the doorjamb, pointing a pistol at Father Mannion. Demi-decrepit he may have been, but the gimlet look in the former intelligence officer's eye indicated that he wouldn't hesitate to pull the trigger of his Heckler & Koch P9. His impassive demeanour suggested that he'd taken care of business on many previous occasions. The years had fallen off him. The oily emeritus professor of a few hours earlier had been left behind in Coleraine. If not quite the relentless killing machine of yore, his assassination engine was still running smoothly.

Taken aback, Father Mannion turned round in astonishment. "Do I know you?"

Abby and Kelley were equally gobsmacked, albeit intermingled with wave after wave of relief. "Perry, old man. Thank God you're here."

"You two," the aging agent ordered, "hands on the table. Where I can see them. Right now!" The captives exchanged confused glances, then did as they were told. Faulkner moved away from the doorway, towards the centre of the room, professionally appraising lines of fire in the event of an attempted escape. The timber floor rang hollow under his tread.

Conn Mannion, arms aloft in surrender, slowly lowered his right hand and, fingers splayed in apparent capitulation, placed the Luger on top of the neatly stacked pile of cash. He nodded toward the towerblocks of tenners, twenties and above. "Take it. It's yours. All of it. Consider it a retirement gift. Your MI5 pension can't be worth much. Her Majesty's government doesn't take care of its loyal retainers like it used to. Buy yourself a villa in Spain."

"Your counterfeit money might fool MI5," Faulkner snarled, his voice crackling with venom. "But it doesn't fool me… Mannion."

Baffled, the ageing cleric stared at the intruder myopically, struggling valiantly to place him. He'd seen and schmoozed so many celebrities, dignitaries and visitors down the years that they were all beginning to blend. But there was something about the old age pistol-packer that struck a distant dampened chord. "Do I know you from somewhere? Have we met before?"

"Interesting photo-gallery outside," the retired spook replied, refusing to enlighten the forgetful holy roller. "God's own glad-hander," he sneered. "You've done well for yourself in the years I've been away. Pity your aeons at the altar didn't make you more honest. I overheard your little fairy story about the Spear of Destiny." He motioned for Mannion to take a seat at the table. "Why don't you tell these… good people… the truth?"

If his many years of charming capricious celebrities had taught the ruddy Redemptorist anything, it was how to handle excitable individuals. However, the hitman giving the orders was anything but agitated. He exuded an air of icy calm. An alternative negotiating tack was called for. "Once an eavesdropper, always an eavesdropper," the priest said tartly, probing for some indication of who, exactly, his captor was and what, precisely, he'd done to upset him. "You know this man?" he shot at Kelley, who remained stony-faced by way of reply.

"An eavesdropper in later years, perhaps. But a paratrooper when I had the misfortune to meet you, Conn Mannion." He cocked the Heckler & Koch with an echoing crack. "It was the bayonet that gave you away, old man. It's my bayonet, you see. I entrusted it to you on the 15th of April 1941, when you were a spotty adolescent, avoiding the war in a monastery, and I wasn't much older but fighting for the Fatherland."

"You're Otto Skorzeny?" Kelley exploded, staggered by the thought that the emeritus in the next office was once the most wanted man in Europe, the six-times-a-night lover of insatiable Eva Peron, the quartermaster who knew where countless looted artworks were hidden, the multi-millionaire with more Swiss bank accounts and money in discreet tax havens than the entire *Sunday*

Times Rich List, and the logistics mastermind behind the Spider, the Odessa network that channelled ex-SS men, including Martin Bormann and the angel of death himself, Josef Mengele, to safety in South America and Southern Ireland.

" 'Fraid not, dear boy," Faulkner replied, smiling condescendingly at his Hustler University colleague. "Scarface died in 1975, taking most of his secrets with him. He borrowed my bayonet one day during training and inscribed his personal spider rune on it. Said it would be valuable one day, the self-regarding bastard. He was right, of course, but I didn't know that back then when I gave it to a star-struck Irish teenager as a wartime keepsake. You should have held on to it, Mannion."

"Or sold it on eBay," Abby interjected sardonically, her suspicions about Professor Peregrine Faulkner finally confirmed. "So you're not O'07, after all, just another murdering SS-man. Not even a famous one. How many concentration camp victims did you herd into the gas chambers? Is that why you have an aversion to showers? What's a bit of body odour when set against the stink of death?"

"I was a Brandenburger, not an SS man!" the raddled paratrooper shouted, then composed himself again. "You know, I was considering letting you escape before King Billy gets here, but on reflection..."

"King Billy? Didn't he die three hundred years ago?" Abby retorted, refusing to buckle or beg. "Or did your mate Mengele find a way round that too?"

"Well, the original King Billy died several centuries back, as Dr. Kelley's distant ancestors can attest. But the current one's dying to meet the person who stole his holdall and priceless item of military memorabilia. He'll be here to collect his property before long. Father Mannion won't be needing it anymore." The aged gunman turned to the equally aged priest. "Do you really think Billy will believe that you didn't arrange this... hand-over?" He waved the gun towards Abby. "Billy knows all about you and Little Miss Moffat here. He's been checking her out."

Mannion ignored Faulkner's cryptic comment, because the mystic chords of memory had struck up a tune that the aged priest remembered well and could play unaccompanied. The unforgettable night in 1941, the moonlit night that turned into flame-filled daytime, was coming back to him. He could hear the incendiary bombs crump, the ammunition dumps explode, the burning buildings collapse, the siren wail of the Irish fire-tenders at the foot of the Antrim Road, where they picked up the Operation Firefly paratroopers with their precious cargo, and returned to Dublin later that night before anyone caught on. "What's your problem, Hoven? It is Jupp Hoven, isn't it? Fair exchange is no robbery. You got what you came for, we got what we wanted. You seemed happy enough at the time. You wouldn't have given me the precious keepsake otherwise. Whatever's bothering you, Herr Hoven, I'm sure there are worse things on your wartime conscience than handling an occult artefact."

"The St. Stephen's Spear was a fake!" Faulkner yelled, his thyroidal eyes bulging to bursting at the memory. "It was Admiral Canaris's fifty-second birthday present for the Führer. It was the Admiral's entrée into the golden circle of advisers around Hitler. Canaris was our only hope of steering the war to a sensible conclusion. But emboldened by your spear, and certain that victory was within his grasp, that madman attacked Russia. Operation Barbarossa, he called it. Six months later he found out that your spear was a fake and had no magical powers after all. He'd swapped the peerless Spear of Destiny for a worthless Irish fake! He lost his nerve. His decision making went to pieces. He turned against the occult powers that had sustained him up to that point. He outlawed astrology, abandoned soothsayers and disparaged Himmler's Camelot thereafter. He imprisoned Canaris and executed him in early '45. He banished our raiding party to the Eastern Front, Skorzeny naturally excepted. Frank Ryan, the wartime leader of the IRA, died in a Berlin sanatorium. Friedrich Krueger was killed in Bosnia, during the attack on Tito's headquarters. Siegfried Grabert and Hermann Munstermann went west at Stalingrad. And all because of a fake!" Sallow complexion ashen with emotion, Emeritus Professor Peregrine Faulkner gestured toward the mini mountain of money. "Once a counterfeiter, always a counterfeiter."

"What are you talking about?" the apoplectic priest shouted

back. "The St. Stephen's Spear wasn't a fake! It was given to you in good faith. I know that for a fact. I was there, remember?"

"Still lying through your teeth, Mannion. I should have plugged you back in '41 when you whimpered 'Halt, who goes there?'" Arms fully extended in front of him, Faulkner had both hands on the cocked Heckler & Koch, steadying himself for a head shot. "The challenge would have been more impressive if your voice had broken beforehand. If I'd known you were still here, I'd have paid you a courtesy call before now."

"Our spear was genuine, I swear to you," the priest reiterated, endeavouring to regain his composure and take some heat out of the situation. "Your best people verified it. Adolf Mahr was here before the war. He vouched for its authenticity."

"That's not what de Valera told Hitler. De Valera informed the Führer that you were a bunch of conmen, that you weren't to be trusted, that he knew you from an old date, from his time in the IRA. He and Hitler were personal acquaintances from way back. Hitler believed him when he said the spear was a fake."

Clutching his chest with disbelief, the tormented man of God emitted a heartrending howl of anguish. "Dev? Dev? The devious bastard! I should've guessed. He had it in for us. He betrayed his former comrades in arms. Dirty de Valera. The conniving, double-crossing, son of a bitch."

"Why don't you tell us what you really think," Abby quipped, determined to kick the unholy father while he was down.

Mannion ignored the jibe. Insistent, he focused all his attention on the ruthless intruder. "That spear was genuine, I tell you. You checked it out yourself, for God's sake. It was the real thing, Hoven."

"Fake or real," the hitman interrupted, "it makes no difference to the outcome. Hitler's faith in the artefact was shattered. That's all it takes." He cleared his throat and pronounced sentence on the unprincipled priest. "Be sure your sins will find you out, Father."

Mannion slumped in his seat, staggered by the revelations. He raised his head as if preparing to say something, or pray something. Suddenly, a loud crack echoed round the silent room. Faulkner whirled round, pointing his weapon at the unseen source.

The priest, seizing his moment, lunged for the Luger and, in the blink of a bloodshot eye, shot Faulkner twice in the torso. Knocked back against the wall by the force of the blasts, the ex-intelligence officer turned round desperately and fired a couple of rounds in the general direction of his aged assailant. The first ploughed through the pile of counterfeit cash, but the second caught Conn Mannion full in the chest. A look of astonishment crossed the priest's face as he staggered, swivelled and slumped to the ground. His breathing was laboured and wheezy as the blood filled up his punctured lungs. He tried to speak, unsuccessfully. He stared with incomprehension at the stain spreading rapidly across his vestments, utterly flummoxed by the sudden flurry of lethal activity.

Kelley was rooted to the spot, equally uncomprehending. But Abby jumped up from the table, darted across to Faulkner, who lay dead against the scuffed skirting board, a plume of blood above him on the wall. She picked up his Heckler & Koch, strode straight over to Father Mannion, placed the barrel between his eyes, pulled the trigger and immediately returned the gun to Faulkner's lifeless hand. "Let's get out of here," she barked, "before King Billy shows his plug ugly face."

Chapter Thirty-Two

Gött in Himmel

Serendipity's the strangest thing, Brodie mused. It could so easily have gone the other way. We might still be none the wiser. When Sergeant Chuck Schmuck was patrolling on this very spot sixty-something years ago, he was probably thinking of his wife and family back in Dingleberry Falls, Idaho. Or maybe he was just enjoying a peaceful, relaxing, wonderfully sunny morning, after the month of hell he'd just lived through. Perhaps he was in a state of high alert, in case some deranged, Hitler-worshipping teenager tried to take him out as a last act of homage to the nation's fallen idol. No doubt that was why he was patrolling in the comparative safety of Obere Schmiedgasse, a narrow street immediately adjacent to the Kaiserburg fortress, where the US Seventh Army was headquartered in the aftermath of its capture of Nuremberg, the heart and soul of National Socialism.

It was the pile of rubble that caught Chuck's attention. In a nothing if not rubble-filled town, there was something odd about this particular pile of rubble. Too neat. Too tidy. Too, well, unnaturally banked up against the side of an old, half-timbered house. Sergeant Schmuck clambered to the top and, in a mind-boggling stroke of good fortune, found himself staring into a long sloping tunnel. At the end of the secret shaft, deep beneath the old fortress where General Patches and his staff officers were billeted, lay an enormous pair of locked steel doors. Two GIs were ordered to guard the discovery while the sergeant scuttled back to HQ to report his remarkable find.

General Patches' marauders didn't know what to do. Some suggested dynamiting the doors open. Others advised cutting through carefully with oxy-acetylene torches. In the end, they found a couple of soldiers with safe-breaking skills – every American regiment has at least a dirty dozen, right? – who twiddled the dial and listened to the tumblers and duly opened the doors of the bomb-proof bunker.

As per the movies, only for real, the air-conditioned vault was packed to the rafters with looted Nazi treasure: gold bullion, silver plate, religious artefacts, priceless paintings, precious antiques and the crown jewels of the Austro-Hungarian Empire, the Reichklein-odien, appropriated from Vienna's Hofburg Palace in October 1938. Not since Howard Carter stumbled on Tutankhamen's tomb 23 years earlier had such a fabulous hoard been found in such a serendipitous manner.

The uncovering of Nuremberg's treasure trove occurred on a very auspicious day, moreover. The very day that Adolf Hitler committed suicide in a bunker beneath the rubble-strewn streets of Berlin…

But that was more than sixty years ago. Brodie was two at the time. Today, the Historischer Kunstbunker is a major tourist attraction. It's presented as an act of selfless artistic conservation, of courage in the face of non-stop carpet bombing. Brodie didn't believe a word of the airbrushed tourist spiel, though he didn't really care. His fourth Schwabacher Goldwasser, an allegedly alchemical liquor – complete with floating gold flakes – had reduced his post-presentation fury somewhat and raised his blood alcohol levels accordingly. Pleasantly pissed, he sat in Kuchlbauer's bier-garten, watching the crowds ebb and flow across Tiergärtnerplatz, a picture postcard Bavarian square with its much-photographed statue, Der Hase, The Hare, a tribute to Albrecht Dürer, the great medieval artist, whose house around the corner was one of the old town's top tourist attractions.

Brodie could spot them a mile off, of course. The Nazi nerds, balding, bespectacled, middle-aged Brits who'd grown up with Airfix kits, *Commando* comics, sets of *Battle Picture Library* – all kept in sequential order – and who knew everything there was to know about the secret bunker beneath the Kaiserburg. *Gött in Himmel. Donner und Blitzen. Achtung Schweinehund.*

Savouring his Goldwasser, the half-plastered professor could see the nerds line up outside the Kunstbunker, waiting their turn to experience the place where the fabulous Spear of Destiny was discovered. They knew how the imperial regalia, including the alleged Holy Lance, had been moved from Vienna to Nuremberg at Hitler's command. They knew how the day of its reparation was declared a national holiday in Nazi Germany and how cheering crowds had lined the streets between the central station and St. Katharine's church, where the precious wares were placed on display. They knew that the Reichkleinodien were secretly relocated to the Kunstbunker in late 1944, after an elaborate decoy operation involving re-routed trucks and a misinformation campaign about indiscriminate dumping in Lake Zell. They knew that when Lieutenant Horn, Colonel Thompson, Sergeant Schmuck and the rest of the Seventh Army crew cracked open the subterranean safe in April 1945, the spear sat on top of the plundered Viet Stoss altarpiece, Poland's priceless equivalent of the Liberty Bell-cum-Magna Carta-cum-Stone of Scone.

Except that it didn't. The original spear was back in Belfast, where it nestled in a wooden box beneath Napoleon's Nose. Napoleon Bonaparte, the terrible threat who triggered the transfer of the spear from Nuremberg to Vienna in 1806 – for safekeeping, allegedly – was having the last laugh.

The Kuchlbauer Bar was laughing too. Even in his less than ebullient state, Professor Brodie still managed to charm the Altstadt barflies. The kilt, needless to say, attracted them like Loch Lomond midges in midsummer. The tartan eye-patch was also a talking point for thirsty tourists and bibulous Bavarians alike. But it was when he removed the patch and performed his legendary eye-rolling routine – imagine Mad-eyed Moodie with two peripatetic peepers – that the Kuchlbauer Bar dissolved into convivial communitas. Before long, the entire bar was singing *"Deutschland, Deutschland über alles"*, followed by a chorus or two of the *633 Squadron* theme tune – da, da, da, da, da-da, da-da – followed by a heel-tapping, thigh-slapping *Schuhplattler* and an amateurishly improvised Highland Fling. Great fun was had by all, even the Nazinerds who drifted in after their underground adventure, drawn by the bacchanalian bellowing, beer-fuelled bonhomie, unbeatable Bavarian hospitality and Pitcairn Brodie's magnetic personality. In Victorian times, he'd have been a sideshow attraction akin to petomanes, missing links and the Elephant Man. Instead, he was the Wild Man of Portobello, working the management consultancy circuit like the Midways and Medicine Shows of yesteryear. Not that there was much difference, really.

The cobbled streets were heaving when Brodie left the bar. Or perhaps they just felt that way. Being the life and soul of the party comes at a price. That price is the line of free drinks donated by grateful nobodies, whose drab lives had been given an unexpected and enormously welcome boost. Some burdens are heavier to bear than others, but the burden of downing several Schwabacher Goldwassers was a burden that Brodie's broad shoulders could carry.

He wasn't so sure about his feet, though. They weren't carrying him as well as they were a few hours earlier. The streets of the old town were definitely steeper than before, and the cobblestones of Bergstrasse were giving the paralytic professor what for. At least there was no Citroën-sponsored bunting to remind him of the Kaiserburg debacle.

This banner-free zone didn't last, however. A couple of twists and turns and stumbles and lurches brought him back to the Rathausplatz, where the unsightly Citroën insignia still covered the sacred frontage of St. Sebaldskirche – whose sculptures of wise and foolish virgins didn't know where to look – and where the giant Transformer robot pranced and pirouetted around the Picasso tableau like an embarrassing uncle at a wedding reception.

Professor Brodie swaggered and staggered across the seemingly cambered square, giving an Edinburgh evil eye to the massive robot en route. The clanking Citroën creature glared back at him, its glowing headlights directing a kind of automotive malocchio at the meandering kilt-clad scholar. Brodie refused to be intimidated by the phoney evil eye. He could see the Transformer's beefy operator in a booth by St. Sebaldskirche's side entrance, wearing an electrode-covered bodysuit that transmitted his every move to the C4's cavorting components. With an impetuous flick of his middle finger, Brodie walked by.

But the robot wouldn't let him pass.

Chapter Thirty-Three

Better Nouveau Than Never

Café Vaudeville is the place to see and be seen in Belfast city centre. Such is its gaudiness, though, that no one's looking at other people. They're way too transfixed by the candy-striped pilasters, gilt-on-gilt mirrors, neon-lit ceilings, ornate wrought-iron staircases, strategically positioned clumps of potted palms and the camp, carefully contrived evocation of Belle Epoque decadence to cast an admiring eye at anyone else.

A former bank, psychedelically reimagined as day-glo bordello, Café Vaudeville is not a modest place, let alone low-key or demure. It sells expensive snack lunches, overpriced evening meals and wallet-emptying champagne cocktails. But most of all Café Vaudeville sells kudos, cool, cachet and a curious kind of class. It offers pseudo exclusivity for home-grown celebrities, local soccer stars and what passes for beautiful people in a plain-spoken, plain-featured, plain-and-simple city. It is two parts eye-candy to one part see-you-Jimmy, especially on Friday and Saturday nights, when the queues stretch halfway down Arthur Street and the world wants in. It's almost as busy on Saturday evenings, when the day's deluxe shopping is done and a stiff drink is needed before the weary journey home.

Most normal people prefer to avoid crowds of self-obsessed status-seekers preening themselves in a neon neo-Art Nouveau confection. However, if you're hiding out in plain sight or prefer not to be seen, then it's the perfect place to be. Having used his aristocratic influence with the burly bouncers – a fistful of fivers'll do nicely, sir – Kelley managed to secure a spot in the busy Bollinger bar on the mezzanine floor. There are few pleasures in life to compare with slipping surly doormen counterfeit cash, except paying for exorbitant Bolly specials from the same wodge of bogus lolly. It seemed to fit the ersatz setting somehow.

An additional benefit of luxury champagne bars, where conspicuous consumers indulge in conspicuous relaxation, is that rows, hissy fits, temper tantrums and analogous exhibitions of inter-personal strife are not unusual. This is especially the case on Saturday evenings, when males of the species, having been dragged around the shops by their better halves, simply can't take any more and let slip clumsy remarks like "Why didn't you buy the first one?", "Did you really have to go back to the same shop three times?" or the almost unforgivable, potentially life-threatening "You've got enough pairs of shoes as it is."

Kelley and Abby sat in the classic strained relationship pose, looking at everything apart from their opposite number. The euphoria of their hair's-breadth escape from two grumpy old hitmen had faded into a funk of silent suspicion and mutual recrimination. Abby's admiration for Kelley's presence of mind – loudly crushing those stale nibbles underfoot was a brilliantly effective diversionary tactic – was counterbalanced by his sheer stupidity. Taking a few fivers from the bullet-riddled stash of cash was one thing, but stealing the reliquary on the way out was unimaginably foolhardy.

She took a tiny sip from the fluted glass and addressed her ordinarily loquacious but currently silent sidekick. "What are you thinking?"

He held her stare and said nothing, obviously biting back what he really felt. He slugged his Bolly insouciantly and replied in an uninflected monotone. "I think we're done. We're quits. Show's over."

"How do you work that out?" she snapped, unconvinced by his blasé attitude.

"King Billy will get his money back. The dead bodies will be discreetly disposed of, or if not, it'll take the police years to piece together what went on. Two old men settling an ancient score, a priest and a professor, an IRA godfather and an ex-intelligence officer. They'll hush that one up sharpish or bury it under the Official Secrets Act."

Abby couldn't believe her ears. "You don't think anyone will notice King Billy's henchmen removing a couple of freshly killed corpses from a Roman Catholic retreat?"

Kelley shrugged. "The post-conference party was just getting started when we left. Can you imagine the state they'll in by now? A posse of property developers could acquire the site, raze the existing buildings, and put up a bunch of one-bedroom apartments, and not a sinner would notice, much less make a complaint about the noise. There's no sign that we were there. As far as the conference is concerned, we left after my disastrous speech and your unpalatable interruption."

Incandescent, Abby was fit to be tied. "And do you really think King Billy is going to be satisfied with getting his money back, especially since we've left a mess that he has to clean up?"

"Something tells me that the death of an IRA godfather won't cause him too many sleepless nights," Kelley replied casually.

"Well," she answered angrily, "something tells *me* that the sudden death of his business partner might just tempt him to hunt the perpetrators down."

"Even if the UVF does come looking for us," Kelley continued, fretfully thumbing his right earlobe, "we've both got something to negotiate with. You've got your Yeats manuscript. I've got a reliquary that once held the spear. They're easily worth a million apiece. Even if Billy holds us responsible for the counterfeits, though that's unlikely as he was in on the scam all along, we've got sufficient collateral to cover ourselves." Kelley set the beautiful rosewood spear-holder on the table and admired it from several angles. Livid, Abby pulled the Yeats manuscript from her commodious Hermès handbag and started flicking through its pages noisily. "Unless you want to swap," he said coldly. "Otherwise we're done."

"I can't believe you stole that box," Abby shot back, infuriated by his studied obtuseness. "Do you really think the church isn't going to miss its property? Do you really think the novitiate who saw us in the woods won't say anything? Do you really imagine that if we somehow persuade the UVF to leave us alone, the IRA and the Catholic Church won't come after us?" Abby shook her head in disbelief.

Pointedly polishing the rosewood reliquary with a crested

linen handkerchief, Kelley dismissed her concerns about the Catholic Church, claiming that the Pope was unlikely to care about the comings and goings of a one-horse Redemptorist retreat in Belfast.

Abby tried to explain that the Catholic Church was a flat organization before flat organizations became fashionable; that there were only two organizational levels between a priest in Belfast and the Pope in Rome; and that, as a former member of the Hitler Youth, Benedict XVI's interest in the Spear of Destiny went without saying. "I can't believe you stole that container," she reiterated.

"I can't believe you stole that manuscript," he retaliated, in a petulant tit-for-tat tone of voice that did him few favours.

"I didn't steal it! Father Mannion gave it to me, in case you've forgotten, Dr. High and Mighty Kelley."

"And what proof do we have of that?" he barked. "You think the owners will take your word for it, Miss Shoot First Think Later?"

"Ah," Abby sighed, as the interpersonal sleeves finally rolled up. "Now I see what this 'we're done, we're quits, show's over' routine is all about."

Kelley raised the champagne glass to his lips and drank deeply. "Stealing stuff is one thing. I think we're entitled to it after all we've been through, and anyway, it's for insurance, not personal gain. But shooting someone in cold blood is way, way, way beyond the pale."

"He was going to kill us, Dave. Didn't you notice?"

"He was a priest, a man of God. How could you, Abby?"

"He was no man of God, or if he was, he'd long forgotten what godliness is. He was an IRA godfather, up to his neck in God knows what. He betrayed you and your country during the Second World War, Dave, while your forefathers were fighting the fascists."

"That's no excuse for taking someone's life. You didn't even hesitate... casual as you like... right between the eyes... killed him in cold blood..."

Abby reached across the table and put her hand on his. He withdrew it instantly. "You're forgetting something, Dave."

"What's that?" he answered hollowly, only to be interrupted by an argument breaking out at an adjacent table, where a long-suffering boyfriend had just made an unconscionable remark about his girlfriend's bum looking big in the YSL trouser suit she'd bought that afternoon. Cutting comments were made, personal insults started to fly and, to cap their perfect day, a glass of expensive Bollinger was hurled in his uncomprehending face. From post-purchase regret to post-traumatic stress disorder in less time than it takes to enter a PIN code. Such is life in contemporary consumer society.

Turning back from the Bolly-fuelled battle of the sexes, Abby attempted to empathize with her partner in crime. "You're forgetting that I used to work in an abattoir, Dave. The killing shed. I've shot more cattle and sheep between the eyes than you've given lectures... or played gigs... or bagged grouse on your father's country estate." Ever forthright, she couldn't help herself. "Or were you too squeamish for that too?"

"Field sports were never my thing," he said haughtily, opening and closing the beautiful but empty reliquary.

"I never found it very sporting, either. Ripping pigs asunder is no way to make a living. But when you're struggling to keep the wolf from the door you'll do anything, even slaughtering innocent animals. The crucial thing is to ensure they don't suffer. Father Mannion was dying. I put him out of his misery. End of story."

Kelley shook his head sorrowfully. "I saw the look on your face, Abby. It wasn't a look of compassion. You enjoyed killing him." He stared across the table at her, his boyish features striated with distaste. "He may have deserved to die – probably did – but you shot him like a helpless dog."

"He was a dog, Dave. He wasn't helpless, though. He didn't hesitate to kill Faulkner and he would have killed us as well." Abby was unrepentant. "He was a ruthless bastard. He deserved to die. I'd shoot him again if I had to."

Kelley couldn't disguise the look of loathing. He didn't try to. "Yes, I'm sure you would. That's what disgusts me about you."

A large weight was crushing Abby's chest; her throat was constricted to the point of strangulation. She felt as if she had been slapped in the face repeatedly. "I'm... I'm... I'm sorry if I disgust you," she stuttered while attempting to stand, her knees almost buckling. "You're right of course, Dr. Kelley. We're done here." She straightened her dress, threw the bulky Birkin over her shoulder and, without so much as a backward glance, forced her way through the crowd at the bar.

Kelley made no attempt to stop her. He stared fixedly at the table in front of him, sipping his champagne with what little dignity he could muster. "You forgot your manuscript," he shouted at Abby's rapidly retreating figure.

"Shove it up your ass, dickhead," she yelled from the turn in the wrought iron staircase. The crowd at the champagne bar cheered loudly. Their evening's entertainment had started already and it was only 7.00 p.m.

Keeping his head well down, Kelley flicked through the yellowing Yeats manuscript. Its typewritten pages looked strangely out of time in an era of high speed laser printers, akin to an illuminated manuscript in Gutenberg's brave new world of moveable type.

Albeit deeply engrossed in the manuscript – sufficiently engrossed, he hoped, to eradicate the unwelcome attention he'd attracted – he sensed a malevolent presence nearby. Kelley glanced up, only to see Abby's enraged face. She was swinging at him with the Skorzeny bayonet. "You can keep this too," she spat, and stabbed the razor-sharp weapon into the rosewood receptacle. The precious artefact disintegrated with an almighty crack, as Kelley looked on, appalled. The entire bar turned round as one, but there was nothing to see because Abby was already pounding down the staircase. She sped through the main downstairs bar, dodging the punters and planters alike, then disappeared into the foyer and the gathering gloaming beyond.

Chapter Thirty-Four

Rosa Alchemica Caledonia

Kelley polished off his Bolly with as much savoir-faire as he could muster and started gathering up his possessions. Splinters of holy rosewood tumbled from the fractured reliquary as he lifted the vandalized container. Fearing further damage, he set it down gently. Slowly, painstakingly, he sorted through the remains, hoping against hope that repairs were possible. But the lid was completely destroyed and the bayonet had penetrated the base, such was the force of the blow. As he picked away at the debris, however, he discovered something that would change his life irrevocably.

He had to find Abby.

The downstairs bar was heaving. Kelley took forever to fight his way outside. Although Arthur Street was remarkably busy – replete with shell-shocked platoons of shoppers retreating from the front lines of the retailing redoubt – there was no sign of his student. He didn't know where she lived and, even if he accessed the university's on-line records, there was no guarantee she'd return there that evening. At a serious loss, he trudged back to the car park, while keeping a weather eye out for an open internet café.

Ordinarily, the evocative streets of old Belfast would have fuelled and fired up Kelley's gothic imagination: the site of the original Elizabethan castle; the market house and hangman's gibbet; the crepuscular graveyard at St. George's; the narrow alleys, entries and courts, where all sorts of skulduggery went on. But not on this occasion. Lost in thought, Kelley rushed past Joy's Entry, once the lair of the city's sedan chair agents and dealers, only to be confronted by a morose retail marketing undergraduate. "Abby!" he shouted with relief, holding her tight and hugging for all he was worth, like a little lost child. "Thank God. There's something I've got to show you."

Untangling herself from his eager embrace, she was seriously tempted to retort "Later, big boy." Instead, she stuck with the explanatory speech she'd rehearsed while waiting for him to return to his car. "There's something I've got to tell you, too."

"Okay, fire away," he said, his puppy-dog face as effervescent as she'd ever seen it. The Vaudevillian disgust had passed, evidently, like wind on the F-Plan.

Abby hesitated. Maybe the speech wasn't necessary. "No, you go first."

Dave didn't need much persuasion. Waving a sheet of paper as if it were a winning lottery ticket, he beetled down Joy's Entry, Bontoni brogues echoing off the enveloping walls. "There's an internet café around here somewhere." Except that there wasn't, nor were the next two entries any better e-quipped. At the third attempt, they encountered the E-spresso E-mporium, a down-at-heel hard-drive-dive, whose sticky floor covering made from reconstituted pre-chewed chewing gum was surpassed only by its tacky-to-the-touch keyboards, blackened by the grime of unwashed fingers from the adjacent public conveniences. The owner was equally unspeakable, MRSA made flesh. Evidently unhappy about their late arrival, he banged, clattered and hissed his grubby Gaggia, dropping less than subtle hints that he planned to shut up shop, asap, before repairing to the cess pit called home.

Kelley and Abby ignored his steamy signals – not that they'd dare drink the stuff he served – while wishing they'd come equipped with rubber gloves. Fearful of infection, they tentatively booted up Hell's Dell, its former flat screen spattered with gobbets of either chocolate chip cookies or congealed bodily fluids. It was hard to tell. And hard to the touch. Yuck.

"As a fellow Yeatsian, you'll never believe what I just found," he said, clicking on to HAHA, the Hustler Arts and Humanities Archive. "In the false bottom of the reliquary!"

Abby glanced at the sheet of notepaper that was burning a hole in his hand. "Let me guess. W.B.'s laundry list? A letter to his German pen pal, Adolf? A limerick? A limerick about Limerick? *There once was a lady from Limerick / Who wrote humorous poems for the hell of it / Five lines full of laughter / That choked rhymers thereafter / A curse on the Limerick Heimlich."*

"Err, err, err, err," Kelley called in a sing-song voice. "Anachronism alert! The Heimlich manoeuvre dates from the 1970s. Yeats couldn't possibly have been aware of it. If he were, mind you, he'd probably have given it a go, hoping that it'd enhance his libido. The man swallowed more monkey glands than smiler there's served cappuccinos."

The pestiferous barista muttered imprecations from behind the feculent counter, while wiping his noisome nozzles with a cloth that had more bacteria on board than the superbug bus service from Belfast City Hospital.

"Just letting off steam," Abby smiled across at him. A Nick Cave look-alike with a ferocious five o'clock shadow – five o'clock three days past, that is – the bad-tempered barista yanked on his jet and grumbled over the gaseous tumult. "Heard it before, sister. Drink up and log off. This isn't fuckin' Starbucks."

Kelley raised an eyebrow at his companion. "Well, maybe Starbucks in Seattle the day after the WTO riots."

"I take it we aren't leaving him a tip, Dave."

"The tip of your bayonet perhaps, darling."

"Not funny."

With a suit-yourself shrug, Kelley passed a piece of paper to his shoulder-surfing companion. It was a handwritten poem. "The Spear of Destiny", by W. B. Yeats. The title index of the Yeats Variorum database filled the screen: "The Song of Wandering Aengus", "The Sorrow of Love", "The Spirit Medium", "Spilt Milk", "The Spur". "There's no 'Spear of Destiny'," Kelley said with a silent swearword. "He wrote one called 'The Arrow'. Another called 'The Hawk'. Yet another called 'The Rose of Battle' and naturally 'The Second Coming'. But nothing remotely like 'The Spear of Destiny', I'm afraid."

"So it's a fake… a forgery of some kind?"

Every inch the academic, Kelley hummed and hawed, while running a hand through his attractively dishevelled dark hair. Then instantly wished he hadn't. The lifeforms from the keyboard were already frogmarching across his scalp in formation, determined to dig in beyond the reach of Head & Shoulders or just about any shampoo short of prussic acid. "Hard to tell," he said. "I mean, if there's an entire novel that nobody's heard of, a thriller no less, what price a poem or two?"

"There are more things in the corpus, Horatio, than are dreamt of in your database."

"Indeed," Kelley replied in a monotone. "Mind you, Yeats was a terrible man for chopping and changing his work. Maybe it's an early draft." He hammered the minging keyboard viciously. "With this database, there's an easy way to find out." *Swan, sing a song of stolen glory*, the first line of "The Spear of Destiny", appeared in the search box. An alphabetical list of Yeats's first lines materialized on the screen: *Surely among a rich man's flowering lawns; Swear by what the sages spoke; Sweetheart, do not love too long*. Kelley sighed heavily. He was starting to sound like the barista. "I'll need to talk to an expert."

"Do you know any?"

He nodded sagaciously, as the door of the café opened. An eager punter popped his head in, obviously anxious for a caffeine infusion. Then popped it out again on receiving the glare of death from Conan the Barista. The sudden draught lifted Yeats's poem off the table and wafted it on to the floor, where it stuck fast on the filthy linoleum. Frowning, Kelley peeled it up with distaste, then slowly cracked an enormous smile. "Yeatsian schmeatsian, darling!" If not quite back to his bubbly self, Dave bipolar Kelley was doing a pretty good impersonation. "The clue's on the other side of the page! Check it out."

Abby turned over the scribble-filled sheet of paper. The obverse was completely blank. With the exception of a small but striking company logo. Yeats's poem had been composed on a scrap of headed stationery. As logos go, the Nazi swastika with a rose in the middle, surrounded by a snake swallowing its tail, wasn't likely to give Nike sleepless nights – nightmares, possibly – but the company name and accompanying slogan were very suggestive. Rosa Alchemica Caledonia. Established 1934. Edinburgh's widest selection of military, magical and monastic memorabilia.

Kelley was staring at her expectantly. "Father Mannion

mentioned that the counterfeit money, plus bayonet, was an up-front payment for someone in Scotland, someone with information about the Spear of Destiny. It's too much of a coincidence to ignore. If we want to track down the missing spear, Rosa Alchemica Caledonia's the place to start."

"I thought we were all done, Dave."

Flustered, he blustered. "Yeah, well, I've been thinking about that, Abby. The best way to get them off our backs for certain, for ever, is to find the spear. That's what the Catholic Church is after, and they're best placed to call off the dogs of war, their psycho Protestant pit-bulls included. The manuscript and the dagger and the poem give us sufficient collateral to negotiate with any memorabilia dealer, whatever their speciality. Just as the spear is useless unless you believe in it, so too dealers believe in one thing and one thing only..."

"Doing deals."

"Exactly," Kelley replied with a smile. "You were listening in class, after all."

"Sorry, Dave. I hate to rain on your academic parade, but I borrowed someone else's lecture notes."

"Bang goes your First, darling."

"So, *darling*," she retorted, "are we off to Edinburgh, then? Is there a late flight tonight? Try Expedia."

Kelley speedclicked through the travel site, while holding forth at the same time. Abby, he decided, should fly to Edinburgh that night, with his sister's passport as proof of identity. She could case the collectables shop while he saw a man about the poem. He'd join her there tomorrow. Decision duly made, he handed over the rest of the fivers and paternally warned her not to spend them all in one shop.

Abby returned the wad with a wiggle of the index finger and a pert purse of the lips. "No more counterfeits, Dave."

"It's either that lot or we can withdraw genuine fakes from the airport ATM."

Abby smiled ruefully and gestured toward the baleful barista. "Do you think our host with the most surly expression has a photocopier we can use? Or a scanner? I'd like a copy of Yeats's poem."

"I'm sure he'll be happy to oblige," Kelley replied with ironic assurance. "While we're waiting for the photocopier to warm up, perhaps you'll tell me what you were going to tell me earlier, then didn't."

Abby shook her ringlets again as they switched off the Dell from Hell and made their way to scowler's festering counter. The coffee-stained melamine surface had more rings than Van Cleef & Arples. "It's not important, Dave. I'll tell you another time."

"Tell me now, Abby," he said earnestly. "Or the deal's off. I mean it."

Although she was tempted to test his new-found resolve, Abby suspected it was time for the truth. "Well, Dave, if you must know, I stayed at St. Stephen's not long after my father committed suicide. I had the family to take care of. I had a breakdown. I was suffering from eating disorders. I needed to go somewhere to recuperate, to get my act together. My extended family didn't want to know, not a single one of them. The priest was very sympathetic. Too sympathetic. He took advantage of my vulnerability, shall we say. He didn't recognize me when we showed up for the conference, nor during our little tête-à-tête, though Juliet D'Anger isn't as slim as Husky Maguire used to be. God knows how many tormented kids he's exploited in the interim. Or how many there were before I passed through his hands."

Slack-jawed with astonishment, Dave stared at his companion as he finished the photocopying and paid for the less than stellar service. "I see."

"The bastard deserved to die," Abby said flatly.

"You're right. He did. I hope he burns in Hell."

Chapter Thirty-Five

Kingdom Come

Malone Road, in the south of the city, is the most desirable residential location in Belfast. Its salubrious streets are lined with mature trees and high hedges, behind which lurk large gardens, larger cars and the largest detached houses in town. Only the most affluent local citizens, or the most crooked, can afford to live in Malone, and only the most pretentious would want to.

Malone, of course, is internally variegated. Just as certain districts on the periphery claim to be "Malone" when they're not – the golf umbrella of Maloneness doesn't cover them and they are forced to stand, shame-faced, in the pouring rain of social disapprobation – so too certain streets are much more "Malone" than others.

The most Malone part of Malone is Malone Park. Malone Park is a private road, a very private road, where run-of-the-mill villas run to well over £1 million and especially desirable properties go for many times that.

Brought up in a castle outside Carrickfergus, Kelley was unlikely to be impressed by the moneyed manoeuvrings of Malone Park life, though his car looked out of place in SUV central. He cruised along the lime tree-lined thoroughfare, carefully negotiated the Himalayan speed bumps – hey, those 4x4 owners have to have something to hone their skills on – and turned left into a leafy cul-de-sac, where he parked in front of a brash, brand new red-brick. Situated in an attractively weathered streetscape, it was testament to the rapaciousness of Ulster property developers, who think nothing of converting big Victorian gardens into pricey executive apartments, bijou pieds-à-terre and compact family residences, as in this particular instance. Isambard Kingdom's carbuncle stood out like a Burberry-bedecked chav at Henley Royal Regatta. Not that he gave a damn.

Isambard Kingdom, formerly of Brunel University, was a Reader in English Literature at Northern Ireland's self-anointed equivalent of Oxbridge, Queen's University Belfast. Situated at the apex of Malone's urban imperium, the Queen's main building is modelled on Magdalen College, Oxford, as is its ethos of intellectual superiority.

Akin to most academic institutions, however, its salaries remain fixed at the bottom end of the church mouse scale (vice-chancellor and senior officers excepted). Queen's readers can't afford to live in Malone Park, as a rule, not unless they're siphoning off student top-up fees or taking back-handers in return for first class degrees.

Or both.

Kingdom's kingdom was honestly made. His residence may have been more spit than polish, but at least he earned it by entrepreneurial acumen, perhaps the rarest of qualities in academia. An iconoclastic outsider among the ossified in-breds of English Literature, Izzy embraced computers, quantitative analysis and literary number-crunching while his colleagues were still fighting tooth and nail over trochees, enjambment and iambic pentameters. He digitized and databased canonical works from Marlow and Milton to Melville and Mailer, then used search and compare algorithms to answer those supposedly unanswerable questions: did Shakespeare write his own plays; were the gospels based on an earlier lost work by Q; how much, exactly, did W. B. Yeats owe to the automatic writings of his unsung wife, Georgie Hyde Lees; and to what extent did Dan the man Brown plagiarize *Holy Blood, Holy Grail*? Isambard's proprietary software had also been adapted to identifying cheating in undergraduate essays and assignments, thereby providing a source of unearned income that makes Croesus look like a panhandler and Warren Buffett a bum. Granted, his income stream suffered grievously on account of plagiarists plagiarizing his plagiarism programme, but such is the price of success in the service industries nowadays.

Despite his decidedly unacademic affluence, Izzy remained utterly unaffected. Hale, hearty, hairy and high-coloured, a classic casting from the bluff Yorkshireman foundry, Kingdom had a handshake like lockjaw. Kelley's metacarpals crumpled under the pressure, as they always did, though four-fractured phalanges were a small price to pay for Isambard Kingdom's expertise. He'd helped Dave on several previous occasions, when he was an indentured doctoral student of the estimable Emer Aherne. Aherne hated Kingdom, because he'd called her much-vaunted Yeats poem into question. But Kelley had always found him funny, friendly and unfailingly helpful. Given that Dave was enrolled in a rival institution and studying under an academic adversary, this was assistance above and beyond the call of collegial duty.

Kingdom's generosity of spirit notwithstanding, there was something about him that Kelley found consistently disconcerting. His eyebrows. Like a pair of ferrets fighting in a sack, they rolled and roiled and rippled with every tiny change of expression. Indeed, having wrestled each other to a post-civilities standstill, they got stuck in with a vengeance when Kelley raised the subject of a new Yeats poem. "Not another one," he growled. "Aherne's handiwork, I take it?"

"No, no," Kelley insisted. "I discovered this one myself."

Dr. Kingdom scrutinized the scrap of paper disdainfully. "Damn and blast," he grumbled, "looks a bit like the old goat's handwriting. You'd better come through to my study." He led the way past a plasma-screened, home-cinemaed, movie-postered, leather-loungered living area, via a granite-topped, breakfast-barred, Aga-ranged, Le Creuset-clad kitchen, with a Smeg the size of an iceberg, to a plain, simple, surprisingly bookless and frighteningly tidy office, where an Apple Mac Pro hummed quietly in the corner.

"I'll call back another time if this is inconvenient, Izzy."

The stereotypical Yorkshireman grunted, in his characteristic grump-with-a-heart-of-gold manner. "Nay lad, it should only take a few minutes. I have to be out of here in half-an-hour. But that should suffice."

"Are you going somewhere nice, somewhere sunny?" Kelley inquired politely as Kingdom typed the first stanza of "The Spear of Destiny" into his search, sift and spit-out-the-answer engine.

Swan, sing a song of stolen glory
Quiet cave, the spear lies in repose
Green eyes aglitter, as the red rose
Dreams of Deirdre's devious story
Valiant Uaithne strikes a chord forlorn
X marks the spot where flint tears fall
Come back my beauteous brown-haired angel, when all
Heaven's cloths enwrap the golden dawn.
A man is but a man of old
Cu Chulainn weeps for death foretold.

Eyes flicking from page to screen, Kingdom coughed up a consumptive cackle. "I'm heading off to Lusty Beg. It hasn't seen any sunshine since the Middle Ages."

"Lusty Beg?"

Kingdom cackled again. "It's an outdoor pursuits centre in the middle of Fermanagh Lakeland. I've organized a team-building weekend for the postdocs. Paddling canoes, climbing trees, crossing chasms, composing sonnets when not indulging in group hugs. The usual."

Sun, angle on the rood of time unholy
Vain demon, pay the price of fame
Murthemne melts in raging fury, the name
Foresworn as love's doves circle slowly
He wishes it were otherwise; the rage
Dies quickly, like a hawk descending
Dart-sharp on its purblind prey, a cunning climbing
Vixen in the sally gardens of the stony age.
Kiltartan calls the cruel killer to him
Neither forgive the sinner nor forget the sin.

"Horrifying."

"Yes, I know. I don't know which is worse, the soakings or the sonnets."

"Actually, Izzy, I was thinking of the horrifying name of the place. There's really somewhere called Lusty Beg? The mind boggles."

A hairball of gruff good humour rolled across Kingdom's neat and tidy desk. "Oh, I don't know, David. I often beg my wife when I'm feeling a little lusty."

"A frightening thought." If he says something about Kingdom Come, Kelley reflected, I'll make my excuses and leave.

"An even more frightening sight!" Isambard roared with self-effacing laughter as he typed the third and final stanza of Yeats's "Spear of Destiny".

Hail, reign heavy in the land of Daanan
Yellow bracken broken on the cruel cross
Will mighty mother Dana regret the loss
Foretold of faithful Fergus, man of men?
Just as curlew cower in the corn fields
Ruadan snoops on Donn's discordant smithy
Perchance the sacred, spellbound spear of destiny
Fights Formorii forever, yet never yields.
Neath holy walls the answer lies
On ancient mound the lance resides.

Even before the software expectorated its answer, Kelley knew what was coming. Kingdom's sceptical look as he scanned the poem to double-check his input spoke volumes. Volumes that weren't written by County Sligo's celebrated son.

"I'm not a lover of Yeats, David my lad, but I examined a lot of his stuff for an analysis of his wife's automatic writing." He handed the scrap of paper back to Kelley. "This poem is a fake. I'm sure of it. The handwriting is a fairly good imitation, the metre and imagery are undoubtedly Yeatsian and some of the slant rhymes and enjambments are… Yeatsish, at a pinch. But it's a pastiche at best and a hoax at worst. I hope you didn't pay too much for it."

Kelley pocketed the poem. "No, no. I found it in an old box, just by chance."

The software excreted its result. Negative. Unrelated strings. Not a match. "Bring me something sexy next time, Dr. Kelley. Yeats's legendary novel would be nice. Now that's the Holy Grail of Yeatsian scholarship."

"A novel?" Kelley asked innocently. "*The Speckled Bird*, you mean? The abortive book he was working on in the early 1900s?"

"Hah!" Kingdom replied, untangling himself from the swivel chair and politely ushering his visitor through the trophy rooms in his trophy house on the trophy street in a trophy part of the city. "Not that piece of trash. I mean the thriller he talked about in the mid-1930s. He was obsessed with pulp fiction, detective stories, cowboy adventures and all the rest. He was devouring them on his deathbed. Despite his Nobel Prize and all the acclaim, he longed for a huge bestseller like Agatha Christie. Partly for the royalties, I grant you, but partly to prove that he had the common touch." He laughed dismissively at the very thought of Yeats slumming it. "Rumours have been circulating about a Yeats pot-boiler for years, though the general academic consensus is that it's probably a prank. Oscar Wilde's estate is plagued by fake manuscripts written by a practical joker in the 1920s. Ironically, though, the prankster publications themselves are extremely valuable. Would you credit it? So even if Yeats's thriller was a fake, it'd still be worth a bob or three, lad."

Kelley extended his hand to the outward bound-bound money-bags, knowing full well that a crush was coming and a pinkie was going to the undiscovered country from whose bourn no traveller returns. "If ever I come across one, I'll be in touch."

"You do that, David. No more poems, okay?"

"Okay Izzy. Got it."

Crunching across the gravel to his cherry-blossom Morris, Kelley heard Kingdom call out behind him. He turned, as the burly Barnsley-man barrelled toward him, ferrets flailing. "Fulcanelli," he barked.

"Sorry?"

"Fulcanelli. The alchemist." The reader with the Midas touch looked at Kelley expectantly, as if he should be familiar with the name. "You know, the famous French alchemist of the 1930s. There is a rumour that Fulcanelli's books were written by Yeats, who was a bit of an alchemist himself. I ran them through the software once. I had to check Fulcanelli out as part of the Dan Brown case. There was a match."

"With Dan Brown?" Kelley laughed.

Kingdom smiled inscrutably. "Have you considered that the poem might be in code? Fulcanelli wrote in code. Yeats was familiar with codes and ciphers on account of his Golden Dawn connections. A code might explain the awkwardness in its scansion."

"What kind of code, Izzy?"

Kingdom patted Kelley on the shoulder. "I will arise and go now, and go to Lusty Beg."

Chapter Thirty-Six

Bury My Braveheart at Wounded Knee

Brodie thought he was imagining things, which was understandable enough given the state he was in. He thought for a moment that the Transformer robot was deliberately blocking his admittedly meandering path across Rathausplatz. He thought that the monumental Meccano set was planning to make him pay for his impertinence, for the damage he'd done to the Citroën brand during its birthday celebrations.

He wasn't wrong.

With a blast of horn and a squeal of brakes and a howl of hip-hop from its in-car stereo, the Citroën Transformer stood in front of Brodie, mechanized arms outstretched, legs planted apart. The professor moved to his left. The Transformer moved too. Chuckling at the stupidity of the situation, Brodie moved resolutely to his right. The Citroën showpiece stepped across, with a rippling rattle of metal and glass. Semi-stotious though he was, the Scottish professor wasn't going to be messed around by a heap of scrap metal. He stared up at the monster then looked over toward its operator beside the church. The message was crystal clear. The operator paid no attention.

Steeling his resolve, as he had done on numerous Friday nights in Edinburgh's Grassmarket, the professor took a couple of preparatory deep breaths, then performed the kind of quick sidestep that had taken him through countless drift defences in his rugby playing days. He knew how to sell a dummy. But the robot wasn't buying. It leapt in front of the professor once more, hydraulics whooshing and wheezing with the effort. The thing then crouched down like an aluminium sumo wrestler, about to charge at its puny opponent. Brodie was a tall, muscular man, 189 cm. and counting. Citroën's Transformer was more than twice that height, with muscles of titanium and thermoplastic talons to boot. This was David versus Goliath. This was Robin Hood versus Little John at the ford. This was Mel Gibson in *Braveheart*, before the blue-faced battle against overwhelming odds.

This was man against machine.

Brodie dropped to a crouch too, facing his mechanized nemesis. Eyes locked, they were akin to American footballers on the gladiatorial gridiron, listening intently for the first down call.

The call never came.

Incredibly, the Transformer rearranged itself in real time. Its metal plates slid this way and that, morphing into another combatant entirely. The bonnet became a chevroned shield. The engine block became a mace-headed war-flail. The toughened glass windows turned into an impenetrable breastplate. The dashboard display shape-shifted into a plastic helmet and dial-dotted visor. Its wing mirrors metamorphosed into a pair of fearsome antler-like horns. Citroën's Transformer was a Teutonic Knight reborn.

The milling, night-time crowd gasped at the sudden transformation and rapidly backed away to the side of the brightly-lit square, leaving the cobbled space clear for the combatants.

Swaying from side to side, as though he were a goalkeeper facing a penalty shootout, Brodie attempted to bamboozle his adamantine antagonist. He leaned to the left, then leaned to the right, then made a dash for the operator in his booth behind the malevolent machine. But the robot wasn't fooled, thumping Brodie with its shield, sending him flying. He fell on to his unprotected knees, with his back to the brute. Screams from the crowd warned him that something was coming, as did the sudden whoosh of displaced air. Brodie dived to one side as the engine block crashed into the cobbles where he'd crouched on all fours a few moments before. With a frustrated shriek from its bespoke Bose sound system, Citroën's Transformer wrenched its war-flail aloft and swung again and again and again. It was all Brodie could do to dodge the massive blows, the shockwaves of which surged underfoot and rattled the windows in encircling buildings.

Two hardy souls from the astonished crowd rushed to Brodie's assistance, but the robot swatted them like gnats with its tempered steel shield. They careered across the plaza and back into the baying crowd, where they lay limp, bloodied and broken.

The Transformer lifted itself to its full height, raised its transmission-knotted arms aloft and emitted a Wagnerian battlecry, its windscreen wipers flip-flapping furiously across the blood-spattered breastplate.

Brodie ran toward the triumphant Transformer, jinking and dodging, trying to get under its defences. The massive engine-block club came crashing down once more, scattering the tables and overturning the seats of surrounding restaurants. He hurdled the al fresco wreckage, swerving one way then the other as the relentless robot tried again. The monster mace smashed into the Picasso tableau, like a vandal in an art gallery. Brodie clambered over the mangled recreation of *Les Demoiselles d'Avignon* – though it looked closer to *Guernica* – leaped on to the still-shuddering weapon and grabbed the tangle of timing chains, carburettor cables and coolant hoses that attached the mace head to the handgrip. The professor pulled for all he was worth. The robot, caught unawares, stumbled slightly and dropped to one knee. Brodie jumped on to its back and somehow managed to straddle its velour upholstered shoulders. Airbags popping, the monster flung its sparkplug-studded head from side to side, in a desperate attempt to shake the pugnacious Scotsman off.

But he held on for grim life, digging his fingers into the high beam eye sockets, pulling frantically on the wiring. The shrieking creature dropped both shield and mace, reached behind its rapidly swelling head, ripped the kilted commando from its shoulders and hurled the Highlander away.

The pain of the four-metre fall was excruciating. Brodie struggled to pick himself up as the Transformer attempted to stomp on its prostrate victim. Brodie rolled away from the monstrous wheel arches – this way, that way – and somehow scrambled to his feet, sprinting for the edge of the square. He ran as hard as he could, arms pumping, legs pounding, lungs bursting. The narrow side streets around Rathausplatz might give him a better chance against the creature.

But he never made it.

Swinging a fan belt like a sling, the bloodthirsty Transformer hurled a selection of headrests, door handles, cup-holders, indicator stalks, tyre irons and spare wheel nuts immediately in front of him. Brodie dodged the Citroën cluster bomb, but slithered on a pool of spilled transmission fluid, then pitched forward face-first, as a seat belt wrapped itself round his ankles like a bolas. He landed on his outstretched hands and already damaged knees, weakened from years of rugby and cross-country running. Winded, he rolled over and struggled to untie the seat-belt lariat.

Howling with victory, the Transformer was upon him, its immense left arm pinning Brodie's heaving chest. The brute unsheathed an entire steering column from a compact storage compartment at its side and made to run him through. With an enormous effort, Brodie managed to shove the creature's arm off his half-crushed chest and he wriggled through its legs, a slippery bar of Scottish soap. The robot turned with a roar, but Brodie had just enough time to pull out his dirk, tucked as per tradition at the top of his tartan knee-socks. He stabbed his razor-sharp weapon into the rear tyres of the beast, which were functioning as knee joints. An almighty jet of pressurized air whooshed out as one of the tyres instantly deflated. The robot lurched and staggered alarmingly and immediately dropped the steering column sword as it reached for the punctured patella. Brodie pierced its other vulcanized kneecap with another almighty whoosh. The Citroën Transformer collapsed on the cobblestones, writhing and thrashing helplessly, its motor functions compromised.

The crowd roared as Brodie rammed the steering column into its unprotected face, smashing the speedometer and rev counter. The shrieks of the in-car six-speaker entertainment system were terrifying to hear, but the attack had damaged its fuel lines and gasoline was pouring in a steady stream from its upper body. The stench of petroleum was overpowering.

Professor Pitcairn Brodie stared at the disabled beast, flat on its back, flailing pitifully. Transformer stared back, acknowledging defeat, a pleading look in its headlamps. The robot knew what was coming. Brodie extracted the cigarette lighter from the

C4's dashboard, checked that it was glowing brightly and threw it toward the pool of petrol. The mechanical monster erupted in a sheet of flame, a 21st century Wicker Man. Like a latter-day Frankenstein, it somehow clambered to its feet, twisting, turning, tumbling and trumpeting all the while. It lurched back towards St. Sebaldskirche, flapping at the rapidly enveloping flames, howling with sub-woofer rage, only to collapse in a clanging, clattering heap, horn blaring and intruder alarm running through its lamentable repertoire. The arching flames caught the bottom edge of the enormous Citroën flag draped across the exterior of St. Sebaldskirche and, in an instant, the artificial fibre vaporized, as though it were tissue paper.

The professor dusted himself off and continued walking back to his hotel. It had been a long day.

Chapter Thirty-Seven

The Witchery

They used to say that if you build a better mousetrap, the world will beat a path to your door. Nowadays, people dispose of mouse and trap together, so the challenge is to build a cheaper mouse-trap, not a better one. China, consequently, has cornered the global mousetrap market. There's no point trying to compete with the mousetrap sweatshops in Guangdong Province, where specially trained teams of Chinese field mice make crappy traps to snap their western cousins. So desperate has the capitalist rat-race become that outsourcing is making the leap from species to species, from man to mouse. Chinese rodents'll be assembling televisions soon, making motor cars and washing machines, running call centres and help lines and telemarketing scams and spam farms and eekk-commerce operations. As it warns in the Bible, albeit in a frequently mistranslated passage, the mice shall inherit the earth.

If global warming doesn't kill us, cutthroat capitalism will.

The west may be trembling, awaiting the tide of wise rodents from the east, but at least we've got one last trick up our sleeves. We know how to build better tourist traps. True, the mice have got Mickey and Minnie on their side, as well as Rémy from *Ratatouille*. However, the Pixar-ed attractions of Disneyland can't compete with the authentic appeal, the grass roots appeal, the granite appeal of Edinburgh. Despite ravening hordes of visitors, conventioneers, festival-goers and citybreakers, Edinburgh effortlessly takes the tourist strain and copes with just about anything Travelocity and Lonely Planet throws at it. Unlike analogous destination cities like Venice, Prague, Tallinn and Dublin, the Athens of the North somehow transcends the tourist tat-trap – year-in, year-out, year-round. Even in August, when the world not only beats a path to Edinburgh's door, but mimes, juggles, dances, somersaults and sword-swallows a path to its door, Auld Reekie accommodates the influx without debasing its intrinsic appeal.

Certain parts of the city, admittedly, have surrendered to the tour-bus multitudes. The Royal Mile, in particular, is clogged with pseudo-Scottish souvenir-scavenging sightseers. Kilts-U-Like, Tartans-R-Us, Haggis-à-Manger, Tattoo-2-Go, Dunkin Dewars and similarly saltaired retail stores stretch from the Esplanade to St. Giles in serried ranks of McThistle that'd make Walter Scott weep and Greyfriars Bobby abandon his master's vault. But even here attempts have been made to ameliorate the heathered highland horrors, foremost among which is The Witchery.

An upmarket theme restaurant-cum-hotel, situated near the brow of Castlehill, The Witchery is a postmodern pick-n-mix of historical epochs, architectural styles, decorative motifs, anachronistic antiques and hyperreal enchantments. With only seven sumptuous suites on offer, plus two tiny dining rooms, The Witchery hovers happily above the slough of surrounding Caledoniana. Super-premium prices ensure that it is the haunt of A-grade celebrities such as Catherine Zeta Jones, Andrew Lloyd Webber, Jack Nicholson, Pierce Brosnan and Matt Groening, as well as lesser but no less luminous lights.

Abby didn't know any of this when she checked in, nor did she scrutinize the famous visitors' book with its signed self-portraits by Homer Simpson. She was fretting about her wad of fake fivers and whether it would pass muster with bellhops, doormen, maître d's and similar leisure sector mendicants. She needn't have worried. Even in today's hopelessly cynical and horribly debased society, no bellhop in his right mind would hold a folding gratuity up to the light or assess its authenticity in an overt manner. On the contrary, the alacrity with which tips are trousered, especially in Scotland, puts drug-pumped Olympic sprinters to shame. Getting change out of Stornoway shopkeepers, some claim, is akin to running a marathon in one of those giant ostrich suits, while carrying a piggy-backing passenger and dragging a ball-and-chain for good measure.

But that is by the bye.

Settling into The Witchery's sumptuous Tarot-themed

restaurant, Abby abandoned her day-long diet for a gourmet gut-buster of Baked Scottish Crotin and Pistachio-crusted Wild Seabass. A secret handshake of five fake fivers rustled up a free-range Apple laptop. She fingered and thumbed her way through cyberspace in search of Rosa Alchemica Caledonia. The long-established memorabilia dealer didn't have a website, but the obvious source of inspiration was readily to hand. "Rosa Alchemica", perhaps inevitably, was a short story published by W. B. Yeats in 1897, at the height of his obsession with the occult. Like most of Yeats's fiction, it was as long on imagery, symbolism and atmosphere as it was short on plot, narrative drive and the necessary twist in the tail. The climactic yarn in his seventeen-story collection, *A Secret Rose*, "Rosa Alchemica" recounted the adventures of one Owen Aherne on his initiation into a secret society called The Order of the Alchemical Rose. This initiation took place in a ruined temple at the end of a seaside pier in Sligo. The local yokels took exception to the godless alchemists and drove them out of town. End of story.

No clue there, then. Abby looked around the magical, candle-lit restaurant. Dominated by a statue of the Greek god Pan, though Dionysus would have been more appropriate, it was comfortably full of silent couples celebrating their silver wedding anniversaries and besuited businessmen making the most of expense account opportunities. Abby was the only diner without a companion, apart from Kong Dong in her Birkin, of course.

Dipping into a delicious blackcurrant delice dessert, Abby clicked on to a Yeats for Dummies website, where she discovered that the rose was the central symbol of the Nobel prize-winner's early poetry, an all-encompassing image of love, purity, perfection, sensuality, synthesis. It not only represented the attraction of opposites – pleasure/pain, past/present, purity/profanity, physical/psychical – but referred to his personal commitment to the immemorial tenets of Rosicrucianism.

Descended, according to the so-called cipher manuscripts, from the medieval Rosicrucians by way of the Temple of Hermanubis, a magical lodge based in Nuremberg, the Hermetic Order of the Golden Dawn was the pre-eminent occult society in the late nineteenth century. W. B. Yeats was one of its leading lights. He was a member of the inner circle of high-ranking adepts. He developed many of its secret ceremonies. He designed most of its colourful vestments and was responsible for choosing its central symbols, including the ouroboros and Celtic cross. So deeply immersed was Yeats in the quasi-kabbalistic, neo-neoplatonist, astrolo-alchemical precepts of the retro-Rosicrucian society that he was known as *Demon Est Deus Inversus* (DEDI), or "the Devil is God Inverted".

"Coffee, madam?"

"Decaff cappuccino, please."

"Coming right up."

Even in Yeats's day, however, the rose was an overworked, hand-me-down symbol of beauty, truth and love. From the Ancient Greeks onward, the rose stood for purity and innocence and allure and sensuality and carnality and fertility. For Christians, it simultaneously represented the bloody wounds of Christ on the cross and Mary Mother of God's virginal fecundity. It inhered in everything from the rosary, which provided a largely illiterate population with reminders of Christian doctrine, through the allegorical rose windows of medieval cathedrals, via the sexual frustration-filled songs of the Troubadours, who wept tuneful tears of pleasurable pain in *The Romance of the Rose*, to Dante's peerless *Divine Comedy*, where paradise comprised a vast celestial rose surrounded by ministering spirits.

In the pantheon of Christian iconography, only the cross ranked higher than the rose.

The energetic waiter, Hector Handstand, bounced up to Abby's table and efficiently swept away the last of the diner's detritus. "Have you finished with the laptop, madam, or do you want to keep it overnight? All our suites are wi-fi enabled. Scotland the Broadband, we call it."

"I'm almost done, thanks. Just a couple more sites to surf."

"More coffee?"

"No, I'm okay, thanks all the same. I need to be up bright and early tomorrow. Too much coffee and I'm climbing the walls."

"Just as well it's decaff."

Abby laughed. "That *is* me on decaff. You should see me after a couple of espressos."

"Would you like a straitjacket with your continental breakfast, madam?"

"Only if it's relaxed fit, Hector." Chuckling and clicking, Abby unearthed an e-soteric website, WorldWideWitches.com, which revealed that the Rosicrucians, in an act of breathtaking symbological chutzpah, combined the rose and the cross into a superpowerful emblem, known as the Rosy Cross. This, they believed, was the *prima materia* that gave life to the four archetypal alchemical elements, earth, air, fire and water; its petals comprised a five-point pentagram, which depicted the sacred wounds of Christ while keeping witches at bay; and, according to Count Cagliostro, the eighteenth-century adept, it was the original and true symbol of the Ancient Eleusinian Mysteries, the Garden of Eden, the isle of Avalon, the centre of the universe.

Wow.

Head spinning, Abby logged off, slipped out of The Witchery's welcoming embrace and took a breath of Edinburgh's bracing air before retiring for the night. The chilly breeze swept her along Castlehill, steered her round The Hub, heaved her down Upper Bow, eased her through Victoria Street, and carried her deep into the throbbing ventricles of Grassmarket, the old town's palpitating heart, where systolic pubs were pumping out, and diastolic clubs sucking in, their intoxicated clienteles. She stared through the darkened display windows of Rosa Alchemica Caledonia, a tiny, narrow-fronted, one-storey retail outlet on West Bow, at the eastern end of the marketplace. There was a swastika-shaped mosaic in the centre of the shopfloor. The swastika, she'd discovered to her surprise, was a much older cross than the Christian variant. It was a symbol of good luck, healing and happiness in many Asian cultures, nothing less than the key to paradise among Buddhists, and a type of sun wheel in Nordic mythology, its crooked arms an allusion to Thor's heroic hammer, Mjollnir. The Celts embraced the swastika as well. Countless thousands of visitors to the National Museum gaze upon the awesome Ardagh Chalice, Ireland's greatest Celto-Christian artefact after the *Book of Kells*, without noticing the swastikas engraved on its foot cone panels.

The swastika, needless to say, also formed an essential part of the Yeats-inspired iconography for the Hermetic Order of the Golden Dawn. The swastika was one of the Order's most central symbols. Staring into the darkened store, Abby wondered if Yeats had discussed it with Hitler when they met way back in 1912. Perhaps he planted the idea in young Adolf's infatuated head.

Nothing would surprise her any more.

Chapter Thirty-Eight

The Vomit Comet

Mirror, mirror on the wall, who's the gayest of them all? Dave Kelley looked like shit. Despite his best efforts with Biotherm's eye-balm, Clinique's anti-ageing unguent and Molton Brown's best wrinkle retardant, the after-effects of two awful days were showing on his otherwise immaculate appearance. His boyish features were not only losing their lustre but showing their age. The rings of Saturn were materializing under each eye, all seven of them, in frighteningly polychromatic hues. A lank hank of hair flopped across his prematurely wrinkled brow, not so much a cow lick as a dung-covered cattle grid. A Stromboli-sized boil was coming up on his chin, moreover. He could sense the subcutaneous pus preparing itself for a Krakatoa-type cataclysm. The caldera would require serious dermal abrasion in due course.

All in all, he looked more Samos than Mykonos, more Majorca than Ibiza, more Réunion than Mauritius. Though he was still more presentable than most. Gay by affectation yet straight by inclination, Kelley didn't consider himself a metrosexual. He was more of a retrosexual, insofar as his presentation-of-self was predicated on dandified days of yore when men were peacocks and proud of it. Nowadays, men are peahens in the main, peahens in Tesco polo shirts, off-white Asda trainers and artless combinations from the House of Lidl, the Aldi Atelier or Pret à Primark.

Nevertheless, the high-speed dash to Belfast International Airport, which involved a stop-off at Castle D'Anger to replenish Abby's wardrobe, then an early morning charge for the first Stena ferry, had taken fearsome physiognomic toll. If eyes are the mirror of the soul, then Kelley was in the seventh circle of hell and Satan's little helpers were getting medieval with their pitchforks.

"Oh behave," Dave said to himself, as he checked a lower eyelid for an incipient sty.

The Vomit Comet is very aptly named. A high-speed hydrofoil, it plies the route between Belfast Harbour and Stranraer, on Scotland's west coast. When the crossing is rough, which it often is, the ferry resembles a Crimean War field hospital during an outbreak of haemorrhagic yellow fever. Its bile-filled bathrooms beggar belief. They reverberate to the groans, moans and retches of the fallen, the legless and the unsteady on their feet. Only the bravest of the brave, or the vainest of the vain, venture within.

Dave Kelley was neither. He was there in a professional capacity. He had a thing about mirrors. Having finished his PhD under the imperious eye of Professor Emer Aherne, he was looking for further academic fields to conquer. As academic preferment depends on publications and as everything that could possibly be written about retail marketing had already been published, he needed a new angle, something different, a Unique Scholarly Proposition. In light of his Love Pump experiences, Dave seriously considered studying the influence of background music on shopper behaviour. But the impact of up-tempo tunes in fast food restaurants – makes diners chew faster – and the effects of slow mood music in shopping centres – makes spendthrift customers tarry – had already been studied to death. There were opportunities for analyses of background music/retail brand dysfunction, such as heavy metal in Marks and Spencer and gangsta rap in Muthafuckin Mothercare, though the law of diminishing academic returns was rapidly setting in.

Dr. Kelley was thinking of mirrors instead. He'd interviewed thousands of shoppers down the years and was struck by how often mirrors popped up in the conversation. Whether it was consumers catching a glimpse of themselves in shop windows, the glitterball feeling that great department stores exude on account of their shimmering displays, or the infuriating suspicion that changing room mirrors are rigged, because the outfits never look that good back home, reflection was a fundamental part of the whole retail experience.

The secret of successful personal selling, furthermore, involved mirroring the behaviour of the prospect. As Kelley discovered during his years as a pharma sales rep – ills sell pills, no pains no gains, create the condition, count the commission – reflecting the buyer back to themselves was vitally important when establishing rapport and sealing the deal. They smile, you smile. They nod encouragingly, you nod in agreement. They drive a Range Rover, you're buying one too. Their favourite pastime is fishing, you caught a whopper that very weekend. And are in the process of reeling another one in.

Mirroring also provided the key to Kelley's lecturing and interpersonal prowess. He unfailingly reflected what the students wanted to see in class and consciously adapted himself to any interpersonal situation – upper crust types, old school tie types, regimental ramrod types, lonely looking-for-love types.

When Kelley discussed mirroring with Aherne, however, she dismissed it with professorial disdain. "Trivial," she said. "Ho-hum," she yawned. "So what?" she asked, the ultimate academic put-down. "The visual side of marketing is so *fin de siècle,*" she stated with finality. "New times call for new senses – touch, taste, smell, hearing. We listen to the customer these days. We sniff out market opportunities. We savour the flavour of Whole Food Markets. We are in thrall to the haptic erotic of iPods." Dave didn't know what haptic meant, but it didn't really matter. As far as Aherne was concerned, seeing was no longer believing in the new sense dispensation.

A man was gazing at him right now. He was standing at a Vomit Comet urinal. Instead of staring straight ahead, as per the manly etiquette of public conveniences, he was glaring in Dave's general direction. Kelley ignored him. He was used to being looked at askance. Students gawped as he wafted down Hustler's grotty corridors (and watched, transfixed, as he delivered his Flash-filled lectures). Colleagues cast a wary eye, or looked down their noses, as he passed (instead of scrutinizing their own sartorial shortcomings). In the heady days of Love Pump, he loved being the focus of ogling audience attention (his vocals weren't great but he looked the part, strutting, swaggering, doing the splits).

Dave was tempted to stick his tongue out at the wizened old

git. But like many small bald men who've been beaten by the ugly stick, he seemed to have several sizeable chips on each stunted shoulder. The size thing. The hair thing. The looks thing. The prostate thing, judging by the production he was making of taking a pee. All these things militated against making mock, much less poking fun at the old fart, so Dave focused on what he focused on best. The mirror.

Peripheral vision's a terrible thing, though. Even as he checked for errant nose and ear hair, Kelley could sense the senior citizen's baleful scrutiny. His heart sank. The chippy crumbly must know him from somewhere, presumably an outreach programme, or a life-long learning lecture, or as guest speaker at some God-forsaken grocers' convention. The things you do for careerist brownie points. As soon as he'd finished micturating, the desiccated old sod was going to come over and shake his hand. He knew it. Gross.

Kelley made for the automatic hand-drier. A fatal mistake, because they take for ever to kick in, cut out a millisecond later, then take ten minutes to catch their emphysemic breath before starting up again for an entire nano-second. The staring slaphead was upon him. He had a speech defect to boot.

Click. "Do I know ye?" Click.

"I don't think so," Kelley replied politely, rolling his hands under the obstinate nozzle in an attempt to initiate the reticent air flow.

Click. "I've seen ye recently, soahave," the puny pensioner said emphatically. His palate was making the most revolting rattling noise, which got worse the more agitated he became.

Dave smiled modestly. "On television perhaps. I'm on the news from time to time."

The pushy old-timer refused to take the hint. He obviously didn't understand the rules of the game. Low-level local celebrities don't like being pestered, particularly in public conveniences that are swimming in vomit during a heavy swell.

Click. "Nah. Not that. You live in Carrick, don't ye?" Click.

"Afraid not. I'm from Coleraine. I teach at the university up there."

Hostility is not a nice look, especially on the afflicted in years and inches and tresses and teeth. Click. "Fuckin' teachers. Long holidays. Short hours. Lazy cunts." Click.

Ordinarily, Kelley would patiently explain that lecturers are underpaid, overworked, underappreciated and expected to be polite at all times, even towards grumpy old gits with an attitude problem. But he couldn't be arsed. "Yes, it's a great life. No work. Lots of money. All the sex I can handle." Kelley winked at the slack-jawed senior citizen and made his escape.

He couldn't get away from him, however. The cantankerous codger continued to evil eye Kelley in the open-plan passenger lounge, where the high-backed seats offered no protection, since his malevolent stare could bend round corners, like light through a prism. Kelley repaired to the cafeteria for a much-needed coffee and a blueberry muffin. Mad-eyed Loony wasn't far behind, glowering for all he was worth. A nazar, or similar source of symbolic protection, would be nice, since something more than a Starbucks was needed to ward off the old coot's voodoo hoodoo. Kelley returned to his seat and spent the rest of the journey with his head in *All Fall Down*, Yeats's unpublished page-turner.

On reading through the manuscript, Kelley got more and more excited. "No way!" he said aloud, just as the ferry was entering Loch Ryan. He was tempted to ring Abby with the incredible news. But he'd be seeing her soon enough.

As the Vomit Comet disgorged its cargo – articulated lorries, people carriers and an inexplicable smattering of diced carrots – Kelley half-expected to see Balor's kid brother lurking among the vehicles, glaring at him like a BMW on high beams and clicking away like Skippy the stuttering kangaroo. But there was no sign of him, thankfully.

He didn't notice the old man on deck, peering over the rail as the cars spewed out of the hydrofoil's vast belly. When a pink Morris Minor appeared, he nodded with recognition, turned away from his vantage point, picked up his shiny leather briefcase and made his way to a nearby railway halt.

Chapter Thirty-Nine

A Room With a Pew

Abby slept in. She didn't mean to. But the strain of the previous day, coupled with an uncomfortable night in Castle D'Anger – the mattress was more solid than the battlements – conspired against her. Only the most iron-willed could withstand the king-sized comfort of her magnificent four-poster. The sumptuous splendour of The Witchery's flower-filled, cushion-covered Inner Sanctum suite was beyond her powers of resistance. It was a world away from the student flats and halls of residence she'd grown accustomed to, and as for the family farm, a full night's sleep was never on the agenda, not with cows to milk, muck to spread, hay to bale and pigshit to shovel. If it weren't for the psychopaths on her trail, the priest she'd topped and the up-coming trip to swastika-central, everything would be perfect. Well, apart from the missing person investigation that was on-going back home…

Fearing an impromptu attack of self-pity, Abby forced herself out of the delicious embrace of the bed made in heaven and crawled into the bathroom. Nefertiti herself could not have asked for more. A massive cast iron, claw-footed, Victorian bath stood brazenly in the centre of the room. Complete with onyx, gold and marble fittings, it was a full-body baptismal font dedicated to Aphrodite, Adonis and analogous gods of beauty. Bottles of bath oil, bath foam and bath salts lined the William Morris-wallpapered walls, thick white towels warmed gently on a free-standing radiator rack, scented candles stood sentinel beside large, carefully-lit mirrors that flattered as they deceived. This wasn't the place for a quick shower, brisk blow-dry and lick of lippy, but a tabernacle to temptation, seduction, allure. She half expected asses' milk to come coursing out of the taps, baby porpoises to frolic like rubber ducks in the fragrant foam and toga-wearing attendants to pour perfumed water on her back and hair from a golden urn, while lyres played plangently in the background.

It was simply irresistible.

A therapeutic soak, Abby reckoned, was just what the doctor ordered. But no sooner had she settled into its balmy benediction, than her well-woman wallow was interrupted by the inevitable telephone call. A frisson of apprehension surged through her, as she feared she'd been tracked down to the lair of luxury. Prudence said she should ignore its nagging insistence, but prudence and Abby weren't on speaking terms. She picked up. It was the good doctor himself. "Hi Dave… Just about to leave for Grassmarket… Called by late last night… Opens at eleven… You're where?… A restaurant outside Ayr… Decided to drive… Ferry at first light… The Yeats poem's a fake?… It might be in code… Is it a fake code, though?!… You're reading the novel… It's amazing… Amazingly good or amazingly interesting? What do you mean, amazingly significant?… You'll be here around two… See you then."

The Grassmarket was three minutes away. Ten minutes more wouldn't do any harm. It would be a shame to waste the water. The shop won't open until quarter past, anyway. Memorabilia retailers aren't renowned for their punctuality, nor do customers queue outside waiting anxiously for the CLOSED sign to turn around. She didn't want to appear too eager. Better give it an extra twenty minutes or so. Just to be on the safe side. Half an hour, maybe.

It was approximately 11.45 a.m. when Abby stood outside Rosa Alchemica Caledonia. There was no sign of life. Edinburgh's foremost purveyor of Military, Magical and Monastic Memorabilia was either playing the reverse psychology game of making life difficult for customers, thereby increasing their desire and urge to acquire, or else the owner was still sleeping off Saturday night's overindulgence. Or else, as she noted on reading the opening hours notice in the clear light of day, the emporium didn't open until 12.00 p.m. on Sundays.

Abby retreated to The Witchery, where she grabbed a late breakfast in the Secret Garden restaurant. It was served with commendable dispatch by Heather Hatchett, an extra-efficient Witchery waitress, who more than earned her ample tip. Fortified by a feed of finest Scottish porridge, Abby walked it off in the New Town and wandered back to memorabiliaville by an enchanting circuitous route, a route that was a tad too circuitous for her borrowed Jimmy Choos.

Abby's feet were aching as she pushed her way into the musty emporium. If not quite the black hole of Ikea, Rosa Alchemica Caledonia was a dark, dusty and deeply disturbing retail store. On the left side of the shopfloor, old teak cabinets containing coins, medals, badges, buttonhole ribbons and commemorative SS rings abutted malevolent mahogany display units filled with peaked caps, arm patches, cuff titles, sleeve diamonds, lapel badges, collar flashes, belt buckles and Nazi brassards in all manner of regimental trim. Other cabinets held decommissioned weaponry, including grenades, gunsights, daggers, binoculars, ceremonial swords and coal-scuttle helmets with death's head, sig rune and Nazi eagle insignia. A rack of tunics, leggings, Gestapo greatcoats and SS jodhpurs with silver piping – colour coded by theatre of operations, everything from Western Desert to Eastern Front – was situated close to the counter, behind which several flags, standards and blood banners stood silently to attention.

It was a Nazi party rally in miniature.

Incongruously, the opposite, right-hand side of the shopfloor was given over to rosewood bookshelves and display units replete with illuminated manuscripts, calvaries, psalters, hymn books, prayer-books, catechisms, encyclicals, missals, inlaid incunabula and massive family Bibles. There were murky oil paintings of pietas and the Good Shepherd, plaster statues of the Virgin Mary and Christ on the Cross, as well as St. Andrew, St. Columba and several other saints Abby didn't recognize. There were crucifixes in all shapes, sizes and materials – gold, silver, ebony, ivory, plastic and pewter, among others. There was a monumental Celtic cross in soapstone, several cut-glass censers and all sorts of sacred hearts, votive candles, altar screens, gilded triptychs, lacquered reliquaries, sunburst monstrances and an impressive prie-dieu. An elaborately carved pew sat directly opposite the racks of Nazi uniforms, bookended by an angular aspersorium and a complete confessional stall.

It was bric-a-brac-a-bishop, the flotsam and jetsam of the Holy See.

The space between the left-hand and right-hand retail offers was empty, filled only by the mosaic Abby had glimpsed the previous evening. The rose in the centre of the swastika was bad enough, but the angled arms of the obscene symbol were encircled by a fearsome serpent caught in the cannibalistic act of swallowing its own tail. She shuddered as she walked over the grotesque object towards the counter.

There was no sign of life. The silence was spine-tingling, the emptiness unbearably oppressive. The till was unmanned, though Abby doubted if it contained anything, bar a few bob float. "Shop!" she shouted. "Anyone there?" No reply. There was a service bell on top of the scuffed cedar counter, akin to those in old-fashioned hotels and department stores. In for a penny, Abby banged the call button con brio. She half expected it to ping *"Sieg Heil"*, but it chimed the opening bars of *"Ave Maria"*. There was a back room or storage facility of some kind, though it was difficult to tell quite what. A beaded bamboo curtain covered the doorway. A sign above the lintel said *Sigillus Sigillorum*. "Hello?"

Undeterred by the indifference, Abby rounded the counter, swept aside the stock room curtain, which rustled and rattled noisily, and poked her nose inside.

"You're not allowed in there, lassie," a deep brown voice said behind her. "Not without an appointment."

Startled, Abby leapt a couple of centimetres into the air. It would have been higher but for the earlier plate of Witchery porridge which still clung to her innards and wouldn't be releasing its grip anytime soon. She whirled round, only to be greeted by an empty shop as before. Either the sales assistant was wearing Harry Potter's invisibility cloak or was blessed with *Britain's Got Talent*-calibre ventriloquism skills. The door of the confessional swung open with a creak and an unforgettable figure emerged.

The owner of an emporium that sells an unholy combination of Nazi collectables and Curia curios might reasonably be expected to look like Dr. Mengele in a dog collar, complete with rimless glasses, beatific smile and giant syringe filled with scopolamine. Not in this case. He was tall, athletic, muscular, of military mien with a big bushy beard, light blue eyes and a combover that resembled a haystack on a flatbed.

"Sorry if I scared you, lassie." What his mocking apology lacked in sincerity it substituted with warmth. "What can I do you for?" He took up his position behind the counter, with the impassive air of a Grenadier guardsman. It was an air that told Abby, in the nicest possible way, to step away from *Sigillus Sigillorum*.

The directness of his question threw Abby completely. Foolishly, she hadn't given any thought as to how she might handle this encounter. "Do you have the Spear of Destiny in stock?" seemed a bit forward, albeit not as forward as "An IRA godfather sent me to ask about his property." She settled for, "What does *Sigillus Sigillorum* mean, when it's at home?"

"If you have to ask that, you've come to the wrong place." The affability leached from his craggy features, the light blue eyes lost their sparkle. "Or perhaps you're not into arcana, esoterica, hermeticism, chiromancy."

"Military memorabilia's more my kind of thing," Abby bluffed. "Well, my grandfather's. His seventy-fifth's coming up."

"Thank God for that," he replied. "Thought you were another one of those Harry Potterites for a second. We've been plagued with them ever since J. K. Rowling put Edinburgh on the map." The lack of admiration in his encomium to Edinburgh's first literary citizen was palpable. "Our initials have given us all sorts of problems with the Harry hocus-pocus Potter set."

"RAC?"

"Aye, we've had no end of telephone calls about broomstick breakdowns, Floo Powder accidents and flying Ford Anglias that won't take off. It was funny the first time, but not the four hundredth. We shut down our website because of it."

"Ah, I was wondering why you weren't on-line."

He smiled and held out his massive hand, the shaggy back of which looked like a ginger gerbil with alopecia issues. "Selkirk Brodie's the name. Can I interest you in a King's Cross with oak leaves and diamonds? Very rare. Perfect for your grandfather's diamond jubilee." He reached under the dusty glass counter display and extracted a small jewellery box. He held it in one hand and opened the little lid with the other. A Tiffany sales associate couldn't have done it with more panache.

Abby feigned interest in the black, diamond-edged metal cross. "Hmmmm. How much?"

"Nine hundred and ninety-nine pounds, ninety-nine pence."

She grimaced. "My budget doesn't stretch that far." Unless you take fake fivers, she thought, suspecting that she'd never get them past a memorabilia dealer. Unless, of course, he was expecting them. "Would you consider a trade in?"

Brodie slipped the padded jewellery box under the counter while appraising her professionally. "Depends," he said. "What are you offering?"

Abby removed the Wehrmacht bayonet from her borrowed Hermès handbag and placed it carefully on the scuffed counter, a counter that hadn't seen French polish since the Napoleonic Wars.

He glanced at the weapon then burst out laughing.

That's when an explosion ripped through the calm of Rosa Alchemica Caledonia.

Chapter Forty

Brand Flu

"Rise and shine."

"Whaaaa..."

"It's your wake-up call. Get down here, right now!"

Professor Pitcairn Brodie held the telephone away from his head and stared at the receiver. Either he was still steaming drunk or having an especially vivid nightmare. Or in the middle of a drunken nightmare. "Piss off," he croaked and slammed the phone down, after a couple of erratic sighting shots. His nondescript bedroom gave no indication of his whereabouts. Surely Nuremberg. Maybe not. On the road is all the same. Airport, taxi, hotel, conference, hotel, taxi, airport. Surely Nuremberg. Maybe not. On the road...

Every day is Groundhog Day.

A few minutes later, the phone rang again. "Reveille was at zero eight hundred, Brodie. You're late for brunch."

"Bugger off, ya bawheid," he growled, slamming the phone down for a second time. When Brodie slams a phone down, it stays slammed. Glaring at the instrument of torture, he threw off the covers and made for the bathroom. His knees buckled beneath him. Raw and red and scuffed and scratched, they'd been in the wars, as had the rest of his trim but still sexagenarian body. "Oh God," he groaned, suddenly remembering the lacerating events of the previous night. He'd really gone and done it this time. He'd done worse things while drunk. Such as the time he shinned up a flagpole during a royal command performance of Edinburgh's military tattoo. He squatted on the button on top, a Scottish Simeon Stylites, shouting obscenities at the countermarching soldiers below. Luckily, most tourists thought it was part of the performance – each regiment boasts a mascot, every platoon a buffoon – and he was let off with a warning. At one stage, they talked about permanent participation in the po-faced display, but the top brass put the kibosh on it. The Queen was keen, though.

Still, he couldn't see the Nuremberg polizei being so understanding. Knowing Teutonic efficiency and Bavarian bureaucracy, there was bound to be a seventeenth-century statute banning abuse of automatons in the Altstadt between the hours of 8 and 10 p.m. during the months of September and October.

Time to face the music.

Head pounding like Mons Meg with a 12" shell stuck in its barrel, Brodie groped his groggy way to the front lobby. No sign of arresting officers or indeed any polizei personnel. Only the usual comings and goings of a busy Sunday morning – suitcase scrimmages, check-out confrontations, taxis tooting outside.

A set of gleaming teeth bore down on him. An immaculately manicured hand pounded him amiably on the shoulder. He winced. His grinning assailant didn't notice. "Let's eat," he said, steering his brunch buddy in the general direction of Nichraucher's, the conference hotel restaurant.

Encased in several layers of synapse-slowing cotton wool, Professor Brodie's cranium wasn't working as well as it normally did. It wasn't until he'd been to the brunch buffet, where he rapidly quaffed several large glasses of organic orange juice, that he recognized his new-found life-long friend. However, he'd no recollection of arranging a meeting with the cheesy American management consultant who'd spoken at the Citroën conference the day before. He couldn't recollect too much about yesterday evening, come to think of it, but he knew that he'd never, ever agree to a one-on-one meeting with that orthodontically enhanced airhead. Even after a garrulous night on the gargle.

"Man," the airhead said as he plonked himself down at their table with a halogen grin. "That was some performance yesterday. Wow. Punching out those security guards. W-O-W. Did it take much rehearsal? The way you pushed over the podium. Man, oh man." He shook his head in bogus admiration. "I've seen laptop computers crash before, but not like that. How did you persuade the organizers to permit it? Was it a dummy Dell?" He picked up his knife and fork, then thought better of the calories on his plate. "That impassioned speech at the end. Man, that was so Mel Gibson, so *Braveheart*. It must have taken you hours to write."

Being reminded of the fiasco was bad enough, but being accused of faking it was unacceptable. "It was'ne rehearsed, laddie," Brodie barked. "It was spontaneous."

Affected affability was the airhead's speciality, along with power networking. However, even he struggled to disguise his surprise. "Okay. Whatever. If you can fake sincerity, right?" he grinned knowingly, his incisors glittering like a Swarovski display cabinet.

Brodie was ready to nut the guy. "I don't recall arranging a meeting with you, laddie." He struggled to compose himself. "Especially at... brunchtime."

"Oh, we didn't arrange anything," the gladhander answered airily. "I just thought it would be nice to network before it's too late." Shooting a Gieves & Hawkes cuff, he checked his Girard Perregaux tourbillon. "I'm heading back to Vegas in an hour. Took a chance on calling you up. Reckoned you wouldn't mind. What time does your Gulfstream leave? "

A sizzling sausage paid the price of Brodie's bad mood. His back-bacon hadn't a chance. Even the egg ran scared. "There wasn't one booked before my speech and I can't see Citroën splashing out now."

"You're on YouTube already," the alpha networker sighed with pseudo admiration. "Someone even added a backing track to your departure speech. It's awesome."

"Oh aye?" The cholesterol-cum-coffee combo was kicking in and, bearish though they may be on occasion, even ironclad Caledonians can succumb ever so slightly when exposed to American orthodontics.

"Sure thing," the cheesy consultant replied. "You're famous. Seriously famous. That's why I thought we should hook up going forward."

Brodie held his head disbelievingly. In his fragile state, he couldn't quite process what he was hearing. It sounded as though this consultancy guy was offering him a job or partnership of some kind. He poured himself another cup of coffee as the charm-force

Yank waxed lyrical about partnership possibilities. He ran SA, a management consultancy hotshop in Las Vegas. They'd been responsible for lots of brilliant breakthrough ideas, none of which Brodie had heard of. They sold their transformational concepts to blue-chip corporations, who attempted to implement them. Usually unsuccessfully, but hey. Their ideas were copyrighted; they earned millions from licensing fees; and when the concept cratered they sold their clients another, then another, then another. US companies were quick fix junkies and his organization was their pusher, their dealer, their supplier, their bitch.

Unimpressed, Professor Brodie had no desire to become a corporate snake-oil salesperson. Selling alchemy was just about acceptable, because it gave bottom-line, stats-obsessed multinational corporations serious pause for thought. But pitching the output of an ideas factory, regardless of the efficacy of the ideas themselves, was too much like Big Pharma for comfort. Big Phucka, more like.

The American gladhander wouldn't take no for an answer. When Brodie demurred, the demurral only encouraged him. He waxed even more lyrical than before. He had this idea, you see. Brand Flu. The corporate equivalent of SARS: Sudden and Accelerating Reduction in Sales. It was a deadly marketplace virus – spread by buzz, viral and word-of-mouth means – that was set to sweep through the brandscape. It was the commercial equivalent of the bubonic plague. The brandbonic plague. He envisaged Brodie storming on stage at industry conferences, wearing a white coat and a stethoscope. He gets the audience to say "aaaahhhhh." He gets them to stick their collective tongue out. He checks their vital signs. He tests their blood pressure and shows the results on a giant screen behind. The scores look bad. Urgent intervention is needed. He pulls out an endoscope and suggests an exploratory proctology examination. If the audience remains unconvinced, he throws a hissy fit as per the Citroën conference. Think John McEnroe. You cannot be serious. Think Elton John going postal at Taipei airport. Rude, vile pigs! Think Björk going bananas and attacking the paparazzi, while wearing that skirt with the swan.

"This could be massive, Pitcairn. *We* could be massive..."

When Brodie made it clear that he wasn't interested, SA's ever-smiling supersalesman indicated that he'd just have to make the millions himself. He was thinking of getting back on the road full-time. He was fed up being a desk jockey, being an ideas man. Yesterday's session reminded him of what he was missing. He and Brodie'd make a great double act. Not to worry. He'd find someone else.

Brodie had no desire to be turned into a freak show act by an American management impresario. He could manage that himself.

"If you ever change your mind, give me a call." Smiler slid a glitzy business card across the breakfast table and said his farewells. But not before Brodie explained that SA, in German, stood for *Sturmabteilung*, or Stormtroopers, and that the hotel they were billeted in, The Carlton, headquartered the marketing department of the Nazi Party during the Nuremberg rallies.

Airhead thought that was pretty cool. Way cool, in fact. He shimmered out of the restaurant, grinning and gladhanding and pointing a semi-automatic finger gun – catch you later! – at fellow guests. His Gulfstream awaits.

Still suffering from the mourning after the night before – did I really destroy that robot? – Brodie went outside to clear his head. A brisk walk round the old town would sort him out, and a quick trip to St. Katharine's church, still in ruins after the Second World War, would remind him that he was right to say what he did about Citroën's crypto-fascist symbology.

The neo-fascists didn't agree, however. No sooner had he walked outside than a platoon of skinheads, loitering in a doorway across the narrow street, rushed toward him shouting and swearing. The leader had a swastika tattooed on his forehead, his second-in-command sported sig runes on either cheek, their back-up boasted a diagonal duelling scar which cruelly distorted his already cruelly distorted features. All three were wearing the regulation neo-Nazi uniform of black death's-head T-shirt, baggy camouflage cargo pants and burnished, ruby-red Doc Martins. They were on Brodie in an instant, kicking and punching and cursing his YouTube-streamed sentiments.

It takes more than a fascist flashmob to faze a Scotsman,

though. He fisted the first on the chin, elbowed the second in the solar plexus and kicked the third just below the left knee, which is not only excruciating but immobilizes the miscreant for good measure.

Brodie's triumph was short-lived. Another squad of skinheads stormed in from a side street and swept down on the kilted colossus. The weight of numbers was overwhelming. Brodie's last stand was looming.

"*Schwanzlutscher*! *Verpisst euch, ihr Glatzendildos*!!"

The fascist aggressors stopped in their tracks, staring at each other in confusion. An ursine security guard, who looked like a secret service agent from central casting – dark glasses, black suit, on-going conversation with his shirt cuff – stood in the centre of the street, immobile, impassive, imperturbable.

A black SUV with tinted windows and cowcatcher-style grille idled behind him. The skinheads rapidly dispersed, pausing only to inform the professor that he was a dead man.

"Thank you, officer," Brodie gasped, dusting himself down for the second time in two days. He hadn't seen anything like it since chucking out time at The Dome, when the Accountancy Association conference hit town.

The man in black said nothing. He opened the rear door of the SUV and indicated, with a curt flick of the head, that the professor was expected to get inside. When Brodie declined politely, he pulled open his Armani jacket to reveal a bulging shoulder holster that brooked no argument. The driver's side window slid down silently. A second security guard, with a physiog like pickled red cabbage, turned to the dishevelled Highlander. "You have an appointment, Professor Brodie. We're running late. Get in."

Chapter Forty-One

The School of Hard Knox

The one o'clock gun isn't fired on Sundays, though cannonades are commonplace when dignitaries hit town. Preoccupied, the sandy-haired shopkeeper ignored the explosive interruption from the Castle above as he scrutinized Abby's precious possession. "Looks like a standard Wehrmacht bayonet to me. Not even in especially good condition," he said. "They're two a penny, lassie. There's been a rise in demand thanks to the Europe-wide emergence of the neo-Nazi movement. They're also popular among wartime re-enactment enthusiasts, middle-aged men who re-fight the Battle of the Bulging Waistline at weekends. But it's only worth a couple of pounds at most. I'll allow you twenty on a trade in. That's the best I can do."

Abby wasn't having any agents and dealers bullshit of the buy low/sell high variety. "Look on the boss. It bears Skorzeny's rune."

Talking all the while in his beautiful baritone brogue, Selkirk Brodie picked up the bayonet, popped in a loupe, scrutinized the hilt and set it down on the unpolished counter once more, with a soft click. "Skorzeny wasn't in the Wehrmacht. He was an SS man through and through. He wouldn't have owned anything like this, lassie. It's a fake, I'm afraid. You've been had." He eased the rogue bayonet from its battered scabbard and re-sheathed it several times, listening to the action. For such a big muscular man, he had a very delicate touch. "Even if it were authentic, it wouldn't be worth much. Skorzeny's reputation has taken a hit in recent years. The man was a blowhard. He was a fantastic self-publicist, but that's all. He propagated extravagant stories about himself, most of which were..."

"I thought he was Hitler's bodyguard," Abby interrupted, "Mussolini's rescuer, the brains behind the Spider..."

The military man raised an appreciative eyebrow. "You certainly know your stuff. I'm impressed. But serious memorabilia collectors aren't interested in spin. They prefer items associated with front-line, two-fisted soldiers, real soldiers like Siegfried Grabert, the Brandenburgers' boy wonder, or Ulster's own Paddy Mayne, the Robocelt who founded the SAS with David Stirling, earned three DSOs for valour in action and was unforgivably denied the Victoria Cross because he pissed off his superiors. War's a dirty business, but it's nothing compared to the politics of military decoration."

Abby understood. Medals, evidently, were the armed services' equivalent of haute couture designer labels, only more exclusive and coveted. "You sound as though you speak from personal experience. Iraq? Falklands?" His craggy face was stony. She knew the answer already. "Where were you based? South Armagh? The Bogside? Falls Road? Fermanagh?"

A vein was throbbing at Brodie's right temple. Even in the dimly lit shop interior, she could see the heightened colour in his flushed features. "Well lassie, if I can't interest you in a King's Cross," he said with an exaggeratedly gregarious voice, "is there anything else that tickles your fancy?" He caught her glance at the bamboo curtain and scowled. "Everyone's a Harry Potter fan nowadays!" Placing his massive hands on the counter, he launched into an oft-repeated routine. "I'm afraid we're out of Magic Wands, Floo Powder, Fizzing Whizzbies and replica Quidditch kits. We might have threstral testicles in stock, though…"

Abby cut him off. "It's okay. I'll try elsewhere." She made for the door, knowing full well that if the Skorzeny bayonet was genuine – as events in St. Stephen's indicated – then he'd call her back to re-negotiate. She'd crossed the centre of the rosy-swastika mosaic before he spoke up.

"You haven't asked about the snake. Everyone asks about the snake. Even Harry Potter fans. They believe it's a basilisk of some sort."

Feigning lack of interest, Abby glanced down at the grotesque image of the serpent gorging on its own tail and, without turning round, called over her shoulder. "I know an ouroboros when I see one." Desperately trying to remember the rest of the Wikipedia entry she'd studied the night before, Abby continued authoritatively. "It's a symbol of recurrence, of cyclical time, of what goes around comes around, of Nietzsche's eternal return of the same, of Yeats's occult Second Coming. It was appropriated by the Nazis and it featured in a lot of their anti-Semitic propaganda, the supposed Jewish plot to take over the world."

"Very good," he acknowledged, "though the alleged plot was as much Masonic as Jewish, and it was rooted in robber baron capitalism. One hundred years ago, many thought big business was devouring the world."

"Many still do," Abby retorted and made for the door. "Didn't the ouroboros have something to do with alchemy too?"

"I'm not sure," he answered, in a testy tone of voice. "You'll need to talk to my big shot wee brother about that. He's our specialist in alchemical and ecclesiastical matters. I just mind the till, handle the militaria and keep the Harry Potter pests at bay. I'm muscle not management, or so bro Brodie keeps telling me."

"Where can I find him?"

"He's probably up at the college, working away."

"The college? He's an academic? He's working on Sunday? Miracles will never cease."

"Well, he *is* a theologian," Brodie chuckled. "Sunday's the busiest day of the week for theologians, funnily enough." The strapping shopkeeper came to see Abby out. He marched briskly across the shopfloor, held open the grimy glass door and gave directions to nearby New College, Edinburgh University's world-renowned department of divinity.

"Who do I ask for?"

"Professor Pitcairn Brodie."

"How will I recognize him?"

"Oh, you'll recognize him, don't worry about that." Regretfully, he handed her the Skorzeny bayonet. "You forgot this," he said, with an expression that suggested he knew more than he was saying. "Unless you want to leave it with me. I can check it out on DeutscheTotsche.com, the Nazi collectables website."

Abby accepted the offer, since she quite fancied seeing Selkirk again, and set off for New College. Several steep flights of steps later, Abby found herself outside its fiercely spiked frontage. If ever a building were designed to put the fear of God into slothful Scottish sinners, it was surely New College. The design seemed to be based on Satan's pitchfork and, as Edinburgh's premier shopping street was situated beneath its bristling barbs, New College reminded sybaritic consumers that the wages of sinful self-indulgence were death. Not that anyone paid a blind bit of notice, not even on the Sabbath day. Praise the Lord and pass the MasterCard.

Pitcairn Brodie was certainly distinctive. But not as Abby imagined him. Tall, thin, with an alarming mop of ginger hair and a decidedly anxious demeanour, he could only have been in his mid-twenties, at most. He was backing out of his office door, carrying a cardboard box full of books. "Need a hand, Professor Brodie?" Abby ventured.

Gasping, the ginger-haired man with the bright red face struggled to reply. The office door closed automatically on inadequately damped hinges, trapping the professor and his armful between the heavy door and its wooden frame. "I'm not Brodie," he panted in an incongruous Home Counties accent.

"You're just stealing stuff from his office." Abby opened the door to its full extent, releasing the captive. "On a Sunday."

"Hardly. He's moving out. I'm his dogsbody. This is my third load already this morning."

"You definitely need a hand."

"Well, if you could grab that box there, I'd be very grateful."

The professor's office was all but empty. The bookshelves were bare. The desk was devoid of life. Filing cabinets rang hollow. Most of the watercolours had been removed, leaving dark patches on the leached lilac wallpaper. Abby hefted one of the brimming cardboard boxes on the bile-green carpet. Compared to a bale of hay it was a breeze, though Professor Brodie's dogsbody looked suitably impressed. They carried the boxes past the reception desk and airy foyer, across a perilous flagstone courtyard to a heavily-laden 2CV illegally parked beside a statue of John Knox. The surly Sabbatarian didn't look too happy about the imposition, his outstretched arms raised to the gods of traffic control. Thou shalt not park in a reserved space, on pain of death, eternal damnation and a three-point penalty on your driving licence.

"So, where can I find Professor Brodie?"

"He's out of the country at present."

"Oh yes? Where's that?"

"I'm afraid I can't say. He doesn't allow me to give out personal details. I'm very sorry."

Brodie's gofer struggled to close the door of his car. It was filled to overflowing with cardboard boxes and looked as though the chassis was about to collapse, depositing a trail of textbooks behind it.

"When will he be back?"

The ginger man wiped a bead of sweat from his forehead. "Can't say, sorry." He rested against the bonnet, rubbing the aches out of his long thin arms.

Abby could tell he was intrigued by his angel of mercy and, from her experience with angels and demons costumes in Some Like It Hot, she knew how to handle a man whose curiosity had been piqued.

"Are you from Ulster, by any chance?"

"Tunbridge Wells, actually," Abby replied.

Startled, the Struwwelpeter look-alike leaped off the bonnet like a scalded tabby-cat. "No way."

Abby laughed at his gullibility. "Tunbridge Wells, County Fermanagh."

She could see the coils of confusion wrapping themselves around the Garden of Englander. "But, surely there isn't a Tunbridge..." He wouldn't last a minute in Belfast, Abby concluded.

"I've just been interviewed for a job in Ulster," he announced apropos of nothing. "I'll be moving over there quite soon, I trust."

It was all Abby could do to stop herself snorting with derision. You'll be eaten alive, she thought, but limited herself to polite expressions of congratulation. "Oh yes? Who will you be working for?"

"The University of Hustler."

Abby didn't snort this time. "I'm a student at Hustler," she said, smiling.

"Really? Which faculty? What are you studying?"

"Business. Marketing. Retail marketing, actually."

"I'm marketing, too!" he said, in a genuinely delighted, good-natured manner. "Simon Magill's my name."

"Pleased to meet you, Simon. I'm Abby. Perhaps I'll see you round the campus sometime."

"Do you fancy a bite of lunch… er… Abby?"

"Is God a Catholic?" she asked playfully.

Magill clambered on to the plinth of the adjacent statue and placed his hands over the religious reformer's brass ears. "Don't let on to John."

Chapter Forty-Two

Depicting the Pict

There was something about Simon Magill that bothered Abby Maguire. Perhaps it was his plummy accent, which reminded her of Peregrine Faulkner, the double-double-agent who'd double-double-crossed them in Belfast. Perhaps it was the unfortunate fact that he was a man, and men – Kelley possibly excepted – were nothing but trouble, big trouble. Perhaps it was his ludicrous claim to be Irish, which was disconcerting enough coming from American tourists whose great-great-great grandpappy hailed from Galway, allegedly, but it was deeply weird in someone with public school written all over him and who looked as though he'd competed in copious Three Day Events. Albeit not as a rider.

Nevertheless, at least he had bright ginger hair, which suggested something Gaelic in the gene pool alongside *equus asinus* Oxbridge. His family came from Eden, of all places, and he'd spent numerous summer holidays on Ulster's frigid North Coast. Hence he knew what it was like to build sandcastles in the pouring rain and eat Morelli's ice cream in the teeth of a force nine gale. He wasn't all bad, in short. But being a true-blue stiff-upper Brit, he refused to divulge anything about Professor Brodie's whereabouts, because he "wasn't allowed to". She tried to explain that he'd never get anywhere in Ireland with that kind of attitude. It was like talking to an offshored call centre, a complete waste of time.

Still, at least the ginger toilet brush deigned to explain Brodie's background as they descended all eighty-seven Playfair Steps en route to the New Town's lunchtime attractions. The tourist-rich Old Town is best avoided on Sundays, Magill said, since its watchwords are "Give me freedom or give me AmEx," "You take the high road and I'll take your wallet," and "The banks and brands o' bonny doon."

A pile of tartan blankets was heaped on the time-grooved sandstone staircase. Abby dropped a fake fiver into the homeless Highlander's begging bowl, hoping that he or she wouldn't get prosecuted for passing off counterfeits, though a night in the cells might be preferable to Playfair Steps. They sauntered across the piazza between the National Gallery of Scotland and the Royal Scottish Academy, those neoclassical buildings that appear in every establishing shot in every movie set in Scotland's capital city, *Trainspotting* included. The piazza is street theatre central during the Festival and best avoided at all costs during the dog days of August. However, it's an exceptionally pleasant place to be on a balmy Sunday in September. Not that Simon Magill seemed to notice. The ginger man was much too busy rabbiting about Brodie.

A world-renowned authority on the Celtic church and its symbols, the professor was a walking, talking embodiment of Scotland wha hae. Pictland, to be precise. True, he didn't smear his face with bright blue woad – not during the working week, anyway, and not with Boots No. 7 on special offer in Jenners – but he exuded that characteristically Caledonian conviviality concealed beneath a carapace of candour and combativeness. If not quite a stock character from the Glasgow kiss school of savage Scottish stereotypes, Brodie had more than a touch of the tartan-clad caber-tosser about him. What's more, he was one of Lothian's legendary tourist attractions, a larger than life individual who roamed the streets of Auld Reekie barking belligerently at innocent visitors. They loved him for it, by all accounts, because they'd seen *Braveheart* and *Highlander* and were wondering if they'd arrived on the wrong day and missed the recreational pugnacity that the brochures gleefully promised.

According to Simon Magill, that is.

Despite her lingering distrust of the gangly ginger monkey, Abby was looking forward to meeting his OTT organ grinder. Something told her Brodie was the big banana behind everything that had happened to date. Here was a theologian who specialized in Celtic symbology and was the power behind the throne of a swastika-swaddled arcana outlet, with occult leanings. Here was someone with a possible link to St. Stephen's splintered spear-holder and the phoney poem it contained. Here was someone Abby had to collar, even if he was as aggressive as his carrot-coloured spin-doctor intimated. He couldn't be any worse than Igor and Billy No-dick, that's for certain.

The only problem was that Magill wouldn't spill the beans on Brodie's location. He informed her that Brodie never informed him when he went walkabout, which wasn't much help, though she suspected he had something up his sleeve. Abby decided to bide her time and work on him over lunch. Failing that, she'd work him over after lunch.

Much to her surprise, the henna-headed popsicle didn't lead the way to a fuggy pub or fashionable New Town eatery. He skipped down the steps into Princes Gardens East, where the National Galleries harboured a semi-subterranean restaurant. Luckily, it was nearly empty because the current exhibition wasn't pulling in the punters. Entitled *De-picting the Pict*, it was one of those challenging counter-memory-driven shows beloved by museum curators trained in the dubious delights of deconstruction, post-structuralism and anti-metanarratives. It was incomprehensible, in other words, a mish-mash of monumental standing stones, untranslatable Pictish pictograms, the curious studded balls that had baffled just about every archaeologist bar Indiana Jones, and all manner of pop culture references from Pendragon role-playing games and Terry Pratchett's Nac Mac Feegles in *The Wee Free Men* to Pink Floyd's hallucinogenic classic, "Several Species of Small Furry Animals Gathered Together in a Cave and Grooving with a Pict", which played in a continuous loop in the background.

All that was questionable enough. However, the exhibition catalogue also debunked the Scythian origin myth – the much-loved legend that the Picts came from the Middle East by way of Ireland – and didn't slaughter the Roman Ninth Legion, as countless hand-me-down stories suggested. The Picts were just one among many nondescript Iron Age tribes who held out in the hilly, forested, infertile margins of the civilized world. Not exactly what today's red-blooded post-Picts wanted to hear, let alone the Ninth Legion of Italian-American tourists.

The accompanying poster was eye-catching, though. It was

a reproduction of *The Spell*, one of the National Galleries' most popular paintings. Unusually arresting, it depicted an Arthurian necromancer raising the dead in a rough-stone dungeon, the walls of which were incised with indecipherable Pictish runes. Obviously a work of late-Victorian whimsy, *The Spell* was post-pre-Raphaelite in style, pre-post-Impressionist in content. However, in a world where Harry Potter is the talisman of popular culture, the Holy Grail is right down the road in Rosslyn, and Edinburgh's tourist chiefs talked of raising a statue to Dan Brown, the patron saint of weekend mini-breaks, it seemed appropriate somehow. There is considerable evidence, after all, that Avalon was situated in the Central Belt of Scotland, as Arthur's Seat and Guinevere's Grave bear New Age witness. The exhibition catalogue debunked that tale too.

At least it kept the Gallery Restaurant empty. Over a nourishing bowl of home-made Scotch broth, Abby turned the conversation to Hustler University's unlikely recruit. He babbled excitedly about the challenge facing him in the Business School and how much he was looking forward to working with the eminent academic Emer Aherne. Abby hadn't the heart to tell him that Aherne was the queen bitch of marketing scholarship, who'd recently royally shafted her boon companion, Dave Kelley. Instead, she talked about the St. Stephen's conference and the outraged reaction to her "intervention".

Magill looked appalled. A beta-male or below, challenging authority was way outwith his comfort zone. The very idea than an uppity marketing undergraduate could interrupt the world's foremost thinkers was far beyond his ken. Too bookish for his own good, the guy needed to grow up, otherwise academia would rip him limb from limb.

"When I was an undergraduate," he spluttered apologetically, "I spent all my time in the library and computer lab. I suppose I should've got out more. I must have missed the misspent youth that everyone misses so much."

"Programming skills are very useful nowadays," Abby said as diplomatically as she could manage. "I wish I'd spent more time in the IT suite."

The regretful redhead took this as an invitation to dilate on his adventures in e-commerce. Some of his ideas were excellent, though he obviously lacked the ruthless entrepreneurial edge that's needed to turn good ideas into paying propositions. BuySpace, a social networking website for tyro businesspeople, many of whom are sadly deficient in the inter-personal skills required by successful start-ups, had very real potential, Abby reckoned. She was no less impressed by BuySpace's segment-specific subsidiaries – StySpace for pig farmers, TieSpace for S&M enthusiasts, WhySpace for undecided existentialists, ShySpace for executives crippled with social anxiety issues, TrySpace for ex-rugby players whose days in the first team are over, CrySpace for passengers who'd flown British Airways and rued the three-day delay and DieSpace for those abandoned aeronauts whose Ryanair flights were cancelled without warning.

She wasn't so sure about his other ambition, retro-cryptography. Bewildered but bedazzled, she nibbled on a bread-stick as Magill expatiated on Paypal, prime numbers and the fact that no encryption protocols are perfect. Despite the assurances of on-line payment providers, every code is breakable in principle and the mathematics employed by contemporary cyber-encryption systems remain unproven. Cyber systems will be cracked sometime soon, and when that happens, the world will go ape for a sufficiently secure set up.

"And you think the history of cryptography is hiding something that nobody's discovered to date?"

"There are countless old-fashioned codes that remain uncracked. The Voynich Manuscript. The Beale Papers. The Dorabella Cipher. The Kryptos Sculpture. The Shugborough Shepherd's Monument. The Pictish pictograms in this very exhibition." He waved his arms in the general direction of the upstairs galleries. He only looked half crazy. "And they're at least fifteen hundred years old."

"So, you're an expert in secret codes, are you?"

Magill blushed. He looked like a hirsute chili pepper. "No, no, not really. It's more of a pipe dream," he said.

"So if I placed a coded poem in front of you, you couldn't crack it?"

He shrugged. "Depends on the code, of course. But probably not."

"So you're good in theory but not in practice?"

"Something like that."

"You'll do well in academia."

Chapter Forty-Three

Storm in a Teabing

Although the A77 is the Antrim Coast Road's poor relation, the Ayrshire equivalent is not without its splendours. Ailsa Craig, an imposing egg-like island just off the coast at Turnberry, is particularly impressive on a sunny day, as is its local nickname, Ayr's Rock.

Kelley was in no mood for sightseeing as he made his way from Stranraer Docks to Salisbury Crags. He was preoccupied by the Yeats novel he'd started on the ferry. Given the title, which was reminiscent of mid-period Agatha Christie, he was expecting a sub-Poirot story filled with the usual stock characters – suspicious butler, scatterbrained parson, society beauty, besotted beau, bumbling professional detectives, savvy amateur sleuth called Gimlet Tweed or somesuch. He suspected, furthermore, that Yeats would simply transpose the setting from England to Ireland (the scatterbrained parson became a drunken priest, the country house an Ascendancy mansion) and that the characters would all fall down thanks to liberal doses of poison (or unfortunate encounters with candlesticks or wayward revolvers that went off accidentally on purpose).

But he was wrong.

Come Maybole, Kelley couldn't bear the suspense any longer. He pulled over at a wayside restaurant, ordered a cairn-sized carafe of coffee and Monroe of warm wheaten scones, then settled down to finish *All Fall Down*. Yeats being Yeats, the novel was clunkily written and filled with evocative descriptions of the countryside. *All Fall Down* was full of glimmering, shimmering, twinkling, trembling trees, lakes, hills, hares, swans, stars, roses, glades and, naturally, sally gardens. The essence of the novel, nevertheless, involved an occult secret society called The Priory of Ryan which was determined to protect a two-thousand-year-old secret concerning the royal bloodline of King Arthur and Queen Guinevere. The book contended, in Yeats's characteristically didactic manner, that Christianity ruthlessly usurped Celtic myths about King Arthur for political and nationalistic purposes. It further claimed that the Holy Grail was actually the Ardagh Chalice, which had been unearthed in 1868 and occupied pride of place in Ireland's National Museum. The first murder, in fact, took place in the museum and it was only by cracking a code on the Chalice's runic inscription – followed by several other ciphers in a complex poem called "The Cryptex" – that the Irish protagonist Robert Lenahan was able to outwit two plodding British detectives, Bill Trilby and Fred Fedora, and uncover the real killer, a country-house-owning English archaeologist, Sir Basil Bingley.

Kelley was stunned. Either the manuscript was a fake, yet another scam by the shysters in St. Stephen's, or else Dan Brown had borrowed the idea for his bestselling novel, *The Da Vinci Code*, from an unpublished manuscript by the foremost poet of the twentieth century. The allegation that Brown had plagiarized his multi-multi-multi-million selling novel from *Holy Blood, Holy Grail*, a non-fiction confection by three crypto-historians, was inconsequential compared to the W. B. Yeats calumny. Fake or real, the manuscript was dynamite. It was likely to be the biggest literary sensation since the Hitler Diaries hoax. It also contained a coded poem. He had to tell Abby.

Lunch hour was almost over by the time Kelley got to The Witchery. The stop-start section from Hermiston Junction to the city centre had taken nearly as long as the drive from Stranraer to Edinburgh. Or perhaps it just felt that way. There was no sign of his student and, in retrospect, he regretted sending her ahead. Much as he loved the girl – in a brotherly manner – she could be a bit unpredictable. Forthright at the best of times and a ferocious force of nature at the worst, he suspected Abby lacked the delicate negotiation skills needed to extract meaningful information from the proprietors of Rosa Alchemica Caledonia. Mind you, if its swastika-shaped logo was any indication, the owner might need some serious persuasion involving orthodontic equipment before spilling the beans about the spear. Abby, Kelley reckoned, wouldn't be averse to extracting an incisor or two without anaesthetic. He could see her now in a latex SS uniform, one knee on the terrified victim as he struggled desperately in the dentist's chair, while holding up a monstrous pair of gleaming pliers and laughing maniacally. "Ve hav vays of making you talk."

Still, she meant well, and if it hadn't been for her presence of mind when the panther was preparing to pounce he'd be missing a limb or three. She'd saved his bacon at the conference itself, when her Yeats-the-fascist outburst rescued him from a savage pack of professors and analogous academics – academics who were much wilder than anything caged, or uncaged, in Belfast Zoological Gardens. She'd also outfoxed the inquisitive policeman at The Frosses…

Miraculously, Kelley managed to find a parking space in Grassmarket, an attractive pub- and restaurant-swaddled square sadly defaced by a double line of parked cars where rinky-dinky market stalls should be. Kelley wasn't complaining, though the parking fee was stiffer than a quadruple malt whisky with Viagra-impregnated ice cubes. Rosa Alchemica Caledonia wasn't open. An old-fashioned CLOSED sign hung askew behind the grubby, glass-panelled door. Kelley peered inside, shielding his eyes from the bright September sunlight. But there was no sign of life.

Disappointed, the good doctor repaired to Biddy Mulligan's Irish pub across the square. From there he could keep a weather eye on the memorabilia emporium. It was late in the year for an al-fresco repast, but the unseasonable sunshine made the observational ordeal less onerous than it might otherwise have been, and a hearty helping of Scotch-Irish stew took the edge off his travel-heightened appetite. With its enormous hunks of mutton, mountainous mounds of carrots, tatties, neeps, barley and something that looked suspiciously like Highland Cattle pizzle, the stew was a three-course meal in itself. There was still no movement at RAC. No comings, no goings, no customers, no window shoppers even.

As a lecturer in retail marketing, Kelley was familiar with this particular sales tactic. Widely used by designer fashion outlets, where intimidating exteriors and black-suited bouncers are used to discourage time wasters, bargain hunters and the hoi polloi, the sinister swastika, unkempt window display and general air of dowdy dilapidation attending Rosa Alchemica Caledonia were designed to deter everyone bar the most determined collectors. Even the unintelligible Latin name on the faded fascia served this off-putting purpose. Dave had seen it all before and wasn't remotely impressed, never mind deterred. What did surprise him was the absence of customers, especially on a sunny Sunday afternoon when one or two anorakish obsessives might be tempted out of their attics for a window shopping expedition. Too busy bidding on eBay, perhaps.

Kelley settled up and strolled across the square once more. He peered into the gloomy interior of the run-down retail store. There'd been more life on his plate of Scotch-Irish stew. Undecided about the next move, he was preparing to turn away, when a slight movement behind a bead curtain caught his hand-cupped eye. He knocked on the glass-panelled door. Nothing. He rapped again, harder this time. The CLOSED sign bobbled slightly on its rubber sucker. Kelley grabbed the handle and rattled it vigorously. The shop door flew open with a crash. Kelley paused at the entrance, uncertain how best to proceed. There was something about the smell of the interior that alarmed him. He'd recognize his sister's customized Patou perfume anywhere. Abby had been here already.

Apprehensively, he walked over to the old wooden counter, crossing the swastika, rose and ouroboros-emblazoned floor without a second thought, let alone a shudder. Nor did Kelley pay any attention to the beyond-good-and-evil store layout, Wehrmacht memorabilia on one side, Catholic collectables on the other. Incompatible retail arrangements had curiosity value in the seminar room or lecture theatre, but not when something real, something untoward, something very wrong was afoot. Kelley leaned across the counter, upsetting an impulse-purchase display of plastic Iron Crosses, *Totenkopf* key rings, Virgin Mary fridge magnets and Jesus Saves piggy banks. There was no one there, nor any reaction to the cascade of cheap-gifts-for-geeks. He clambered over the counter, scattering the rest of the crapulous till-side set-up, and fought his way through the beaded curtain. Once again, he didn't pay any attention to the bottles of bat blood, flagons of rat entrails, decanters of rose attar, phials of poppy seeds, demijohns of frog spawn, glass jars of mandrake root and amphorae of unicorn horn, much less the pre-prepared love potions and inflatable voodoo dolls which deflate with a satisfying whine when pierced by pins or similar sharp instruments. Nor did he hear the rattling and clashing and swishing of the bamboo curtain as it swayed to a stop behind him.

He was preoccupied with the crumpled figure in the corner. Propped up against a bookshelf, filled with enormous, leather-bound, gilt-edged grimoires, he was tightly bound hand and foot. Evidently, the store had been robbed or something valuable taken, or both. The spear? Abby? Kelley dashed over to the recumbent figure, roughly trussed up in black insulating tape. There was a thick strip of tape across his mouth and beard, and an ugly bruise on his forehead where he'd been hit with a blunt instrument. He was not a puny man, by any means, so there must have been more than one assailant or a particularly vicious one. Kelley knelt down and shook his face. He was still semi-conscious. Kelley slapped him sharply on the cheek. Then slapped him again. He came round with a start and started speaking rapidly, though nothing intelligible penetrated the strip of gaffer tape. His startled blue eyes were staring frantically over Kelley's shoulder and he somehow emitted an enormous warning moan.

Kelley turned to look, but it was too late. A knife-wielding figure sprang out from behind a cast iron cauldron. The speed of the assault was incredible and took Kelley completely by surprise. He hardly had time to register that it was the mad old man from the bog on the boat when the dagger sank deep into his thorax, twisting, turning, tearing, ripping. Everything began to spin, swim, swoon, sink.

He thought he heard someone shout "I never forget a face, you fucker." But Kelley was beyond caring.

Chapter Forty-Four

Room 600

The SUV slipped into the flow of traffic swirling round the Altstadt ring road. The old town's towers and walls and moat-spanning bridges weren't breached on this occasion, as the black bruiser muscled its way along Frauentorgraben, past the pretty Art Nouveau opera house at Richard Wagner Platz and headed in the general direction of Fürth, Nuremberg's sister city. Less than ten minutes later, they pulled into the car park of an imposing public building, and less than five minutes after that Brodie found himself in the well of a wood-panelled, cedar-ceilinged, crucifix-dominated courtroom, where he was ordered into the dock. The cellulite-faced enforcers stood silently on either side. The prisoner's questions went unanswered. His Celtic curses were ignored.

A heavy oaken door, surmounted by a massive marble bust of Medusa, opened dramatically. A diminutive figure entered the room. Brodie half-expected a shout of "all rise", but there were only four people in court, all of whom were standing. The judge, a petite, pert, power-suited woman with expensively cut, shoulder-length hair, took her place behind the bench and coolly appraised the prisoner. Clearly, she meant business.

"I thought this setting would be appropriate," she said in a mellifluous French accent, "in light of your misdemeanours."

The Scotsman wasn't in the mood for deference. He had a thunderous hangover. He'd been attacked in the street by neo-Nazis. He'd been given the silent treatment in a blacked-out SUV by a couple of pistol-packing heavies with physiogs like sweaty cottage cheese. He wasn't going to apologize for his behaviour.

"We haven't met," she continued coldly. "I'm Gabrielle Duchamp, the marketing director of Citroën worldwide. My team hired you for the centenary celebration. They claimed you were an inspiring motivational speaker. They were wrong. You embarrassed my company and yourself. Your behaviour was unprofessional, unconscionable, unforgivable. You should be ashamed of yourself."

Brodie shrugged and tried to extricate himself from the dock. The swing door was securely locked. He could have vaulted out with ease and confronted the cheeky cow. But he couldn't be bothered. He took a seat instead. "Sorry about your robot, lassie. I didn't mean tae kill him. He started it."

The global marketing director was bamboozled. Brodie's left-field response had thrown her. She had that look that non-native speakers always have when they encounter an idiomatic expression for the first time. "Ze robot? Ze Citroën Transformer?" She waved her hands in that uniquely expressive French way. "Has it broken down? It was dancing in the square when I left my hotel fifteen minutes ago." She pouted in that uniquely perplexed French manner prior to saying *pof*. "You think you… killed it? I think you are imagining things, Professor. I think you are starting to see the… pink elephants, *oui*?"

"So, if it's not your robot, lassie, why am I standing in the dock?"

"Because this is Schwurgerichtssaal 600, the courtroom where Nazi leaders were tried sixty years ago. Ribbentrop, Göring, Hess and many others sat where you're sitting now, Brodie." Elegantly, she wafted an arm toward the computer screens, polished floor and fresh paintwork. "The court's still in use, as you can see. But not at weekends. They let us borrow it for the day. Why? Because the Citroën conference is good for the city. Nuremberg is pleased to see us. That's why the city council approved our banners, our flags, our posters and our symbols that you take exception to. Business is business. The convention market is very competitive. We could have gone to Prague or Budapest or Krakow or any number of other cities. But we chose Nuremberg because the city's coat of arms includes red and white chevrons, though that obviously escaped your notice. More importantly, we chose Nuremberg because it's close to the headquarters of BMW and Audi. We want to remind them that Citroën is coming good again. You have to roll your tanks on to competitors' lawns from time to time. That's why we're here, Brodie."

"Unfortunate allusion, lassie. They made panzers here during the Second World War. Tiger tanks too. Have you no sense of history? Didn't it occur to you that flaunting your logo in such a flagrant fashion would stir up terrible memories? Don't you appreciate the power of symbols? Didn't you stop to think that André Citroën looks a lot like Heinrich Himmler, right down to the wire-rimmed glasses?"

"The Nuremberg Visitors Bureau doesn't see it that way. They're delighted we're here, pumping millions of euros into the local economy. We're the biggest thing to hit Nuremberg…"

"Since the Nazi Party rallies!" Brodie spat. "Or the firebombing of January 1945. Or the street-by-street assault of the American Seventh Army." He'd had enough. "If you're withholding my appearance fee as a punishment, Ms. Duchamp, so be it. I don't give a flying fortress. I don't want your blood money anyway. You can shove it up your cheese-eating arse, lassie."

The marketing director took several moments to savour the Scotsman's anatomically challenging advice. "I don't intend to pay your fee, Professor. I'm here to agree appropriate reparation. I think you need to be taught some manners." She signalled toward the Trappist thugs. "Perhaps you'll be more respectful in ten minutes. *D'accord*?"

A quarter of an hour later, Brodie was slumped on a metal chair in a holding cell several storeys beneath the courtroom, a holding cell accessed by a lift installed to transport prisoners to and from the dock, a holding cell where Hermann Göring had taken cyanide rather than submit to the embrace of the Allies' hangman, a holding cell where Otto Skorzeny, the most wanted man in Europe, found he didn't need to do the decent thing, because the prosecutors erroneously believed he was only following orders. Brodie's captors weren't so sympathetic, as the upper-body bruising and cigarette-lighter burns bore witness.

With an imperious aroma of Fragonard, Madame Duchamp breezed into the basement cell, set a glass of water on the battered aluminium table in front of her insubordinate prisoner, and settled herself into a metal chair opposite. "Okay, Brodie. Let's get down to business. You have embarrassed my company. Your performance is on YouTube already. You are going to pay for your rash remarks. If they'd been made in the heat of the moment I might overlook the incident. But they weren't. Your premeditated outburst was either malicious in intent or part of the conspiracy against us. Which was it?"

It was Brodie's turn to look baffled. "Conspiracy?" he rasped. "Malice?" he croaked. Breathing was painful, almost impossible. He feared a broken rib or two. "I don't know what you mean, lassie. My outburst wasn't malicious or conspiratorial or premeditated."

"But you were rehearsing in the hotel the night before, yes?" She smiled coldly, registering Brodie's angry reaction to her sneaky surveillance tactics. "You should cut back on the cocktails, Professor. Your liver, *aïe*!"

"It's my ribs I'm worried about," he wheezed. "And my kidneys. I'll be pissing blood for weeks on account of your goons. I think I've paid the price for embarrassing your caring organization. Now let me out of here." Wincing, he attempted to stand up. The metal chair scraped agonizingly on the tiled floor, false nails across a blackboard. He sat down again, slowly. "Once I've had a wee rest."

She pulled out a cigarette and lit up, blowing the smoke into the harsh light of a naked bulb that dangled from the ceiling. "You haven't answered my question, Professor. Tell me about the conspiracy. Any more of your denials and I'll take another fifteen minute break, *compris*?"

Threats seem less threatening somehow when they're made in a sultry French accent. But less in this case was still pretty unpleasant. "If I could answer your questions, I would," the Scot said, panting. "I don't know anything about a conspiracy. You'll have to fill me in."

"My guards will fill you in – *non*? – if you lie to me, Brodie. I can spot a lie a mile off. Women's intuition." She dragged deeply on her Gitane, then came out with a tale so bizarre that Brodie would have laughed if he hadn't been incapacitated. Her department had been receiving threatening emails and letters. Threats that went way beyond the usual customer complaints, even the especially irate complaints the car industry receives day and daily. The complaints Duchamp was dealing with centred on the Citroën logo. Its double chevron was a representation, apparently, of the "blade", a primordial symbol of tumescent masculinity. It was a denial and denigration of the "universal feminine", epitomized by the "chalice", an inversion of the Citroën logo. Worse, the company's logo was an unforgivable celebration of freemasonry. It was a blatant advertisement for the secret organization that is behind just about every cover-up, conspiracy, calamity and corporate slight of hand, everything from the sinking of the *Titanic* and the Roswell incident to the design of the dollar bill and the death of Princess Diana. The Freemasons were behind the Rosicrucians, who were behind the Illuminati, who were behind the Priory of Sion, who were a front for the Knights Templar, the Trilateral Commission and Opus Dei. They were all in it together and Citroën's suspicious Masonic chevrons lay at the heart of the labyrinthine tangle.

"Logos are powerful things," Brodie agreed. "But they're not *that* powerful. I don't know why you're so worried. Conspiracy theories are popular nowadays, especially after those egregious books by Dan Brown. But they're hokum, by and large."

Madame Duchamp drew deeply on her cigarette and, after looking round for an ashtray in an ashtray-less room, dropped the smouldering butt into Brodie's tumbler of water. "We think there's an ulterior motive. We think there's a guerrilla marketing stunt in the offing. We have heard that Dan Brown's next book is about the Freemasons. If the threats we've been receiving were to leak out, or are leaked by an unscrupulous publicist – the publicist behind the threats, maybe – Citroën would end up in the same position as the Catholic Church did, as Opus Dei did, as the National Organization for Albinism did, in his previous books. We are not going to be sucked into some cheap marketing stunt."

"You think Dan Brown is behind the letters?" Brodie asked in amazement, his burns and bruises all but forgotten. "Don't be daft."

"It all fits. The blade. The chalice. The eternal feminine. The

Freemasons. The writer's record of stirring up controversy in order to sell his dreadful novels."

"And you think I have something to do with it?"

"You did mention Brown and the Freemasons during your presentation. What else do you expect us to think?"

Professor Brodie was at a loss. He had no recollection of mentioning Dan Brown. The Nazis, yes. The Brownshirts, possibly. But Dan Brown, the American author of penny dreadfuls, whose appalling books he'd skimmed some years back when he was stuck in an airport with nothing better to read? He didn't actually mention him, did he?

Gabrielle Duchamp threw a dog-eared copy of *The Da Vinci Code* on to the desk. "I believe you're a theologian by training, Professor Brodie. You're supposed to be ze beez kneez in religious symbology and hidden meanings, a real-life Robert Langdon. I understand from my contacts in Procter & Gamble that you sometimes advise companies confronted by conspiracy cranks. Advise me on how best to outmanoeuvre Brown, Brodie, and we'll call it quits."

"How long have I got?"

"Until 5.00 p.m."

"Do I have to stay here? Can't you find somewhere more comfortable?"

"I don't think you quite get it," she said, rising from her seat and making for the cell door. "Failure is not an option, Professor. You either find a way of beating Dan Brown or my... assistants will beat you instead. *A bientôt*."

Chapter Forty-Five

The Witchery Code

Abby was livid when she left the Gallery Restaurant. She knew she was right to be wary of Magill. She should have realized he was full of it. His bright idea for cracking the poetic cipher involved taking the first letter of each line. It might be an acrostic, he whined. An acrostic that spelled SQGDVXCHAC SVMFHD-DVKN HYWFJRPFNO.

What a twat.

Still, at least she got Pitcairn Brodie's location out of him. Or, rather, a riddle containing the professor's top secret location, which Magill had uncovered somehow:

My first is in National but not in Galleries
My second is in Turret but not in Castle
My third is in Cipher but not in Code
My fourth is in Edinburgh but not in Glasgow
My fifth is in Marketing but not in Retailing
My sixth is in Brand but not in Name
My seventh is in Sales but not in Promotion
My eighth is in Maguire but not in Abby
My ninth is in Magill but not in Simon.

Abby was certain it spelled SIMPLETON, but the letters didn't fit.

Puffed out, Abby was perspiring slightly by the time she reached The Witchery. The setts on Castlehill didn't help, not when you're a see-you-Jimmy Choo wearer. Oh for a pair of Crocs. She wondered if Dave the Rave had arrived yet. He should be here by now. Just time for a quick shower and change of outfit. Something a bit more relaxed. Flats too.

Abby hobbled down the narrow entranceway, heading for the wonderfully winding stairs to the Inner Sanctum above. Preoccupied with bloodthirsty thoughts about men's congenital stupidity – pity them or put them down? – she failed to notice the desk clerk's attempts to attract her attention.

"Miss D'Anger! Miss D'Anger!" the clerk called, scampering after her rapidly evaporating guest.

Abby paused on the landing outside the first floor suite and looked down at the employee below. A portrait of Mary, Queen of Scots, the Britney of her day, loomed gloomily over the assistant assistant-manager's shoulder. She had an anxious air. Somewhat discomfited. Almost imploring. The desk clerk didn't look too happy either.

Intrigued, Abby returned to the ground floor, where the flunkey whispered that the manager wanted a word with her. Heather Hatchett, the extra-efficient waitress she'd tipped that morning after breakfast, was sitting outside the manager's office, watching events unfold while refusing to meet Abby's eye. Abby also noted that the uniformed concierge had positioned himself at the far end of the entrance passageway, presumably to foil any escape attempt. He'd nothing to worry about. Jimmy Choos weren't built for speed.

The manager was wearing a smartly-tailored Jaeger suit. Thin faced, narrow-lipped, beetle-browed and slightly freckled, her closely cropped fair hair showed no sign of the bottle, much less hint of a tint. Aside from her seen-it-all-and-then-some expression, she looked calm, collected, courteous and cloned. In that seemingly super-efficient hospitality industry manner, her slimline, vanity-boarded, beech-veneer desk was uncluttered, completely empty apart from an Anglepoise lamp, flat screen computer, brass name plate and... a crisp five pound note, all on its own-e-o.

"Can you explain this, Miss D'Anger?"

Abby looked her up and down, holding and returning her ice queen stare. "Well, it's either the frustrated spinster look or the woman-in-a-man's-world routine. They're hard to tell apart." Abby wasn't going to be browbeaten by anybody, especially not an uppity hotel manager called Florence Housemartin.

Frozen Flora bristled. "Very good, Miss D'Anger. Danger by name, danger by nature. Perhaps you could tell me what this counterfeit note says about *you*."

"That I must have passed it on by accident?"

"Try again."

"That I'm a mystery shopper who circulates fake fivers to gauge hoteliers' and retailers' reactions?"

The Witchery's chief witch drummed her fingers on the desk. "Try again."

"That it's a work of art, an attempted critique of mindless consumerism, rapacious capitalism and the co-option of Scotland's authentic traditions by multi-national corporations and the theme park industry?"

Ms. Housemartin touched her hands-free headset. "Front desk? Call the police. Ask them to be discreet this time. No flashing lights or sirens." Frozen Flora smiled coolly at her troublesome guest. "They upset the celebrities," she explained, "especially those with a coke habit. With so many A-listers staying here, we get used to their foibles. We do our best to keep them happy and out of trouble. Shoplifting's a particular problem for some reason, so we have the necessary arrangements in place. The misappropriated merchandise is returned, no questions asked, no leaks to the Sunday papers." She held up the fiver by its outer edge, as if the loathsome object were contaminated. "Now, are you going to explain this oversight or would you prefer to talk to several tough policemen?"

"How tough?" Abby quipped. "In uniform? With the pointy policeman's helmet and big rubber truncheon? Hmmmmmm. How many, exactly, is several? I'll have to think about this."

Fortunately, Florence laughed. Then waited for an explanation. Once again, it was not forthcoming. She reached for her headpiece, with a slight oh-well-I-tried hike of the eyebrows.

As Abby had no real alternative, other than using the heel of her Jimmys as an offensive weapon, then hopping down the Royal Mile to freedom, she decided to tell all. She briefly summarized her bizarre situation, from the shoplifting boyfriend in Some Like It Hot to her lunchtime encounter with a crap cryptographer, expunging only the bits that might give Manager Housemartin the wrong impression. Shooting Father Mannion, for instance.

"I've never heard the like of it," Florence declared, raising a hand to her headset for the third time. Abby slipped off a shoe. "But I believe you, Miss D'Anger. Front desk, a pot of coffee, please. And a tray of shortbread. Thank you Mabel." The Witchery's wonder-woman smiled sympathetically. "When you've been in the business as long as I have, you get to know who's lying and who's not. Strange as your story is, it has the ring of truth." The ice queen may not have melted but a welcome thaw was setting in. "I'd have shot that bajin priest if it were me."

Abby nodded and said nothing. She slipped her Choo back on.

Heralded by the most wonderful smell imaginable, a huge pot of freshly brewed coffee materialized on the manager's desk. The accompanying side-plate of shortbread looked delicious. A minion poured and promptly disappeared. Florence took a tiny sip, then a nibble, and sank back into her chair with a sigh. "It's been a hard day, Miss D'Anger." She took another revivifying sip. "It's also the final day of your stay, I believe."

"Yes, it is. It is. I'll gather my stuff and get out of your hair. Thanks for being so understanding. I'm very grateful. I'll just go and check out…"

"Not before we crack your code."

"Sorry?" Abby couldn't keep the astonishment out of her voice.

Florence set her coffee cup down with a contented clatter. "The Witchery provides a free cryptography service." The look of disbelief crossing Abby's face was, if not quite priceless, certainly close to its MasterCard limit. "Ever since *The Da Vinci Code*, we've been invaded by Grail hunters, Templar seekers, Rosslyn Chapel connoisseurs. It's only a couple of miles from here. The stars stayed with us while they were making the movie. Tom Hanks, Audrey Tatou, Ron Howard, Dan Brown. We organized treasure hunts around town for their kids and what have you. We run Unsolved Mysteries and Hidden Conspiracies weekends in conjunction with the ghost tour people. One of our newest suites, The Abracadabra, has a hocus-pocus theme. J. K. Rowling sometimes stays there when she can't write at home. Reminds her of the good old days in Nicolson's coffee shop. We aren't called The Witchery for nothing."

"And you have a professional cryptographer on call?"

Florence snorted at the very suggestion. "You're looking at her! I studied sub-atomic physics at uni and, as there aren't too many jobs for quantum crunchers, I ended up here. Let me see your coded poem."

Still surprised, Abby passed across the crumpled scrap of paper. Florence slipped on a pair of owlish reading glasses and picked it up with a sniff. "My first is in National but not in Galleries..."

"Whoops, sorry about that," Abby interrupted. "The poem's on the other side. That's just a silly conundrum concocted by the ginger gofer from New College."

The Witchery's in-house cryptographer kept reading, however. Then shook her head. "Easy-peasy. The answer's NUREMBERG. Apt given the logo, I suppose." Exuding efficiency, she immediately turned the RAC invoice over and scanned "The Spear of Destiny". "Well, it's definitely polyalphabetic. See this little glyph at the bottom?" She pointed to a tiny scribble at the foot of the page, which Abby thought was a doodle. "It refers to John Dee, the Elizabethan alchemist and spymaster, who was widely regarded as the foremost warlock of his time and who conversed with angels via a scrying plate."

"He had a signature cipher, did he?" Abby asked, fascinated by the sight of Flo in full flow.

"Well, he wrote a lot of stuff in Enochian, the language of the angels, but the code he normally used was Trithemius's."

"So, what's the Trithemius code when it's at home?"

A look of confusion crossed Florence's face as she scribbled rapidly on a blank Witchery notepad. "Hmmmm. The biggest problem with monoalphabetic ciphers is that certain letters of the alphabet are more common than others, and this means that, although they're quick and convenient to use, they can be cracked by letter frequency counts. Trithemius got round this by a twenty-six by twenty-six alphabetic grid, each line of which was shifted one letter to the right. The first letter of the plain text message was coded according to the letter sequence in the first line, the second by the letter sequence in the second line and so on."

"Sounds complicated."

Florence shook her head vigorously. "No, it's actually very simple. It sounds more complicated than it is in practice. The beauty of Trithemius's cipher is that it makes frequency counts very difficult. Words like, say, COFFEE in plain text, lose the second F and second E in cipher text, because of the sequential alphabetical shift."

"So what does the poem say?"

Florence grimaced. "I'm not quite sure. It doesn't make sense. I can only assume that the poet is using a keyword of some kind. The keyword's a later refinement of the Trithemius, introduced by Vigenère. Basically, it shuffles the order of the alphabetic grid, which makes life quite difficult for would-be code-breakers." She took her glasses off and heaved a sigh. "They're not impossible to crack, by any means. They just take a bit of time and cryptographic brainpower."

"It's not an acrostic, then?" Abby asked sarcastically. "That's what Mr. Magoo – sorry, Mr. Magill – from New College claimed."

The hotelier started scribbling furiously once more. "Out of the mouths of babes…"

"He's no babe, believe me."

Florence looked up, her peaky, pinched face flushed with pleasure, like a successful Su Doku samurai or Rubik's Cube wrangler. She ripped a sheet from her pad and slid it over to Abby in triumph. It contained three words:

SPEARSWAST IKASTONESU NDIALSPELL

Chapter Forty-Six

Dan the Man

Taking her ballpoint pen, Florence swiftly rearranged the spaces:

SPEAR SWASTIKA STONE SUNDIAL SPELL

"Okay. Fair enough. But what do they mean?" Abby asked.

The business-like hotel manager reached into her drawer for a pad of tear-off-and-keep city maps, the kind of synoptic diagrams doled out by concierges the world over. She placed a map on the desk between them, as if she were giving directions to a nearby attraction such as the Camera Obscura or the Museum of Childhood. "We're in Dan Brown territory, Miss Dobbs."

With a look of look-at-me glee, the look that all crossword addicts adopt when casting aside a completed *Times* Cryptic, Florence rattled out the answers. "SWASTIKA must refer to the memorabilia store's logo." She made a mark on the map in the Grassmarket. "STONE is almost certainly the Stone of Scone in Edinburgh Castle." She made a second mark. "There's an occult SUNDIAL in the gardens of Holyrood House, at the bottom of the Royal Mile." A third mark appeared, though there was no obvious overall pattern, apart from a vague "V" shape, somewhat reminiscent of the symbolic "chalice" in *The Da Vinci Code*.

Flora clicked the tip of her pen absentmindedly. She stared into the distance, the lazy Sunday afternoon silence interrupted by a lone piper busking on the Esplanade outside. "SPELL, I'm not so sure of. Perhaps this is where it gets complicated."

Abby's moment of cryptographic glory had arrived. "There's a painting in the National Galleries called *The Spell*."

"Ah, of course," the manageress cried with delight. "Of course there is! I should have remembered. Silly me." Flora made her fourth mark.

"What about SPEAR?"

With another smile of deep satisfaction, the manager of The Witchery passed the marked-up map to her exclusive hotel's esteemed guest. A perfect Christian cross connected Edinburgh Castle, Holyrood House, the National Galleries of Scotland and Rosa Alchemica Caledonia. The lines intersected over New College. "The Spear of Destiny is either hidden in the bowels of New College library, or on open display in Professor Brodie's office. Knowing the professor as I do, the latter's much more likely. Pitcairn Brodie's the man you need."

"Riddle solved, in double quick time."

"All part of the service, Miss D'Anger. The Witchery prides itself on customer care beyond the call of duty." She picked up the contaminated counterfeit note. "I'll dispose of... this... shall I?"

"It's time I left, isn't it?"

"I think so."

As Abby was gathering up her stuff, such as it was, a sharp knock rat-a-tat-tatted on the manager's door. Mabel, the anxious desk clerk who'd collared Abby earlier, popped her hangdog face into the room. "The police are here, Ms. Housemartin. Shall I show them in or ask them to wait in The Secret Garden?"

"Show them in," the manager replied curtly.

Abby was completely taken aback. She couldn't believe that Flora was leading her a merry dance, keeping her talking till the cops arrived.

But Flora was. And Housemartin did.

Ensnared, Abby didn't know whether to be impressed by the hotel manager's ability to fake sincerity – a tremendous boon in the service industries – or to feel utterly betrayed by a woman who seemed sympathetic to her plight, who took evident pleasure in cracking the code. Mind you, Abby'd bonded and bullshitted herself on quite a few Some Like It Hot occasions. She should have known better than to fall for it. She cursed her own stupidity.

Two uniformed policemen walked into the office, one cold and calculating, the other pale and pustular. The older, cannier officer immediately removed his cap and tucked it politely under an arm. The younger, whey-faced constable was preoccupied with his short-wave radio, which crackled incomprehensibly on his lapel. A glare from the senior officer appraised his assistant of policing *realpolitik*. Caps had to be doffed in the presence of a VIB, very important businessperson. The callow recruit did as he was bid, revealing an unattractive number one haircut and a line of oozing pimples across his forehead, where accumulated sweat under the headband had played havoc with his sensitive skin. He looked as though he'd been skelped in the kisser by a scalding skillet.

"We received a report about forged notes, Ma'am," the older officer said deferentially. "Has someone been passing them off in the restaurant?"

"Yes, I'm afraid so," Ms. Housemartin replied with a weary tinge of regret. "It's Inspector Sinclair, isn't it?"

The officer nodded, suffused with pride at being recognized.

"This is Miss D'Anger," Florence Housemartin continued, "the guest who discovered the forgery. She was given it in change at the bar, unfortunately. It's very embarrassing for us, as you can imagine." The manager's presence of mind was mind-boggling.

Abby rose from her seat in acknowledgement, convinced that the deception was etched on her deeply relieved face. It may well have been, because the inspector was looking at her warily.

"You're familiar with counterfeit money, Miss D'Anger?" he inquired, with a sceptical lift of the eyebrow. "That's very unusual. Most consumers don't notice counterfeits. They just pass them on, inadvertently. It's the shops, pubs, hotels and retail trade generally who usually spot such things. They're encouraged and instructed to do so. But most ordinary people never notice."

Abby had to think fast. Fortunately, she was up to the task. "I'm doing a doctorate on fake goods and counterfeit fashions. Clothes, watches, cosmetics, perfumes, CDs, DVDs, car parts, pharmaceuticals, handbags, holy water and, of course, cash. You name it, they fake it these days."

"Oh aye?" the pasty-faced constable cut in. "And whit did ye find oot?"

It's not easy to invent an entire PhD thesis on the spur of the moment. Even as a final-year undergrad, however, Abby had had enough experience of hair-splitting, nit-picking, self-congratulatory academic articles to know the kind of guff that was needed. "Oh, that there's no such thing as a fake. The boundary between fake and real is indistinguishable. Designer labels steal their haute couture ideas from kids on the street and the designers' ideas are pirated in turn by fast fashion chain stores which are then plagiarized by cheap knock-off manufacturers whose goods are worn mainly by the kids on the street, who can't afford designer labels and who are then ripped off again by designer labels. Who's doing the stealing here? Where's the fake and where's the real? Illegal downloads, likewise, are killing the music business. But nobody really cares because the music business has been ripping customers off for years. It deserves to die."

"That's not how we look at it, Miss D'Anger," the narrow-eyed inspector said. "If convicted, counterfeiters can face up to ten years in prison." His distrustful disposition yelled "liar", though his language remained within the bounds of procedural acceptability. "And people who knowingly pass off counterfeit notes are also looking at a long stretch."

"Just as well I informed Ms. Housemartin of my suspicions, then."

"Indeed." He picked up the dodgy fiver and studied it carefully. "This is a good forgery. You have a good eye, Miss D'Anger. Very good." Deftly pocketing the counterfeit, almost as if he were trousering a see-no-evil backhander, he invited Abby to join him at Gayfield Square police station. A statement was necessary.

"Is it really necessary?" the manageress intervened, with a look that spoke volumes about the hotel's relationship with the local constabulary. "Miss D'Anger is one of our most important clients and, as you know, we prefer to keep ourselves strictly off the record, Inspector Sinclair."

Well aware of the side-of-bread-buttered scenario, Sinclair had no alternative but to accept Ms. Housemartin's endorsement of her guest's good character. The police officers withdrew, but not before the pustular constable shot a departing question as he was pulling on his constrictive cap. "Not too many students can afford The Witchery. Are the student grants that big noo-adays?"

Abby had seen enough episodes of *Columbo* to know that the cops always saved a killer question for the end of the interview, when the prime suspect starts to relax. She was surprised that the police persisted with the ploy when everyone knew it was coming. Perhaps cops didn't watch cop shows. They should. They could learn something. "Trust fund," she said apologetically. "I'm afraid the D'Anger family is really… um… quite prominent in Northern Irish society. Perhaps you should… um… check us out." Abby hoped that the studied diffidence would convince the grunting constable. She wasn't so sure about the inspector, though, whose general attitude had grown more and more suspicious.

"We'll do that," Sinclair confirmed. "Do you have any identification?"

As calmly as she could manage, while cursing herself for over-confidence, Abby fumbled around in her handbag then pulled out Dave's sister's passport. She handed it to the inspector with a pretend imperious glare. Far from scrutinizing her ID carefully and making Abby sweat, he flicked though its pages disconcertingly quickly. With a sidelong glance at the tetchy hotel manager, he returned it with a knowing smile. "Everything seems to be in order."

Florence showed them out with suitable words of gratitude, plus some amiable Old Town small-talk. Before Abby could express her heartfelt appreciation, however, the manageress hushed her with the palm of her hand. She sidled round to her sleek flat-screen computer, performed a quick flamenco on its cordless mouse and hissed, "Sssssh, listen to this."

Abby was confused. "Don't tell me. An illegal music download. The Police, presumably."

"Don't tell me," Florence countered, "you've never heard of plodcasts, police radio in real time? They're password protected. But easy enough to hack into. Hoteliers need to know what's going on around town. We all listen in." She increased the volume on her surround-sound speakers.

It was almost as if they were in the back seat of the police car as the inspector chatted on the radio. "Could be her. Fat Ulsterwoman with fake fivers. Fake ID too. We'll pick her up when she leaves the hotel. No point making a scene. The idiot manageress has fallen for her story."

Silly as it sounds, the gratuitous fat remark bothered Abby more than the prospect of capture. "It wasn't a story, Florence," she said in her most persuasive manner.

"I know," Florence replied. "I may be an idiot manageress but I can still tell truth from lies. You'd best go out though The Secret Garden restaurant. This building used to be a grammar school and there's a hidden flight of steps under the floor. They lead to the girls' entrance on Dunstone Terrace. You'll be okay from there. Just keep heading away from the castle."

"Got it." Abby gathered up her stuff, thanked Flo profusely and made for the door.

"Before you go," the hotelier said. "There was a message for you."

"Oh yes?" Abby answered, expecting to be handed a post-it note or something similar.

Reading from her screen, Florence continued, "It's from a Dave Kelley. He called by while you were out. Says he'll meet you at RAC."

Abby took a wrong turn on exiting The Witchery. She had almost reached the Usher Hall before she realized that Grassmarket was the other way. A friendly local, well used to redirecting discombobulated tourists, pointed her in the right direction and five minutes later she was standing outside Rosa Alchemica Caledonia. The shop door was wide open, a sharp contrast to the consumer deterrence strategy she'd detected before. However, the change in sales tactics hadn't made any difference to customer footfall. It was still eerily empty, despite the crowds milling around Grassmarket in the Sunday afternoon sunshine. The swastika, presumably, was sufficient to dissuade all but the most psychotic shopaholics. The customer, they say, is always right wing, though comparatively few are *that* far right.

She was just about to thump the press-for-service bell, when a moaning sound caught her attention. Selkirk Brodie was sprawled on the shop floor behind the counter. His arms and legs were bound with black insulating tape, the phone was off the hook. It looked as though he'd been trying to get in touch with the police, without success. Impulse purchase gee-gaws were scattered on the floor around him, like confetti at a Nazi wedding ceremony.

Jumping into action, Abby lifted the counter flap, crouched down beside the bruised, somewhat groggy shopkeeper and reached for the thick strip of tape that covered his bushy bearded mouth. She was hesitant to pull at first because she knew all about depilation and could tell that his pain to date was as nothing to what was coming. Needs must, however. She yanked with all her might. The ex-SAS man must have experienced worse. His voice was full of urgency and concern. "Back room. Hurry."

Abby ripped the bamboo curtain apart. Dave was lying on the floor. In an enormous pool of bright red blood. He was deathly pale. He was deathly silent. He was dead.

Chapter Forty-Seven

I Love You, You Love Me

The history of torture makes hideous reading. From racks and thumb screws to iron maidens and electric shock apparatus, the technology of pain infliction advances inexorably. Powerful psychotropic drugs, heavy metal music played at excruciating volumes and mobile phones with inane ring tones have all been pressed into persecution service. The latter are especially effective on crowded commuter trains, when entire carriages can be reduced to confess-all, admit-anything telltales by the simple repetition of da de la da, da de la da, da de la da.

Despite continual technological development, which surely reached its apogee when Iraqi prisoners endured prolonged exposure to the theme tune of *Barney*, the kiddies' TV favourite, many of the most effective torture methods are among the oldest. Dripping taps, water boards, branding irons, bamboo shoots under the fingernails, beatings on the soles of the feet, holding the arms outstretched for hour after hour, relentless questioning and personal abuse that goes on for several days without respite. The list is endless.

Of all the currently available interrogation options, perhaps the most inhuman is *The Da Vinci Code*. Being forced to read the giga-selling blockbuster is on a par, surely, with the most extreme forms of sensory deprivation. For many high-brow aesthetes, it is the intellectual equivalent of Russian roulette, with every chamber loaded. American misdeeds in Abu-Ghraib and Guantanamo Bay are a mere bagatelle compared to the damage being done to collective IQs by *The Da Vinci Code* and its partners in crime – *Digital Fortress, Angels and Demons* and *Deception Point*. The masses tremble at the horrors soon to be visited upon them when *The Solomon Key* is released.

Pitcairn Brodie was made of sterner stuff, however. Wrestling day in and day out with delicate illuminated manuscripts, water-damaged incunabula and cryptic medieval grimoires in riddling pig Latin, he had no qualms about swallowing several penny dreadfuls at a sitting. It took him less than two hours to digest *The Da Vinci Code*. By the time Gabrielle Duchamp and her tapioca-faced henchmen returned to the tile-lined cell beneath Schwurgerichtssaal 600, he had formulated a plan of action. Naturally, he refused to divulge the nitty-gritty immediately, since that would only invite instant rejection. Human nature is such that if things are too readily obtained, they are considered valueless. Instead, he treated Citroën's marketing director to a brief history lesson.

The founding father of public relations, Brodie explained, was Edward L. Bernays. A nephew of Sigmund Freud, he set up one of the world's first PR companies and invented the techniques that every cynical spin doctor and savvy publicist employs nowadays. He not only wrote the book on the black art of media manipulation, but his infamous 1928 volume, *Propaganda*, was used to chilling effect by none other than Josef Goebbels.

The key to Bernays's ability to outspin the spindoctors, Brodie continued – despite Duchamp's get-to-the-point impatience – was what he called "appeals of indirection". Here, the object of the PR exercise wasn't approached head-on, but tackled by subtle Machiavellian means. Bernays promoted Harcourt Brace, the book publisher, less by advertising individual titles than by persuading architects, housebuilders and property developers to design dwellings with built-in bookshelves. Where there are bookshelves, Bernays contended, there will be books. When a leading bacon producer was in a flap about falling sales, on account of the growing popularity of Kellogg's breakfast cereals, he organized a campaign to change America's eating habits. He conducted a pseudo survey of doctors who maintained that hearty breakfasts were beneficial. The newspapers splashed on this "finding", sales of bacon and eggs soared and the full American breakfast was born. When hired to promote Lucky Strike cigarettes, he set out to make Lucky's green livery into the latest thing, the new black, the shade to be seen in. He did so by means of a star-studded Emerald Ball, a cascade of green-related stories in the media and a series of learned lectures on the symbology of the colour in western art, as well as Ireland's imperishable contribution to American culture. He invented the St. Patrick's Day parade in order to sell Lucky Strikes.

"Very interesting, professor," Madame Duchamp said with asperity. "But how does this help with Dan Brown? Are you suggesting we make brown an unpopular colour and that this will somehow affect the public perception of the person? Brown is already a horrible colour!" She clicked a finger. The heavies stepped forward. One had a face like Beth Ditto's arse. The other looked like a cauliflower ear, with a purple fungal infection. They extracted their cigarette lighters and clicked in unison. The message was clear, if unsubtle. "You are wasting Citroën's time," Duchamp warned. "You may think this is a joke, but Dan Brown is not funny!"

After re-reading *The Da Vinci Code*, Pitcairn Brodie was inclined to disagree. "Bananas," he said.

Thunderstruck, Citroën's marketing director was lost for words. "Bananas?" she repeated in an incredulous tone. Flicking a quick you-know-what-to-do glance at the goon squad, she made for the cell door, muttering under her breath.

"Bananas," Brodie called out, "were Bernays's greatest triumph and the key to defeating Dan Brown."

Stopped in her tracks by the surreal lunacy of the Brown Bananas scenario, Madame Duchamp turned to face her Caledonian captive. Her patience, if not exactly exhausted, was definitely running on empty. However, she'd been to sufficient short courses on creative thinking to know that the best ideas sometimes come from the strangest juxtapositions. "This better be good," she said curtly.

"Back in the 1930s," the Scottish theologian sermonized, "there was an urban myth about bananas. It was said that bananas caused polio in children. This unfounded rumour was adversely affecting the sales of America's biggest banana dealers, the United Fruit Company. The company brought in Bernays to refute the allegations. Bernays knew that he couldn't deny the polio-mylitis slur outright. Denial would only give it credence. The denial wouldn't be believed in any event, because the denier was in the business of selling bananas. It was a classic 'they would say that, wouldn't they' situation. So, rather than attack the polio myth head on, Bernays set up a front organization called the National Foundation for Infantile Paralysis, which was dedicated to tackling the terrible disease. The organization was secretly funded by the United Fruit Company and, as part of its remit, duly issued an 'independent' report on the causes of polio in children. The bananas rumour was ridiculed in the much-publicized report. As it was quashed by a supposedly disinterested body, the allegation faded away, and banana sales soared. The technique is used to this day in American politics, where it is known as 'astroturfing'."

A frown line that a bucket of Botox couldn't assuage appeared on Duchamp's perfectly-preserved features. "Are you suggesting that we set up an Official Commission on the Holy Grail to refute the story that Jesus and Mary Magdalene were married and had children and their descendents are alive and well and living in Scotland?"

"No, of course not," Brodie scoffed. "The object is to ensure that you don't get involved directly. The mistake the Vatican made and Opus Dei made and the Albinism society made was that they responded to the book's insinuations officially. And because their critiques and counter-arguments weren't disinterested they added to the controversy surrounding *The Da Vinci Code* and contributed to Brown's bottom line. They fell into his PR trap. He set out to antagonize them and he succeeded. Madonna, Damien Hirst, Michael O'Leary, all successful self-promoters, employ variations on the same tactic. Some victims ignore the provocation..."

"Ignore it?" interrupted Duchamp. "We let Brown say what he likes about Citroën? Never. Never! *Non*!"

Brodie smiled. He had her where he wanted her. "As I was about to say, some victims ignore the provocation in the belief that 'no comment' is sufficient, that by refusing to engage with the controversy the issue will fade away. It won't. It never does. The rumour has to be crushed, but it must be crushed by a third party, someone or something that doesn't appear to have a personal stake in the outcome. Ideally, as with Bernays's bananas, this refutation should ridicule the provocateur's position. There's nothing like ridicule to stop someone in their tracks."

The face that launched a thousand cars, and shipped a whole lot more, was a furrowed mask of doubt. Or as furrowed as a crateful of collagen filler would allow. "Let me get this clear, Professor Brodie, your advice is that we sent up an independent front organization to ridicule Dan Brown?"

Brodie dismissed the suggestion with an airy wave. "It doesn't have to be an organization as such. A book would suffice. The challenge is to show that the factual basis of Brown's novels is incorrect. Remember, he claims that the information in his stories is true. If you fund someone to show otherwise, someone with no obvious connection to Citroën, then you're well on your way to calling Brown's bluff."

"Someone like you, Professor Brodie?"

"*Pof*!" the Scotsman replied with a grin.

Duchamp remained unconvinced. "What sort of facts would you ridicule?"

"Well, as a professional theologian, I could show that the religious basis of Brown's argument is faulty. I could undermine his claim that Jesus and Mary Magdalene were married. I could demonstrate that his treatment of the Council of Nicaea is historically incorrect. I could question his discussion of the Dead Sea Scrolls, the Gnostic Gospels and the Q-hypothesis. I could challenge… I could do all of these things, Ms. Duchamp. But they've been done already. The Catholic Church and Opus Dei made the very same points, so they can't be aired by someone like me, because they're old news. Brown, I believe, can be beaten by showing that the tiny details are wrong. Albinos don't have pink eyes, as a rule. Versailles is not north of Paris. The Gare St-Lazare railway station doesn't serve Lille. Rue Haxos is nowhere near Roland Garros stadium. Vinegar doesn't dissolve papyrus, even when encased in a cryptex. Polyalphabetic substitution ciphers were invented by Trithemius, not Abu Yusuf Ismail al-Kindi…"

"Is this the best you can come up with, Brodie?" Duchamp demanded contemptuously. "That vinegar doesn't dissolve papyrus? That Brown got a cryptographer's name wrong? That albinos' eyes aren't pink!?"

Brodie shrugged, scratched his heavily stubbled chin and sat back in the uncomfortable metal seat, which screeched on the uneven floor. "Rhetoricians tell us that the best way to defeat an argument is to expose its factual shortcomings. Listeners extrapolate the tiny flaws to the whole. It's the halo effect in reverse. The entire edifice can be brought down by the tiniest erroneous detail, just as great leaders can be tripped up by seeming trivialities. Jack Welch's pension. Martha Stewart's phone call. Al Capone's tax evasion. Bill Clinton's cigar holder. When Brown writes his book on Citroën and the freemasons, an outsourced nitpicking strategy will pay big dividends, trust me."

"The thing is, Professor Brodie, I don't trust you. You are uncontrollable. You are a drunken buffoon. You have embarrassed my organization and me. You have twenty-four hours to come up with a better plan. Otherwise..."

"Otherwise what, lassie?" the Scotsman growled.

"Otherwise we inform the world about your little ... peccadilloes in Ireland. We know all about you, Brodie. We did a background check. We are aware of your propensities, *oui*? We found out about your love of... *les enfants*. The world will hear about your paedophilia." She turned to her minders, who'd been listening to the exchange impassively. "Take him away. Teach him a lesson. He makes me sick."

Chapter Forty-Eight

Abby Go Lucky

Distracted, disturbed, distraught, Abby turned the pages of the Yeats manuscript. Nothing was sinking in. Her eye scanned the text but her brain was elsewhere. She couldn't get Dave Kelley out of her mind. The sight of his boyish body sprawled in a pool of bright red blood would stay with her forever. Dead bodies didn't bother her, ordinarily. Workers in slaughterhouses soon become immune to annihilation. Abby could eviscerate a hippo in double-quick time, with nary a second thought or flicker of emotion. However, the sheer amount of blood on the floor of that retail store shocked Abby to the core. And then some.

In retrospect, she realized she shouldn't have pounded and pummelled the prostrate body – scene of crime officers, be damned – nor cursed Kelley aloud for leaving her in the lurch. Especially as he'd had sufficient nous to pass on a message to the shopkeeper before he too passed on. As last words go, "Read the manuscript, recover the spear" weren't exactly in the "Bugger Bognor" league, let alone "Kiss me Hardy" or "I may be gone for some time." Nonetheless, Kelley's parting message was the one thing Abby had to cling to, and she wasn't going to let Dave down. For all her faults, Abby Maguire was faithful to friends, unforgiving with enemies and, on this occasion, fearful of what the future had in store.

Her fears, of course, didn't stymie the retail marketing student's innate resourcefulness. Ever clever, she emptied the cadaver's pockets of anything that might assist the police, cash and credit cards included. "This is a private matter," she whispered to the trussed-up shopkeeper, as she slit his swaddling bonds with a felicity honed on the boning line. "I know who did this. Revenge shall be mine. When the cops get here, keep me out of your account." The ex-soldier nodded his assent. He knew the score. She dialled the emergency services then passed the handset over to him, just in case the authorities were recording incoming calls. She made her escape, shutting the shop door firmly behind her, and hailed a taxi to the airport. She was securing her back-seat seatbelt when a police car sped into the Grassmarket, lights flashing, siren wailing. The response time was such that Abby was sure it was The Witchery twosome.

Damn, she'd forgotten to reclaim the Skorzeny dagger. Abby had no personal protection, not even her trusty can of delay spray. That had fallen foul of the onboard liquids restrictions at Belfast International Airport, though it gave the grunting security guards something to keep themselves occupied.

Air Berlin claims to be a low-cost airline. Certainly, its prices are competitive, not that Abby was worrying, since Kelley's credit was taking care of business. On looking round the cabin, though, she could tell that German consumers were much too fond of their Lufthansa-inculcated comforts to fully grasp the no-frills, low-cost concept. Hell, Air Berlin even offered complimentary newspapers and in-flight snacks, which was positively sybaritic compared to the rough and tumble of Ryanair. Still, Air Berlin provided the quickest route to Nuremberg, via Stansted, and time was of the essence. The police were looking for her in Ulster. The cops were keeping a cell warm in Edinburgh. The passport she was carrying wasn't her own, though she passed for a plus-size version of Juliet D'Anger. The money in her purse was counterfeit, albeit sufficiently real to fool the harassed desk clerk at the foreign exchange kiosk. All in all, Abby was skating on ice that was extremely thin, melting fast and cracking ominously.

Passport control was oblivious, fortunately, as were the officious jobsworths on security. Having worked on a production line, Abby knew all about the deadening effects of workflow blur. People passing, passing people, people passing people, passing people passing people, all indistinct and indistinguishable. The brain turns to mush, the daydreams begin, the heightened state of alert soon reverts to torpor, indifference, absent-mindedness. They say that if terrorists really want to get through airport security, they can. And they do. Much more easily than many might imagine.

When it comes to chubby Caucasian women, the chances of being intercepted are slim, unless accident intervenes. But Abby's luck held. She even had the gumption to call the ginger widget, Simon Magill, from Edinburgh airport and, on revealing that his NUREMBERG conundrum had been cracked, managed to extract the name of Pitcairn Brodie's hotel. It cost her a date with the Hustler-bound redhead, but she'd find some way to wriggle out of that in due course. Continued survival was her more immediate concern.

Abby struggled to concentrate on the Yeats manuscript. She was reading in a waking dream. *All Fall Down* contained a clue of some kind. What kind of clue, she hadn't a clue. It was obviously written by a poet – all style, no content – though it seemed awfully familiar somehow. But then literary types were always ripping off each others' ideas, just like the designer label fakers, the haute couture copyists and the iffy lippy pirates she was doing her doctorate on. She was a phoney too. Who wasn't nowadays? Even the dear departed Dave Kelley was a serial dissembler. Was he gay or straight, goth or metal, ordinary bloke or calculating aristocrat? She never really got to know him. Morbid thoughts crowded in as the plane ploughed on and Abby ploughed through the hackneyed whodunnit.

The taxi driver had either been on a customer care training course or was being tipped like an ante-post favourite at Nuremberg's Norisring Races. The latter, Abby surmised, because he was driving a high-specification Mercedes and wearing one of those luxurious leather car coats that are two-a-penny in Germany but cost an arm and a leg elsewhere. Roman Abramovich's arm and leg, that is. With embarrassingly effortless command of the English language, Kurt took evident pride in his home town, summarizing its history as the Merc glided citywards. The history lesson was somewhat sanitized, since he didn't mention the war, though home town hero Albrecht Dürer, the medieval Meistersingers, the birthplace of Germany's railway network, the world famous Christmas market – news to Abby – and the city's latter-day stand on human rights all figured prominently in his well-practised spiel. Bar Bavarian domestic architecture, the sights were few in number until the old town loomed into view. In a world of cheap and cheerful city-breaks, old towns are decidedly old hat. They are the urban equivalent of seen-one-seen-'em-all heritage parks with their working water wheels, immaculate rustic cottages, tasteful displays of obsolete agricultural implements and frighteningly well-nourished farmworkers wearing authentic reproduction costumes while reminding visitors how wonderful things were way back when, hundreds of years before they were born.

Nuremberg's Altstadt, nevertheless, is a noteworthy exception to the same old old town rule. A crenellated castle looms over a compact riverside settlement, its four squat towers and defensive walls impressively intact. The winding streets are stuffed with Gothic churches, cosy squares, outdoor cafes, striking sculptures, magnificent museums, waterside walkways, stop-and-stare footbridges, money-no-object public buildings and designer boutiques that bespeak Bavaria's on-going economic miracle. It's hard to believe that most of it is new build. The old town, according to Abby's complimentary in-flight magazine, was all but obliterated by Allied bombing during the Second World War. In the dying days of the Third Reich, it was the scene of intense hand-to-hand fighting. The spiritual home of National Socialism, Nuremberg couldn't be seen to fall to the godforsaken Americans. Hitler commanded that the city be defended to the last drop of blood and, Stalingrad notwithstanding, the exquisite medieval settlement duly witnessed some of the most savage fighting of the Second World War. The tooth-and-nail defence of Nuremberg was all the more remarkable, because everywhere else in Germany, the once-invincible Wehrmacht had thrown in the towel. Towel emplacement, admittedly, is a German strategic speciality, as countless commandeered sun loungers, requisitioned deck chairs and annexed poolside spots in numberless Mediterranean holiday resorts attest. The end result of this last ditch defence was a devastated city centre and a subsequent rebuilding programme that is remarkable in its fidelity to the old. Nuremberg's Altstadt may be a fake, but who's complaining when the fake is just like reality, only better?

Kurt dropped her off at The Carlton, a nice but nondescript hotel within easy walking distance of the anything but nondescript

Hauptbahnof. The lobby was ubiquitous hospitality industry modernism – grey on grey sofas, with blond wood and glass coffee tables and abstract objets d'art. It was deserted, apart from a couple of leather-clad bratwurst lookalikes conversing in the corner. The striking display of tiger lilies behind the check-in, coupled with the crystal bowl of complimentary apples on the counter, yelled £200 per night.

Abby asked for Professor Pitcairn Brodie.

"The Scottishman, yes?" Emma, the smiling receptionist, rang Brodie's room and cheerfully confirmed that he wasn't there. She suggested trying the bar, where the once-seen-never-forgotten Celt could unfailingly be found. More often than in his room, evidently.

Her heart rapidly sinking – all she needed was an och-aye-the-noo scenario – Abby made for Boynann's Bar across the lobby, which was empty apart from a lone bartender polishing his steins for the night ahead. Returning to reception, as the fat bratwursts looked on with amusement, Abby informed the impeccably groomed clerk that Brodie was her father and she needed to speak with him urgently. Did she know where he could be?

Smiling encouragingly, Emma suggested that she speak with Heinrich behind the bar, because he'd run several errands for the Scottishman over the past couple of days. Headache tablets, mainly. Gloomily, Abby ambled back to the bar. She *gutentagged* toward the grinning bratwursts while concluding that this professor was certain to be a complete prick – par for the academic course – only to be informed that he was attending the big conference in the Kaiserburg. "Citroën, *ja*? Not good."

Abby debated whether to make her way to the fortress, which was on the opposite side of the old town, according to the map in the in-flight magazine. On reflection, she decided that waiting in the lobby might be her best bet. The bratwursts in suits introduced themselves.

"You are the daughter of Brodie, yes?" the taller, tapioca-faced bratwurst asked deferentially.

"Yes, yes, I am. Do you know where he is?"

"Ve do," the smaller one with a schnozzle like beetroot strudel confirmed. "Ve are his... bodyguards... *ja*? He is special guest of Zitroën... protected at all times."

Abby wondered why they weren't doing their protective duty. Unless they had multiple teams working on the tartan terror. Who the hell was this Brodie guy?

"Ve take you to him, yes?" beetroot bratwurst suggested.

By this stage in the proceedings, Abby really should have known better. But she was susceptible to the charms of smooth-talking, sauerkraut-complexioned German sausages.

Some people never learn.

Chapter Forty-Nine

He Who Hesitates

Abby didn't like lifts at the best of time. But sharing a cramped elevator with two beefy bratwursts, perspiring heavily and reeking of garlic, was a fate worse than the February Fetish Fayre in Some Like It Hot. Actually, Brodie's minders reminded her of Terminator Vibrators – purple heads, knotted veins, an aura of mingled awe and disgust. They looked a lot less fun than the Terminator, though.

She wasn't wrong. No sooner had the lift lifted off than the big bratwurst ripped Abby's handbag from her shoulder and quickly rifled through its clotted contents. The bigger bratwurst grabbed her jaw with his massive left hand and squeezed her cheeks together. She couldn't speak, let alone shout for assistance. He leant into her face and promised pain like she'd never experienced before, though his breath was so bad that the threat was the least of her worries.

The lift doors slid open with a ping. Abby was frog-marched down a minimalist corridor, peppered with reproduction Impressionist artworks and unfortunately devoid of residents or housekeeping staff or anyone who could render appropriate assistance. They shoved her into a bedroom at the end of the passageway. Spare and unornamented in the international hospitality industry style, it was as bland as bland could be, apart from the bowl of black irises, monstrous wall-mounted flat-screen and a scattering of minibar empties, like rose petals in the honeymoon suite. A half-packed suitcase filled with half-quaffed duty-frees lay spread-eagled on the floor and a kilted Scotsman sprawled semi-comatose on the king size. He looked less like Sleeping Beauty awaiting Prince Charming than an RTA on a mortuary slab. There were wheals and cuts and burns all over his naked torso.

Heaved hard into the room, Abby stumbled against the corner of the bed and tumbled on to the floor in an ungainly heap, her handbag tangled beneath her. Big bratwurst grabbed her by the hair then pulled back forcefully. He shook the recumbent Scot with his booted foot. "Guess who's here, Brodie? Your daughter's come to take care of you." The purple-nosed provocateur snorted with guttural laughter, his companion harrumphed. Hilarity was unbounded.

The prostrate professor sat up with a start, wincing in evident pain. Bushy beard excepted, he was a clone of his older brother in Rosa Alchemica Caledonia, even down to the muscular build. An elaborate combover, reminiscent of a mendicant's begging bowl, lay by the side of his head. He swept it back into place with a well-practised move, where it perched like the shell of a tortoise. The movement must have caused considerable discomfort, because he groaned noticeably on completion, his bright blue eyes flashing with suppressed rage. This was someone with battered bratwurst in mind.

"I dinnae have a daughter," he growled, then lay back on the bed staring up at the suspended ceiling.

Big boss bratwurst vibrated with unrestrained glee. Bigger bratwurst, the gargantuan sidekick, throbbed in concert. "You will have to do better than that, Scotlandman," bigger announced. "Look, she squeals just like you when we hit her, *schweinehund*." A massive punch caught Abby in the kidneys, but she bit back the excruciating spasms, which surged to the end of every ganglion in her body. Bigger punched her again and again. She refused to cry out. There's a lot to be said for a spare tyre at times, and Abby's spare had sufficient air to absorb the bratwurst's best body shots.

Abby raised herself to her full height and looked contemptuously at the ugly assailant. "You'll have to do better than that, *schweinehund*."

Infuriated, bigger bratwurst pulled out his underarm pistol and planted the snub-nosed Glock between Abby's eyes. Her contempt never wavered, as she stared at him unblinkingly. He pulled back the hammer. The click reverberated round the silent bedroom.

"Am I supposed to be frightened?" Abby asked, struggling

mightily to control any waver in her voice. She turned her eyes into the barrel, held the cross-eyed look for several seconds then blinked slowly, disdainfully. She was tempted to add insult to injury by sticking out her tongue or placing her thumbs in her ears and wiggling her fingers. But she could see he was about to explode and cleaning up the resultant mess would have been unfair on housekeeping.

"*Nein*, Karl," big bratwurst commanded from a Barcelona chair, where he was wiping the perspiration off his empurpled brow with a pad of paper tissues.

The ginormous subordinate bratwurst did as he was bid. He released the Glock hammer silently, using a podgy thumb to control the pressure, and shoved the lethal weapon into his leather holster with a resounding thunk. Abby relaxed momentarily, which was the wrong thing to do. A vicious left hook caught her in the solar plexus and she went down like the proverbial sack of spuds, coughing and retching, yet unable to breathe. Gasping, hawking, she staggered painfully to her feet, then collapsed on the carpet again, still spluttering. She grabbed the side of the bed and tried to pick herself up, up, up once more. She wasn't going to be beaten by a bunch of Boss-wearing Blutwursts. "I'm here to escort my father home," Abby gasped. "My mother's worried about him."

While she was still on her knees, big bratwurst seized her by the hair again and wrenched her round to face him. Perspiration was cascading down the moguls of his maroon countenance, dripping on his captive. Abby felt herself recoil with disgust. Sweaty Betty bratwurst felt it too.

"Do I disgust you, little Miss Brodie?"

Abby said nothing.

"*Ja*, I disgust you," he sighed with mock regret. "Your father..." He nodded in the direction of Pitcairn Brodie, who was struggling to sit up in bed, though the pain defeated him once again. "Does he disgust you, too?"

"Of course not," Abby spat. "I wouldn't be here if he did."

Sweaty Betty bent over and placed his perspiring face by the side of Abby's head. He whispered loudly into her ear. "He should disgust you. We know what kind of man he is. Do you know what kind of man he is? We know he interferes with *der kinder*. We know he played with orphan boys in Belfast. Little orphan boys. Little boys in a home where no one cared for them or could hear the screams. Did you know that about your father, Little Miss Brodie?"

"You're a liar!" Abby retorted. She had never met Brodie before. She knew next to nothing about him, apart from the reports she'd received from his brother and research assistant, one glowing, the other less so. She wasn't going to give big boss bratwurst an inch. "You're a liar," she repeated, if only to convince herself.

The sweaty sausage giggled. "No, *fräulein*, you're the liar," he said in a grisly girly voice. "Brodie crept in to see you, didn't he? When you were little. While you were trying to sleep. Late at night. He slipped into your bed. You didn't know what was happening. He told you not to tell anyone. He did it night after night. He told you to do what daddy said. You didn't want to. He wanted you to. You didn't want to. He wanted you to. You didn't want to..."

Big bratwurst was panting and wheezing by this stage, his breath coming in short excited gasps. He was obviously projecting a grotesque fantasy of his own on to Abby and Brodie. Perspiration was pouring to the floor. She hoped it was perspiration. She didn't dare look at his piggy, port-wine stained face, flushed with sexual fantasy frenzy. Listening to his guttural gasps was bad enough. Unfortunately, Abby was facing his sweaty crotch which was starting to bulge as eenie, meenie, miney bratwurst responded to its owner's ithyphallic urgings. It wasn't much of a bulge, more like a slight swelling, but the sight was enough to turn Abby's stomach. He continued with his obscene tirade, getting louder and louder, more and more excited, increasingly disgusting in his perverted paedophilic ramblings. Even his partner was staring aghast at the psychotic and pornographic filth pouring from Sweaty Betty's tormented psyche.

Abby couldn't take any more. She sank to the floor, weeping uncontrollably. Huge sobs wracked her trembling body. Although Brodie was the butt of the repellent tirade, bratwurst's nauseating remarks were too close to home, too painful to relive, too reminiscent of her own experience. Her father's suicide. Bringing up her brother and sister. Her predatory uncle. The killing line at the abattoir. Father Mannion's unfatherly fumblings at St. Stephen's, where she'd gone to recuperate but found further depravity. She'd bottled it up for years and got on with her life. She had no choice. She had a family to feed, a farm to run, with further education on hold and only comfort eating for comfort. However, the horrific events of the past two days, coupled with the sickening sight of big bratwurst's wiggling wiener, was just too much.

She cried her heart out. The bratwursts didn't know what to do. They'd never seen such a situation before. Begging for mercy, yes. Pleading for the pain to end, certainly. But exhibitions of uncontrolled and uncontrollable anguish were way beyond their ken and indeed their thuggish comfort zones. They looked at each other mutely, uncertain how best to proceed.

He who hesitates is lost. Professor Brodie didn't hesitate. With a roar that would do Hampden Park proud, he jumped up from his prostrate position and leapt on the baffled bratwursts. Although he was sixty if he was a day, the craggy Scotsman had the advantage of surprise and a raging fury that could only descend on someone falsely accused of unspeakable crimes. His blood was up. The bratwursts went down.

Big and bigger crashed to the floor, which shuddered under the impact. They went for their weapons but Brodie was too quick for them. He banged their heads together then banged them together once more. Sweaty Betty swung a haymaker that caught the Scotsman in the ribs. Groaning involuntarily, the Highlander carried on through the pain, as he kicked red cabbage-complexion full in the face, though it was hard to tell if any damage had been done.

Brodie turned to the second German sausage, but his sexagenarian reflexes, slowed by the punishment beating and burning he'd received an hour or so earlier, weren't up to the mark. Bigger bratwurst was crouched in position, his snub-nosed Glock pointing straight at the Scot's muscular chest. He licked his lips as he pulled back the hammer. He was finally getting what had been denied him earlier. He smiled and squeezed.

But he smiled too soon and squeezed too late. In the confusion, Abby had picked up a half-empty bottle of Famous Grouse. She hurled it at the heavy. It hit him smack on the bridge of the nose, which was painful enough. Luckily, the gout of arcing spirit also splashed into his eyes. He dropped his Glock like a red hot poker, such was his desire to wipe away the burning liquid. Abby barged the bellowing brute aside and picked up his gun. She was standing over him in an instant. She pointed the pistol between his streaming eyes. She pulled back on the hammer, relishing the satisfying click. Then, in traditional Ulster fashion, promptly shot him in the kneecap instead. A volcano of blood and bone spewed out of the shattered patella. He passed out with the pain.

Abby swivelled to deal with big boss bratwurst. Professor Brodie had Sweaty Betty in an armlock. He looked terrible. Sweaty Betty didn't look too good, either. Bigger's superior raised his free hand in surrender. But Abby wasn't in the mood for taking prisoners. Jamming the Glock into his crotch, perhaps the only part of his sweat soaked body that wasn't twitching with terror, Abby generously informed him that he needed professional help with his perverted paedophilic fantasies. But in case professional help wasn't forthcoming she'd give him something for his problem in the meantime. He nodded vigorously, thankful for small mercies.

Pausing momentarily, Abby reflected on Peregrine Faulkner's advice about keeping her emotions in check. She checked. She felt nothing. She shoved the Glock into his gonads again, looked deep into his panicking piggy eyes and pulled the trigger.

"Time to check out, Professor Brodie."

"The airport awaits, lassie"

"Don't forget your suitcase, popsicle."

"Lucky I have a lovely daughter to remind me."

"Where would you be without me, daddy-o?"

"Down the pub, lassie. Down the pub."

Chapter Fifty

The Emerald Tablet

"*Sláinte.*" Abby Maguire knocked her whisky back in one. She didn't drink alcohol as a rule, but she needed a stiffener to settle her nerves. Terrifying though the encounter with the bratwursts had been, it was as nothing compared to Professor Pitcairn Brodie's driving. He'd commandeered an SUV belonging to the ugly brothers, despite never having driven one before, claiming that he needed it more than they did. He conveniently overlooked the fact that Europeans drive on the "wrong" side of the road and took exception to those who begged to differ.

There's road rage, then there's Brodie rage.

Worse, he had difficulty with Nuremberg's traffic management system and ended up some way south of the Altstadt, instead of due north where the airport was. Still, the Nazi Party parade grounds are well worth visiting, if only to see how a place of unspeakable horror can be turned into peaceful parkland. As if that weren't enough to be getting along with, the great theologian was driving without his glasses, kept swigging from a hip flask the size of a milk churn – for medicinal purposes, lassie – and was wearing the full Highland monty, sporran included. They also had a couple of stolen weapons in the car, repatriated from the bratwursts.

It was a miracle they weren't stopped by the police. But they somehow managed to dump the fully-loaded, slightly-dented SUV in the long-term car park and deposit the liberated handguns in a bin outside the terminal building. Brodie made straight for the departure lounge bar, where he promptly concocted a celebratory cocktail. When asked what he called the bespoke libation, Brodie thought for a moment and considered a couple of unacceptable options – Snotgreen Sea and Hubble Bubble among them – before settling on the Emerald Tablet. He explained that the Emerald

Tablet not only summarized the wisdom of the ancients, but contained the secrets of mysticism, alchemy and all true knowledge. Originally written by Hermes Trimegistos, albeit brilliantly reimagined by Fulcanelli, it was endlessly intriguing, deeply addictive and a single sip was never enough.

So marvellous was the story surrounding Brodie's new-born brew that Abby was tempted to try one, especially when he explained that the Emerald Tablet was an alchemical allegory that actually referred to Ireland. But when the bubbling green gloop – a fetid mixture of crème de menthe, absinthe and horseradish sauce – materialized by his elbow, she immediately changed her mind.

"*Sláinte,*" the professor replied, and chucked the cocktail back with a single epiglottal glug. He exhaled through his teeth, shuddered from stem to stern and immediately ordered another. "Nervous flier," he winked at the barmaid, a flaxen-haired stunner from Saxony. "So," he said, turning to Abby, "who exactly are you, lassie, apart from my delightful deliverance?"

"I'm your long lost daughter. I thought we'd established that."

The professor appraised her appreciatively, as if wondering whether it were possible. Then he smiled to himself and shook his massive head. "Well, long lost daughter, what brings you here, apart from sharing a snifter with your dear old dad?"

Abby started from the beginning, back in Some Like It Hot. She told him everything that had happened in the last two tumultuous days. He listened attentively, laughed out loud occasionally and interrupted her once to explain the eerie noise in the hidden chamber beneath Carrickfergus. Ireland's ancient megaliths operated on similar principles, he said. When the druids performed ceremonies in Newgrange and Emain Macha, their chanting was designed to resonate within the corbelled vault. The resultant sound was enormously amplified and its harmonics made the entire edifice shake. It was considered very powerful magic, magic that reinforced the priesthood's importance. The Gods had spoken.

When Abby finished her incredible story, Brodie sat silent for a minute or two, staring through the serried bottles of liquor behind the bar and into the polished mirror beyond. "So you're here for the spear," he sighed, while absent-mindedly running a knotty finger round the rim of his empty glass. "Be careful what you ask for."

She placed her hand over his great gnarled paw, and squeezed. "I'm sorry, Professor, but if I don't secure the Spear of Destiny I'm doomed. The Catholic Church is after me, the IRA is after me, the UVF is after me. I wish it were otherwise…"

Brodie cut her off before she talked herself out of what she had to do. "You've told your story, lassie. Now it's my turn." Some time ago, he said, he'd done a very foolish thing. Like many marooned middle-aged men, he'd fallen for a younger woman, an ambitious marketing academic called Emer Aherne. He taught her the druidic art of memory, which enabled her to shine on the conference circuit. He got her to think out of the business box by explaining that the best marketers aren't always found in marketing departments. Smitten idiot that he was, he wrote verse after verse of sub-Yeatsian poetry for her, while emphasizing that W. B. Yeats was a very astute marketer, notwithstanding his pronouncements to the contrary. Aherne was a quick study. She organized conferences at St. Stephen's to showcase her presentational skills; she wrote a paper on Yeats's marketing prowess that rocked the foundations of Irish academia; and, ruthless bitch that she was, Aherne charmed the pants off a republican priest at the retreat, who spilled the beans about Yeats's connection to the Redemptorist facility. He gave her one of St. Stephen's treasures, an unpublished poem by the master, a poem that confirmed Yeats's commercial mentality. It was dynamite in the rarefied world of Yeatsian scholarship. The ensuing commotion made Aherne's name, she wrote a shock-horror book about the marketing savvy of Ireland's greatest literati and, having been elevated to the academic empyrean, she dumped the sad middle-aged bastard who set her on the road to glory. "I introduced the two of them, you know. Father Mannion and Emer Aherne. I brought this on myself. I created a monster and it gobbled me up."

He ordered a third Tablet.

Abby found it hard to be sympathetic toward libidinous men with more testosterone than sense. But she was a sucker for charm. For all his congenital masculine failings, Professor Brodie was a charmer first class. "Where does the spear fit in, Pitcairn?"

He sipped his cocktail slowly, savouring the taste, awaiting the wallop. "Father Mannion was a collector, Abby. He collected Catholic memorabilia. Holy relics. There's something you must understand about holy relics. They were a huge industry in the middle ages. They were the church's main source of income. They were fakes, one and all. There were more crucifixion nails in existence than there were rivets on the *Titanic*. If all the wood from the True Cross were gathered together, it'd supply a B&Q superstore. At least eighteen holy prepuces existed and, as prepuce is a polite word for foreskin, we can only assume that either His circumcision went horribly awry or the Son of God was unusually well endowed."

"No wonder Mary Magdalene married the Man of Men."

"Anyway," the Scottish theologian continued with a wry grin, "my point is that today's Far Eastern sweatshops, producing phoney Prada, Pucci and Paddington bags, are amateurs compared to the pre-Reformation church. To this very day, supposedly holy relics can be picked up, if you know where to look. I used to unearth lots of stuff on my travels – that's why I acquired Rosa Alchemica Caledonia when the original owners retired – and Father Mannion was one of my best customers. He was an inveterate collector and, like many collectors, he was driven by an overwhelming desire to possess, to have, to own. Once he acquired something, of course, he usually lost interest in it. Most collectors are motivated by the thrill of the chase. They're constantly searching for the next item, and the item after that. Many don't even open, much less display, their expensive treasures."

"A bit like shopaholics?"

"Exactly like shopaholics, Abby. Countless consumers buy clothes and shoes and handbags uncontrollably, yet never wear the clothes or use the handbags or do anything other than keep the shoes safe in their boxes. It is an illness akin to drug addiction, gambling addiction, bulimia, anorexia…"

"Bulimia? Anorexia?"

"The binging and purging cycle is similar to what shopaholics and alcoholics and addicted collectors go through, an uncontrollable cycle of self-indulgence and self-loathing, the cycle that drives contemporary capitalism. We don't need most of what we buy nowadays. The capitalist system teaches us to binge and purge, binge and purge. It's grotesque. Love of Miu Miu is the root of all evil."

Professor Brodie was drifting off the point, presumably out of self-loathing, because he was one of the people behind the people who taught people to binge and purge. But also because he was pissed. She doubted if they'd let him on to his flight. "The spear, Professor?"

He chuckled into his designerless stubble. "Och aye. The spear. As I said, Father Mannion was one of my best customers. I knew that the Spear of Destiny was his pride and joy. When I discovered that he and Aherne were having a fling behind my back, I decided to exact my revenge. They were away at a republican boot camp one weekend. I dropped into St. Stephen's, removed the spear from its reliquary and, just to let them know that I knew what they'd been up to, I wrote a sub-Yeatsian poem that could only have been penned by me. I also included sufficient clues to help Mannion track down his oh-so-precious artefact. I placed it in the reliquary's secret compartment and waited for an explosion of bile. I waited and waited and waited. But nothing happened. I think Aherne moved on to some other sucker and Mannion, like most collectors of his type, obviously didn't notice that the spear was gone. And when he did, didn't think to check the hidden drawer of the reliquary. I suspect he never knew the secret chamber was there. They rarely do. The myopia of collectors is unbelievable. But what do I care? It keeps Rosa Alchemica Caledonia in business."

Brodie finished his drink and stood up. Successfully. Amazingly. "The shop's full of fakes you know, Abby. But collectors want to believe in them. They really do. Who am I to spoil their fun or ruin their dream? Give the customer what they want, right?"

"All capitalists say that, Professor Brodie. But that doesn't make it true. Should people be given what they want if what they want damages their health or their wellbeing or wider society or the environment?"

He nodded sagely. "Good question, lassie. Good question."

"I have another question for you, Professor. Where's the spear now? What happened to it? Is it back in your Edinburgh office, as per the poem?"

Brodie scratched his granite jaw. The bristles sounded like someone pulling Christmas crackers. "I'm afraid I can't tell you, lassie."

"Can't or won't?"

"I'll answer any question you ask. I owe you that much. But the Spear of Destiny's beyond the pale."

"Okay then, since you put it like that. Are you a paedophile, Professor Brodie?"

The question hung in the air. The theologian lowered his head, his combover lifting slightly like a badly laid paving stone. "Yes. Yes, I am."

Abby turned her back on him and ordered another whisky.

Abashed, Brodie wandered off to his gate.

Chapter Fifty-One

Black Swan Down

Abby finished *All Fall Down* with a smile of grim satisfaction. Terrible though it was as a novel, Yeats's manuscript contained an escape route, a possible way out of her on-going nightmare. Looking up, she caught a glimpse of herself in the mirror behind the bar. She seemed to have lost a bit of weight. Her cheekbones had miraculously regenerated and her steadily advancing double chin was in headlong retreat. If only her long lost dimples could find it within themselves to return, she'd almost be back to her best.

A craggy figure was staring at her in the mirror, his bloodshot blue eyes blazing.

"Sod off, Brodie," she said, without turning round. "I've nothing to say to a monster like you. People like you should be put down. Shot. The goons didn't hit you hard enough."

A massive hand was placed on her shoulder. She tried to shrug the thing off, but it was made of granite. "Piss off and play your bagpipes elsewhere, Bonnie Prince Charlie." Abby was surprised by her own vehemence. She didn't know she knew words like that, let alone how to use them.

"You're not exactly Flora MacDonald, lassie."

"Aye, and I'm not rowing you over the sea to Skye, Brodie. Not unless there's an anchor tied to your ankle and I get to throw it overboard."

He let the provocative remark pass. "Lucky I'm a strong swimmer." Wincing with pain, in a blatant attempt to elicit sympathy, he settled himself into the barstool beside her and adjusted the hang of his kilt. She looked the other way, then made to leave. A second slab of granite gripped Abby's shoulder and pressed her back into the seat.

"I'll scream," she said.

"No you won't," he said. "You don't want to get the police involved. Neither do I. Just hear me out for a couple of minutes, and then if you want to leave, that's okay."

She forced herself to face the brute. "Make it quick, laddie. I've a flight to catch."

"You didn't ask me *why* I'm a paedophile, Abby."

"I'd've thought that was fairly obvious, Brodie. And I'd really rather not hear the sordid details."

"That's where you're wrong. You should never, ever, accept anything at face value or jump to conclusions without establishing the facts. It's true that there's a dusty police file somewhere that says I'm a paedophile. But I was taking the fall for my godson, an army officer in Northern Ireland who got caught up in the Kincora scandal, a child prostitution racket involving politicians, churchmen, civil servants, intelligence operatives, terrorist godfathers and prominent Orangemen. They had their wicked way with the children and when the scandal was exposed, immediately ran for cover. My godson, an entirely innocent adjutant for a high ranking army officer, was left holding the baby. Literally. It could have destroyed his career. His father wouldn't help. So I used my connections to take the rap on his behalf. No one was prosecuted. They hushed it up, as was standard practice back then. But my name is on a police file somewhere. And these things can come back to haunt you."

"How can I believe what you say? You've just told me not to accept anything at face value. Why should I accept what you've said?"

"You can't. And I wouldn't expect you to. But what's the first thing convicted paedophiles always say?"

"I am not a paedophile."

"What was the first thing I said to you, when you asked?"

"Yes, I'm a paedophile." People skills were never Abby's strong point, and as a judge of character she was pretty woeful, at least where men were concerned. However, Brodie's explanation had the ring of truth. She asked what happened to his godson. He was killed in a dubious honey trap, possibly set up because of the Kincora connection. So the professor's sacrifice was in vain in any event. He'd since taken his dead godson's kid brother under his wing. He was working as Brodie's research assistant. An enthusiastic young man who had a lot to learn, though Brodie feared he'd end up like his big brother.

Abby hadn't the heart to tell him that she'd met Magill and was decidedly unimpressed. "Yes, I ran into him in Edinburgh. We had lunch. He spent most of the time talking about ciphers and codes and cyberspace. Is that where you got the idea for the coded Yeats poem? Or did he develop his interest from you?"

Brodie chortled, then explained that it was one of those serendipitous things, an entirely unpredictable black swan event. Back in 2000, he'd been reading a trashy novel called *Angels and Demons* by an unknown American author, Dan Brown. He borrowed a bit of the story, the geographical criss-cross clues to the Vatican City conspiracy. The book was so bad and so clichéd that Brodie was amazed when its author went on to enormous fame and fortune with a later book, an even worse novel called *The Da Vinci Code. Angels and Demons* then became a retrospective hit. Brodie thought that its popularity would lead to his conundrum's exposure, especially as the Catholic Church was the butt of Brown's books. But no one at St. Stephen's caught on. "Until you worked it out, lassie."

"Well, I had help."

"But you did discover the connecting factor, correct?"

"Well, we cracked the acrostic, if that's what you mean."

Rubbing his rasping chin absentmindedly, Brodie's drink-dappled physiog appeared perplexed, uncomprehending. "I don't know what you're talking about, lassie," he said, while attempting to catch the busty barmaid's attention.

"Yes you do… the acrostic. The secret code based on the first letter of each line of the poem." Abby looked at him in anticipation, nodding eager encouragement as if she expected to be congratulated for her cryptographic perspicacity.

It didn't come. Brodie stared at her blankly. He raised a frayed eyebrow. "You've been reading too many conspiracy theory thrillers. The clues are in the poem itself. Stony age, cruel cross, sun angle, spellbound spear, X marks the spot. It's all there, as is my anger, bitterness, jealousy, heartache, desire for revenge. Green eyes aglitter, Deirdre's devious story, Murthemne melts in raging fury, come back my beauteous, cunning climbing vixen, neither forgive the sinner nor forget the sin. It includes references to the stolen spear and its current whereabouts. The spear lies in repose, 'neath holy walls the answer lies, on ancient mound the lance resides. The poem even alludes to angels, demons, Dan and brown. It couldn't be more blatant, lassie."

It was Abby's turn to look blank. She wasn't sure if he was bluffing or not. "But the acrostic, Professor. The Trithemius cipher. The thirty capital letters that spelled out SPEAR, SWASTIKA, STONE, SUNDIAL, SPELL. Thirty's an important alchemical number, isn't it? A magic number?"

The craggy Scot rolled his massive shoulders and scratched his shaggy head, while trying not to disturb his delicately balanced coiffure, which bobbled slightly under the strain. "Yes, thirty's a very magical number. Ramon Lull, Giordano Bruno, Simon Magus, John Dee, Johannes Trithemius; they all based their spells and incantations on the number thirty. There are thirty known ways of conjuring angels and demons..." His voice tailed off. "But there's no acrostic built into the poem, lassie. It's a coincidence... a fluke... a miracle."

Abby finished her drink. "But the chances of that must be millions to one."

Brodie ordered another. "That's the way it is with conspiracy theories and magical thinking generally. In a pattern-less world, people see the patterns they want to see and they interpret the world accordingly. The ancients looked at the night sky and saw the future in the stars. Seers stared at the entrails of sheep and goats and based their predictions on the disposition of the giblets. Fundamentalist Christians identified signs and wonders and, with the aid of ambiguously worded verses in the Bible, happily anticipated the end of the world. Conspiracy cranks scrutinized the backs of dollar bills, or Procter & Gamble's logo, and recognized the malevolent hand of the Freemasons or equally heinous secret societies. Inexplicably serendipitous events like the assassination of JFK or the death of Lady Di are explained with recourse to grassy knolls, white Fiats and so forth. Social scientists find what they want to find in their data sets, sometimes with the assistance of multivariate statistics, sometimes with the assistance of qualitative analysis software. They code their data in more ways than one."

Abby scrutinized his rum-raddled face carefully, determined to detect an ironic glint in his strabismic eye. There really was an acrostic, wasn't there? Of course there was. Any minute now he'll burst out laughing and tell her he's kidding. Unless she too was over-interpreting a patternless pattern of ambiguous body language…

"Marketers are particularly prone to magical thinking, lassie. They see patterns where there aren't any. They extract cause and effect from a mass of discrepant information. The contents of academic articles are exercises in necromantic numerology. The diagrams that pepper marketing textbooks, with their arrows and circles and pyramids and squiggles, wouldn't be out of place in medieval grimoires. The contents of strategic marketing plans or scenario planning exercises are contemporary forms of augury and no more oracular, frankly, than tealeaf readings."

While Abby didn't disagree with his assessment of marketing academia – she'd struggled through sufficient hieroglyphic articles to last a lifetime – she knew Brodie was bluffing. There's no way he could say all that and still believe in the Spear of Destiny's supernatural powers. So she interrupted his flow and repeated the questions she'd asked earlier. "Where's the spear, Professor? What happened to it?"

The Scottish symbologist was silent for what seemed like ages. He adjusted his sporran nonchalantly. Abby hoped it was his sporran.

"I gave it away, lassie," he sighed. "For a very good reason. The spear is a double-edged sword. Ownership gives an enormous sense of power and achievement and well-being and self-belief. I've never been so successful professionally as I was during my spear-holding years. But it corrupts. It eats away at you. It destroys as it gives. When the Holy Roman Empire owned the spear it became more and more rotten and degenerate and venal and perverted. When it was ensconced in the Hofburg, the Hapsburg Empire reached its zenith and collapsed from within. When Hitler repatriated it in 1938, the Nazis quickly conquered the world, then lost the plot, and millions paid the price. When the IRA had access to the spear via St. Stephen's, they were motivated by Irish nationalist ideology. Now they're racketeers and counterfeiters and drug runners and bank robbers. The Catholic Church likewise enjoyed a period of unprecedented success in the post-war era. Until the spear was stolen and things fell apart, thanks to the abusive priests scandal, the ordination of women issue, the death of Pope John Paul II and the election of a Hitler Youth alumnus, to say nothing of the dramatic loss of belief after *The Da Vinci Code* controversy, et cetera. So you see, I had to get rid of it. It was too much for me."

"Where is it now?"

"I can't tell you."

"Can't or won't?"

"Both. I gave it to a client. I can't tell you who. As I said earlier, that information's beyond the pale. Client confidentiality and all that. You know how it is. Sorry, lassie."

Abby's efforts to persuade him were useless. The management consultancy industry is one of the most rapacious on the planet, yet, like chivalrous knights of yore, its exponents adhere to a code of conduct that would be laughable if it weren't so fatuous. They aren't so much Knights of the Round Table, as Knights of the 2x2 Table, Knights of the Round Up the Fees Table. Realizing her efforts were futile, Abby tried another tack, a last desperate fling. "There's something I don't quite understand about your explanation, Professor. There's something that doesn't add up."

"What's that lassie?"

"The phoney novel by W. B. Yeats, *All Fall Down*. I take it you wrote that as well as the fake poem. But if you wrote the phoney novel in 2000 and Dan Brown's *Da Vinci Code* wasn't published until 2003, how did you anticipate his plot? Was that a fluke too, a coincidence, a miracle, a chance in a million?"

"What are you blethering about, lassie? I'd nothing to do with any novel. What novel? What's *The Da Vinci Code* got to do with this?

"Oh, that's a shame. I guess you'll never know. I'd love to tell you, but I can't and I won't. Client confidentiality and all that. You know how it is. Sorry, laddie."

Chapter Fifty-Two

Doors to Manual

They say that fair exchange is no robbery. When a master negotiator is involved in the process, though, a fair exchange can feel like grand larceny, never mind no robbery. In return for access to *All Fall Down*, Abby received a copy of an academic journal, a journal containing a clue to the Spear of Destiny's whereabouts. Or so Brodie assured her. He wouldn't tell her who his client was. But if she worked it out for herself, then they were in business…

Not only did Abby get the short end of the negotiating stick – the Emerald Tablets evidently hadn't affected the Scot's selling prowess – she was short-changed in the pleasure department. Whereas the good professor, wedged into the seat beside her en route to Edinburgh via Stansted, was getting an enormous kick out of Yeats's alleged thriller, Abby was forced to work her way through a series of sluggish scholarly scribblings. Academic articles aren't exactly airport reading at the best of times, and especially not at a time like this. The journal was about "Celtic Marketing Concepts", the suggestion that old-style, number-crunching, Anglo-Saxon marketing should be replaced with approaches based on art, poetry, storytelling, song, magic, mystery, the call of the Celt.

Holy Mary, Mother of Mingers. Don't academics have anything better to do with themselves?

"If this manuscript is authentic," Brodie bellowed excitedly, "it'll cause the biggest literary rumpus since Clifford Irving's fraudulent biography of Howard Hughes, since Mark Hofmann's bogus Books of Mormon, since the spoof Ossian poems of James Macpherson, since the counterfeit Shakespeare plays of William Henry Ireland…"

"Dan Brown spent some time at St. Stephen's. Father Mannion told us. There's a photograph of him. He's definitely been there."

Brodie looked fit to burst. So much so, that Abby found it difficult to concentrate on her assigned reading. It contained long boring articles on Guinness, on pseudo Celtic theme parks, on contemporary witchcraft as practised in wicca and whatnot, and on the so-called Cu Chulainn of civil aviation, Michael O'Leary. Abby thought she was going to scream… with tedium.

"Aaarrrrggggghhhh," Brodie roared from the next seat. Several panicking passengers in front turned anxiously, wondering whether to reach for the lifejackets under their seats. "Aringarosa!" He slapped himself dramatically on the forehead, though not so hard as to disturb his concrete coiffure. "The evil cardinal in *The Da Vinci Code*. I should have guessed the name was a hint: 'Ring a Ring a Rosy/Pocket Full of Posy/Hush-ah, Hush-ah/We all fall down.' Brown's got a nerve on him."

Rapidly losing patience, Abby interrupted the professor's performance. "Can you give me a clue, here?"

Delighted, evidently, with his share of the bargain, Brodie retreated a fraction. "Well, daughter dearest, what's the most important lesson you've learned thus far?"

"That the world is full of fakes!" Abby snapped.

"Precisely," the professor of divinity replied. "Look for the fake, lassie."

Abby skimmed the articles, but the entire issue appeared to be about fakes: fake Celtic theme parks, the new breed of pseudo witches who bear no relation to the enchantresses of yore, how Guinness's image is cool and youthful in America, old and conservative in Ireland and another word for aphrodisiac in Africa. Huh? There was even an article by Dave Kelley's nemesis, the unspeakable Professor Aherne, and it too was a spoof of some kind. Her idea of humour, perhaps. Abby was no better off.

"Who is Brian Boru, professor?"

"Brian Boru was the undisputed King of Ireland this time last millennium. He out-manoeuvred the O'Neills and defeated the Vikings at the Battle of Clontarf in 1014. His harp is in Trinity College Dublin, on every bottle of Guinness, on every government document and on many public buildings. Every true-bred Irishman and woman knows who Brian Boru is. Call yourself Irish, lassie?"

"No," Abby interrupted, waving the journal under his nose. "I meant who is *this* Brian Boru, the Brian Boru who wrote the article on Michael O'Leary and Ryanair?"

He smiled a guilty smile, bloodshot eyes a-twinkle. "No idea." Changing the subject, he continued calculating the apocalyptic implications of *All Fall Down*. "You know, if this is genuine, then there are ramifications for Baigent and Leigh, the authors who accused Dan Brown of plagiarism. It predates their book as well."

"Don't change the subject, Professor."

"I always thought that court case was odd. I assumed they sued Brown, not because he appropriated their ideas, but because Brown's book is so badly written. *Holy Blood, Holy Grail* is complete tosh. But it's well-written tosh. It must have rankled when badly written tosh sold countless millions on the back of their idea, which was based on a hoax about the so-called Priory of Sion."

"You're Brian Boru. Aren't you, Professor? You wrote this article on Ryanair."

Brodie ignored her. "They were also motivated, I suspect, by the Trevor Ravenscroft case. In 1980, the author of *The Spear of Destiny* sued James Herbert, who used Ravenscroft's ideas in his best-selling novel, *The Spear*. Ravenscroft won and was awarded fifteen per cent of Herbert's royalties."

"Hold on," Abby interrupted. "Father Mannion told us that Ravenscroft's *Spear of Destiny* was based on a planted newspaper article by Max Caulfield."

A roar of laughter erupted from the OTT Scotsman. "So it was based on a hoax, too? How apt. How apt."

"Is the article on Ryanair a hoax, Professor? The fake that you mentioned?"

"Why don't you read it and decide for yourself, lassie."

Abby did as she was bid. The mismatched duo settled into their seats, concentrating on their respective reading material. Brodie raced through *All Fall Down*, the pages rustling like a rapidly spreading forest fire. Abby struggled to focus and only managed to remain awake thanks to incessant infusions of caffeine and chocolate, chocolate and caffeine. The professor, with four Emerald Tablets under his belt, was more than adequately infused already.

Catapulted back to tiresome afternoons in Hustler University library, where she attempted to read unreadable articles by self-styled marketing gurus, Abby tried to make sense of the Ryanair story. It began life as the runt of Tony Ryan's business litter, a slightly cheaper clone of the national carrier, Aer Lingus. But it was turned into a ravening attack dog by Michael O'Leary, a rabid Ryanair accountant who was bitten by the low-cost bug when he paid a courtesy call to Herb Kelleher, the hell-raising Irish-American behind Southwest Airlines. Inspired by Kelleher's business model, O'Leary crucified costs, slaughtered prices, adopted the fast-turnaround, full-flights model that maximized aircraft productivity, and did everything in his power to generate free publicity. He antagonized politicians, competitors, pilots, trade unions, air traffic controllers, merchant bankers, travel agents, airport authorities and even the Vatican in an attempt to attract shock-horror attention. Every frill or frippery or artsy-fartsy fancy was stripped from the company's rock-bottom, bare-bones, no-bullshit jetliners, even reclining seats and sickbags. He packed customers into his flying cattle trucks. He refused to refund fares, even when flights were cancelled. He had no time for strategic plans or marketing experts or brand consultants or any of that "bolloxology". He abandoned the customer-coddling, love-you-all, because-you're-worth-it palaver that's par for the course in marketing-led organizations. He worked on the assumption that the customer is always shite. He offered the lowest prices bar none and if passengers didn't like it they could fuck away off and fly with rip-off, full-service embezzlers like British Airways, Lufthansa or Air France.

The more Abby read about O'Leary, the more she liked him. There's so much bullshit in business that it's refreshing when someone tells it the way it is. "O'Leary's quite a character," she muttered to her travelling companion.

"Yes, he's featured on my website about supreme self-publicists, Paspi.biz. You should look it up sometime."

Abby turned back to her article. She'd never been besotted by an academic paper before, much less captivated to the point of forgetting to belt up, straighten her seat back and stow the tray table for landing. It was the climax of Boru's article that was so true it was untrue. Ryanair, apparently, had made steady but uninspired progress until 2002, then made a massive grab for market share, adding destinations like an American tourist doing seventeen European cities in ten days. The overstretch almost ruined the company. The stockmarket vultures started circling. O'Leary's professional obituaries were being written by those with scores to settle, which added up to an awful lot of eff-off eulogies. But Ryanair somehow recovered and got back on its feet, stronger and meaner and more aggressive than ever. It may not have been the world's favourite airline, but by God it was the most profitable.

As AB8594 flew into Stansted, Abby knew what she had to do. Her conviction was reinforced by the concluding paragraph of Boru's article which highlighted the inherent paradoxes of Michael O'Leary: an accountant by training but a bone fide marketing genius; a foul-mouthed force of nature renowned for his rarefied art collection; a horny-handed son of the soil who was educated at Ireland's Eton, Clongowes College; a man of the people who's one of the richest people in the country, with a mansion in Mullingar; a populist pleb who plays football with the baggage handlers and dresses like a navvy after a hard day digging ditches, yet who also owns a herd of pedigree cattle, and a stable of thoroughbred horses. The customer may not be king, as far as O'Leary's concerned, but the sport of kings was another matter entirely. King Michael hardly qualified as an out-and-out fake, unless his straight talking was a double-, double-, double-bluff. Abby was convinced, however, that he was the fake Brodie referred to earlier.

"Professor Brodie, I've decided to fly to Dublin instead of Edinburgh. I have to see a man about a spear, a man who lives in Mullingar, which is a place beyond the Pale."

He winked at her conspiratorially. "I'll come with you, lassie. I know Michael from an old date. You'll never get to meet him otherwise."

"I thought you had an appointment in Edinburgh tomorrow morning."

"Not to worry," he replied. "It's only another disciplinary hearing. The university's determined to sack me."

"Shouldn't you be there?"

Brodie avoided the question. A look of regret flickered across his rugged features as he studied his fingernails attentively. "Have you been to Mullingar before, lassie?"

"No, but it's farming country round there. I'll be right at home."

"Let's hope so."

Chapter Fifty-Three

The Gathering

Hell on wheels. That's what it's known as. And with good reason. Dublin's traffic congestion is the nearest thing to Hades this side of the grave. On two days of the year – Christmas and Boxing Day – things ease off from exceptionally congested to very congested. But on every other day it's Old Nick's worst nightmare, with added carbon monoxide. The nadir of noxiousness is the M50 ring road, which was constructed to ease traffic flow. In classic Irish fashion, though, it simply added to the congestion and exacerbated the national road rage epidemic, known locally as the forty shades of magenta.

Little wonder then that the sainted Michael O'Leary circumvented the magenta carriageway by acquiring a taxi driver's licence. For the modest sum of €6000, he is entitled to use the city's infuriatingly uncongested bus and taxi lanes. Even more infuriatingly for his airline rivals, O'Leary's taxi action attracted worldwide front page publicity, which recouped the financial outlay many times over and added another chutzpah-enriched chapter to the Ryanair story.

The drive from Dublin airport to Mullingar – in a hire car, with Abby at the wheel – was rather less hassle-free than O'Leary's daily commute. There were few arresting views or picturesque panoramas to compensate, since the landscape of the Irish Midlands was either as dull as ditchwater or ditchwater itself. Abby didn't mind, though. She came from a drab country townland up north, so Westmeath seemed like home from home. Only more congested.

Brodie wasn't bothered either, because he spent the time babbling about the Brown bloodline. In Celtic countries, the surname Brown was traditionally associated with tribes of wandering gypsies who were deeply versed in occult lore, magical rituals and clairvoyant practices. Their storytelling skills were legendary, as were their musical abilities and, because they made a living from the tinkering trade, their sales acumen was unrivalled.

"You can't have too many clothes pegs, right?"

But akin to wandering Jews, Brodie continued unabashed, the Browns were despised and prosecuted. They moved from place to place, encampment to encampment, spiritual site to spiritual site. Rosslyn Glen, south of Edinburgh, was the venue for the Brown tribe's Mayday celebrations, as a figurine in Rosslyn chapel signifies to this day. They also have connections to the Knights Templar and…

Abby got the picture. Dan was typical of the Brown breed. An ex-musician turned storyteller, he was obsessed with occult lore and hidden histories and secret codes and so forth. He was also an astute salesman and attracted worldwide opprobrium with his ruminations on Rosslyn Chapel and all the rest. Ho hum. Abby would kill for a hot bath, with scented candles and lashings of foam and a good book. Anything but Brown. A glossy magazine would be just the ticket.

The sun was going down as they skirted the metropolitan Mardi Gras that is Mullingar. O'Leary's lair lay a couple of kilometres outside town. Surrounded by a newly built sandstone wall and ornate ornamental gates with equine motif, Gigginstown House was an impressive spread. Brodie was unable to ring in advance because Michael kept changing his home telephone number. He'd been plagued by countless callers ordering taxis to the airport, so his privacy policy was understandable, if frustrating for his friends. As his friends were few and far between, however, no real harm was done. The Fiat Rattletrap pitched up in front of the gates and Abby punched the intercom. Through the crackle, she could just about make out the words, "Will you fuck away off out of here."

Professor Brodie leant across the driver, exuding a not unattractive whiff of whiskers and whisky, and bellowed at the intercom, "Open up, O'Leary, you tight-arsed bastard. It's Brodie here."

There was silence for several seconds. Only the crackling of the connection, the cawing of the crows and the clanking of the Rattletrap cut through the ethereal hush of dusk. "Pitcairn, you wanker.

What are you doing here, you old gobshite? Who's that beside you, you geriatric fuck bunny?"

Abby hadn't noticed the CCTV cameras sitting on top of the towering gateposts, though she suspected they were zooming in on her cleavage. With an audible clunk, the gates opened automatically. Abby gunned the Fiat up O'Leary's lengthy driveway. Pop-gunned, rather. The grounds were rolling parkland, dotted with stands of imperious elm and spreading horse chestnut. Freshly fenced and carefully levelled trackways bespoke Gigginstown's ancillary function as an equine stud farm, plus racehorse training facility. Herds of plump Aberdeen Angus peered at the passing pair, chewing the cud cretinously.

Gigginstown House was surprisingly small, a classic Georgian two-storey country abode, complete with original windows, steeply pitched roof, thrusting chimney stacks and mandatory front door ensemble: brass knocker, sunburst fanlight, pilaster flanked portico and three feldspar steps. The semicircular forecourt was decorated with a Land Rover, a Range Rover and a big black Mercedes bearing hackney cab plates. O'Leary himself was standing at the front door, awaiting their arrival. In idle moments, she'd hoped that The Michael would be the antithesis of his public image, an Oscar Wilde-style figure in quilted, quince-coloured smoking jacket, dispensing bons mots and witty quips. BA is the curse of the travelling classes. I can resist everything except surcharges. I have nothing to declare except No Refunds. A little customer service is a dangerous thing and a lot of it is fatal. Sadly, he was just as she would have expected – check shirt, blue jeans, cheap trainers, cheeky grin, greying hair and a feline demeanour that was reminiscent of the panther she'd encountered in the hills overlooking Belfast. O'Leary was a salt-and-pepper panther.

After pumping Abby's outstretched hand vigorously – she counted her fingers immediately afterward, only one ring missing – then battering Brodie with the curses and imprecations that are a token of undying friendship in Ireland, O'Leary showed them round the mansion that low fares built. Impressive coving, immaculate cornices and great gilded chandeliers dripping from splendid ceiling roses were the order of the day. The hallway was magnificently light and airy, the golden glow of sunset filtering in from an enormous clerestory window above a sweeping flight of stairs. Every wall was covered in gilt-framed oil paintings, predominantly of sub-Stubbs horseflesh and eighteenth-century gentry, resplendent in velvets, silks, bustles, big hair and hunting dogs. Michael had a thing about bloodlines.

And success. The exquisite ground floor reception rooms were filled with trophies and display cases, commemorating O'Leary's equine achievements. Homey they weren't. Horsey they were. The Michael led them through to his den at the rear, which was equipped with the requisite home cinema, a smattering of soft-rock CDs and bulky bookshelves filled with hefty biographies and business strategy success stories. If, as O'Leary often claimed, business books are bullshit and written by wankers, he seemed strangely partial to defecating masturbators. Still, it takes all sorts.

"I've opened a bottle in your honour," O'Leary announced. "Got it duty-free. Nothing special. East European rotgut. But good enough for you, you old bastard."

"*Sláinte* to you too, you miserable shite." They clinked glasses, Brodie drank deeply and then spluttered and coughed at what must have been a mixture of Polish turpentine and Lithuanian antifreeze. Abby set her brimming glass back on the gleaming walnut table, untouched. It hissed.

O'Leary laughed at the sight of the gasping theologian. "So, how's it hanging, Pitcairn?"

"I'll show you if you like, Michael. That's the beauty of the kilt. Easy access."

Michael declined, though Abby could see that the *Braveheart* ensemble had struck a chord. The boss of Ryanair, according to the Boru article, was famous for his publicity stunts, many of which involved dressing up in ludicrous costumes. No record of *Highlander*, as far as she knew. There Can Be Only One. Ryanair's mission in a nutshell.

After exchanging pleasantries, bringing each other up to date on family matters and discussing Michael's future plans, which seemed to involve a breathtakingly bold bid for Aer Lingus – a run-down regional airline, as O'Leary cruelly described it – the conversation finally turned to the purpose of the visit. Brodie outlined the back-story, with occasional contributions from his companion, then asked for the return of the holy relic he'd loaned him.

O'Leary's bantering manner changed abruptly. "It's mine, Pitcairn."

"No Michael, it was a temporary loan," Brodie asserted.

"It belongs to me, you fucker," O'Leary replied acidly, the merriment draining from his voice.

An exasperated look crossed the theology professor's craggy countenance. "Come on, Michael. Don't play games. You're not negotiating with a regional airport now. The spear was a loaner until you got through Ryanair's rough patch. That was our agreement."

Astonishingly, O'Leary was out of his seat, shouting in Brodie's weather-beaten, whisky-pickled face. "It's fucking mine, you fucker. The Spear of Destiny belongs to me. You can't have it. Now get the fuck out of here."

To Abby's awestruck amazement, the symbologist kept his cool as O'Leary ranted and raved. He must have dealt with The Michael before. Calmly and deliberately, he reminded Ryanair's boss of their agreement and reiterated what he'd evidently emphasized on earlier occasions, that possession of the artefact is accompanied by paranoia, megalomania and delusional notions of invincibility.

Brodie's avuncular endeavours were wasted. Ryanair's CEO became more and more irascible and abusive, if such a thing were possible. A tirade of swear words, most of which Abby hadn't heard before, let alone uttered in anger, spewed out of The Michael's mouth.

Bravely, Abby leapt into O'Leary's torrent of c-words and f-words and every imaginable four-lettered combination. She reckoned that if appeals to Michael's sense of fairness wouldn't work, appeals to his financial sense just might. She told him about the Yeats manuscript. He wasn't interested. He didn't collect books, only paintings. She intimated that it could be worth millions, because *All Fall Down* was an unpublished novel, a thriller no less. O'Leary offered to take it off her hands for one hundred grand. But only if it's authenticated. She let slip that Dan Brown's *Da Vinci Code* was based on Yeats's original and that the publicity surrounding its exposure might be beyond priceless and possibly ongoing if Brown were to sue O'Leary for defamation of character.

Abby could see he was interested. She also knew she was dealing with a master deal maker. So she got up to leave. "We're wasting our time here, Professor Brodie. I've got a better idea."

Brodie wasn't used to being ordered about. But he did as he was bid, pausing only to polish off the Polish-Lithuanian antifreeze alliance.

"Look, it's getting late," O'Leary observed, his mood reverting from Mr. Hyde with a hernia to Dr. Jekyll on laughing gas. "Stay the night. We'll talk in the morning. Let's finish the bottle."

"That bottle'll finish you, Brodie," Abby said sharply and made for the door. "Let's go." Brodie was stuck to the seat, immobilized by the effects of the East European ambrosia. Registered blindness was a very real possibility.

Neither Abby nor O'Leary noticed the professor's distress. "Okay, Ms. Maguire," Ryanair's CEO said, with resignation. "You have a deal. The manuscript for the Spear of Destiny."

Abby spat on one hand then reached across the table. "Done."

"Done." O'Leary spat and shook. "Provided the manuscript's authenticated."

Resolutely, Abby refused to release his hand. From farming stock, like O'Leary, she knew weasel words when she heard them, and refused to allow any wriggle room. "No, Michael. Even if it's a fake it'll still generate all the publicity you want. And then some. Do we have a deal?"

"Yes," he replied, with a scowl. "We have a deal."

"My *All Fall Down* for your Spear of Destiny?"

"Your *All Fall Down* for my Spear of Destiny," he echoed.

"Lead on Macduff."

Chapter Fifty-Four

Gigginstown House Party

The trio walked through O'Leary's commodious dwelling, though one walked much further and less steadily than the others. An impressive glass-panelled extension, modelled on the Orangery at Kew Gardens, had been added at the back of the house. One wing was filled with a swimming pool, hot tub and fitness centre. Another was lined with luxurious guest rooms, all of them unoccupied. The third wing, directly opposite the main house, was given over to a suite of offices, meeting rooms and laboratories, where the work of the Gigginstown Stud took place. Beyond the administrative block, across a floodlit flagstone courtyard, lay the stables themselves. Finished to the highest possible standard, the fourteen pristine stalls were filled with a wide range of horseflesh, everything from a couple of Connemara ponies for the kids, through a pair of Irish hunters for riding round the estate, to the peerless prize-winning thoroughbreds, Economy Drive, No Refunds and War of Attrition.

As per every racehorse owner with a captive audience, O'Leary took the opportunity to recount his thrilling victories, most notably the Cheltenham Gold Cup. It was like a Celtic *Seabiscuit*, complete with injured horse, grizzled trainer, close finish and lashings of schmaltz. The Michael excitedly re-enacted every jump, every crack of the whip, every lung-bursting furlong to the finish, charging round his yard and thwacking his backside like a middle-aged teenager. The horses stared out of their stalls, looking laconically at the crackpot making an exhibition of himself. Abby could almost hear them snickering.

"Anyway," O'Leary concluded with a yee-haw, "War of Attrition came in at seven to one. I haven't had so much fun since British Airways sued over our 'Expensive Bastards' knocking ad. The judge ruled that it was fair comment! BA *are* expensive bastards! Jesus, I love the airline business."

Abby was wondering when he was going to get to the point. She knew enough about Irish horse dealers to know that when Irishmen started recounting stories about horseflesh, some kind of chicanery was afoot. In a minute he'll be telling us he doesn't know too much about it. Exactly sixty seconds later, O'Leary announced that the Gigginstown Stud was run by his brother, Eddie, and he himself wasn't directly involved in the business. In another minute or two, Abby calculated, he'll spin some yarn about the pedigree of a particular horse; the more illustrious the bloodline, the worse the broken-winded nag invariably is. Sixty seconds or so later, O'Leary introduced them to No Refunds, which was descended from none other than the Byerly Turk, one of the three Arab founders of the original thoroughbred line, a stallion that took part in the Battle of the Boyne in July 1690. "You're an Orangeman, Brodie. Think of the history here. History on the hoof."

Utterly impassive and undoubtedly paralytic, Pitcairn Brodie wasn't buying any of The Michael's palaver. He'd heard it all before. Abby wasn't buying either because she knew that one in three thoroughbreds is descended from Byerly Turk and, on peering into No Refunds' mouth, reckoned that its next race was the UHU Superglue Stakes.

"You know a bit about horses?" O'Leary inquired, eyeing his statuesque guest with something approaching admiration.

Abby shrugged. "My da dabbled for a while."

"Oh aye? You'll enjoy this then." He sauntered to the stall between Economy Drive and War of Attrition, swung it open with a flourish, shucked the mane of the big bay within and announced triumphantly. "Behold my Spear of Destiny!"

"What?!" Abby turned to Brodie, who was just as astonished as she was, then set about O'Leary. "You bastard! You son of a bitch! You think this is some kind of joke?"

One of the walls of the stable block was lined with damp tack. But not for long. Abby hurled every item imaginable at Gigginstown's grinning boss – bits, bridles, girths, cuppers, stirrups, numnahs and more. If there'd been a saddle, that too would have been pitched at the smirking double-dealer. She lashed at him with a martingale. It cracked like a bullwhip under his nose.

"Enough!" O'Leary shouted, just as Abby started eyeing up the shovels, rakes, pitchforks, horseshit scoops and ancillary items of mucking-out equipment. "You're frightening the talent." A worrying whinnying had started up as the animals sensed the angry commotion outside. War of Attrition was particularly feisty, stomping and rearing and kicking at his stable door.

When calm descended, O'Leary remained resolute, impenitent, unmoved. Abby had agreed to exchange her *All Fall Down* for his Spear of Destiny. A deal's a deal. They'd shaken on it. The horse was hers, the manuscript was his.

"Very funny, Michael," Brodie said, his voice slightly slurred. "But why would you want to exchange a valuable racehorse for an iffy work of literature? There's either something wrong with the horse or you've taken leave of your senses. What's going on?"

O'Leary picked up a pitchfork to defend himself from the attack that was sure to come. "I swopped the Spear of Destiny – the spear you gave me, Brodie – for this Spear of Destiny. I don't have your spear any more. I only have this nag!"

"Nag?" Abby yelled, despite herself. "You're telling me this horse is crocked?"

" 'Fraid so," The Michael admitted. "At first, we thought it was laminitis, but it's congenital. The horse is a bum steer. I was sold a pup."

Abby took a close look. Gently caressing the big bay on its lightning-like blaze and shapely crest, she muttered a few words into Spear of Destiny's ear. He responded with a gentle whinny, like they were having an intimate conversation. "Well, if you've been sold a pup, you've got grounds for undoing the deal and getting the original Spear of Destiny back."

"Can't do that," O'Leary swore. "It would make me look like a bad judge of horseflesh." Gamely, he joined Abby by the stricken nag's head and produced a gnarled carrot. Spear of Destiny chomped contentedly, as O'Leary slapped him on the shoulder. "I've got a reputation to uphold."

Professor Brodie roared with ironic laughter. "Reputation?

What reputation would that be, Michael? Everyone knows what your reputation is and it won't be changed by a badly chosen bay. You aren't the first Irishman to be robbed blind over a lame horse and you won't be the last."

"And anyway," Abby added, "you told us a few minutes ago that you'd no knowledge of horses, because your brother Eddie did the business."

O'Leary blushed at being caught out, possibly for the first time in his professional life. "Aye, well, you shouldn't believe everything you hear."

"I'll tell Ryanair's passengers that, shall I?" Abby retorted.

"Tell them whatever the fuck you like!" Caught with his metaphorical pants down, O'Leary went on to justify himself at length. It wasn't simply a matter of undoing a deal – he'd reneged on one or two deals in the past, after all – it was a matter of getting even. He was going to get his own back on the bugger who pulled the wool over his eyes. No one gets one up on The Michael. No one fucks with the king of low-cost airlines. The Yeats manuscript would help him wreak his revenge. So he couldn't undo the deal with Abby. It was her horse and she was stuck with it. She might get a good price at the glue factory. He'd throw in free transportation to the rendering plant, though obviously there'd be taxes and insurance to pay. Plus a fuel surcharge.

Abby wasn't rolling over for anyone, not after what she'd been through. It was time to play her trump card. She reached into her borrowed Birkin, and pulled out a bag of Ryanair peanuts, purchased on the flight from Stansted to Dublin. It was an empty bag, carefully smoothed out. She held it up so that the CEO could see.

"Hope you paid for those."

"I did. They were awful. They were stale."

"What do you expect for €4.50?" O'Leary replied, unrepentant.

Abby painstakingly examined the back of the foil wrapper. "What I expect in a bag of peanuts is peanuts."

"D'oh."

A tiny smile of victory crossed Abby's face. "I have a peanut allergy, Michael."

"And you were cured by a bag of our choice selection? Another Ryanair miracle. The good Lord be praised. Hold the front page and nobody leave…"

Abby cut him off. "Mr. O'Leary, if your bag *had* contained peanuts – real peanuts as opposed to recycled rabbit droppings – I'd've been very seriously ill, rushed to hospital with anaphylactic shock. But nothing happened. Your nuts are nutless."

"Think yourself lucky, then."

He was wriggling. She could sense it. He knew where this was going. "Just think what the press could do with a story like that. I can see the headlines now, can't you Michael? Your nuts, or lack of them, are going to be all over the newspapers. How does that make you feel, you prick?" Abby folded the package carefully and returned it to her handbag.

O'Leary was nothing if not a tough nut, though. He accused her of bluffing, because anyone with a nut allergy would have noticed. Not when you think you've bought pretzels and were given peanuts instead, without warning or explanation, and wolfed the packet down before realizing the mistake. Stung by the accusation of sloppy in-flight service to go with the nutless nuts scenario, Ryanair's boss continued to bluster, to abuse, to "do your worst because all publicity is good publicity". Abby patiently reminded him that the tiniest things can bring great companies down. Gerald Ratner's cut-price jewellery empire being a classic case in point. He was the loud-mouthed O'Leary of his day and look what happened to him.

O'Leary laughed in her face.

Clearly, there was no negotiating with the man. So Abby resorted to the ultimate sanction. She opened the door of the stall beside Spear of Destiny and led War of Attrition into the floodlit courtyard. The Michael started to panic. He urged her not to do anything silly. He promised he'd sort something out. He swore on his mother's grave. He crossed his heart and hoped to die…

But it was too late. Abby had had enough of his bullshit. She punched War of Attrition between the eyes, right on the star in the middle of its forehead. It wasn't the mightiest of blows. Accuracy is all that matters, though. The thoroughbred was completely poleaxed. It sank to the ground, legs splayed out as if it had slipped on a sheet of ice. Abby straddled the horse's withers, grabbed him by the neck and twisted it right round. The horse's head was over her left shoulder. One more jerk and War of Attrition was a goner.

To his credit, O'Leary stood his ground. He called her bluff. She couldn't kill an innocent creature. All of Ireland would be horrified. She couldn't murder the Gold Cup winner. Everyone would hate her. He knew the feeling. No one could do a thing like that. Not even an Ulsterwoman.

"I used to work in an abattoir," Abby said abruptly. "Many's a day the stun guns weren't working. I've killed countless animals by hand. Cattle. Pigs. Sheep. Horses. You name it, I've killed it. It means nothing to me." She twisted War of Attrition's neck even tighter, the spinal column started to creak and the Gold Cup winner's eyes began rolling alarmingly. "I'm indifferent to pleas for mercy. You must feel the same way when passengers pester you with sob stories. We're not so different, Mr. O'Leary. You know I'll do it."

Chapter Fifty-Five

The Eejit Has Landed

O'Leary cracked. It was a terrible sight. He was crying, wailing, tearing his hair. He was on his knees, begging her to reconsider. He'd do anything. Anything. Free flights for life. The life of a hamster, that is. Okay, a cat… a dog… a pony… a thoroughbred. A donkey? No fuckin' way!

Abby enjoyed watching him squirm. She only wished she had a camera, because YouTube would love to watch him as well. Ever so gently, she released her grip on the thoroughbred's neck, patted him gently on the withers as she dismounted and whispered a few words of encouragement into his flickering ear. The horse snickered softly, tossed its mane a couple of times and struggled up from its ungainly pose. There was a stupefied look in its eyes, but all things considered it was none the worse for its experience. Abby led him back into his stall, whispering all the while, and bolted the stable door. "You were saying, Michael?"

"There's just one small problem," O'Leary replied, flinging himself in front of his prizewinner's stall to forestall any further incursions.

"Don't mess with me," Abby hissed, grabbing the pitchfork that O'Leary had abandoned in his haste. "Forget the horses, Michael. Your nuts are mine." She motioned towards her uncharacteristically subdued sidekick. "Ever tasted testicular shish kebab, Brodie?"

But Brodie wasn't listening. His corrugated iron combover was bobbing like the lid of a boiling kettle. Smoke, admittedly, wasn't coming from his ears, nor was he whistling shrilly. He seemed pretty ticked off, all the same. "What the pair of you seem to have forgotten is that, firstly, Ms. Maguire and I have already negotiated a deal on the Yeats manuscript and, secondly, that the Spear of Destiny belongs to me. It wasn't yours to give away, O'Leary.

It isn't yours to trade for, Abby, even if you do manage to arrange some kind of restitution with the pseudo agent or phoney dealer who turned Michael over so comprehensively."

Ryanair's CEO was well used to insults. They were water off a jumbo jet's back. But having his business abilities mocked by a goddam academic – a fucking divinity professor to boot – was more than the chief executive could stand. He lost the rag completely. He screamed that they'd been through this already, that Brodie was a wanker, asswipe, tosspot, jerkoff and worse, that the Spear of Destiny was his to do with what he chose.

"Prove it, Michael."

With a look of fury, O'Leary shouted for assistance. Across the courtyard, the door of the Gigginstown Stud offices swung open.

Professor Brodie's jaw dropped. He was either drunk or dreaming. Or both. "What are you doing here?" he snarled.

"That's a nice way to greet your big brother," Selkirk Brodie replied, strolling casually toward the stable block. He too was wearing the Brodie tartan ensemble. They were mirror images of each other, except Selkirk was carrying a lethal weapon.

"As I said, Pitcairn," O'Leary interjected, "the spear belongs to me. I bought it from your partner."

Professor Brodie guffawed and blustered. "Selkirk's job is to mind the till and keep the Harry Potter pests out of the shop. He has no authority to negotiate. He's the muscle, I'm the brains. He had no right to sell you the spear. The deal is null and void."

"That's where you're wrong," Brodie's brother shot back. "You put me in charge of Nazi memorabilia and I let Mr. O'Leary buy the weapon he had on approval."

"The spear isn't a Nazi artefact," the senior partner exploded. "It's theological, you bloody idiot. It's the bloody spear that pierced the bloody side of Jesus bloody Christ on the bloody cross. That's my domain, you bloody bampot."

Abby hadn't a clue what bampot meant and neither did O'Leary. Something like eejit, perhaps. Whatever it was, it must have been pretty bad, because within a few seconds the belligerent brothers were in each others' faces, hurling insults that clearly went back a very long way, certainly to adolescence, possibly to childhood.

Pitcairn was too big for his boots. Selkirk was their parents' favourite. Pitcairn got all the educational opportunities. Selkirk was too stupid to avail himself of them. Pitcairn was a prude, a bookworm, a drunk. Selkirk was a skirt-chaser, a knucklehead, a sociopath, if he even knew what that meant. Pitcairn was facing the sack from New College and not before time. Selkirk couldn't sell to save his life and was probably ripped off by O'Leary. Pitcairn was wrong, because he talked up the price by dropping hints to another interested party from Belfast.

Enraged at Selkirk's display of business idiocy, not to mention the Ulster trouble he'd triggered, Brodie minor bellowed like he was going to bite the balls off an Aberdeen Angus. Equally enraged, Brodie major waved the lethal weapon under his wee brother's drink-disfigured nose.

"Hold on a minute," O'Leary announced. "Don't mess with the merchandise, Selkirk. If that bayonet's damaged, the deal's off. I'm serious!"

"Hold on a minute," Abby reiterated. "That dagger. That bayonet. That's mine. That belongs to me and my…" She was going to say partner but had to make do with ex. "You've no right to sell that."

Brodie and Brodie were staring at each other intently, slowly circling in the centre of the yard. Things had gone beyond a fraternal spat. Selkirk flicked a quick glance at Abby. "Your boyfriend said I could keep it for saving his life." The sidelong glance was an error of judgement, though. His kid brother charged toward him, kilt flying, arms flailing, head lowered like an American footballer during first down. He even had the rock-hard helmet. But then so did his sibling, who was equally afflicted with terminal psilosis.

The stable block echoed to the roaring and shouting of the brotherly loveless brothers. Punches were thrown. Kicks were exchanged. Combovers were tugged, albeit carefully. Horseshit was hurled. Pitchforks were wielded. Shovels clanged like medieval halberds. The bayonet was brandished by Brodie major. A dirk was drawn from Brodie minor's stocking top. There was much rolling around on the flagstones. Abby covered her eyes. The thoroughbreds were transfixed.

O'Leary soon got bored. "We need to talk," he said to Abby.

"Are you sure they won't hurt themselves? I think we should separate them."

"Abby," O'Leary deadpanned, "I come from a family of six. I've two younger brothers. That's nothing compared to what we used to do to each other. My sisters were worse. Let's leave them to it. It's just handbags."

"Sporrans, I think you mean."

The CEO laughed as the Brodie combovers collided like a clap of thunder above Ben Nevis. He led the way back through Gigginstown's extension, past the swimming pool and hot tub, to his book-lined den. He let it be known that his Spear of Destiny problem had nothing to do with horse dealers or bloodstock agents. But a tosser author, someone who must remain nameless, someone who had a monster world-wide bestseller and was stricken with post-success performance anxiety. They'd met in America by chance. They'd hit it off. They'd a surprising amount in common. The guy was a natural salesman, who had published a cheap and cheerful novel that'd taken the world by storm. He was the Ryanair of writing, basically. Everyone hated his books but they were enormously successful all the same. The Catholic Church hated him too. They had a shared interest in bloodlines…

"Dan Brown, you mean?"

The Michael refused to comment. The anxious guy had confided in O'Leary. O'Leary told him about the spear's miraculous properties. The guy had been given a pure-blood thoroughbred by a besotted admirer. Or so he said. They did a secret deal. The spear for the Spear. It was only when he put the horse through its paces he realized he'd been had. He'd never live down the shame if it got out. The boss of Ryanair being bested by a writer of fucking potboilers.

"So you reckon the Yeats manuscript, if genuine, might enable you to get your own back on… the person who sold you a pup?"

"Precisely."

"But Brodie wants the Yeats manuscript for his own anti-Brown purposes, some arrangement with Citroën. And I've been thinking that even if I don't get the Spear of Destiny back, the Catholic Church might accept something that'll help them settle the score with someone who accused them of distorting history, who perpetuates the view that the Vatican is a hotbed of devilry, who's made all sorts of allegations about Opus Dei. I reckon I'll hold on to *All Fall Down*, Mr. O'Leary. I'll sort things out myself. I've had enough of this horseshit."

Ryanair's CEO is considered by some to be a commercial genius. Others regard him as a foul-mouthed, bad-tempered bastard who's set customer service back several decades. But there's no denying that he's a canny operator. "Why don't we just photocopy the fucking thing? We can all have a copy! Everyone's a winner."

The manuscript was 450 pages plus, and The Michael's photocopier was an old model, slow and cantankerous. As they copied, O'Leary offered Abby a job at Gigginstown stud. That punch on the forehead routine, if surreptitiously applied to rival racehorses, could do wonders for War of Attrition's chances. Abby wasn't interested. He suggested that once she'd finished her retail marketing degree, she should come to work for Ryanair. The retail side's where the real money's made. He was impressed by her negotiating skills. They needed female executives. O'Leary was looking for a charismatic successor. He was CFO at 29, CEO at 33. She could do likewise. He could see that the world was Abby's oyster, but Ryanair could offer a pearl or two. Cultured, naturally. Abby was flattered, although she knew better than to take The Michael's promises at face value. She told him about Some Like It Hot. He got hotter and hotter, especially when the costumes came in to the conversation. He'd worn a frilly French maid outfit on occasion and really quite enjoyed the experience. He was working on a Skorzeny stormtrooper get-up for the German market, which was proving difficult to crack, hence the memorabilia deal with Selkirk. He had a number of Nazi-themed promotions in mind: The Great Escape, The Price Busters, Free Seat Blitzkrieg, Where Seagulls Dare, Stalingrad Specials, El-Alamein Weekends, Battle of the Bulge Breaks. What did she think?

Fortunately, the photocopier had stopped excreting sheets before Abby had time to mutter anything other than "Mmmm, controversial. Just think of the free publicity, Michael."

O'Leary quickly gathered up the copies, still warm from their exertions, and handed them all to Abby. "That'll be €675."

"What?"

"Four hundred and fifty pages by three at 50 cent per sheet. €675 all told."

Abby was staggered. "You're charging me for the photocopies?"

"This is Ryanair, for fuck's sake. If you want free copies talk to British fucking Airways. Or go to Easy fucking Copy. Think yourself lucky I'm not imposing surcharges for sorting, staples and toner depletion."

Talk about a brass neck. "What do you mean, three copies? You only made two copies, you chancer! Two copies, one original."

"Oh aye. So I did." O'Leary brazened it out. "That'll be €450."

"I've only got English."

"Not a problem," he said. "Today's exchange rate is parity. One pound gets you one euro. That'll be £450."

Truly, there was no end to his cost-consciousness. With a sorrowful shake of the head, Abby pulled the depleted wad of fivers from her handbag and counted out £450 as O'Leary looked on, smirking.

"Nice doing business with you, Miss Maguire."

"You too, Mr. O'Leary."

"No one gets the better of The Michael."

Abby stuffed the copies of *All Fall Down* into her handbag and got ready to depart. "You're just too canny for me."

Never let it be said that Ryanair's CEO is a heartless swashbuckler who crows over the fallen. In a moment of weakness, he extracted a fiver from his newly acquired pile and handed it back to Abby. "That's for the peanuts." He looked her up and down. "You don't really have a peanut allergy, do you?"

"No, I don't. And Spear of Destiny isn't really a nag. He's got a very mild case of Triple E, I reckon. There was an outbreak in New England a while back. Eastern equine encephalitis can be hard to detect, but it's easily rectified with dietary supplements and appropriate antibiotics."

O'Leary looked astonished, gobsmacked even. "Gee thanks, Abby. I owe you one."

"Actually, there is one thing, Mr. O'Leary."

"What's that, Abby? Anything."

"If the Catholic Church doesn't nibble at the Yeats manuscript and if you get the spear back from Brown, I'll be looking for the artefact. Either that or a full refund."

Staggered, O'Leary clutched his chest and collapsed on the sofa. "No fucking refunds," he wheezed. He struggled unsuccessfully to get up. "No. Fucking. Refunds." Gasping for breath, he pointed toward the door and the Fiat Rattletrap parked outside. "NO FUCKING REFUNDS."

Chapter Fifty-Six

The Queer of Destiny

Abby was almost back in Dublin before the significance of Selkirk's comments hit her. She was racing along the M4, gratifyingly free of traffic late at night, when Brodie's throwaway remark struck home. So forcefully did it connect that she almost lost control of the vehicle, which was travelling at top speed. Fortunately, the top speed of a Fiat Rattletrap is 90 km. per hour, less against a head wind. Hence no real damage was done.

With a bit of strategic banging and thumping at the Ryanair desk – having bested the 600lb silverback at the top of the organization, the baboons at the bottom weren't going to beat her – she managed to talk herself on to the last flight to Scotland. Unfortunately, Ryanair doesn't fly to Edinburgh. It doesn't fly to Glasgow either, since Prestwick is fifty kilometres outside town on the Ayrshire coast, closer to the Glens of Antrim than Glasgow's West End. Still, compared to some of Ryanair's destinations, which are not only infamously far from the cities they allegedly serve but are sometimes in completely different countries, Prestwick counts as pretty convenient, all things considered.

Convenient or not, it was another ninety minutes before Abby's taxi pulled up at Edinburgh's Royal Infirmary, six kilometres southeast of the city centre on the Old Dalkeith Road. The Glasgow taxi driver had never seen a payday like it and just so long as he didn't look too closely at the fistful of fivers, he'd never have another so remunerative. If he did look closely, of course, he'd never have another so deceptive. However, it was practically the last of her stash and Abby didn't care. Her only regret was that she wasn't there to see O'Leary's face when his photocopying profit centre proved chimerical. Poetic justice, surely, was served by paying for copies with copies.

If she'd learnt anything from her brief encounter with Ryanair's main man, the Dirty Harry Callaghan of civil aviation, it was not to take no for an answer. Not even from Doris Drawbridge, the formidable night receptionist at the Infirmary's A&E. Visiting time was over. Dr. Kelley was out of immediate danger. Call back tomorrow morning after 11.00 a.m. Abby was having none of it. She was his beloved long-lost half-sister. She'd heard the news on holiday in Mustique. She'd flown in to be by his side. Didn't Doris know who she was?

The blether cut no ice with the growling gatekeeper, who'd heard it all before. However, Abby's evident anxiety about her loved one got through doughty Drawbridge's defences and she was allowed to see her injured brother. Kelley was asleep when she tiptoed into the private room off Ward 5. His boyish face looked beautiful in the pool of light from a bedside lamp. The torso was less attractive, unless swaddling bandages, surgical strapping and saline drips are considered cute nowadays. That said, nothing would surprise Abby after several months in Some Like It Hot. Hospital fetishes were a perennial favourite, though Doctors-and-Nurses were the preferred carnal scenario over Patients-and-Visitors. She bent over to kiss him before leaving. She didn't want to disturb his rest, his recovery. As long as she could see with her own eyes that he was alive, that'd be enough for the meantime.

Her lips brushed his cheek ever so gently. He smelled of baby lotion mixed with hunky musk. He looked awfully pale, which was accentuated by a light dusting of five o'clock shadow. She kissed her fingertips, placed them on his rosebud lips then stood up to go. Kelley opened his eyes. The best Abby could've hoped for was "I must be dreaming." But Dave went one better. He smiled broadly and said, "You look beautiful, Abby. Absolutely beautiful." He almost went and spoiled it by adding "You've lost weight." Even in his heavily medicated state, however, he had enough Ulster gumption to focus on how fantastic she looked.

"You've heard of the hip 'n' thigh diet?" Abby asked. "Well, I've been on the high anxiety diet. Near-death experiences are real calorie burners, believe me. Not eating between meals helps too."

His little face lit up with delight. Throwing caution to the whatever, Abby hugged him like she'd hugged none other. If it weren't for his cries of agony, hurriedly suppressed to avoid disturbing the adjacent ward, she'd be hugging him still. At least the pain yanked Kelley out of his soporific stupor. Abby couldn't get a word in edgeways. Drugs don't work, they say, but in Dave's case they were working overtime. He rambled on about how much he loved her, cared for her, had never met anyone like her.

Whatever he was on, Abby wasn't complaining. After, oh, an hour or so, she attempted to staunch the love-struck flow. "But you're gay, Dave."

"Oh yes, so I am." Kelley laughed.

Abby joined in. She couldn't help it.

Eventually, they ssshhhhed each other into silence, albeit with difficulty because the more they ssshhhhed, the funnier it became. When the merriment subsided, Abby managed to extract a cogent account of what went on in Rosa Alchemica Caledonia. Had Dave been more alert, had he turned to face his assailant more swiftly, he'd almost certainly have been killed. The knife came within a fraction of the thoracic aorta, clipped the edge of his left lung and just missed the major organs. Apparently, he'd passed out with the sudden loss of blood but the police got there particularly quickly and they kept him going till the ambulance arrived. He was very lucky.

Abby was astonished. "But Dave, there was blood all over the place. Gallons of it. You couldn't possibly have survived after that."

"Ah, no, not exactly," Kelley said coyly. "Much of the blood was... ahem... attar of roses. I knocked a container over on my way down, apparently."

"I thought you smelled beautiful in death."

"I'll take that as a compliment." Despite his attempted grin, Kelley was deeply disturbed by the retelling. The speed and unpredictability of the attack. The shock and surprise and sudden realization that this was The End. The evident enjoyment on the pint-sized psychopath's face. The slashing sound as the blade cut through the air and the thump when it hit him. Abby could see that the horrific events had been playing on his mind, sedatives notwithstanding. It was time to go and let him rest.

Kelley was unwilling, however. He propped himself up on the pillows, insisting that Abby tell all. Nothing less than a blow-by-blow account of what went down since he went down would suffice. There was no talking to him. So she talked to him. It wasn't the most coherent of narrations, since she herself hadn't had time to make sense of what'd happened in the thirty hours since he'd dropped her off at Belfast International Airport. Hesitantly, with many contradictions and backtrackings and mixed metaphors, she laid out the events as she remembered them. The conversation with Selkirk in RAC, the futile meeting with Brodie's research assistant, the dramatic turn of events in The Witchery, the discovery of his body in a big pool of blood, the flight to Nuremberg, the fight with Brodie's bouncers, the secret of the spear's whereabouts, the meeting with Michael O'Leary, the fracas between Pitcairn and Selkirk, the flight to Prestwick, the late-night dash to the Royal Infirmary. But it was worth it. They had an escape route. St. Stephen's would surely leap at the Dan Brown deal. He was the Pope's public enemy number one. They'd call off their psychotic Protestant subcontractors. If, for some reason, St. Stephen's wouldn't play ball, she'd extracted the promise of a refund from O'Leary. And as The Michael would demolish the Vatican City brick by fucking brick before issuing a refund, she was sure they'd be safe. "Is that worth an A in my assignment, Dr. Kelley, or what?"

Clearly deeply impressed and awestruck with admiration, Kelley sighed and replied, "It's worth an A double plus, Abby."

Abby licked the tip of an index finger and touched her right buttock with an exaggerated hiss. She was hot. "First class honours, here I come."

"The only problem is that I won't be around to see it."

"Don't be daft, Dave," she joshed. "Your injuries can't be that bad. A couple of days and you'll be up and about."

He reached out and stroked her hand. "I've decided to quit academic life. I'll be handing in my resignation as soon as I get out of here. I'm going to give music another go. Bad as the music business is, it's a lot less loathsome than academia."

"You're re-forming Love Pump?" Abby sighed, trying not to laugh.

Kelley smiled wrily. "No, not Love Pump. I'm going solo. I posted some stuff on the web and, you'll never believe this, but I'm Most Viewed and Top Rated on YouTube. Someone spliced one of my songs on to a clip of a crazy kilted Scotsman throwing a strop at a conference. He kicks over the laptop, nuts a couple of bouncers and flounces out. It's very funny. I got a call from an agent this morning. The major labels are offering all sorts of lucrative deals..."

"That's... that's... that's great, Dave." Abby was struggling. "I'm delighted for you." She felt like she too had been stabbed. "You deserve your chance." Time to leave. "You'll be a big hit, I'm sure of it." Bit late to find a hotel. "Maybe I'll come and see you sometime." Wonder when the first Belfast flight leaves. "I've always wanted a backstage pass." She told him he needed to rest and, holding back the tears, leant over for a goodnight kiss. A goodbye kiss.

But Kelley didn't reciprocate. Not so much as a pucker, much less a love-you-always snogathon. If anything, his general attitude had cooled considerably. Guess that's the way it is with bipolar rock stars. "You didn't get the spear, then?"

"No, no I didn't," Abby replied, a bit taken aback by the sharpness of her ex-tutor's tone. "But it doesn't matter. We don't need the spear. As I explained, we're off the hook without it. You can go and become a big star without continually looking back over your shoulder."

With a glare that would paralyse War of Attrition, he pushed her away. "You were supposed to recover the Spear of Destiny!"

Abby wasn't upset. She had witnessed his mood swings in the past. She knew how much his career meant to him. "Dave, you don't need the spear. You can make it in the music industry without artificial aids. You have the talent, now go out there and prove it. The Spear of Destiny's a poisoned chalice."

He didn't laugh. Not even a flicker. "This has nothing to do with the music business," he barked. "This is about you getting the spear for the organization I represent."

"What are you talking about, Dave?"

The look he gave her was two parts pity to one part scorn. "I'm a cop, Abby. I work for the Assets Recovery Agency. We've been trying to crack the IRA/UVF strategic alliance for years. We know they launder money through Discount DIY, Some Like It Hot and the University of Hustler. We know Emer Aherne is involved. I posed as a deep-cover doctoral student, lecturer thereafter. We were getting nowhere. We needed a wild card to crack the case open. When I uncovered your distant connection with the Biggars and not so distant connection to Father Mannion, I placed you in Some Like It Hot. I waited for the inevitable explosion, hoping that things would fall apart because the Semtex cannot hold. We badly need the spear, though. Our organization is getting a lot of flak because it costs more to run than it recoups from criminals. If we can show that the IRA/UVF are trading priceless religious artefacts like bent car dealers or dodgy estate agents, it'll do terrible damage to their brand images and give us a massive publicity boost. You failed us, I'm afraid."

Astonishment isn't the most attractive look on a lady, even as attractive a lady as Abby Maguire. She couldn't help herself, however. She couldn't believe what she was hearing. She was so stunned she couldn't speak. "You're kidding me, right?"

"Do you really think the policeman on the road to Belfast would have waved us on if I hadn't given him a signal?"

"Well, yes, frankly."

"Do you really think the Edinburgh cops would have backed off without prior arrangement?"

"Well, yes, frankly. Florence Housemartin could scare anyone off with her ice queen act."

"Do you really think I'd have time to leave a message for you before passing over?"

"Well, it worked in *The Da Vinci Code* and *All Fall Down*."

"Do you really think it was genuine counterfeit money? Get real, woman!"

"So it was counterfeit counterfeit money? Is that what you're saying?" She glared at him. He glared at her. "This is complete bullshit isn't it, Dave? You're having a laugh. Aren't you?"

"Yes I am, Abby! But I had you going for a minute! You should see your face! That's what you get for cursing me up and down in RAC and pummelling me while I was lying on the storeroom floor with a serious knife wound!"

"Bastard!" she shouted at the top of her voice. "That's so not funny!" she yelled. Abby grabbed him by the shoulders and shook him vigorously. Ow, ow, ow, ow. He deserved it. The so-and-so. She shook him again. If she'd had the Spear of Destiny to hand, it'd be disappearing where the sun don't shine.

The commotion was too much for night duty nurse Kitty Cathcart, who burst into the room, insisting that Abby leave. Right Now. She was disturbing the other patients. She should have some consideration. What on earth did she think she was doing wrestling an injured man like that? If she didn't leave right away, she'd be banned from the hospital. Permanently.

Kelley, the sod, was feigning injury. Moaning and groaning to get Nurse Cathcart's sympathy. Abby knew he was bluffing. He knew she knew he was bluffing. He winked at her as she was shepherded out of the room. Abby wasn't going to argue. She'd get her own back in the morning. She'd get her revenge in Some Like It Hot, a window display of vibrators in the shape of Castle D'Anger. D'Angerous Dildos, she'd call it.

"Love Pump sucks," Abby whispered by way of a parting shot.

"Licks, darling. I think you'll find it licks."

Abby stuck her tongue out, then placed a thumb on her nose and wiggled her fingers. It wasn't very adult. But then again, adulthood's vastly overrated.

Chapter Fifty-Seven

I Can't Believe It's Not Billy

There was no room at the Holiday Inn. Abby managed to snatch a couple of hours' sleep in the Infirmary's reception area, before a friendly cleaner took pity on her. With a nod and a wink and her final fake fiver, he found an unoccupied bed on a side ward. Braving the wrath of Kitty Cathcart, Abby slipped upstairs to see the patient once again, before catching an early flight back to Belfast. She wasn't sure whether to forgive him. If he played that kind of trick on her now, what would he be like later on? She had asked for it, admittedly, though it was very harsh punishment for a perfectly reasonable outburst. She should've realized he was bluffing when he claimed to be a deep-cover doctoral student. Nobody, but nobody, is that dedicated. That daft.

In the cold light of Dawn French, as she checked her slimmer but still sizeable self in a full-length bathroom mirror, Abby concluded that there was no future for them together. Aristocrats and abattoir workers don't mix, not even ex-members of the minor nobility and past pupils of Strabane slaughterhouse.

But Kelley didn't see it that way. He was wide awake and wondering whether he'd been dreaming the night before. She was beautiful, gorgeous, hot, hot, hot. Get a grip, Dave. He had never met anyone like her. True, but steady on, cowboy. He was falling for her big time. Dementia's a terrible thing in one so young, though there's definitely an upside. They talked like young lovers do for half an hour. He wanted her to come on tour with him as Dave the Rave Kelley did the greasy pole-dance of the music business. Abby wasn't the kind of person who carried someone's guitars or humped their equipment.

"Not even my love pump?"

"Especially not your love pump!"

Reassuringly, he informed Abby that her job was on the management side. The music business was tough. He needed someone who'd take no bull from anyone. He needed someone to do the deals, collect the cash, control the merchandise and, above all, intimidate producers, labels, A&Rsholes etc. He needed a bulldozer, basically.

Much as she cared for him – loved him, maybe – Abby didn't want to go down that particular road, even though her extensive abattoir experience was perfect preparation for the bull-filled challenges ahead. When she declined, Dave suggested a knock-em-dead alternative, an Irish equivalent of The White Stripes.

"The Green Stripes?"

"Call me a bigoted Ulster Protestant, but I was thinking of the Red, White and Blue Stripes, actually."

Abby didn't want to go down the tribute band route, either. She couldn't play the drums, for starters, though that never stopped Meg White. The more they talked about the ups and downs of the music business, the more she yearned for the ins and outs of the intimate apparel industry. A potentially stupendous new product development was fermenting in her ever-inventive mind: The Spear of Ecstasy. An occult vibrator that induces feelings of omnipotence, empowerment, superiority. An occult vibrator that taps into the primal power of the eternal feminine. The electrical feminine, rather. An occult vibrator with four speed settings – Jesus Christ! Holy Shit!! Praise the Lord!!! and Hallelujah!!!! – plus an optional afterburner, I'm-Going-Straight-to-Hell-and-I-Don't-Care. The congregation at St. Nicholas's church will love that one. Sundays in Carrickfergus will never be the same, as hallelujahs ring out from all quarters, just like the great religious revivals of the late nineteenth century. Abby was a missionary for lurve.

She had lots of other ideas as well. The highly profitable ice-cream cooler unit could be expanded for a start. They could stock the full I Can't Believe It's Not range. In addition to I Can't Believe It's Not Beaver, she'd carry I Can't Believe It's Not Badger, I Can't Believe It's Not Thrush, I Can't Believe It's Not Chlamydia, I Can't Believe It's Not Todger, I Can't Believe It's Not Minger and many more.

The Yeatsian theme also had potential. W.B.'s monkey glands. Willie's Erectile Embrocation. Gift editions of his love poetry. Maud Gonne's gone but not forgotten. Her allure lives on. She was a big woman. Big bloomers. Big bustiers. Big's beautiful. Big clockwork Victorian vibrators. Wind-up, spring-loaded, steam-driven dildos. She could see them now. The Aspidistra. The Dreadnought. The Prince Albert. The Star of India. The Sun Never Sets.

Inevitably, the unpublished Yeats manuscript wormed its way into an otherwise business-like conversation. After some discussion and not a little disagreement, they concurred that Pitcairn Brodie should negotiate with St. Stephen's. Time was of the essence, though, because they needed the republican Redemptorists' intercession with the Protestant paramilitaries. Abby would have liked an extra bargaining chip, especially since Dave gave away the Skorzeny bayonet, but Kelley believed *All Fall Down* would do. As a practising academic, he had a sense of the sensation that would transpire if the Yeats–Brown borrowings ever saw the light of day. The church could easily extract the spear from the expropriating novelist, if that's what they really wanted, or they could sit on the threat for as long as was necessary to keep the writer in check.

"Or until such time as Citroën exposes the rascal," Abby cautioned. "Or even Ryanair. O'Leary's not the kind of man to keep things quiet."

"Oh, he does when the Priory of Ryan says so," Kelley riposted with a knowing look.

The problem with knowing looks is that they are deeply meaningful for those in the know but not for those in the don't know. Abby pumped the patient for information on the Priory of Ryan. It didn't really exist outside *All Fall Down*, did it?

Kelley held her hand as he recalled some of the horrid events they'd been through together. "The thing that bothered me about the Mannion–Faulkner encounter was that Mannion was obviously telling the truth about the St. Stephen's Spear. They *did* trade the genuine spear, I'm sure of it. But the spear that got back to Germany was a fake, according to Faulkner."

"So what happened?"

Eyes shining, excitement mounting, Kelley struggled to sit up in bed. He looked deliciously helpless. Lovingly, Abby plumped pillows behind him, as he talked non-stop, rattling out his newly-minted conspiracy theory. "De Valera intercepted the thing. Dev was a member of Yeats's Priory of Ryan, which he set up for real in the 1930s. At a time of widespread preoccupation with racial purity, the priory was dedicated to preserving the Celtic bloodline, as per *All Fall Down*. Dev was totally committed to maintaining Ireland's singular culture, something he stressed on numerous occasions. He and Yeats got on very well, despite their obvious differences. Yeats told Dev about the St. Stephen's Spear and when Dev got wind of the spear swap – almost certainly from Adolf Mahr, a close friend who worked for the National Museum – he decided to intervene. The Belfast-bound fire engines were his idea. Indeed, as they had to get his express permission to travel north, he must have been in on it. When the Brandenburgers returned to Dublin with St. Stephen's occult lance, he intercepted the package, kept the original and replaced it with a fake spearhead, which was passed on to Admiral Canaris."

"Sounds plausible, Dave," Abby said, "apart from two obvious problems. Surely the Brandenburgers would have suspected that something was up when the package was appropriated by Dev's people. Faulkner blamed Mannion for the switch. If something untoward went on in Dublin, he'd hardly hold Father Mannion responsible."

"Not necessarily. The package was delivered to the German legation for transportation to Berlin in the diplomatic bag. Dev had double agents inside the German embassy, though I personally reckon he did a deal with Skorzeny. Skorzeny lived in Ireland after the war. He was treated like royalty. The guy was a rabid SS man, remember, not a Brandenburger. He owed nothing to Canaris or the other members of the raiding party. He was a marketer, a businessman. He looked after his own interests. He was arranging a Plan B if the war went against the Nazis. He did a deal with Dev. And eventually received his post-war reward."

"Okay, fair enough. But why would de Valera want the spear in the first place?"

"Well, if the spear had powers on a par with weapons of mass destruction, as everyone seemed to think, it must have been enormously tempting for him. Threatened with invasion by both Britain and Germany, the spear represented the ultimate deterrent. You can see the attraction from his perspective. De Valera was desperate in 1941. His country was defenceless. He was clutching at straws, at spears. When he thought Hitler was about to conquer Russia and turn back to the western question, he informed the Führer that the devious IRA volunteers in Belfast had double-crossed him."

"So the Priory of Ryan carried the day, Irish culture was saved for all eternity and Yeats finally got his hands on St. Stephen's occult spear, albeit in absentia."

"Maybe not in absentia, Abby."

"Huh? Didn't he die in 1939?"

"According to Isambard Kingdom, Yeats also wrote the works of Fulcanelli. Fulcanelli was an infamous French alchemist who translated *The Emerald Tablet*, possessed the philosopher's stone and is reputed to enjoy eternal life."

"But Yeats didn't speak French and he was buried twice, once on the Riviera and subsequently in Sligo."

"His wife was fluent, though, and she helped with all his post-1920s prose. There's long been a rumour that Yeats isn't buried in Drumcliffe Graveyard, under Ben Bulben."

"You're raving, Dave. The drugs have affected your thought processes."

"Maybe you're right, Abby. But I think the Priory of Ryan still exists. Have you ever noticed how many rich and successful Ryans there are in Irish public life? It's no accident. We're on to them, Abby. We have another bargaining chip of sorts. I think we're finally out of the woods."

For the first time in three days Abby felt relaxed. She felt relaxed on the way back to Edinburgh airport. She felt relaxed on the thirty-minute easyJet flight to Belfast International. She felt relaxed in the taxi to Carrickfergus's West Street, where she disembarked with a happy sigh and strolled fifty metres up the street to Some Like It Hot. Passers-by were staring at her happy relaxed face, smiling at the sight of a woman in love.

Abby didn't know what she expected to find at Some Like It

Hot. However, she didn't expect what she found. Two days previously, the store was wrecked, with stock scattered everywhere, display racks all over the place and the counter overturned, its glass panelling shattered. The last thing she saw before escaping down the underground tunnel was a retail establishment that had been hit by an Igor-shaped explosive device.

When she raised the security screen, Abby couldn't believe her eyes. The premises were completely empty. All the stock was gone; the display units had been removed; the fixtures and fittings were nowhere to be seen; the shop window was as bare as Mother Hubbard's cupboard during Lent. The marble-effect floor was spotless. The walls were strangely shelfless. The retro telephone had disappeared, as had the redoubtable cash register. Only the musty aroma of It's a Miracle delay spray lingered around the place, though she might have been imagining that. Even the fitting and ex-stock rooms at the back were bereft. The anchor, armour, armoire et cetera had evaporated into the retailing ether.

Abby was beginning to think that it had all been a bad dream – and it had been a *very bad dream* – when she thought she could hear someone, or something, on the shopfloor. She hurried to the front of the building, where Dick and Betty Biggar were taking a last look at what remained of their intimate apparel empire. After gleeful expressions of delight and relief at Abby's happy reappearance, they explained that they were getting out of retail and into e-tail. No more bricks and mortar, only clicks and eyeballs and Paypal and popups and uploads and downloads and streaming steamy videos. Some may not like it, but Dick knew it'd be hotter than ever. BlueTube, a video site featuring viewers' wives and kinky courting couples, was going to be big, big, big. So were Peepo, Fuckr, MySperm and Sit On My Facebook, though he didn't want to give too much away. Abby was welcome to come and join them at Some Like It Hot 2.0, once they were fully functional. However, as they had to give priority to permanent staff at the other retail outlets, she'd have to wait. They suggested transferring to the new store for the meantime, the shop that's about to open in Some Like It Hot's former premises. They'd clear it with Hustler. She could speak with the new owner, who'd be here in a couple of minutes. They'd give her a glowing reference. Imagine, starting a brand new store from scratch. Best feeling in the world. Wonderful experience that'd stand her in tremendous stead. Takes them back to the happy days when Some Like It Hot was at, well, room temperature, during the depths of winter, when the heating had packed up. What fun. What a laugh. What an opportunity for her.

A large black Mercedes pulled up outside, ignoring the pedestrian zone regulations. A well-dressed man stepped out and, unbuttoning the jacket of his shimmering suit, he sauntered across to Some Like It Hot, as the S-class sped off. He paused for a few moments, taking in the frontage and fascia with a proprietorial eye.

He looked familiar.

Very familiar.

Chapter Fifty-Eight

Some Like It Hotter

Robert D'Anger stared at her quizzically, as he held out his hand. He had that haven't-I-seen-you-somewhere expression on his face. Abby assumed it was his sister's dress, a distinctive Diane von Fürstenberg wraparound, that registered with the imperious aristocrat. But she was wrong. D'Anger knew exactly who Abby was.

"How lovely to meet you, Miss Maguire," he said in an accent that wasn't so much cut glass as diamond encrusted. "I trust you are fit and well and none the worse for your ordeal."

My ordeal, Abby was inclined to reply, is none of your business. Before she could say anything, however, the Biggars interrupted with a guilty, gabbling, self-justifying explanation of their decision to contact the police. How worried they were. The disappearance of their employee. The state of the shop. The work of vandals or kidnappers or... The third alternative hung in the air, unspoken. They might as well have broadcast it from the battlements of Carrickfergus Castle. Namely, the unstable mental health of an employee whose father topped himself and whose mother couldn't cope with the family farm in his absence and who finished up in the funny farm. It's in the blood, you know. It's genetic, congenital, inherited, insidious. They were glad to see her back, looking so well. They didn't mean to let the world know about her, um, their family history. But the media got hold of it. The police could see the publicity potential. She looked so attractive in the old photograph. The press plastered it on every front page. It snowballed. They were so worried. They should never have left her in the shop on her own. Look, let's meet up for lunch after you've had a chat with Mr. D'Anger. We'll be in Dobbins Inn. Then we can sort things out with the police and the university and, well, you know...

As Abby watched them scuttle out of the store, feet pitter-pattering on the faux marble flooring, she understood why the passers-by had been staring at her. Far from looking admiringly at a woman in love, they were wondering where they'd seen her before. D'Anger was also sizing her up, though his expression was closer to triumph than perplexity. If this were a Victorian melodrama, he would be twisting his handlebar moustaches with fiendish relish.

Briskly, D'Anger explained that he was establishing an estate agency-cum-property dealership on the site and she was welcome to join his team. They were short-handed. There was much to do before opening day. It would be excellent experience for her – proper experience, he said, intimating that Some Like It Hot was somehow unbecoming – and, if she passed muster, there might be a job at the end of her placement. Part-time initially, permanent when she'd finished her degree. D'Anger Estates had big plans. She could be part of them. Get in at ground level, as it were. He laughed at his own joke, while twirling those invisible whiskers.

Abby didn't need to ask why Robert was expanding into estate agency. But as someone who loved the sound of his own voice even more than he adored grand opera, D'Anger pontificated and perorated regardless. In the New Northern Ireland property was where the money was. Ulster's post-peace property market had, well, exploded. He smiled at his second bon mot, albeit a tasteless bon mot. The residential property market was booming. Smirk. The commercial property market was thermonuclear. Smirk. Northern Ireland had been undershopped for years. The tourist trade was roaring ahead. Carrickfergus had incredible potential – well-preserved castle, Norman church, city walls, ancient harbour, narrow streets, Georgian buildings, ghosts aplenty. All it needs is a flagship centre, something that'll link the harbour area and the old town, while repairing the blight of the dual carriageway which currently bisects the twin attractions. Thanks to Abby's excellent if unwitting contribution, a new day was dawning, a brighter future was in prospect. The very least D'Anger Estates could do by way of recompense was to offer Miss Maguire a leg up, a foothold on the ladder, a space on the high speed elevator to the glass ceiling. Smirk.

D'Anger was wearing a Valentino suit, Abby noted, with a gratuitously gilded pair of Gucci loafers. An identity bracelet, made from gold links the size of doughnuts, dragged down one arm and would have made him look deformed if it weren't for the counterbalancing Rolex Oyster which was clamped to his other wrist like a de luxe limpet. Never let it be said that the upper crust is an anachronism. Robert Fortinbras D'Anger had property shark written all over him and tattooed on his dorsal. "I'm grateful for the offer, Mr. D'Anger, but..."

"Call me Viscount," he smirked, flashing a quick glance at his Oyster, which shimmered like the mother of all mothers of pearl and was doubtless water resistant to fifty fathoms or thereabouts. Perfect for those who end up sleeping with the fishes or wearing customized concrete loafers.

D'Anger wandered round the empty shop, checking it out, knocking on walls, talking all the while. "This, my dear Miss Maguire, is the property we've been waiting for, the final piece in the jigsaw. Now that we've acquired the freehold on this piece of shit, pardon my French, our flagship centre can go ahead. The Biggars were the only hold outs. We offered them a blank cheque. We offered them alternative premises. We pressurized them with the aid of 'outraged' churchgoers and 'concerned' ratepayers who were worried about the corrupting effect on our young people and complained to the council. Unfortunately, the campaign made them even more popular and harder to dislodge. But thanks to you, my dear, we're home and dry."

"M-me?" Abby stammered, as the scales finally fell from her eyes. She'd been a patsy in a property scam. That's what this was about all along.

"Yes, you. They felt terribly guilty, you know, when your father died and your mother lost her mind. They didn't take your family in, even though they were distantly related. They didn't lift a finger to help, despite social services' attempts to persuade them. They were much too busy making money, building the bawdy business and managing their property portfolio. They couldn't possibly cope with a bunch of traumatized children. Ten years on, when the fire of financial desire had dimmed and when you parachuted in on placement, they had their chance to make amends, to teach you the business, to pass it on to you in the fullness of time. However, when you got… kidnapped, when the store was… wrecked, when you… disappeared off the face of the earth, Dick and Betty were understandably distraught. They'd failed again. Regret's a powerful motivator. People'll give anything away during a guilt trip. And so it proved, especially when I told them that my brother the Hustler lecturer, my brother your dedicated placement tutor, my brother who'd suffered grievously when a previous student went postal, was on the case and that he'd find you if it was the last thing he'd do, even if it meant putting himself at risk."

Reeling from the revelation that Dave was directly involved, Abby felt her knees buckle beneath her. "So it was all a grubby property scam?"

People who dress in Valentino and Gucci are inherently untrustworthy, most neutrals would agree, especially if the rig is accompanied by ingot-sized identity bracelets and watches bigger than the Great Pyramid of Giza. But when the get-up is topped with a look of piteous condescension, the looker is within spitting distance of a slap in the chops. "It wasn't grubby, Miss Maguire, nor a property scam. It was a well thought-out and impeccably executed strategy, a strategy that has delivered the final piece of the flagship project, as we always knew it would. True, it stirred up some savage sleeping dogs and rattled a few unanticipated cages. However, we got there in the end."

Abby refused to listen to the bullshit. "I don't believe you. Dave tried to place me several times before Some Like It Hot turned up. The invitation to St. Stephen's came completely out of the blue. He knew nothing about my connection to Father Mannion. I don't believe he'd get involved in anything so tacky. And anyway your family doesn't have the financial resources to undertake vast property developments."

He shook his head in fake sorrow, pseudo pity. "Dave dissuaded the other student placement takers by hinting at your instability. The St. Stephen's call was prearranged, my dear. Your aunt and uncle were most forthcoming during the negotiations, which have been going on for months, and university records are pretty extensive nowadays, especially those concerning deprived students with special needs. My brother can be pretty tacky when it suits him, darling. He owns the derelict town centre properties that our flagship's built around. He's been supportive from the start."

"What about the money, the finance?" Abby could tell that the taunt had touched a nerve and she pressed home her advantage. "Landed gentry like the D'Angers are as poor as church mice, I hear. You couldn't possibly fund an enormous property development even if you mortgaged or sold off all your estates."

Casually, D'Anger extracted a mobile phone from the innards of his spiv-suit and flicked open the clamshell. Without so much as a scintilla of emotion – despite Abby's attempted provocation – he commanded an underling to collect him in five. He pulled a Montecristo Especial from his breast pocket and, as if auditioning for the role of Don Corleone, rolled it between finger and thumb, listening to the rustling tobacco. "Ordinarily," he rasped, pointing the panatella at his appalled patsy, "I'd take exception to your remarks, especially as they come from a County Tyrone bogtrotter with two fields and a pigsty to her family's illustrious name. But it's true. The D'Anger fortune doesn't extend to serious commercial development. Luckily, we have heavyweight backers, the Ryan Alliance. Have you heard of them? They're big wheels in the merchant banking community."

"Ryan Alliance? 'Fraid not. Means nothing to me."

"Well, perhaps I should give them their full title. I thought everyone was familiar with the International Ryan Alliance, or its initials at least."

"IRA?" The implications of the acronym started to sink in as the Priory of Ryan came back to her, as the prominence of Ryans in Irish public life came back to her, as the names of many leading republicans came back to her, Frank Ryan included, and as the very etymology of the word Ryan came back to her. It was derived from the old Gaelic, *righ an* – Little King.

It was all Abby could do to stay upright. "But I thought the D'Anger family was part of the British establishment, the Protestant Ascendancy, the last-ditch defenders of Ulster since the days of William of Orange?"

"We are. We're proud of it. We owe undying loyalty to the king. But commerce is king nowadays. The customer is king. Business is business. Some of our associates have unsavoury reputations, that's true. However, they've paid their debt to society. They want to go straight. They have money to invest and, thanks to our impeccable name and reputation, D'Anger Estates can help them invest it."

"Launder it, you mean."

D'Anger puffed himself up like an affronted peacock with a penchant for panatellas. "Reparation, we prefer to call it, Miss Maguire. IRA only invests in projects that benefit the community. Carrickfergus's flagship centre is a case in point. The whole town will be revitalized. Think of the new jobs. Think of the tourists. Think of the local economy. Is that really so bad?"

"Think of the money you're laundering. Think of the gangsters you're laundering it for. Think of the small shops that'll go out of business and be replaced by multinational corporations who care nothing for the community and source their stuff from third world sweatshops."

"That's progress," he replied languidly, rapidly losing interest in the conversation. "I take it your answer's no, Miss Maguire. You're refusing our offer. "

"Yes," Abby answered. "It's a no. It's a no because I don't think D'Anger Estates has a future as bright as you suggest. The shops in this street are listed buildings and they're protected from the ravages of money-grubbing property developers like IRA."

The shop door opened with a rattle. D'Anger's flunkey appeared at his side. Abby knew who it was even before she looked at him. It couldn't be anyone else. It was Billy No-dick, the goateed, muscle-bound gangster who'd molested her less than three days previously, though it felt like two lifetimes. Eyes twinkling, pate glistening, he hitched the waistband of his Wranglers lasciviously and hooked his thumbs in his hip pockets like he was some kind of sex machine. If Abby had had her Glock, she'd've shot the skank on the spot, ideally in the balls like big bratwurst, though Billy's were an especially tiny target. She smiled at him while thinking, You're a dead man; I'll see to it if it kills me.

Viscount Robert D'Anger was smiling too. "It's true," he said, raising the panatella to his lips. "The buildings in this area are protected. But there are ways round that." He winked at his muscle-bound companion, who pulled a classic Zippo lighter from his pocket and, with a lazy flick of the flint, emitted a jet of flame that'd do a Bruce Willis blockbuster proud. D'Anger dipped his panatella into the inferno, dragged deeply on the charred stump and blew a cloud of cloying smoke toward the polystyrene ceiling. "Arson's a terrible thing, Abby. There are so many uncontrollable teenagers running around these days. The things they get up to. Carrickfergus's plagued by them."

"Terrible construction materials they used in places like this, Mr. D'Anger. Very flammable. Very dangerous, so to speak. That's gerry builders for you."

"That's the world we live in, Billy."

"Oh well, nobody's perfect..."

Epilogue

Abby Ever After

Abby sipped her coffee disconsolately. She scrolled through the on-line edition of the *Belfast Telegraph,* looking for the coverage she'd been promised. The lead item caught her eye:

CARRICKGATE REOPENS

> The world heritage body, UNESCO, is threatening to step into the Carrickgate controversy. The town's underground warren of tunnels, culminating in the best preserved Irish megalith since New Grange, continues to divide local opinion. "Archaeologists the world over are excited by this find," says Dr. Trevor Trowell of the Department of Arts, Heritage and Leisure. "If carefully managed, it could be turned into a major tourist attraction, on a par with Carrickfergus Castle. As a bare minimum, this fantastic discovery has to be thoroughly and systematically studied. This is the find of the 21st century. I'm amazed it hasn't been discovered before now, but that's what makes archaeology so exciting. It is a site of world importance and UNESCO's interest is indicative of that."
>
> Carrick's town council disagrees. Some councillors remain convinced that a flagship shopping complex – local wags call it Carrickgate Centre – is the best way forward. "Our town needs jobs and investment and modern shopping facilities," says Councillor Sammy Duddy. "We have to stop digging up the past and start building for the future."
>
> Councillor Duddy is in the minority. His impartiality has been called into question, since it emerged that he acted as an "ambassador" for the consortium behind the shopping complex. Straw polls among men and women on the street also suggest that Carrickfergus's past is the best way forward. "The discovery of St. Patrick's

Well is a miracle," says Caroline Crossan, a parishioner of St. Nicholas's. "When the good Lord struck down that den of iniquity, Some Like It Hot, the flames of perdition revealed a blessed well, a place of peace and succour. God moves in mysterious ways."

God isn't the only one. Three weeks on, rumours continue to circulate about the conflagration that inadvertently exposed the underground warren. "Accusations of foul play will be investigated fully," claims local police chief, Martin Cassidy. "No stone will be left unturned."

The concerned citizen who alerted the authorities has yet to come forward. Curiously, the person who found the find of the century can't be found.

What a shame, Abby thought to herself. Carrickfergus's flagship centre scuppered by a concerned citizen. International Ryan Associates can't be too pleased about the outcome. Wonder what D'Angerman makes of it all. According to another on-line story, no one seemed to know:

LOCAL LUCAN LOST AT SEA?

Mystery still surrounds the disappearance of Viscount Robert D'Anger, of D'Anger Castle, County Antrim. The conspiracy theorists are out in force even as the family tries to come to terms with the loss of its most prominent member. "Some of the theories are sick," says David D'Anger, who stands to inherit the family estate should his brother remain missing. "He is not a local Lord Lucan, nor was Shergar's head found in his bed, nor is he managing Elvis in the afterlife like an undead Colonel Parker. The very idea that my beloved brother was involved in criminal activity, or Mafia-style money laundering, is utterly grotesque, as is the suggestion that he's sleeping with the fishes. And as for the scuttleblog suggestions that I myself plotted Robert's downfall, with the connivance of a glamorous gangster's moll, is simply beneath contempt. I was laid up in hospital when my brother disappeared. It grieves me deeply that I was unable to speak with him and talk him out of his mid-life anxieties."

"My wonderful brother," David D'Anger continues, "was devoted to developing and maintaining the D'Anger Castle Estate. A book lover, Robert was particularly proud of the family library, which was once used by Jonathan Swift himself. Accordingly, I'm planning an annual literary festival in my brilliant brother's honour. The event will celebrate Carrickfergus's literary heritage and offer advice for emerging talent. I'm pleased to announce that Dan Brown, author of such modern classics as *Angels and Demons* and *Deception Point*, will lead the inaugural writing workshop. I'm certain my brother won't want to miss it. He's a big fan of Dan. He'll be back. I know it in my waters."

Abby preferred the Assets Recovery yarn. At least she could have forgiven him for being a cop, for misleading her in the pursuit of justice. But being Kelley's dupe in a property scam, a scam that caused a chain reaction which left four dead, was unforgivable. She didn't even want to think about the possibility that the property scam was itself a property scam to reclaim Kelley's inheritance and protect his precious library. Ah, here it is...

WEETUBE – THE CRAIC IS BACK!

Everyone agrees that WeeTube is the place to be in Belfast. Since its opening six weeks ago, on the site of a former internet café in Pottinger's Entry, it has taken the city by storm, as well as the World Wide Web.

"Everyone loves YouTube and rightly so," says Abby Maguire, manageress of the city centre hotspot. "It's the second best thing you can do alone in your bedroom. What YouTube lacks is an authentic sense of community, the craic that comes from groups of like-minded people – real people – being in the same place at the same time, all enjoying the YouTube experience. That's what WeeTube provides. The big screens, the individual monitors, the vote-generated and random-mix programming together ensure that everyone gets an authentic interactive experience and a great night out. Every night is different – comedy nights, music nights, natural history nights, odd advert nights, karaoke nights – but they're all fantastic."

When asked how she came up with the idea, Abby replies that it popped into her head during a lunchtime chat with an e-commerce enthusiast in Edinburgh. She subsequently came into a bit of money, thanks to an unexpected bequest, and decided to go for it. "Giving up my studies at Hustler was a bit of a wrench, but during my course I discovered that some of the world's best marketers don't have formal marketing qualifications. If people like Madonna and Damien Hirst and Steve Jobs and Donald Trump can make it without a marketing degree, I decided to follow in their footsteps. Things have been going very well so far and we've got some great WeeTube developments in store. We're thinking of running X-rated nights, in conjunction with BlueTube, and live music's also on the agenda. The craic is definitely back!"

Not bad, Abby reckoned, all things considered. She couldn't remember telling the journalist that YouTube was the second best bedroom pastime. Such a thought had never crossed her mind. But newspaper people love a snappy quote, even if they have to coin it themselves. Oh well, what the hell. She clicked on the embedded hyperlink and was whisked through cyberspace to the forthcoming attraction flyer:

WEETUBE ROCKS!

WeeTube, the most amazing entertainment experience in Greater Belfast, today announced its inaugural live act. Local legend D. D. Kelley will showcase tracks from his latest album, *Abby Road*. A radical departure for D.D., *Abby Road* is a lovelorn reinterpretation of various Beatles standards including "Abby In the Sky With Diamonds", "Abbyness is a Warm Gun", "Long Tall Abby", "Abby It's You", "DD Kelley's Lonely Hearts Club Band", "While My Attar Gently Weeps" and "We Can Work It Out".

"I owe everything to YouTube, darling," says Kelley from his totsche-filled tourbus. "If it weren't for the phenomenal success of my YouTube video, *See You Citroën*, I'd never have scored a record deal. I'm here to give something back to my local fans and to support Ulster's own WeeTube, which is a fantastic entertainment concept that'll soon go global. I'm sure of it."

Fans with long memories best remember D. D. Kelley as the charismatic front man of Love Pump, the legendary rock band banned from *Top of the Pops* after a live broadcast of their controversial song, "We Don't Need No Lubrication". The band broke up in acrimony not long after. The question on everyone's lips is whether D.D. will play any of his early classics. "No, darling," he says. "Not a chance. However, there's a nostalgic track on my new album that harks back to the good old bad old days. It's called 'All You Need is Love Pump'."

Abby Road, eh? Nice try, Kelley. But you'll have to do better than that, she thought. Still, at least he got the Edinburgh cops off her back. Oddly, they never contacted her again, much less called her back for questioning. Did Kelley use his underworld influence? Or was a different agenda at work? Was it headquarters they were talking to on the radio that day, or were they reporting back to someone else entirely? She didn't know. She didn't care. She had weighty WeeTube matters on her mind. She didn't have time to worry about the past.

As Abby returned to the *Belfast Telegraph* homepage before logging off, an item of breaking news caught her eye:

DOUBLE FIRST FOR RYANAIR

Ryanair today announced its first flights to the United States. A daily service to New York from Dublin and Stansted starts next month. "Transatlantic passengers have been robbed blind for years," says Ryanair's ebullient CEO, Michael O'Leary, who wore a dashing highwayman outfit at the press conference. "BA and Virgin, expensive bastards both, have been ripping people off for decades. We rob passengers too but at least we don't wear a mask and we steal less of our customers' money. What could be fairer than that?"

When asked what is fair about flying to White Plains, 55 miles north of Manhattan, while claiming it is New York in the adverts,

Ryanair's combative CEO replied in characteristically forthright fashion. "The ad says New York. White Plains is in New York State. It's still fucking New York. Is it my fault if people don't read the fucking ads properly? What's their problem, for fuck's sake? The distance between White Plains and Manhattan is hardly anything when you look at it on the map."

Alongside Ryanair's move into the transatlantic market, the company announced a change in its promotional strategy. Its first-ever celebrity spokesperson will be fronting the US marketing campaign. Dan Brown, the best-selling American author, is appearing in a series of newspaper ads and television spots. The deal is quite a coup for Ryanair, because Dan Brown is notoriously reclusive. "I just couldn't resist the slogan," says the celebrity author from his luxury home in Rye Beach, New Hampshire. The ads feature a photograph of Brown, holding a Sherlock Holmes-style magnifying glass, alongside the strapline, "It's a mystery to me why Ryanair's fares are so low."

"Ryanair is delighted to bring Dan Brown on board," says O'Leary. "Our company is a supporter of the arts and is a work of art in itself. Ryanair is the W. B. Yeats of the airline industry. Just as Yeats's style changed from extravagantly embellished to spare and lean, so too Ryanair started as a full-price, full-service operation that became sparer and leaner through time. It's entirely appropriate, therefore, that Dan Brown – the W. B. Yeats of the thriller – should join Ryanair as a celebrity spokesperson."

Abby set down her empty coffee cup. How, she wondered, in a fleeting moment of Yeatsian transcendence, can we tell the bullshitter from the bullshit?

Author's Note

As a marketing lecturer, I've noticed that my undergraduate students are increasingly reluctant to read traditional textbooks. This reluctance is partly due to the price of such tomes, which are becoming prohibitively expensive, particularly for student loan-strapped students. It's also partly attributable to their sheer bulk, since several hundred fact-packed, folio-sized pages is the norm nowadays. True, these pages are usually interspersed with full-colour photographs, all-action diagrams and just about every trick in the graphic design arsenal – grab quotes, colour coding, action points, et cetera – but my undergraduate students still find them very tough going. It's not that today's computer game-addicted kids are reluctant to read per se, since Harry Potter patently proves otherwise; it's that they are understandably unwilling to slog through page after page of dry-as-dust didacticism.

It thus seems to me that the established textbook format, which is fifty years old if it's a day, is going to hell in a hand-me-down handbasket. I further reckon that no amount of revision, renovation, restoration (or indeed price reduction) will change the fact that a pedagogic paradigm shift is required. Big Fat Books About Marketing will continue to be published, of course, but only because textbook publishers have sunk so much time and effort and capital and faith and promotional support into the formulaic format that they can't afford to kill the fatted calf, let alone slaughter the sacred cow.

Agents and Dealers and *The Marketing Code* represent attempts to cure the educational equivalent of BSE – Book Spongiform Encephalopathy. They are written as Dan Brown-style thrillers in the belief that getting students excited about the subject is more important than ensuring that they can regurgitate "the facts" behind psychographic segmentation, integrated marketing communications, the Howard-Sheth model of consumer behaviour and similar pearls of conventional academic wisdom. Such facts have their place, admittedly. But they shouldn't be given pride of place, as they are in most mainstream textbooks. We need to change the marketing script.

This book, then, is my response to the challenge of making marketing writing more interesting, more pleasurable, more exciting. Obviously, I'm not the best judge of whether that ambition has been achieved. I'll leave that up to you. I can say, however, that my overriding concern has been to ensure that the story works as a story and that the key pedagogic themes aren't introduced in an overly ham-fisted or finger-wagging manner. As if!

My themes, on this occasion, are threefold. The first is that marketing is inherently magical. Marketing is not a science or a technology or a toolkit, as traditional textbooks tend to claim, but a place of enchantment, wonder, mystery, allure. Marketers are alchemists, I believe (and Pitcairn Brodie agrees with me!). My second theme is the significance of revenge. Businesspeople, in the main, are not motivated by profit maximisation, as neoclassical economists contend, nor by making obscene amounts of money, as many media types assume, but by all sorts of other factors, such as freedom, fame, self-fulfilment and, not least, revenge. My third point is that there are no holy grails or magic bullets or, for that matter, spears of destiny in marketing. Management gurus claim to possess the "secrets of success" and sell shed-loads of books thereby. However, the brute reality of business life is that no matter how good your product or service or marketing campaign happens to be, its success depends on luck and timing and never-say-die determination.

Lest there is any confusion, I must make it absolutely clear that *Agents and Dealers* is entirely fictional. All the settings are fictional, all the situations are fictional, all the characters are fictional. Although my novel makes many references to real brands, real places and real people – purely for verisimilitude – they are fictionalised versions of real brands, places and people. They bear no relation to reality. The Citroën conference in Nuremberg, for example, is entirely a figment of my imagination, as is the company's marketing executive in Chapters 44 and 47. The Michael O'Leary character in Chapters 53 to 55 is clearly based on the ebullient public persona of Ryanair's chief executive. It has nothing whatsoever to do with the "real" person, though. The same is true of the "Dan Brown" figure described herein, as is my (entirely fictional) hypothesis concerning Yeats's (non-existent) manuscript *All Fall Down*.

That said, some of the places described in the book – most notably University of Hustler, D'Anger Castle and St. Stephen's Retreat – do actually exist, albeit I've changed the names to protect the innocent, as they say in cheap novels. I'll let you work the originals out for yourselves, though the University of Hustler is a tough one, I must confess.

* * *

As an academic, I feel obliged to cite my sources, which are manifold and various. I won't belabour things with an enormous reading list, but on the off-chance that you're interested in some of the topics contained in *Agents and Dealers*, the following should help get you started.

The bombing raid described in the Prologue did indeed take place, as Robert Fisk recounts in his superb book *In Time of War* (Flamingo, London, 1985), and all the characters are based on Nazi spies who plied their wartime trade in Ireland (see Mark M. Hull, *Irish Secrets*, Irish Academic Press, Dublin, 2003). The recent renaissance of Belfast, referred to in Chapter 1, is chronicled by Fred Boal and Steve Royle in their beautifully illustrated *Enduring City* (Blackstaff, Belfast, 2006). Carrickfergus's illustrious history is cogently summarised in *A Stroll Through Time* (Charles McConnell, Carrickfergus Publications, 1994) and plans for comprehensive urban revitalisation are currently afoot. It'll be nice when it's finished, as they say.

The system of tunnels described in Chapters 10 and 11 actually exists (see Samuel Lewis, *County Antrim: A Topographical Dictionary*, Friar's Bush Press, Belfast, 2002), though I've exaggerated things considerably for storytelling purposes. The USE arms dump in Chapter 11 is fictional, though the existence of something similar wouldn't surprise me in the least. Jonathan Swift's adventures in Kilroot are outlined by Joseph McMinn (*Jonathan Swift: A Literary Life*, Macmillan, Basingstoke, 1991), who also retells the tale of Cave Hill's influence on *Gulliver's Travels*. The great man hated Ulster with a vengeance, incidentally.

There are many wonderful stories associated with the Antrim Coast Road, which features in Chapter 15. An excellent collection has been gathered by my esteemed ex-colleague, Alan Turner (*The Glens of Antrim*, Appletree Press, 2005). The Carrick-a-Rede rope bridge is definitely worth traversing, though it's not as rickety as I imply. The dilapidated University of Hustler campus described in Chapters 16 to 21 bears no relation whatsoever to the University of Ulster's verdant campus at Coleraine. How could you even think such a thing? Shame on you!

Moving swiftly along, the history of the Irish Redemptorist Order, sketched out in Chapter 25, is thoroughly covered by James Grant (*One Hundred Years With the Clonard Redemptorists*, Columba Press, 2003). The stories of old Cave Hill, including the coronation stone incident, are recounted in Cathal O'Byrne's 1946 classic, *As I Roved Out* (Lagan Books, Belfast, 2000). As the first volume of Roy Foster's sublime biography reveals, W. B. Yeats really did visit Belfast in 1899; he really did scale Cave Hill with Maud Gonne; and he really was obsessed with the Celtic Order of Mysteries at the time (*W. B. Yeats: A Life*, Oxford University Press, 1997). The stuff about his fascist leanings is also true, though Maud was much more pro-Nazi than her wannabe paramour (see Nancy Cardozo, *Maud Gonne*, New Amsterdam Books, 1990).

Otto Skorzeny, the "most dangerous man in Europe", has been subject to several biographies (e.g. Charles Whiting, *Skorzeny*, Leo Cooper, Barnsley, 1998). Adolf Mahr, allegedly Ireland's top-ranking Nazi, has recently received a book-length treatment, though it errs on the side of hagiography (Gerry Mullins, *Dublin Nazi No. 1*, Liberties Press, Dublin, 2007). De Valera's difficult balancing act is cogently described in Fisk (op. cit.) and Clair Wills's much-praised *That Neutral Island* (Faber and Faber, London, 2007). Whatever else is said about him, Dev played his wartime hand brilliantly.

When it comes to the Spear of Destiny, the seminal work is by Trevor Ravenscroft, although many consider his best-seller to be pseudo-history of the highest order, on a par with *Holy Blood, Holy Grail* (*The Spear of Destiny*, Sphere Books, London, 1973). The literature on the occult roots of Nazism is legion. By far the most scholarly contributions are by Nicolas Goodrick-Clarke, but if you're looking for an uncritical overview, check out Paul Roland, *The Nazis and the Occult* (Arcturus, London, 2007). Adolf Hitler's alleged sojourn in Liverpool is outlined in Michael Unger's *The Memoirs of Bridget Hitler* (Duckworth, London, 1979), and artfully novelised by Beryl Bainbridge in *Young Adolf* (Abacus, London, 2003). The material about Max Caulfield as the original source of the spear story is true, according to Alec MacLellan's *Secret of the Spear* (Souvenir Press, London, 2004), though his imputed links to the conspiracy herein are a fictional figment of my fevered imagination. Caulfield, in fact, is a very distinguished historian, whose work on the 1916 Easter Rising is considered definitive.

The Edinburgh chapters are predicated on *Holyrood and Canongate* (E. Patricia Dennison, Birlinn Limited, Edinburgh, 2006), *Walks in Edinburgh's Old Town* (Michael and Elspeth Wills, Mercat Press, Edinburgh, 2001), *Edinburgh: A Cultural and Literary History* (Donald Campbell, Signal Books, Oxford, 2003) and *The Playfair Project* (Michael Clarke, National Galleries of Scotland, Edinburgh, 2004), plus a lot of foot-slogging and guidebook-goggling by yours truly. The Witchery is as wonderful as it appears in Chapters 37 and 39; the escape tunnel under The Secret Garden restaurant actually exists; and the four clues in the criss-cross, *Angels and Demons*-style puzzle are pretty much as described. True, the tour-guides at Holyrood are unaware of the occult essence of their celebrated sundial and the Stone of Scone looks a bit like a crumbling concrete block, but *The Spell* is well worth a visit (albeit it's hidden away in the bowels of the National Galleries). Rosa Alchemica Caledonia is completely fictional, however.

Turning to the Nuremberg chapters, the historical details are fairly accurate. Everything from the vestigial sculptures on the exterior of the Carlton Hotel to the lift in the courtroom that held the infamous war trials is exactly as described. My principal sources here, apart from several days on shanks's pony, were Maik Kopleck, *Pastfinder Nuremberg* (Pastfinder, Hong Kong, 2007), Peter Heigl, *Nuremberg Trials* (Verlag Hans Carl, Nuremberg, 2001), Birgit Friedel and Ulrich Grossman, *Nuremberg Imperial Palace* (Verlag Schnell & Steiner, Regensburg, 2006), and of course Ravenscroft (op. cit.). FYI, replicas of the entire *Reichkleinodien* are currently on display in the Altes Rathaus (sorry, that should be replicas of the replicas!).

Michael O'Leary, the rambunctious CEO of Ryanair, is not exactly publicity shy. An unauthorised biography, *Michael O'Leary: A Life in Full Flight*, was published by Alan Ruddock in 2007 (Penguin, Ireland), though Siobhan Creaton's earlier book on Ryanair is no less informative (Aurum, London, 2004). I've summarised most of this material in earlier articles (see the pen portrait in my *Fail Better*, Cyan/Marshall Cavendish, London, 2008, for instance) and the caricature of O'Leary contained herein is based on much the same sources.

Finally, it goes without saying that the Priory of Ryan doesn't actually exist. Or does it? I guess you'll just have to read *The Customer Key*, the last volume in my thriller trilogy, to find out …

Stephen Brown
May 2008

Acknowledgements

Like many marketers, I spend a fair amount of time in airports. Like many bibliophiles, I spend a fair amount of money in airport bookstores. It was in Gatwick, for example, that I encountered my first book by Cyan, a beautifully produced volume on the David Beckham brand. I'm no fan of Beckham – and never have been – but I was so taken with the production values in *Brand It Like Beckham* (Andy Milligan, Cyan, London, 2004) that I simply had to work with the wonderful people responsible. For the past few years I've been fortunate enough to do so and I can honestly say that Martin Liu and Pom Somkabcharti are by far the best publishers I've ever come across. I've worked with quite a few first-class publishers down the years but no one compares to Martin and Pom. I'm enormously grateful for their continuing support and only hope that their faith in me is rewarded.

Another thing I've noticed in airport bookstores, while patiently standing in line at the cash register, is that businesspeople often buy two books at a time. One is the latest management tome, the buzzword-filled blockbuster that everyone's talking about and that they have to be familiar with, if only to show that they're up to date with cutting-edge thinking. The other is a page-turner of some kind – a Stephen King or a James Patterson or a Jackie Collins or indeed a Dan Brown. It's almost as if they need a little light relief, something suitably entertaining and escapist, to counterbalance the worthy but dull "lessons" of the management tome.

Agents and Dealers, like *The Marketing Code* before it, represents an attempt to meld management and murder. The novel is set in a marketing context and engages with important marketing issues, but it does so in a thrills and spills-filled manner. It replaces case studies with corpses, bullet-points with bullets and how-to with who-done-it. It's two books for the price of one, basically. It's a time-saver for today's busy managers. It speeds things up at the bookstore checkout. You know it makes sense.

As with *The Marketing Code, Agents and Dealers* would never have seen the light of day if it hadn't been for the help I've received along the way. Kent Drummond, as before, encouraged me in my attempts to emulate the Danster, as did my ever-enthusiastic brother-in-law, Alun Richards. Yet again, Dr. Stephanie O'Donohoe was a fount of useful information on Edinburgh, though I spared her the dialect dilemma this time. Dr. Markus Giesler, my preferred profanity supplier, ensured that the German in Chapter 40 passed muster. Professor Douglas Brownlie, Dr. Hope Schau and Dr. Mark Tadajewski read the work-in-progress and gave me some very valuable feedback. I'm particularly grateful to Paula Durkan and Sherlie Richards, and to Linda Brown, my "preternaturally patient" better half, for ensuring that the female protagonist wasn't too unrealistic. My daughters, Madison, Sophie and Holly, were as supportive as ever, even though my writing schedule meant that I missed yet another summer holiday. Holly, incidentally, helped design the draft front cover, although we went for something slightly different in the end. Maybe next time, Holly!

Quite a few people have been in touch since *The Marketing Code*, some with kind comments, others with nits to pick about the plot, the characters, the foreign translations, et cetera. I really appreciate reader reactions, which have given me considerable food for thought. I've taken your suggestions on board and I hope that *Agents and Dealers* represents a further step forward. If you have any comments on the novel – for good or ill – I'd love to hear from you. I can be contacted via my website: www.sfxbrown.com

If you're planning to read
The Marketing Code, the sequel to
Agents and Dealers, read this first…

The Metaphor Wars

EEEEEeeeee.. The braking Boeing's bellowing engines had barely ceased their banshee wail before Barton Brady's cell phone set the scene. "Viva, Las Vegas," the king of ring tones, tinkled throughout the first class cabin, to the delight of Brady's fellow passengers. High-fliers one and all, their cells soon chimed in, a kitsch chorus of tinny tunes that presaged a weekend of high stakes, high jinks, and high roller high fives.

Although he badly needed several servings from the R&R smorgasbord, especially after an eighteen-hour flight from Nuremberg, via De Gaulle and Dulles, the CEO of Serendipity Associates had something more serious on his plate. Deadly serious, in fact. Unbeknown to Barton Brady, there was a new dish in town.

Casually finger-combing his immaculate coiffure, Brady unzipped a rhinestone smile before answering. A salesman to his back teeth, who worked the smirk incessantly, Brady knew that incisor action was the secret of a successful telephone manner. As head honcho of the hottest hotshop in the management consultancy business, he had smiled his way to the top of a ruthless, grin-to-win industry. He couldn't afford to relax his jaw for an instant.

Brady flicked open his Vertu Vainglory, the most exclusive cell phone on the planet, set his orthodontic halogens on high beam, and imperceptibly intoned his personal empowerment mantra: "Every day, in every way, I get cuter and cuter."

"Shoot," he sparkled.

"Bang, bang. You're dead." Damn, it was Yasmin Buonarroti, Serendipity Associates' hard-nosed, hard-headed, hard-boiled workhorse.

A hard-bitten Bronco from the Bronx, with physiognomy to match, Yasmin Buonarroti had brilliantly bucked the management consultancy system. Together with her Gatling-grinned sidekick, she'd established SA as the foremost metaphor ranch in the west. Once regarded as a waste of corporate resources, a ditzy distraction that took executives' eyes off the bottom line, imaginative metaphors were increasingly considered the key to competitive advantage in today's creative economy. Metaphors were the bits, the bytes, the binary code of the imagination. Metaphor was the new math and Brady and Buonarroti were its Fermat and Fibonacci.

Founded during the great brand rush of the late 1990s, Serendipity Associates was a post-industrial Ponderosa. The organization bred ideas, raised acronyms, herded narratives, lassoed analogies and rounded up rhetorical devices for the management rodeo-cum-circus, where they competed against purple cows, dancing elephants, scampering squirrels, indecisive mice, giraffe strategies, rhino tactics, buffalo brands, fluffy-bunny customer care programmes, the seven secrets of silverback gorilla leadership and the rest of the executive education menagerie.

Luckily, anthropomorphic allusions didn't live long in corner office captivity, especially not in the repressed air of brokeback boardrooms. Thus the demand for SA's free-range figures of speech was constant. A fad a day kept bankruptcy at bay, or so their blue-chip clients believed, and who were Serendipity Associates to disabuse them? It was like taking candy from Baby Bells.

"Anything interesting in Nuremberg?" Buonarroti continued casually.

"It was completely crazy," Brady laughed, despite his exhaustion. "The conference began with a fist fight, continued with a full-blown riot and ended up..."

"Cool," Buonarroti cut in.

Brady could detect the tension in his colleague's voice, but couldn't risk inquiring what the problem was. Espionage was rampant in the management metaphor business and eavesdropping an everyday occurrence. As a good-to-great metaphor was worth its weight in Fortune 500 gold, particularly if it was built to last beyond entrepreneurship, great care had to be taken in unguarded conversation. In a world where words were bearer bonds, and coinages were coinage, James Bondoid behavior was unavoidable.

Sensing her high anxiety, Brady opted for SA's emergency casino codeword. The corporate equivalent of Defcon One to Defcon Five, "Tropicana" flagged a little local difficulty, "MGM Grand" meant a fairly major problem, "Bellaggio" translated into very, very big trouble and "Caesars" was a freakin' raging inferno at their Fremont Street HQ. "How are things on the Strip?" he asked apprehensively.

"Serious, bro."

"Caesars serious, sis?"

"Worse. We're in a Wynn, Wynn situation."

Brady's giga-grin collapsed like a house of marked cards, as the ghost of grifts past glided over his grave. All thoughts of R&R were abandoned. "I'll be there in twelve minutes precisely. Boardroom lockdown. Get Rosenkreutz."

Ordinarily, Brady relished strolling through the marbled, palm-peppered halls of McCarran International, while grabbing glimpses of his gorgeous, Gucci-girt reflection in its marvellously mirrored surfaces. He revelled in the ringing ranks of slots, the gaudy ads for glitzy attractions, the pheromonic, phantasmagoric atmosphere of winning big and breaking the bank. It may have been tacky to the tenth degree, but he loved the smell of gaming in the morning... evening... anytime. Where there's hope, there's life.

Death was on the agenda, unfortunately. Hence his insistence on Rosenkreutz's attendance. SA's bagman, bruiser and big-time bad guy, Rosenkreutz was the consigliere's consigliere, the consultancy industry's Most Valuable Enforcer. A much-decorated marketing veteran, who'd been awarded the New Coke Cross, the Segway Star and the Ronald McDonald Medal of Honor among others, Rosenkreutz was the ideal man for Wynn Wynn situations. He'd even served a couple of tours of duty in 'Nam. Panam, that is.

When the going got tough, Rosenkreutz got tougher.

SA's big, black, sabre-toothed SUV picked Brady up at the Russell Road entrance and, as it loped down Maryland Parkway, he chanted his "cuter" mantra to keep dark thoughts at bay. An English Literature major at Yale – tapped, naturally, by Scroll & Key – he could have made it as a neo-nü-wave poet if Snoop Dogg hadn't cornered the market in doggerel. He cut his literary losses, learnt the slogan shucking business on Madison Avenue, scored a couple of Breakthrough Idea plaudits in *HBR* – McKinsey near misses, Brady maintained – and turned his training to good account when American management went metaphor crazy, a side effect of the millennial madness that caused dotcom delirium.

Seven years on, the consultancy industry was getting awfully crowded. The business was awash with fire walkers, wind talkers, ice dancers, home runners, slam dunkers, jazz strategists, wiki-warriors, Shakespeare spouters, Dilbert devotees, value chain escapologists and sellers of Attila the Hun's HR secrets, to say nothing of manifold metaphor wranglers such as SA. Collectively, they were pushing the envelope up the flagstaff of out-of-the-box thinking to the next level of the learning curve ball, where only the parodied survive. The unscrupulous, also. Twinned with Gomorrah, management consultancy made Las Vegas look like Lake Wobegon.

The workhorse was waiting in the boardroom when Brady arrived. Surrounded by styrofoam cups and half-eaten submarine sandwiches, Buonarroti was hunched over a Sony Vaio laptop, the one with the built-in fire extinguisher. She looked terrible, like Trigger in transit to the glue factory.

"Welcome home, handsome."

"Good to see you, Babearroti. What's up?"

With a worried sigh, Yasmin span her Sony round, albeit with difficulty because of the big red canister of USB foam. The super-bright screen was filled with a blog roll. But not just any old blog roll. It was GoneWithTheWindows.com, the rabid ramblings of Rhetorical Butler, self-appointed scourge of the creative economy in general and management fads in particular. Under the tagline "I *do* give a damn, frankly," Butler deposited his digital diarrhoea day after day to a lap-it-up audience of millions. The posting was called "Mixed Metaphormatosis". A crude summary of the rapid rise of management metaphors, the malevolent motormouse contended that personification and anthropomorphism were getting out of hand. Metaphor ranching was leading American management astray. There was a serious oversupply of metaphors – a figurative glut – and mercy killing was called for, akin to culling baby seals. Metaphors look cute, but they are pests, weeds, the kudzu of commerce, the cane toads of thought, the roaches of discourse. They had to be exterminated, sooner rather than later.

Disney and Pixar'll love that, Brady reckoned, then continued reading.

Butler's loathsome screed climaxed with a repellent call to action: "Metaphors maketh management, some say, but the profusion of confusing messages is making American managers indecisive and denuding their get up and go. The sugar rush of syrupy similes is causing organizational arteriosclerosis, as is the high-cal content of meaty metaphors. When Marx predicted that the contradictions of western capitalism would precipitate its collapse, most thought he was talking literally. However, it's today's contradictory metaphors that are bringing capitalism down. It's time to raise semantic trade barriers, to establish syntax exclusion zones, to do an Abu Ghraib on dangling participles, to support the Personification Liberation Front..."

Brady grimaced. It would have been easy to make mock of Butler's garbled thoughts, asinine prose and penchant for the very mixed metaphors he disparaged. However, as an English Literature major, Brady knew that mixing metaphors was a surefire way of attracting attention. They may be aesthetically unappealing, but in a metaphor-saturated situation, figurative mash-ups have major league impact. Rhetorical Butler's rabble-rousing rant was certain to trigger Richter-scale ripples throughout the management consultancy community. SA's carefully constructed edifice was sitting on dangerously shifting sands. All their eggs were in one basket and the basket was holed below the waterline.

Mixing metaphors was contagious, dammit.

"So, what do you reckon?" Buonarroti asked.

Brady had never seen her look fearful before. Yasmin had the drive of a dump truck, plus the chassis, but even dump trucks have their tipping point. "Reminds me of the management metaphor meltdown of 1999," he said.

"Me too," she whispered with a shudder.

The millennial metaphor war began innocently enough, when Peter Tompkins, an evangelical management guru who'd made his name in the 1980s with the blockbuster buzzword "Transcendence", launched a tongue-in-cheek attack on management by metaphor. The man who'd given the world such timeless figures of speech as "Stick to the Spaghetti, Betty" and "Close to the Customer's Pocketbook" roguishly contended that there were three stages in the evolution of management metaphors: *ornamental*, when they were considered vulgar add-ons; *elemental*, when the realization dawned that figurative thinking was not only unavoidable but invaluable; and *detrimental*, when every wannabe management swami was selling a verminous collection of moth-eaten, fly-blown, rat-tailed, cheese-please concepts.

Tompkins's cheeky critique unfortunately coincided with the belated arrival of accountancy firms, full-service advertising agencies and the upper crust of the pie-chart contingent, who had decided it was time to get a slice of the metaphor action. Cut-throat competition burgeoned at the very moment when the metaphor market was in literal freefall. If it hadn't been for SA's sideline in TLAs (Three Letter Acronyms), which are the PBBs (Peanut Butter Bankers) of the CIC (Consultancy Industrial Complex), their AOK organization would have been in VDS. The day was saved by the timely intervention of Harvard's Hannibal, Bethany Kando, whose troupe of giant dancing elephants cut Tompkins off at the pass.

Elephants are the bees' knees of the metaphor industry. Just as Wall Street turns to gold in times of crisis, so too consultants revert to tusker tropes when the metaphor market wobbles. True, these turns invariably lead to the unedifying sight of blind men palpating bemused pachyderms. Brady sometimes wondered what would happen if the sightless seven groped an ornery hippo in error. The carnage would be indescribable. There might be a reality television show in it, though. He made a mental note to ring his agents, Louis "the linnet" Lambrusco and Mickey "the moose" Morelli.

Brady's musings were interrupted by the rumbling arrival of Chas Rosenkreutz, SA's set 'em upper, shake 'em downer, rattle 'em arounder. Undeniably physically imposing, Rosenkreutz was not a handsome man. He had a face like a Botoxed warthog. Worse, he was wearing a shiny Valentino suit with lapels the size of Stealth fighters. He looked as though he was modelling a kite. Rosenkreutz nodded curtly toward Buonarroti, shrugged his shoulders in that bada-boom manner, placed a protective palm across his double-breasted midriff and took a seat at the head of the burnished boardroom table.

"What's the word on the street?" Brady asked with trepidation, knowing full well that Rosenkreutz's nose for a story, ear to the ground and eye for the main chance were a formidable combination. Elephant Mannish, yes, but formidable all the same.

"Yield?" Buonarroti interrupted sarcastically. "Tow away zone? No turn on red? No parking any time?" When stressed, Yasmin had an annoying habit of interpreting every expression literally, which was a bit of a bummer in a metaphor manufacturing facility. Once, when Rosenkreutz was belly-aching about "fiddling while Rome burns" she jumped up shouting "What, Caesars is on fire? Has Elton's candle caught the wind? Who's the soloist, Yo Yo Ma?" On another occasion, when Rosenkreutz contended "two heads are better than one," she cruelly retorted, "Just don't sign up for Hot or Not, Chas." They'd been mortal enemies ever since. She openly admitted she hated his guts, though the rest of him was okay. He said she was as mad as a Hilton, the one on Penitentiary Boulevard. Brady was worried about her, frankly. At a time like this, he needed lateral not literal thinking.

Luckily, Rosenkreutz ignored the interruption. Although he looked like Rocky Balboa after fifteen rounds with Bigfoot's big brother, Chas was one smart cookie. "Hank Wittgenstein's attempting an end run," he rumbled.

Brady had never heard of the dude. "Who?"

"Wittgenstein's a rogue philosopher," Buonarroti spat, determined to show that she too was streetwise. "Runs a low-rent simile operation outta Reno, Tropes R Us. Calls himself an excluded middleman, the categorical imperative killer."

"A *rogue* philosopher?" Brady repeated with asperity. "What is it with the rogue thing these days? There's rogue traders, rogue realtors, rogue economists, rogue sociologists and rogue geologists, no doubt. What's next, rogue librarians? Rogue beauticians? Rogue morticians? Rogue proct…"

Buonarroti cut him off. "Hank the Skank's no threat to us," she insisted. "He's a bottom line bottom feeder, who doesn't appreciate the importance of alliteration and assonance, much less the rolling rhythm of melodious metonyms."

"Yeah," Brady agreed, "all the great management metaphors have that extra-special snap, the syncopation, the onomatopoeic magic that SA supplies."

"Marketing myopia," Buonarroti ventured.

"A classic," Brady acknowledged.

"Six Sigma."

"That echo of Six Shooter is sublime."

"Customer is king."

"K-sounds are a killer," Brady beamed. "Kotler, Keller, Kanter, Kando, Kirby, Clayton Christensen…"

"… Kelleher, Kamprand, Calvin Klein, Coca Cola, Kellogg's Cornflakes, core competencies, *keiretsu*," Buonarroti added, smiling.

"K-Mart!" Rosenkreutz snapped. "Krispy Kreme, Kraft, Kodak, Kevin Costner, Naomi Klein, Naomi Campbell, KFC, KKR, KKK, Katrina! Not all Ks are As! You've been drinking your own Kool-Aid, sister. Wake up and smell the…"

"*Capisce*?"

"Blow it out your assonance, Buonarroti!"

"That's enough, the two of you," Brady said testily. He was tired, jet-lagged, lock-jawed from two days of fixed grinning in Germany. "What's the deal with Wittgenstein, Chas?"

"Whereof one cannot speak," Buonarroti quipped caustically, "one must be silent."

Rosenkreutz shook his gnarled head with exasperation. "The word on the street is that he's offshoring his metaphor manufacturing operation and plans to flood the market with extra-cheap tropes."

"That's a relief," Buonarroti replied, with an exaggerated wipe of the hand across her corrugated brow. "Just as well he's not outsourcing source domains and targeting target domains."

Brady was losing his patience. This was no time for wordplay.

"They're bound to be low-calibre conceits," she added in a reassuring voice that betrayed her concern. "We're at the opposite end of the figurative spectrum, Barton. They're infra-red, if that. They're microwaves. We're ultra-violet, at least. We're X-rays. We're gamma rays, for goodness sakes."

"Yes, and remember what happened to Neutron Jack," Brady cautioned. "If Wittgenstein destabilizes a market that's twitchy thanks to Butler's witless outburst, we could still be adversely affected. If intellectual offshoring is successful, the entire management consultancy industry could be Y-K-W, W-A-P."

Rosenkreutz raised a ragged eyebrow. "Y-K-W?"

"You Know Where," Brady explained.

"W-A-P?"

"Without A Paddle."

"Look," Buonarroti insisted, struggling to steer her colleague away from his unfortunate TLA fixation, "it's true that many left brain management activities, such as manufacturing and information processing, have been successfully offshored to India, China, Thailand, Vietnam and the like. But today's creative economy relies on right-brain abilities like conceptualization, imagination, storytelling, analogical thinking, metaphor making. These can't be easily air-freighted to gimcrack factories on the festering outskirts of Sweatshop City. As for Rhetorical Butler, maybe Chas here could whack him."

"What," SA's MVE deadpanned, "you mean slap him around the head a little bit and perhaps plant a quick kick up his caboose?"

"No!" Buonarroti retorted, understandably infuriated by his literal rejoinder. "I mean, um, pop him, if that's the correct euphemism."

"He's got trapped wind, has he?"

"This bitching isn't helping, guys." Brady held his head in despair, though he was careful not to disturb the proud prow of his pristine pompadour. As a lapsed literature major who specialized in post-colonial theory, he knew that the most imaginative writing in the English language came from formerly downtrodden colonies, places that once suffered under the yoke of Empire – India, Canada, Australia, South Africa and, when Poe, Stowe, Melville and Emerson were in their pomp, America itself. He also knew that if US cultural hegemony continued to wane inexorably, as it had been doing in recent years, its creative industries would not be immune from intellectual offshoring, outsourcing, downsizing, undercutting. Wittgenstein's decision was a whisper on the wind. Brady may have been an airhead, but at least it was fresh air, unpolluted by the figurative fug found in Hollywood, Broadway, Silicon Valley, Capitol Hill or similar synecdoches. "Where's he moving his manufacturing capacity, anyway? Do you know?"

"Ireland in the first instance," Rosenkreutz grunted.

Clutching his chest, Brady gasped at the heinous implications. The most creative right brains on the planet were about to eat SA's lunch. The country that constructed America was plotting its deconstruction. Even Buonarroti looked spooked.

"You should see the colloquialisms they're coming up with," Rosenkreutz continued lugubriously. "They're either cheaper, or better, or more up to date than ours. Eight day wonder. The whole eight yards. A stitch in time saves ten. If you can't stand the heat, lower the thermostat. Don't count your chickens before they're incubated. As sure as Uggs is Uggs. Keeping up with the Indiana Joneses. The buck stops here today, gone tomorrow. They'll be doubling the triple bottom line, putting lean manufacturing on the Atkins, re-engineering re-engineering and destabilizing the scorecard before you know it. They can also fake metaphors that are not only indistinguishable from the originals but cost next to nothing."

"Impossible!" Buonarroti roared. She stood upright, palms pressed on the gleaming tabletop, rocking backward and forward like an agitated oil derrick, glaring at her gnarled nemesis. "You can't fake metaphors!"

Brady signalled for her to sit down. "I'm not so sure, Yasmin. If you can mix metaphors, if you can extend metaphors, if you can root metaphors, if metaphor creep is our problem, if metaphors can curl up and die, then it stands to reason that they can be faked. Everything else is faked nowadays. Fendi, Ferrari, Ferragamo, Fed-Ex, Frito-Lay... not forgetting Rogaine and Viagra."

Buonarroti glanced at Brady suspiciously. She'd always had her doubts about that pompadour, and as for the blue breath mints he swallowed by the handful... Hmmm.

"I think we should call Chang and Eng," Brady said briskly. "Perhaps they can help us think this through."

Buonarroti and Rosenkreutz shook their heads simultaneously, a rare moment of corporate accord. Generally acknowledged to be the Crick and Watson of Brand DNA, Jack Chang and Jill Eng were, if not quite the creative heart of Serendipity Associates, definitely its defibrillation paddles. Like many right brain wunderkinds, though, they were nervy, highly strung, easily upset and prone to fits of pique.

"Chang's working on the Apollo sneakers account," Buonarroti said; "best not disturb him."

"Oh, of course," Brady nodded. "The one small step for brands project. Better leave him to it. What about Eng?"

"The Dan Brown pitch," Buonarroti answered flatly. SA was hoping to secure the product placement contract for the long-awaited sequel to *The Da Vinci Code*. However, it was proving very problematic because Dan was determined to prove he was a proper author, not just a hack writer of airport novels.

"Is he still tinkering with that sequel to *Moby Dick*?" Brady inquired incredulously.

"No, he's dropped *Moby Dicker*. There's not much demand for books about negotiating tactics in nineteenth-century Nantucket. He's kept the Ahab bloodline subplot, though. *The Queequeg Conspiracy*, I think it's called. *The Pequod Code*, possibly. Something about an on-line marketing scam."

"Call me Phishmael," Brady sighed. Worn out after three days at the face-to-face face, he so wanted to yawn, but his mandibles couldn't take any more. With an exaggerated effort, he pushed his chair away from the table, stood up *very* slowly and, after checking it carefully for creases, slipped on his immaculate Zegna jacket. "Look guys, I need to, ah, gather my strength."

Buonarroti rolled her eyes. "We don't have much time, Bart. We need to reply to the Butler blog before it builds momentum."

Rosenkreutz sniffed. "Wanna arrange a quick hit on Hank? In a light-hearted language game kinda way. Friendly like."

"I need an hour or so, folks. I'm sorry."

Some say that when things get ugly in Las Vegas, Steve Buscemi's in town. The rest of the time Sin City's an ersatz paradise, an immoral utopia, the land of the lotus cheaters. As Brady strolled along the trash-strewn Strip, the spittoon of western civilization, he wasn't so sure. Deep in thought, he sauntered past the topless shows of bottomless depravity, through the throngs of importuning panhandlers flicking flyers at potential punters, trying to make strategic sense of the rapidly unravelling situation. He ended up, as he always did, at the Tropicana, where he took a turn around the *Titanic* exhibition. The story of the doomed liner had always fascinated him. One of his ancestors died on that terrible night in 1912. At Yale, he wrote a term paper on Herman Melville's presentiment of the disaster in his eerie 1888 poem, "The Berg". He'd seen the exhibition scores of times before. Its mixture of reproduction artifacts and mock ups of the passenger accommodation was as familiar to him as Serendipity Associates' boardroom. The thing that drew him back time and again was the passenger ticket issued on entry, which came complete with the real name of an actual passenger, whose survival or otherwise could be verified on exit. Brady hadn't drowned yet, largely on account of his unerring ability to convince the box office clerk that he warranted a first class ticket. For female passengers. He wasn't going down with the boat, not now, not never, not imagined, not real, not without a fight or sleight of hand.

Barton Brady was Bruce Ismay reborn.

As he sprawled across the four poster bed in a perfect recreation of the Wideners' first class cabin, Brady struggled to make sense of SA's dilemma. The nub of the problem, he realized, was theoretical: How does the management metaphor market function? Is it Malthusian, where the oversupply of metaphors precipitates warfare, pestilence and the battle of allusion against allusion? Is it Darwinian, where the fittest metaphor survives and successfully reproduces itself, a kind of Robotrope? Is it Veblenian, where metaphor-based management fads are corporate forms of conspicuous consumption, with the emphasis on con? Is it Marxian, where the contradictions of capitalism's mixed metaphors are harbingers of literal, all-too literal collapse? Or is the metaphor market Porterian, a competitive arena where the five famous forces prevail, and where cost-, focus- and differentiation-based simile strategies co-exist?

A compelling case, Brady knew, could be made for any of these meta-metaphorical models. Perhaps Veblenian demand for management metaphors was insatiable and, if so, SA was in the clear. Maybe a Malthusian metapocalypse was imminent, as Buonarroti and Rosenkreutz believed. If Porter prevailed, the principal challenge was to identify conceit clusters and apply the value chain metaphor to metaphors themselves. A Darwinian scenario seemed plausible, since seminal personifications like the Invisible Hand still held good and would continue to do so, fingers crossed. If the Marxian model was correct, however, America's imagined competitive advantage in imagination was likely to receive a rude awakening in the not too distant future.

Whatever meta-metaphor obtained, Barton Brady knew one thing for certain: he couldn't afford to get into a price war, because his figurative cost base didn't permit it. But he wasn't going to give up the ghost either, not without a fight. What he really needed was a new, improved management metaphor, a disruptive intellectual innovation, a simile so superlative that it changed the rules and convinced the sceptics that SA – and by extension the USA – was unassailable. America was built on metaphors: freedom, the frontier and fighting for the right to party among them. America was a beacon, the shining city on the hill, the light of the western world. Despite the recent metaphor metastasis – what Rhetorical Butler had cruelly described as an "explosion in a language laboratory" – America was not a past participle. It remained the future perfect.

But where should Brady look for the killer figure of speech? There's a world of difference between good metaphors and great metaphors, between long tails and tall tales, between tipping points and tripping points, between built to last and doomed to failure, between shining cities on the hill and squalid sinks along the Strip. Image may be nothing but imagination is everything. The country that gave the world diet water and Death brand cigarettes wasn't so easily beaten, was it? The self-indulgent attractions of the experiential economy, epitomized by Las Vegas, hadn't dulled his country's can-do spirit, had they?

He wondered sometimes.

Hair-loss aside, Brady's worst fear was that right brain rhetoric was a convenient phantasm, a national defence mechanism, a collective attempt to convince one another that losing manufacturing capacity and widget-working savvy didn't really matter, when everyone knew in their heart of hearts that it did. America was fiddling at Caesars while China ignited, Brazil burned, and India fanned the flames.

Brady felt himself slipping asleep. Jeez, he was tired.

Still adrift on an ice-floe of thought, Brady checked his *Titanic* surrogate on the way out. Kate Phillips. She survived the sinking. *Yes!* According to the on-line passenger database, Phillips had not only eloped with a businessman lover, but her adventures formed the basis of James Cameron's Oscar-winning screenplay. Kate Phillips. Hmmmm. He'd heard that name before. Wasn't Kate Phillips the great marketing guru from Northwestern University? Wasn't Kate Phillips the person who invented the metaphor-rich marketing concept? He wondered if there was a family connection between *Titanic* survivor and concept creator. Perhaps it's an omen. Maybe she's the lifeboat he's looking for.

Grinning gallantly at the box office clerk, Barton Brady turned his back on the sinking vessel and set a course for the metaphorical metropolises on Las Vegas Boulevard – New York, Paris, Venice, Monte Carlo and more. The Strip's scintillating haar shimmered before him, incredible, incandescent, insane.

Then all collapsed and the great cloud of casinos rolled on, as they rolled five and fifty years before.

Also by Stephen Brown

"I read *The Marketing Code* from beginning to end in one sitting. I had to know how it turned out. It shows great imagination, clever plotting, and a Rabelaisian scale of outrage and wit."
– Philip Kotler

"A marketing text written as a novel … You cannot fail to be amused, entertained and engrossed by this gem of a book."
– *Marketer* magazine

"Pitch perfect."
– *Harvard Business Review*

SOMETIMES YOU HAVE TO KILL TO MAKE A KILLING

Death stalks the streets of Edinburgh as marketing lecturer Simon Magill receives a gruesome message about a mysterious website. He is plunged into a marketing maelstrom that sweeps from the glitz of Las Vegas to the grime of West Belfast, taking in the Freemasons, the Knights Templar, the conspiracies surrounding the sinking of the *Titanic* and, not least, the insidious marketing campaign behind Dan Brown's blockbuster novel, *The Da Vinci Code*.

As Simon Magill struggles to make sense of the riddle, he uncovers a startling truth about the irredeemably commercial character of the Holy Grail. Racing against time, he discovers that there is, and always has been, a cabal at the heart of Western capitalism – a secret society that possesses the key to business success. Based at a prominent American business school, this clandestine organization has been systematically misleading the marketing community for millennia. As Magill soon discovers, it will stop at nothing to prevent its jealously guarded secret being revealed…

ISBN 978-1-905736-82-9/£7.99 Paperback